Magnificat

PROCLAIMS

A collection of powerful, inspiring testimonies

Magnificat

PROCLAIMS

A collection of powerful, inspiring testimonies

Magnificat® Central Service Team, Inc.
Metairie, LA

Acknowledgments

F irst of all, we want to thank everyone for their prayers to bring this project to fruition! In addition to all of our wonderful contributing authors, there have been many who have played a role in this endeavor. From the initial days of researching the possibilities (Duane Bambusch) and providing advice on the process (John LaBriola) to the actual time of publishing, we have had a number of generous souls who have contributed their time and expertise. We would like to begin by thanking our media angel, Felice Gerwitz, for guiding us through new waters. Many of the testimonies were transcribed from the recorded Chapter Meal CDs by Virginia Shaffer and Marilyn Hollingsworth. Then Marilyn Quirk, Lenora Grimaud, and Joan Lococo were a tremendous help with the review process. We were blessed to have Susan Marlow and Donna Patton edit the work, and Susan Spann provided legal counsel. It is said a picture is worth a thousand words, so we are very grateful to Colleen Swiatek for the inspired new Magnificat graphics and Cathy Behrens, who created the beautiful book cover and layout.

Although it will be difficult to mention everyone who had a part in bringing *Magnificat Proclaims* to reality, we do want you to know how much your support has meant to us. We also want to express our gratitude to the Magnificat Chapters worldwide for their commitment to magnify the Lord, the Magnificat Central Service Team for their confidence in this undertaking and the Communications Ministry for their role in spearheading this anointed mission. To God be the glory!

Dedication

This book is dedicated to Our Blessed Mother Mary, and to the living and deceased mothers of the Magnificat Central Service Team and the contributing authors of this book:

Juliet Nemirovsky (Baber)
Elma DiBacco DePrisco (Bates)
Gloria Dolores Lopez (Beckman)
Johnnette McCaskie Simon (Benkovic)
Josephine Barnes (Bleasdell)
Theresa "Nell" Chiappetta (Bordlee)
Joey Cleveland Caruso (Cleveland)
H J (Giganti)
Rose Capritto Johnson (Heap)
Angela J. Kim (Kim)
Caroline Weeks (MacInnis)
Netta Gallagher (Mansfield)
Brigid McKenna (McKenna)
Elsie Brodsky (Moss)
Carmelita Trifilio Stavale (O'Kane)
Dorothy Eldridge Montalbano (Quirk)
Vera LaPonzina (Razza)
Gloria Michel (Renaudin)
Evelyn "Sprink" Scarnecchia (Ross)
Anne Regina Barry (Skok)
Lois Kerner Schexnaildre (Tate)
Dr. Josephine Kouri, MD (Vadia)

TABLE OF CONTENTS

Magnificat has been proclaiming the greatness of the Lord since 1981. This international apostolate started from humble beginnings in New Orleans, LA. On October 7, Feast of the Holy Rosary, the first Magnificat Meal was held.

The ***Magnificat*** (Luke 1:46–55) is the great hymn of praise that Mary prayed while visiting Elizabeth. Both women had been deeply touched by God. Elizabeth was bearing a long-awaited child; Mary was carrying within her womb the very Son of God. They came together to help one another, to speak of God's action in their lives, to sing, to pray, to share a common table, and to be strengthened for all that was to come.

Magnificat came into being out of a desire to share with all Catholic women the fruit we have experienced through the Catholic Charismatic Renewal. We describe this fruit as:

- a deeper knowledge and love of Jesus Christ
- an experience of the release of the power of the Holy Spirit
- an appreciation and love for Mary, our Mother and Model
- an appreciation and love for the Catholic Church

Magnificat Meals are hosted by local Chapters worldwide about every three months on or around a feast day of Mary to whom we consecrate this ministry in a special way. We call our Meals "Magnificat" because, like Mary and Elizabeth, we want to come together in God's presence. May we too recognize what God has already done in us and call forth in each other a new openness to the power of His Spirit in our lives.

Magnificat® Central Service Team, Inc.
1629 Metairie Road – Suite 3, Metairie, LA 70005-3926
Tel: (504) 828-MARY [6279] ❖ Fax: (504) 828-1060
magnificatcst@aol.com ❖ www.magnificat-ministry.org

Foreword

Magnificat is proud to present its first edition book dedicated to you, the holy women of the Magnificat ministry, who have so generously offered to share their personal testimonies of what God has done in their lives through the power of the Holy Spirit.

For thirty-three years now, within one hundred Chapters formed world-wide, women like you, have voiced the stories of their journey with the Lord so other women could be blessed. The Magnificat Meal is the catalyst for the rivers of grace, which have been like tributaries releasing God's ongoing healing around the world. This book has been a labor of love, prayer, and much joy and excitement.

"A city set on a mountain cannot be hidden. Nor do they light a lamp and then put it under a bushel basket; it is set on a lamp stand, where it gives light to all in the house. Just so, your light must shine before others, that they may see your good deeds and glorify your heavenly Father" (Mt. 5:14–16).

We need to shout our good news from the mountain top! We are the light in the darkness and by our Baptism, we are commissioned to go out and let it shine.

We firmly believe that God wants these wonderful testimonies to be heard. When we share with one another what God has done for us in our lives, hearts are touched. Scripture tells us how powerful and life-changing they are in Revelation 12:11, "They conquered him [devil] by the blood of the Lamb and by the word of their testimony."

We thank each of our contributing authors for sharing their stories of what God has done in their lives. Because of your sharing, all who read your sacred words will be blessed.

The Lord will speak to your heart as you read. We encourage you to go deeper than what is on the surface by questioning yourself during further reflection as to what the Lord is saying to you through these testimonies. You will gain valuable insight that will shed light on your particular life story.

We suggest you ask yourself two questions when you have finished reading each chapter:

1.) How does this testimony speak to me?
2.) Is God asking me to change something in my life?

We encourage you to journal your conversations with the Lord.

We are indebted to the Blessed Mother for wrapping each of us in her maternal mantle and drawing us into her Immaculate Heart. It has been said the surest way to Jesus is through Mary! She has certainly been the one who has shown each of us how to magnify the Lord, as she did so beautifully in her own Magnificat! She has been an incredible role model and an instrument of life and love. Our earthly mothers have been an extension of her in our daily lives. We would like to thank them for cooperating with God's will and accepting the grace to carrying us in their wombs. Without their "yes," none of us would be here today. So whether living or deceased, we would like to say "thank you" to our mothers for their influence in helping us to be Magnificat women.

"Now Jesus did many other signs in the presence of [His] disciples that are not written in this book" (John 20:30). Each testimony continues to tell the "Good News" of our hope and faith in Jesus Christ, Our Lord. As you read Magnificat Proclaims, we hope you will sense the heavenly anointing on this labor of love!

Magnificat Central Service Team
Kathy MacInnis, Diane Bates, Paulette Renaudin,
Donna Ross, and Nancy Skok

Preface

In the Gospel of Mark [Mk 5: 19–20] Jesus casts out the devil from the Gerasene demoniac. When he was delivered, he begged Jesus "that he might be with him." But Jesus refused and told him to "go home to your friends and tell them how much the Lord has done for you, and how he has had mercy on you." And he went away and began to proclaim ... all that Jesus did for him, and everyone who heard him marveled.

Jesus wanted him not only as a disciple, but also as a witness. We can only imagine the power of his testimony among the people.

Today many words are used to inflate the egos of celebrities and the great-ones of this world. By contrast, this book "Magnificat Proclaims" shows us women who witness to what God has accomplished in their lives. They give testimony to all the Lord has done for them. Each one describes the powerful working of God's amazing grace and how it transformed her.

Over the years of my association with Magnificat, I have come to know all of these women and many, many others. They, like all those who come under the sanctifying influence of Our Blessed Mother, seemed to arrive rapidly at a notable degree of holiness. Their stories will touch the hearts and change the lives of many.

Rev. Kevin Scallon, C.M.
Spiritual Advisor to the Magnificat Central Service Team

Annette Miriam Baber

Shalom! I was born to be a Catholic!

I dedicate this testimony to my Jewish mother, Mary, St. Anne, whom I am named after, and to St. Edith Stein. I believe their prayers brought me to the Messiah.

I was born in Des Moines, Iowa, to orthodox Jewish parents. I have two younger brothers and sisters. My grandfather on my mother's side was a Spanish Jew. When I was three years old, he put his hand on my head and gave me his blessing: "This child will be a blessing to God and to her family." I never forgot his hand on my head and that blessing.

My father was a social worker and the athletic director of the Jewish Community Center in Des Moines. His parents were Russian Jews who spoke Yiddish and kept Kosher. We would walk up the hill to Beth El Jacob Synagogue. It was very beautiful, with stained glass windows. I loved my Russian-Jewish grandfather. He was full of love. I loved the rabbi of the synagogue; he too was full of love. I enjoyed looking up at the beautiful Star of David on the ceiling. My grandfather always said to me, "The Messiah is coming in the clouds of Heaven." I would look so excitedly at the clouds and wonder when He would come, hoping to see Him.

Although they loved each other, my parents had a difficult marriage. Because of this, we all suffered. We also suffered a lot of persecution from Catholics. I remember being called a "dirty Jew" and being told I killed Christ. I thought, *Christ, Christ, who is Christ? How did I kill Him?*

As I grew older the persecution continued. When I attempted to find a job, I was rejected, especially when I was truthful and included my religion on the applications. You can imagine my joy when years later Pope John Paul II asked forgiveness from the Jewish people for all those who had persecuted us for so long.

I remember my Catholic neighbors. Marie, the mother of three, had a very abusive, alcoholic husband. I admired her for her faith. Our houses stood close together, and we could hear the constant fighting and suffering that went on. Every Sunday, I watched Marie take her children to Mass.

The priest visited her regularly. I thought how great it was that she had comfort from someone religious.

Our family got a television set. We only received one station, and who happened to be on it? Bishop Sheen! So we watched him. There was something about the bishop's wonderful eyes that struck me. I remember thinking that I could see eternity in them. As I look back now, it was all that love that emanated from him.

Since I was the oldest, I was encouraged to be a little mother to my family. I felt such pressure to make everybody happy, safe, and good. When I was in my teens, I took a deeper look at myself. I believe God gave me the grace to know that I was bad. I knew the Ten Commandments my grandfather had faithfully taught me. By that time he had gone to be with the Lord, and I thought to myself, *I can't keep those commandments.* So, I broke them all, if not in my actions, I did so in my heart. I was pretty smart to know that without a Savior it would be impossible to be good.

Every day on the school bus we drove past St. John's Cathedral. Inscribed above the doors were the words of Matthew 11:28: "Come to Me all you who are weary from carrying heavy burdens and I will give you rest."

I thought, *Rest! What is that?* I felt burdened, dirty, guilty, and inadequate. The doors of the cathedral were always wide open. I remember thinking that if I went in there I would get struck by Jewish lightning. Then again, my whole Jewish family was terrified of death. I thought that if I could get inside I might know the peace I felt emanating from the cathedral.

When I graduated from high school, my art teacher encouraged me to go to art school in Chicago. I applied at the American Academy of Art, which stood across the street from the Art Institute. I worked all that summer as a switchboard operator at Mercy Hospital, run by the nuns, in order to pay for my tuition. I told the hospital I would stay and work for them, since they had to train me and wanted a permanent employee, but I had no intention of staying.

One sister—the head of the operating section—really impressed me. It was obvious she wanted to convert me. She asked if I knew Jesus. I was so dumbfounded I couldn't answer her.

There was a small adoration chapel in the hospital that drew me in. When I walked in I saw statues all around. In the presence of the tabernacle, I felt clean. When I walked out, I felt dirty again. It was an astounding phenomenon. *What is going on here?* I wondered. During this time, Sister Mary Pauline handed me a red rose from her private garden. It was for my younger brother, Michael, who had just been born. That was such a nice gesture.

When it came time to quit my job, I told the office manager. He was furious! I didn't blame him. I'd lied to him. The sister who liked me said something that shocked me. She knew very well that I had lied, but she said, "You have made the right choice, child. You go right on to art school. That's good." I had never known anyone who returned good for evil. I had been raised to believe "An eye for an eye and a tooth for a tooth" (Exodus 21:24). The nun's response to my lie was an incredible act of goodness. I couldn't imagine what in the world made her say a thing like that.

I moved to Chicago, where I stayed with my grandmother and enrolled in art school. One day, the most beautiful Catholic boy walked into the classroom. "I'm going to marry that boy," I told the girl sitting next to me. We have now been married for fifty-four years!

My Jewish mother loved him. "He is a prince," she said. "Marry him!" My father was not so happy. A priest would not marry us; neither would a rabbi. We went to a minister who was a Justice of the Peace. I told him, "Don't mention the name of Jesus because my father will leave the wedding." I'm sure all heaven said in chorus, "Annette, just wait! The time will come when His name will be forever on your lips and in your heart."

We were married, and a year later our son, Daniel, was born. He was born in Evanston, Illinois, at St. Francis Hospital. *I was born to be a Catholic.* Even my pediatrician was a Catholic.

A year later, my mother called. "I want you to come home," she said. "Your father is very ill." I became nervous and depressed. I remember being exhausted. When I lay down and took a nap, I had a dream.

I dreamt that God's hand came down from Heaven. He took the roof off my parents' house in Des Moines, stretched forth His hand, and removed my father into the heavens. A fear seized me after that dream and I quickly made arrangements to go home. While traveling, I remembered that a year before, my father had asked me to read the New Testament. At the time, I thought he was acting like a traitor. We were Jewish! He had taken a course in relative religion at a junior college, where he had to read the New Testament. His face had changed dramatically in front of me as he repeated his request three times.

It was God's anointing for my father's salvation, but I didn't understand it at the time. With the little light he had within him, he acted upon it. The Holy Catholic Church teaches much on the Baptism of Desire. Yet, my father's words disturbed me. I quickly walked away, vowing to put the thought of reading the New Testament out of my mind. Being Jewish, I couldn't imagine why he would want me to do such a thing.

When I arrived at my parents' home in Iowa, I learned my sister Rebecca had called the doctor and discovered that my father had lung cancer. He had three months to live. Because I was the oldest, Rebecca and my mother expected me to take care of the situation. I can't begin to describe how I felt. I was devastated. Because of the Jews' nebulous belief in the afterlife, I felt I would never see, touch, or hear his voice again.

I realized the burden was on my shoulders, thinking, *I have to do something. Everyone is counting on me.* I got up, shaking as if a bomb had burst inside of me. "We are going to the synagogue," I said. "God parted the Red Sea. He fed the multitude with manna and quail, and He can heal our daddy."

My sister and I got into Dad's car and headed to the synagogue. It was early on a Friday night in September. Rebecca sobbed all the way there, but I couldn't cry. I had to be strong. I couldn't let her know how weak I truly felt inside. When we got to the temple, the parking lot was empty. I was concerned because we needed at least nine men for a service. We began to suspect we would not get in. We thought the doors would be locked.

My sister continued to cry. "Even God is locking us out!" she wailed. We got out of the car and walked up to the entrance of the temple. "We can always go back and pray in the car if we have to," I said.

We walked up to the four, large temple doors. Sure enough, they were locked. The back doors were locked as well. By now it was getting dark. We walked around to the front doors and just stood there. Then I fell to the ground, sobbing.

My sister looked down at me and said, "There goes my last hope for any help." Then she reminded me how we used to drive past St. John's Cathedral, where the doors were always open. She shook her fist toward Heaven and said, "If this was a church, those doors would be open!" With that, all four of the temple's ten-foot-high doors opened wide.

I will never forget those doors opening as long as I live. Rebecca and I were petrified. We didn't know why God opened those doors. We hadn't read the New Testament where it says, "If you ask anything of Me in my name, I will do it" (John 14:14). As we approached the chapel, those doors opened! The chapel light was lit. Upon entering, my sister went through the building saying, "Who's here?"

I knew it was God. There was no doubt in my mind.

I entered the chapel, fell on my knees, and began to pray and plead for my daddy's life. My sister continued searching the whole building, still yelling, "Who's here?" Finally, she came back and said, "Annette, there is no one in this building."

"Of course not," I said. "What's the big deal? If God opened the Red Sea, why not the temple doors?"

When we came out of the synagogue and got back in the car, the doors remained open. There were still no cars in the parking lot. Then above the temple, hovering like a helicopter, we saw a huge star. I thought, *This is like a movie.* Again, we had never read the Book of Revelation about Christ being the bright morning Star. We sat there and watched as the star ascended into the sky.

"What is this all about?" my sister asked with astonishment.

I replied, "It's all about God. He will let us know later."

As we drove home, I sensed I had been infused with incredible new strength. I felt strong enough to be able to encourage and take care of my family. I now know it was God's grace instilled within me that gave me this courage. We had gone to the synagogue to pray for our daddy, and we had met our heavenly Father, who had opened those doors for us. We were filled with joy.

When we got home, we burst through the front door and told Mama. She had called one of the men from the synagogue since she was so worried about us. She said, "You couldn't have opened those doors. They were double locked."

She then told us the rabbi was on vacation in Florida, as he routinely was prior to the High Holy Days. Because there had been recent break-ins in the neighborhood, our mother was naturally concerned about the two of us. "Mama, those doors opened!" Rebecca and I said. "God opened those doors!"

"I think I'm going to call our family doctor to get some sedatives for the two of you," Mama said.

My sister and I were so excited because such a great miracle had happened, but our mama didn't believe us! When I called my husband, he didn't believe me either. My sister and I reminded each other, "We are each other's witnesses!" (After my conversion seven years later, we shared the story of this miracle with over 5,000 people at a Jesus rally in Chicago).

Because of the infused grace I received after seeing the doors open, I was able to stay at my father's bedside for the next three months. He was in the Veterans' Hospital just a few blocks from our home. While in the ward, a man walked in who was due to have surgery the next day. He pointed at the television, where Perry Como was singing the Ave Maria. "That is the most important thing in this world," he said loudly. Everyone in the ward heard him. The next day, the man underwent open-heart surgery and died on the operating table. I am certain God was giving my dad and me a great warning, since Jews need signs. This dear man was pointing us to Jesus, His Holy Mother, and the Catholic Church. He was like an angel.

After Daddy died, we moved to Chicago. I joined a temple called Beth Or, meaning "House of Light." The rabbi was an atheist who believed in humanism. I got busy in the temple and involved with the rabbi's humanistic philosophy. I was angry with God because He had not healed my father. The rabbi was very intellectual—something I was not—so I started reading books. I wanted to become "Mrs. Beth Or."

I was busy running from God. I thought if I worked in the synagogue I would become real popular fast. I spent a great deal of money and worked hard. I became the president of the women's club and secretary to the president of the synagogue. This dear man converted years later after I converted.

I became a humanist. I began reading Ayn Rand, Socrates, Plato, and Aristotle, but I didn't understand what they were talking about. I was trying so hard to appear smart and intellectual in front of all the people in the synagogue.

My sister Rebecca kept reminding me, "Annette, don't you remember the temple doors?"

I replied, "I don't want to talk about it."

I ran away from God. In doing so, I ran away from my responsibilities as a wife, mother, daughter, and sister. I was in a downward spiral. My marriage was failing, and Satan had a stronghold on me. My husband and I attended a party where we were asked to draw pictures of our spouses. He drew the best, detailed picture of a perfect witch! It was a pretty good drawing, but I didn't want to think about the implications. He had asked me for a divorce the year before, but I thought, *He doesn't mean it. Who would divorce Mrs. Beth Or?*

I remember getting sick and losing weight. I was very weak and couldn't sleep. I went to several doctors. They found nothing wrong until I was diagnosed by a Jewish doctor, who told me I had psittacosis, "parrot fever." He said this because he couldn't find anything else wrong with me. I looked it up and found out that psittacosis is an often-fatal disease. I panicked and thought that I was going to die. I finally went to a doctor who had retired from the Mayo Clinic. He told me I had a kidney infection.

My younger brother, Michael, had come to live with me. He was two years older than our son, Daniel, who was seven. I was hospitalized for the kidney infection. The hospital was only two blocks from our home. The two little boys would look up at the hospital and wonder what was wrong with me. As I looked down at them through the window, I could see myself, and it was pretty shocking. I thought, *I am that witch! That is exactly what I am.* I decided right there on the spot to change for the better. I recalled Anne Frank's diary: "Most people want to be good, but they don't know how."

I didn't realize at the time that the only way I could possibly change was to follow Jesus. I continued to discount what happened at the temple. I then decided the philosophers were all a bunch of windbags. I decided that somehow I was going to change and become a perfect wife and mother.

I tried and I tried with all my strength. The more I tried, the more I failed, until I had a nervous breakdown. Later, God called it a nervous "breakthrough." I couldn't sleep for months. I had difficulty eating and lost a lot of weight. I couldn't clean the house or make meals. It was like going through hell. My family could not stand me. My husband still wanted a divorce.

Then God gave my husband a dream. He dreamt I was in a church praying in tongues. How could he divorce me? It seemed that God was saving my marriage, but I was miserable and wretched. One night, I decided to commit suicide. I felt the devil telling me that if I did, I would know peace. My family would just have to understand that I was really tortured.

I now realize all this misery was bringing me to God. As I lay in bed contemplating my suicide, I planned to drown myself. It started to rain, and I was annoyed. I had an absurd thought, *Why is it raining when I'm going to drown myself?* Then I thought, *Who is going to love my husband and children like I do?* I wrestled back and forth with myself until I finally decided, "Oh, well, they'll have to learn to get along without me. They would be better off with a maid in the house."

After making this decision, I suddenly saw the bushes outside the window moving from a strong wind. When the wind came through the window, it lifted me out of my body and into the universe. The planets whirled around me. I felt engulfed in a power and love that cannot be explained. St. Paul speaks about being taken out of his body in 2 Corinthians 12:1–4. I could see the planets all around me.

When I cried out to my husband, I heard the sweetest voice say, "Oh, so you don't want to die?"

I said, "No! I don't want to die!"

I have since learned that the fruit of any supernatural experience is the way you judge whether or not it is of God. I no longer wanted to die. The moment I said "yes" to life, I was put back down into my body. I became very frightened and decided I had really lost it. I needed to be admitted to a mental institution. I lay there all night, afraid to move because I didn't want that wind to come back.

I didn't know that in John 3 our Lord says, "Unless you be born again, you shall not inherit the kingdom of heaven. The wind blows where it wills and no man knows where it goes or where it comes from. So it is with those who are born of the Spirit."

The next morning—after a sleepless night—I got up and walked into the living room. I heard an inner voice say, "Welcome home, daughter. I am your heavenly Father. I will make you a perfect wife and mother. You never have to be afraid again."

I thought, *Okay, now I am hearing voices.* I sat down on the couch and began to think. I wasn't taking any pills because I was a hypochondriac. What an interesting contradiction. I wanted to kill myself, yet I didn't want to take any pills that might kill me. I concluded that I was hallucinating.

The telephone rang. It was my best girlfriend from Iowa, who was also Jewish. We had met in junior high and were close friends. At this time, we were both thirty years old. She had gone to college and become a psychiatric social worker. Now she wanted to go to the University of Chicago and get her master's degree. She asked if she could stay with me until she could find an apartment.

I said, "Yes, if you want to stay with a crazy person. I have been taken up into the universe, and I'm hearing voices from God."

"Praise the Lord!" she said. "You've found God. Now you need to find His Son."

"Francine, what are you talking about? We're Jewish."

I didn't know it at the time, but Francine had converted to Christianity a year earlier, when she and her brother had given their lives to Christ. "Francine," I said. "I don't want to talk about this right now. I'm a Jew and *not* a traitor." I was so offended!

She continued to say, "I will see you at O'Hare airport and we will talk more then."

After we hung up I thought, *She's the one who went to college and I didn't. She thinks she knows more than I do.* I asked my husband, "Would you please get me a New Testament?"

My husband was out the door in a flash. I had to read it before my friend arrived so I could refute her. As I began to read, I started to fall in love with this beautiful Jewish Rabbi, Jesus. I thought, *He's a lot like Sister Mary Pauline. He talks about returning good for evil.*

I loved the way Jesus spoke to the Pharisees. I felt I had known a few of them from the temple we attended as a child. They had treated us terribly because we were poor. We were made to sit in the back of the synagogue.

As I read about Jesus, I thought, *This man has chutzpah! He tells it like it is and is not afraid of anyone or what they think.* I really liked that. I admired Him. When they attacked Jesus and scourged Him, I thought, *I know what it's like to be persecuted and beaten as a child for being Jewish.* I had compassion for Him because of what I had experienced. I could relate.

Then I thought, *But is He the Messiah?* I remembered my personal experiences. I had been up in the universe with God. I felt God had spoken to me. I decided to ask Him myself. "Father, is Jesus Your Son?"

He responded, "I have waited years to tell you. 'He is my beloved Son. Hear ye Him'" (Luke 9:35).

God the Father had to draw me to His Son! "No one can come to me unless the Father who sent me draw him" (John 6:44). I ran from one end of the house to the other, screaming and crying out to God, "What about my Jewish family? Why did You wait so long to tell me? For thirty years I didn't know Jesus was the Messiah. How could you do this to me?"

"I will save your entire family," He said. "Every one of them will become a Christian." It happened as He said. They have all become Christians!

I was changed in an instant. I wanted to do everything God commanded me to do. I wanted only His will from that moment on. Because of Jesus, I now felt I could keep His commandments.

I told my husband to get me a Bible and a Pieta. I had seen the real Pieta a few years earlier at the World's Fair in New York City. It was the most magnificent work of art I had ever seen. At the time, I knew there must be something to this Jesus. Michelangelo could never have carved that kind of perfection without divine inspiration. I wanted a rosary and books about the saints. I also asked my husband to build me a little altar, which he did. I now have the real altar in God's Holy Church.

By the time Francine arrived, I was a brand-new Christian. She and I spent weeks sharing the Scriptures, listening to God together, and learning to obey Him. One of the first things He taught me came from Ephesians 5:23: "Wives, submit to your husbands as unto the Lord." I started greeting my husband at the door with a big smile when he came home. I set the table each night with candles. Previously, I had won him for the devil. He had left the Catholic Church because he was fed up with me.

Our Lord said to me, "You have the power to destroy your marriage. Now you have the power to win your husband back to Me and My Son."

I got busy and made the decision to be the sweetest wife you ever saw! With God, all things are possible. It worked. I held my big, handsome husband in my arms as he wept one night, giving his life back to Jesus. He now thinks that instead of a witch, I remind him either of Golda Meier, the former prime minister of Israel, or Joan of Arc. Praise the Lord! He has changed my life. Because of my great love for the Messiah, I constantly witnessed to my family and anyone else who would listen.

Eventually, we moved to Huntley, Illinois. Our post office box password was GJC, God Jesus Christ. I was incredulous that God would make it so clear that He had gone before me.

The Lord says in His Word to pick up your cross and follow Him (Luke 9:23). Suddenly, suffering began, one incident after another. My brother Jacob, who was mentally ill, was in a mini-bike accident and had to have three-quarters of his liver removed. My sister, a wife and mother of four children, was in an automobile accident and incurred brain damage. My brother Michael, nineteen years younger than I, whom I was raising, contracted Crohn's disease.

Despite the grief, I was grateful to be a Christian. I could now suffer without believing God was punishing me. Jesus reversed the whole Old Testament for me. I had always believed that unless I was healthy, happy, famous, and wealthy, I was not blessed by God. As a Christian I realized that because Jesus' suffering was redemptive, my suffering—in imitation of Him—is also redemptive. God permits suffering so good can come from it, for our own salvation and that of others. I had a dream that a beautiful Rabbi was holding me in His arms, crying with me and for me. I woke up and I knew the Rabbi was Jesus. He was suffering with me and for me.

My nephew David was born with a hole in his heart. Knowing that only good can come from suffering in Christ, I witnessed to my sister Rebecca. I told her Jesus could heal her eight-year-old son. David was in Children's Memorial Hospital preparing for open-heart surgery. Rebecca was terrified, and for a good reason. When she had her tonsils out as a child, she suffered blindness for two weeks afterward. I held my cross in my hand and told her that Jesus would heal David.

"Don't tell me about Jesus," she said.

At the same time, my brother Jacob was in another hospital undergoing surgery on his liver. While at my sister's house, my Aunt Molly said, "Take off that cross or your brother and nephew will die."

I replied, "Aunt Molly, if I take this cross off, they surely will die. Jesus will save them."

My sister walked in the back door and said, "Annette, tell me about Jesus!" I was shocked but soon learned the reason. Just before surgery was to take place, the doctors said, "Mr. and Mrs. Marcovitz, your son has had a miracle. The hole in his heart is closed."

Later that night, we learned Jacob had developed an infection after his liver surgery. He would not make it until morning. The Lord, however, told me Jacob would live. Then He told me to share the news with my husband. "The Lord told me my brother is going to live."

He responded, "Annette, I think you had better prepare yourself because he will most likely die."

"Honey," I said. "God told me he will live, and I believe it."

The next morning we received a phone call from my sister at the hospital. My brother had miraculously recovered. He went on to live another twenty-five years and became a Christian!

My mother's conversion occurred while she was on the phone with Aunt Molly. My aunt was very wealthy and lived on Lake Shore Drive in Chicago. She told my mother, "You are suffering so many trials because Annette believes in Jesus. God is punishing you."

With tears streaming down her face, Mother said, "Molly, the problem with you is that you never have problems. You do not know your need of a Messiah. Read Isaiah 53. Jesus is the Messiah."

I grabbed the phone from my mother's hand and added, "And He is also God!"

Aunt Molly hung up, and Mother became a Christian. Aunt Molly did not speak to me for over ten years. Before Mother died, she said, "I want to go home and be with the Lord." Jesus kept her to the end!

Before I became a Christian, my sister Marlene became a Catholic in secret, fearing our wrath. All four of her children were baptized, and she taught CCD for several years. When we found out she'd converted, we persecuted her terribly. She ignored us and continued to worship at the Catholic Church.

My husband led me to a beautiful Pentecostal church to fulfill the prophecy of his dream of me speaking in tongues. I received the baptism of the Holy Spirit in this church, and the Scriptures opened up to me as never before.

Then all of a sudden, Catholics started coming out of the woodwork! A woman named Marge, who had once a vocation to become a nun, said, "Annette, do you believe the Bible? Did you read in John 6, where Jesus said that it is His Body and Blood in the bread and wine?"

I replied, "Yes, I believe it is His Body and Blood. The protestants taught me that every word in the Scriptures is true."

Then she asked, "Why aren't you a Catholic?"

"Because Catholics were very mean to me as a child," I answered. However, the challenge to become a Catholic was a seed she planted. Since

I felt that Jesus talked to me, I decided to ask Him if He wanted me to become a Catholic.

Jesus replied, "Yes, daughter, I want you to become a Catholic. I condescended to dwell among your people. Will you not dwell among mine?"

Even after the Lord told me to become a Catholic, I struggled with the idea. Still, as a Protestant I sensed something was missing. I felt the Lord was always with me, but not inside of me. I now know that it was a longing for the Eucharist.

Then in 1977, God moved us to Kansas City, Missouri. I decided to inquire about the Catholic Church at St. Teresa in Park City. Inscribed over the church doors was a quotation from St. Theresa of Lisieux: "My vocation is to love. I choose all. All is grace." I took that as my vocation.

The church had a Charismatic prayer group, and they treated me as if I was Queen Esther. When they received Communion, I smelled the scent of roses on each one of them. I wondered about this, thinking it might be some exquisite perfume. When I came home all excited about the prayer group, my husband said, "You were born to be a Catholic!"

Our pastor, Monsignor Moser, was on the board of directors of the largest Catholic Interdenominational Conference ever held. It took place in Arrowhead Stadium, home of the Kansas City Chiefs football team. Over 60,000 people were present. The speakers included Cardinal Suenens from Rome, Ruth Stapleton Carter, Art Katz of Jews for Jesus, and Maria Von Trapp. The movie, *The Sound of Music*, portrayed Maria and her family during the events leading up to World War II.

The evening I attended the conference I saw an apparition of our Lord Jesus in the sky. His face was purer than that of a newborn baby. No artist could ever capture the magnificence of that face. I saw His bowed head and the crown of thorns. This took place while 60,000 Christians were praising and worshiping God. I now realize our Lord was letting me know I would be purified through suffering. I told my husband I had just seen God. I was beginning to feel like the Catholic Church was really something special.

I remembered reading in Scripture that the Jews needed signs (1 Cor. 1:22). During one of the day sessions, Art Katz from Jews for Jesus was speaking. He asked, "Are there nuns in the audience?" Two fully habited sisters walked up on the podium. One of them got down on her knees and asked Art Katz and the Jewish people to forgive the Catholic Church for their persecution of the Jews. I thought, *Wow! This Church can't be so bad, after all.*

Years later I met Mother John Marie of the Disciples of the Lord Jesus Christ. When I told her about this incident at Arrowhead Stadium, she said, "I was that nun!" We wept in each other's arms, and I told her she was one of the reasons I became a Catholic. We have been friends for years.

After these incredible signs, I began RCIA at St. Teresa's. I went for nine months, feeling like I was giving birth to a baby I knew nothing about. When I met with Monsignor Moser for the Sacrament of Penance, I told him I didn't understand anything.

"That's okay, Annette," he said lovingly. "You will find out more once you are in."

My Jewish mama said, "Annette, it's okay that you are a Christian, but why a Catholic?"

I was very apprehensive the night before I was confirmed. "Lord, I just can't do this." Then I said, "But I must obey You." I asked the Lord to give me a dream.

God gave me one of the most beautiful dreams of my life. I was in St. Peter's in Rome on the porch of the Vatican. A United States flag was flying in the sky. "Where is my Lord?" I asked.

Then I saw the Lord several feet in front of me, united to the most beautiful woman I had ever seen. Her hands were held up together in prayer. The two were glued together as one. It was an infusion of oneness. I did not realize it at the time, but the Church is the Bride of Christ, and Mary is the Mother of the Church. I also didn't know that the Eucharist is the consummation of souls in their marriage to Jesus. I thought in my dream, *That's what I want! To be one with Him like that, just as she is.*

Finally, the woman walked away. "Good!" I said. "Now it's my turn." I walked up to Jesus, but instead of allowing me to enter into this oneness, He put his arm around my shoulders and led me down the steps of the porch and into a garden. He led me to a priest who had given Life in the Spirit Seminars at St. Teresa's. "Listen to him," the Lord said and walked away. I was brokenhearted as I watched Him leave.

The priest handed me a book titled, *In the Fullness of Christ.* He then said, "Go home and read this."

When I woke up, I knew I wanted to be united to Christ like the beautiful woman. I would become a Roman Catholic and receive Holy Communion. I have not missed one day of Holy Communion for more than thirty-three years, except for an occasional illness. I now understand that the woman united to Christ in my dream was Mary, Mother of the Eucharist, representing the Bride and Body of Christ in the fullness of His Church. Before receiving daily communion I had many fears, all of which soon left me. I now felt like a rock inside, full of incredible peace and security I had never known before. Even my chronic asthma was instantly healed upon receiving Holy Communion.

I became a "cafeteria" Catholic, picking and choosing what I wanted to believe. With the exception of the Eucharist, I struggled with most of the Church's teachings. Then God moved my family again, this time to Texas.

One of my best friends, Diana Ferrante, who helped me lead a prayer group, was a brilliant teacher. She hounded me with the Church's teachings just like "The Hound of Heaven." She invited me to attend a weekend course at the University of Dallas, where Fr. Mitch Pacwa, Fr. Paul Hinnebusch, Dr. Marcellino D'Ambrosio, and Dr. Douglas Bushman—all renowned teachers and speakers—were presenters. At the end of the weekend, all the doors to the Catholic Church opened up to me. I became a completed Catholic. I knew with an infusion of grace that the teachings of the Church were all true. I finally got it!

The Magisterium, the Church Triumphant, the Church Suffering, and the Church Militant—I finally saw their purpose. It was like my dream when the priest handed me the book, *In the Fullness of Christ*, to read. Like the temple doors opening that long-ago day, all the doors of the Church opened to me now to fully grasp, understand, and follow. God was giving me the Kingdom of Heaven on earth through His Holy Church.

I went to Corpus Christi Catholic Church, where I consecrated my life to the Blessed Mother. I learned about the Magnificat Ministry to Catholic Women. Through Our Lady's intercession, I founded the Grapevine, Texas, Magnificat Chapter, as well as the McHenry II Chapter. In 2005, I was asked to be the guest speaker at the Magnificat International Conference in New Orleans. I have shared my testimony at Magnificat Chapters across the country ever since.

One thing I have learned as a "completed Catholic" is that our testimony never ends. God is forever doing something new and wonderful in our lives, and opening more and more doors for us. God has done great things for me, and holy is His name. Thank you for letting me share my story with you.

Bio –

Annette Miriam Baber was born into an Orthodox Jewish family. After she grew up, married, and had a son, she felt her world crumbling, feeling she was a failure as a wife and mother. While suffering from a nervous breakdown and contemplating suicide one night in 1971, God sovereignly spoke to her. The next day she read the New Testament Gospels and cried out to the Father asking who this Jesus really was. At that moment, the Lord spoke to Annette, saying Jesus was "His beloved Son" whom He wanted Annette to know. She immediately committed her life to Christ Jesus and miracles began to happen. Since 1984, Annette has led charismatic prayer groups, Bible studies, and has spoken at numerous conferences and Magnificat meals. She was the founding coordinator of both the Dallas, Texas, and McHenry, Illinois, Magnificat chapters.

Diane Bates

My story is a tender love story between God the Father, full of wisdom and unconditional love, and one of His beloved daughters—me. God has gently guided me through what I call "lesson plans." Each lasted about two to three years. As I reflected on each of these lessons, I noticed a common thread. I was significantly different before and after each one. In addition, I realized that at the end of each lesson, God seemed to lead me to gifts. I call them graduation presents! These presents helped prepare me for future lessons.

Before I explain the lessons, I feel I should share the "before" picture, the old me before my walk with the Lord. I was born the first of two children to Dr. John and Elma DePrisco in Philadelphia, Pennsylvania. Early on, my parents realized I was exceptionally bright, especially when I set IQ records at all of the schools I attended. As a result, my family, friends, and teachers pushed me to achieve.

On the spiritual side, I was a cradle Catholic. Our family attended Mass regularly. I received all of the sacraments on schedule, but like most Catholics in my generation, I didn't receive any religious instruction after my Confirmation at age twelve. These two diverging trends in my life—increasing pressure to achieve and decreasing opportunities for spiritual direction—caused me to become very worldly.

I wasn't a bad person. I didn't break any laws. I didn't intentionally hurt anyone. Like most of today's youth, though, I was arrogant, prideful, impatient, and uncompassionate. One could say I wasn't steeped in the virtues.

As time went on, I attended college and majored in chemistry. Science became my religion. I stopped going to Mass. I didn't pray anymore. I seriously doubted if God existed. I wasn't even sure if I believed in an afterlife. God wasn't on my radar screen. I had walked away from Him completely, and I seemed to be doing fine without Him.

My life rolled merrily along. I graduated with a BS in chemistry from Rutgers University. I went on to the University of Rochester, where I received my Ph.D. in physical chemistry, and from there I attended Duke University in Durham, North Carolina, and did two years of an American Cancer

Society post-doctoral fellowship in biochemistry. Finally, at the age of twenty-eight years old, I started my first job. My uncle used to tease me that I would be the only person who was going directly from school to Medicare.

I landed my first job in Irving, Texas, at Abbott Laboratories. Abbott is a Fortune 200 company. They deal in health care and had three divisions: pharmaceuticals, hospital products, and diagnostics. I worked in the diagnostics division and developed the blood tests for glucose, calcium, and cholesterol screening, to name a few. I also helped design the instruments. Eventually, I climbed the corporate ladder. I was responsible for many products, millions of dollars, and many people. I earned several patents and had my research on the cover of a national magazine.

I'm sharing this to give you a perspective of the enormous amount of pressure I was under, as well as the depth of the goal-oriented, high-achieving culture in which I was immersed. During that time I met my husband, Tom. We were married, bought a house, and started having children. I had it all! I had the exciting career, the six-figure salary, the family, the beautiful home, and the Porsche in the driveway. I was the classic, Type A personality. I was in control, and for me, life was perfect.

Then, something happened that would change my life forever. My younger brother fell sick, and he was dying. On Labor Day weekend of 1989, our family flew up to Philadelphia. I had the privilege of being in his room and holding his hand the moment he died. In that moment, an incredible energy went through me from the top of my head to the tips of my toes. I knew it was his spirit. It really shook me. I had never seen anyone die. I had never seen a body with a spirit and then suddenly lifeless, without a spirit.

When I returned to Dallas, I was very fragile. I had trouble eating. I couldn't watch movies where anyone died. If anyone came up to me at work and even said "boo," I was on the verge of crying and falling apart. This in-control person was in trouble.

I went to the company nurse, and she suggested I see a psychologist. For six months, I went to the psychologist's office. For six months, I sat on her couch with a box of tissues and cried. That's all I did. Every week for an hour I sat on her couch, cried, and then went home. I was in so much pain over my brother's death. Pain and suffering were all I could see. Not only my own pain, but I saw the pain in my parents' eyes at losing their son.

My brother was only twenty-nine when he died. He died two days before his thirtieth birthday. I remember sitting in the funeral home on his birthday with my parents. My dad said, "All my life I bought my son birthday presents. I never dreamed one of them would be a casket." All I could see was the pain. My intellectual brain was trying to understand this, but I couldn't see the purpose.

Then one day, the psychologist asked me a pointed question. "Diane, has anything good come out of your brother's death?"

I had to think hard about it, but after a moment, I said, "Yes, one good thing has come out of my brother's death. I have become a better person. Before, I didn't know how to comfort anyone with the pain of loss. I usually wouldn't do or say anything because I didn't know what to say. Now, I know the things people said or did that comforted me when I lost my brother, and I can share that with others."

With that thought, I was healed. I never went back to her office. Right then, I vowed, that if the one good thing that came out of my brother's death was that I became a better person, then I was going to strive for that with all my strength. I wasn't going to let my brother's death be in vain.

And so I did.

I comforted many people with the loss of a loved one, and eventually I went back to church. Then my family began going back to church. We started to develop our relationship with the Lord. We received not only the gift of the Church, but the gift of the sacraments as well. It was wonderful. I am now convinced there are many reasons why my brother died, but one of them was for the salvation of my family. We were lost, and now we were found!

At this point in my life though, I was still very spiritually immature. For the whole six months that I sat in the psychologist's office, I was actually mad at God. I remember thinking, *Well, God, you can take one of my loved ones out of this world, but I have the ability to bring another loved one into this world.*

Tom and I were interested in having more children. One year later our beautiful son, Jonathan, was born on October 4, 1990, perfectly healthy. It didn't take long, though, until we realized something was wrong. At eighteen months, my son couldn't understand anything we said to him. He couldn't talk to us or express himself. Jonathan was in his own world most of the time. We could put a beautifully wrapped present in front of him and he wouldn't acknowledge it was there. He would look right past it. He didn't respond when we called his name. He didn't look us in the eye or acknowledge that we were speaking to him.

Something was terribly wrong.

After several months, several doctors, and several tests, we finally had our answer. I will never forget that day for as long as I live. I can still see it as if it were yesterday. Tom and I were looking through a two-way mirror. We were watching Jonathan at the Callier Center for Communication Disorders as he took a test.

When the test was finished, four assessors entered our room. My husband and I were sitting on the couch. The assessors sat in the four chairs opposite us. Then the lead psychologist spoke words that would be the sword that pierced my heart.

"Your son is autistic," she said. "It is a severe, lifelong disability with no known cause and no known cure."

I was devastated. I remember sitting there feeling like I had gone into suspended animation. I remember thinking, *This is really weird. What is going on?* I was looking at the four assessors sitting opposite me. I knew they were talking to me because their lips were moving, but I couldn't hear anything they were saying.

A friend of mine later explained I must have gone into shock and temporarily lost my hearing. It can happen sometimes.

The lead psychologist said, "The only thing that can help your son is play therapy."

Being action-oriented parents, Tom and I immediately put Jonathan in the best play-therapy program in the city. However, at the end of the summer, the director met with us and told us it wasn't working. She had noticed no progress in Jonathan.

I was devastated to learn that the play therapy, the only thing that would help my son who had a lifelong debilitating disorder, wasn't working! I was hysterical, absolutely hysterical. I was on the verge of a nervous breakdown. I couldn't eat; I couldn't sleep. I would go to my friend's house and sit on her couch with a box of tissues and cry.

I remember pacing back and forth saying, "You know, when somebody is bad and something bad happens to them, I can understand that—there is some justice in that. But what has this child done? What has this little, innocent child done to deserve this lifelong sentence?"

All my friend said was, "Diane, pray. Just keep praying."

And pray I did. I went into Jonathan's room every night after he fell asleep. I knelt next to his bed and prayed back-to-back rosaries.

Then one day, I took Jonathan and Christopher to McDonald's. They were playing in the balls, and I was sitting at the table ragging on God. Not out loud, of course, as there were other people there, but in my mind I was really ragging on Him.

I was saying, *Now God, You don't answer any of my prayers and You know I was thinking about quitting work and doing ministry work for You, and now I can't. I am going to have to work for two lifetimes, mine and Jonathan's.*

Then I heard God speak to me! Right then! I unequivocally knew that it was God. I knew because He interrupted my train of thought. I was so taken back that I grabbed the first thing in front of me to write down as much as I could remember of what He said.

The first thing in front of me was a McDonald's napkin! To this day, I carry that McDonald's napkin with me everywhere. It is always in my Bible. God said, "Now wait a minute. I do too answer your prayers." Then He started naming prayers He had answered.

Oh, You did answer that one, I thought. *Oh yes. Thank you, Lord. I forgot about that one also.*

He reminded me of all the prayers He had answered recently. Then He said, "I will heal Jonathan in a slow process."

I then wrote: *And now I have the logic behind this and I feel more at peace because I know Jonathan's disability is a preparation for me to do God's work later. He knows I am planning on retiring early to do His work.*

God said, "You will be more effective, more understanding, and more devoted to this mission having gone through what you are going through now." The Lord was telling me, "I have Jonathan in the palm of My hands, and this is a lesson plan for you."

I was so excited! I drove home as fast as I could. I ran to my husband and said, "Tom, you aren't going to believe this! God spoke to me in McDonald's." I told him what God had said, and he just shook his head.

"You know Diane," he said. "You're pretty stressed out about this. Are you sure this isn't just wishful thinking?"

But I had my answer, and I knew this was from God. It had to be! Those close to me knew I was in a fragile state. I couldn't put two rational neurons together, and I certainly couldn't conjure up an idea that made perfect sense. I could not have figured out anything so complex during this state in my life. So, I really believed this was from God.

But as the days passed, doubt started creeping in. I wondered, *Okay, did I really hear from God at McDonalds?*

Two months later in October, another dear friend said to me, "You know, Diane, you should take Jonathan to the healing Mass at St. Michael's Church."

I was desperate and willing to go anywhere so Jonathan and I went to the healing Mass at St. Michael's. This was my first experience with anything charismatic. At the end of the Mass, the priest called everyone up to form a single line across the base of the altar. He proceeded to anoint people with holy oil, making the sign of the cross on their foreheads.

I watched as he made his way down the row. People were falling on the floor! I didn't know what was going on. I had never seen anyone "overcome with the Spirit." I remember thinking to myself, *I don't know what they are doing, but I'm not leaving.*

I held Jonathan on my right hip as the priest came down the row. When he got to me, he put his thumb up to make the sign of the cross on my forehead. Out of my mouth came the words, "No, not me, my son—"

I didn't even finish the sentence before *boom*, I was on the floor. I lay there crying in deep, deep sobs. My hands were stretched out in front of me. In each palm I felt an energy the likes of which I have never felt before or since—like two balls of lightning. It was so powerful that my hands tingled for hours afterwards.

While I was on the floor, a special nun from the Disciples of the Lord Jesus Christ prayed over me. "She is generating so much heat," she said. I was! I was one big ball of energy.

When I rose, I saw a gentleman standing behind me who had been praying for me while I was down on the floor. "Where is my son?" I asked him. (They had to carry Jonathan out of the church because he was crying and hysterical. He didn't know what was happening to me when I was on the floor crying). I kept asking, "Where is my son? I want him to receive an anointing."

The gentleman looked straight into my eyes and said, "No, it is you God wants to heal. He healed your son before you were ever born."

I looked at him and thought, *Wow, this is the same message God gave me at McDonalds—that Jonathan is in the palm of His hands and this is for me. God is trying to do something with me.*

I went to the back of the church and found Jonathan. Then my friend said, "I have to introduce you to my friend Annette. You need to let Annette pray over your son."

Annette came and laid her hands on Jonathan. Then she abruptly took her hands away and said, "God has a message for you."

"Great! What is it?"

"I really want to pray about it some more," Annette said. "Let me call you in a couple of days."

I gave her my number. A couple of days later, she called and read me the prophecy the Lord had given her: "Tell My Diane that 'I Am that I Am.' Jonathan is in My hands. His healing will be gradual. She is not to be impatient but to wait on Me. Jonathan is united to My Christ like a little lamb. He too will bring many to salvation."

A perfect stranger, someone I had never met before, had just given me the same message I had received in McDonald's—that God was going to heal Jonathan gradually. I was now able to be at peace and go on. I could appreciate the blessings of Jonathan and enjoy watching him achieve each little milestone.

Jonathan taught us so much. Before he was born I was such an impatient person, primarily because things came so easily to me. When someone couldn't keep up, I became impatient, frustrated, and even angry. I thought they were being lazy or they didn't want to learn. It never occurred to me that they *couldn't* get it. Because of Jonathan, I began to have tremendous compassion for people who couldn't do things.

All the people at work I had wanted to fire, I now wanted to help. Not only did Jonathan help me feel this tremendous compassion for people who couldn't do certain things, but I also developed a deep appreciation for people who *could* do things; for people who were gifted with talents from the Lord. I was even in awe of something as simple as an eloquent presentation, because *my* son couldn't even talk.

Jonathan also helped our faith and trust in God. I was the in-control person, so God handed me something no human being could help me with. Only He could help me. The expression, "It brought me to my knees" proved true. Jonathan brought me to my knees in prayer.

Jonathan also taught me humility. Once a prideful person, I learned humility every time people sneered, rolled their eyes, or uttered a hateful remark about my son's odd behavior.

Our family always remarks about how much they have learned from Jonathan. In our society, the way we learn is primarily through language. We learn through books and teachers. But with Jonathan, we learned so much without a spoken word.

I was transformed in many ways. I could never go back to being the person I used to be. I saw the world through completely different eyes. I was a new creation!

At this time, God in His graciousness led me to two profound gifts. I received them both on Pentecost weekend, 1995. The first was the Baptism in the Holy Spirit; the second was my introduction to Schoenstatt, a Marian Apostolic Movement in the Catholic Church. The Baptism in the Holy Spirit is a deepening of the release of the Holy Spirit we receive from our Confirmation. It is a release of the charismatic gifts from 1 Corinthians 12. For me, this deepening of my relationship with the Holy Spirit provided the desire, the enthusiasm, and the passion to want to draw closer to the Lord, strive for holiness, and serve Him.

Schoenstatt is a deepening of our relationship with the Blessed Mother. As Fr. Langsch likes to say, "Union of the Blessed Mother and the Holy Spirit is what produced Jesus Christ. So it is a very powerful union."

For me, it was as though the Holy Spirit provided the *zeal* or the *passion*, and Schoenstatt provided the *way* to get to know, love, and serve Him better.

One of the themes in Schoenstatt spirituality is Mission Consciousness. It is thinking about your God-given mission. What did God intend for you to do with your life the day He created you? This captivated me at the time, because my life was growing so hectic. I had more and more responsibility at work. I also traveled a lot. On the personal side, I had more responsibilities at home. Not only was I taking care of my kids, but I was beginning to take care of parents too. I was rapidly getting to the point where something was going to have to give.

I prayed about it and felt the Lord showing me that my primary mission was my family. No matter how hard I worked, I couldn't make the difference there that I could make with my family. I prayed and talked to Tom. In prayer I felt I heard the Lord say, "Leave everything and follow Me."

This was going to be tremendously difficult for me. I was walking away from a career I had worked my entire life to achieve, a six-figure salary and all the implications that would have on my family. I would be stepping out in faith in God's promise to me that He was going to heal Jonathan, and I wouldn't have to work for two lifetimes. That was a lot!

Tom and I decided we needed a sign—*a big sign*. We decided that our sign would be if our nanny resigned. Our nanny was wonderful with our children. They loved her, and she had become my best friend. She had been with us for four years, and there was never a sign she might quit. And, I knew that if she ever did quit, I was the only person who could replace her. So, we prayed for about six months, "Oh, Lord, if I should quit working, please give me the sign." The Lord took me at my word. The day came when our nanny told us she was quitting.

So, what did Tom and I say? "*No!* Oh, God, we are not ready."

"Why do you want to quit?" I asked the nanny.

"My son is having trouble in school, and I feel I need to be home to help him."

"I have lots of experience with that," I told her. "I'll help you."

I went to her son's school, set up team meetings, came up with a comprehensive plan, and followed up to make sure they were being carried through. Her son began to do much better at school, so she decided not to quit. *Whew! The crisis was over!*

However, Tom and I soon realized we had circumvented the Lord's plans. *What did we do? We had been praying to Him to give us a sign, and when He did, we said, "No!"* We felt so badly. It grated on us for the next six months until we couldn't stand it. We finally agreed I had to quit. But now, after we had convinced our nanny to stay, how could we tell her she had to go?

One week before we planned to tell her, she came to us and said she was quitting. This time she was giving us notice because her husband was starting a jewelry business and she wanted to help him. He wanted to start after Christmas, in January. Coincidently, that was the exact date Tom and I had decided I was going to quit. God worked it all out in His perfect timing.

Now I had made it through another of His lesson plans. I was able to place myself on the altar and let go of the secular world, let go of all those achievements and success, let go of all the material things, let go of the money, and really learn to put my life in order with God first and my family second.

Immediately, God began working on my graduation present. It was my ministry work for Him because shortly afterward I became the leader of the Wednesday prayer group, district leader in Schoenstatt, and on the service team with Magnificat.

One may ask, "How is ministry work for other people a graduation present for me?"

The answer comes from the words of St. Augustine: "Only then do we possess a truth completely when we teach it to others. Only then do we truly love a virtue when we wish others to love it also. Only then do we wholly love God when we desire to make Him loved by all. Give money away or spend it and it is no longer yours, but give God away and you possess Him more fully for yourself." It is so true! My ministry work has brought me so much closer to the Lord and made me more of an instrument in His hands, and in the hands of the Blessed Mother.

At the same time God was working on my graduation present, He was also starting the next lesson plan.

I quit working in January, and the very next month, in February, my dad's health took a significant turn for the worse. Up until that point, Dad's health was fine, but when I quit working, everything changed. Two years later, my mother-in-law was diagnosed with terminal uterine cancer and she moved in with us. I now had three people with special needs—my mother-in-law, my dad, and my son. In addition, I had the other two kids, my husband, and two houses I was trying to take care of—ours and my dad's. Every day was a challenge. I might have a plan for the day, and in the blink of an eye my day would turn into fifty-two-card pickup. I had crises in three places at once: I needed to be at school, the hospital, and home. Coping with this was very stressful.

However, God speaks to us in many ways. Sometimes it is through books; sometimes it is through another person. For me one day, it was through EWTN. I was watching a program where Alice Von Hildebrand was talking about her husband, Dietrich's, writings. Dietrich Von Hildebrand is a famous Catholic theologian.

Von Hildebrand wrote, "Impatience is at the root of many other sins. If you have a plan for your day and then you get angry and frustrated if things don't go the way you planned, then what you are really saying is, God, I didn't like your plan for the day. I wanted my plan."

I knew right there *that* was my lesson plan from God. I needed to learn how to let go of every activity in my day and let God plan my days. I had to get to the point of being able to go to sleep at night knowing I may not have accomplished all the things I wanted to get done that day, but that I'd done everything *God* put in front of me, and I did it to the best of my ability. I had to learn to live every day and do each activity in it with a heroic holiness. I had to find the peace of Christ that surpasses all understanding.

Sometimes life seems like a random walk, but it's not. God is in every day, designing it with opportunities and lesson plans to help you grow. Reflect on your lesson plans from God. Cooperating with His plans transforms us into new creations as we become strikingly different before and after each one. The grace that abounds from each graduation present facilitates our journey toward holiness, and ultimately toward the Lord.

God is fulfilling His promise to me. Not only is Jonathan talking, but he is also reading and writing. He is in the seventh grade and doing fifth-grade work, which is phenomenal.

Praise be to God for His enduring faithfulness. Amen. Alleluia!

Bio –

Diane Bates is the wife of Deacon Tom Bates, mother of three boys, and grandma to one precious granddaughter. She has a Ph.D. in Physical Chemistry and worked in Research and Development for Abbott Laboratories for seventeen years. Her testimony has aired on EWTN radio and tells the tender love story of how, through the intercession of Our Lady, she became a new creation, especially when she learned that her youngest son was autistic. Diane was a founding member of the Magnificat Chapter in Grapevine, Texas. She has also served as the Magnificat South Central Regional Representative and as a Diocesan Leader in Schoenstatt, a Marian Apostolic Movement in the Catholic Church. She leads the Prayer Group at her Parish and is the Treasurer for the Magnificat Central Service Team that oversees the ministry worldwide.

Kathleen Beckman

I marvel at God's patience with me and my family. My story is a mixture of blessings and crosses. However, it reveals the merciful love of God actively pursuing and protecting us. I share my story to proclaim the Lord's marvelous deeds and to bring hope to those suffering in similar ways. Many suffering families and marriages need encouragement from those who have walked a similar path. My heart quickens to comfort those who are challenged in the same way I was challenged to "fight the good fight" St. Paul speaks of in defense of marriage and family.

My life with Christ before my adult conversion was "all or nothing." If I pushed God aside, I did so completely. For ten years I led a life of selfish ambition. Worldly enticements took priority over my relationship with God. Our lumber business was successful because of my husband's hard work. I enjoyed working as a medical assistant and quickly moved into a managerial position. I became more self-reliant, empowered by money, and put aside the pious practices of my youth. I was convinced that it was fine to enjoy the good things of life. Surely God would be pleased with how successful we had become because of our hard work.

This is what I told myself when we moved into a million-dollar neighborhood, Nellie Gail Ranch, at the age of thirty.

At that time, we had one son. I continued to work as a medical assistant until our second son was due, then I stayed home to care for the children. As the children grew we returned to Sunday Mass, but I did not pray outside of Mass. At first we sent the children to public school since we lived in a good school district. But when we heard our neighbors were placing their children in a prestigious Catholic school so they could be taught two languages, we decided to do the same.

One morning when I dropped the children off for class, one of the school mothers invited me to join a rosary prayer group. I quickly refused. She persisted to invite me for a year, and I repeatedly declined. Realizing I was not going to accept the invitation to the prayer group, she gave me Fr. René Laurentin's book about Mary's many messages around the world. This book remained unopened on my nightstand for months.

Then one day I felt prompted to read a page. I randomly opened the book to a message from the Blessed Mother that asked people to form prayer groups to intercede for the conversion of sinners. The message also said that we should pray as much as possible, and that three hours a day is not too much.

When I read this a powerful grace came with it. I was convinced about the call to pray the rosary, that it was urgent, and that my life would depend upon it. This was a big grace. My whole attitude about prayer changed almost instantly after reading one page of the book.

When I accepted an invitation to join a rosary prayer group in 1991, my spiritual conversion began. The prayer group consisted of mothers from St. Jeanne de Lestonnac school and parishioners of the Cathedral parish, men and women, young and old. Their dedication to prayer, their lively faith in God, and their love of Mary quickened my faith again.

At the beginning of the prayer meetings everyone stated personal intentions. One evening, a beautiful married lady closed her eyes and calmly prayed, "I offer my rosary tonight for the woman my husband is involved with. Lord, please bless her and her son, and find a suitable man to help them. Please keep my husband safe."

I was stunned to hear such a selfless prayer. I wondered, *How does a person become so big-hearted?*

Shortly afterward, this lady was diagnosed with cancer, suffered, and died. During her battle with cancer, her husband converted and was faithful to her. At the funeral he confided, "She was a saint. She helped save me from myself."

I found myself in the midst of committed disciples who wholeheartedly loved Jesus and Mary and were willing to sacrifice for love of God and souls. This small faith community became a school of prayer for me. For twenty years we gathered at weekly Friday night cenacles to pray the holy rosary as Our Lady asks, because souls are perishing for lack of prayer.

Another lovely lady in the prayer group named Lorraine spoke to me about starting Magnificat, A Ministry to Catholic Women, but I had not heard of this ministry. She had also spoken about Magnificat with other women regarding the start of a chapter in our area.

Lorraine intended to go with this group of women on a pilgrimage to Lourdes to ask for the grace to start Magnificat. Just prior to leaving she had a serious stroke that left her paralyzed and unable to speak. I visited her in the hospital before leaving on the pilgrimage. She held my hand and said in broken speech, "I can't start Magnificat now, so please do it for me." I heard her heartfelt plea but did not understand the ramification of what she asked. Lorraine suffered for a time as a victim soul and then passed to the Lord.

Members of the prayer group and I traveled to Lourdes, France, with a group of Catholic medical volunteers from the St. Jeanne de Lestonnac free medical clinic. Sr. Marie Therese Solomon founded this facility to provide medical care for indigent patients, the "poorest of the poor," as she called them.

Sister asked me to organize a pilgrimage for the clinic directors and volunteers. She was very interested in our spiritual formation since she knew it would be the basis of our continuing commitment to serve the medical needs of the people. Sister Therese and I joyfully planned the itinerary for approximately forty people. Fr. Raymond Skonezny, who served on the board of directors of the clinic, accompanied the pilgrimage group to provide the sacraments each day. At that time he was not yet my spiritual director, nor did I recognize that he had been my freshman religion teacher from St. Anthony's High School in Long Beach, California, years ago.

This would be my first trip to Europe. My husband and sons planned to accompany me on this pilgrimage. As it turned out, my eldest son and I went on the pilgrimage while my husband and youngest son remained at home due to our business.

The pilgrimage itinerary included flying into Paris and then a bus trip to Lourdes. In Paris, we visited Rue de Bac, the place where Blessed Mother appeared to St. Catherine Laboure and gave the message of the Miraculous Medal. We visited the incorrupt body of St. Vincent de Paul at Notre Dame Cathedral and many other magnificent Catholic churches, stopping to pray at each one. Then we traveled to Lourdes, visiting Paray Le Monial, where St. Margaret Mary Alacoque received the revelation of the Sacred Heart. We visited Ars, where St. John Vianney lived. Fr. Ray offered a private Mass for the pilgrimage group in the downstairs chapel. Some unforgettable, even miraculous, graces came for all of us during the Mass.

We visited the home of a little-known French mystic named Marthe Robin, a victim soul who existed on only the Eucharist. She bore the wounds of Christ in her body and was bedridden due to extreme physical infirmities. Upon entering her room, the Holy Spirit was so powerful that several of us, including Father, fell to our knees and prayed in awe.

These holy places and what they represented (the saints and their stories) made a deep, lasting impression on me. I prayed intently at each site and asked the saints whom we venerated to take me into their spiritual family, to make me their spiritual child. The stirring in my heart was intense with the desire to become like the holy ones who gave themselves completely to God in the service of the Church. The rich tradition of the Church and the colorful lives of the saints formed a beautiful, unexpected, spiritual tapestry that captured my heart in a way worldly things never did.

One particular night in Lourdes, tired from sightseeing and the hot weather, I retired to my tiny room and quickly feel asleep. In the middle of the night, awakened from a deep sleep, I perceived the powerful presence of Jesus in an unprecedented, tangible way. He allowed me to see Him in a mystical way that was clearer than if I'd seen Him in person.

Christ's presence was penetratingly majestic, yet gentle and kind. I somehow experienced the Incarnate Word—His indescribable majesty and beauty not of this world. He was full of light and alive with ineffable love radiating outward from His heart toward me.

I immediately responded with the words of St. Peter that welled up in my heart, "Lord, depart from me, a sinner." In the presence of Jesus I perceived my sin-sickness so clearly that it was painful. I felt it was unjust that King Jesus should gaze upon an imperfect creature in need of such tremendous purification. There should be a chasm between us, yet He seemed as close as my breath, as tangible as my heartbeat.

I kept repeating Peter's words to Jesus, "Lord, depart from me, a sinner," but the Lord remained for a good portion of that night. He worked in my soul in ways I cannot articulate even to this day. I share this only to bear witness that Jesus is truly alive, and that He manifests His Presence so the soul can experience His divine love that captures it for the sake of His glory.

When I awoke, I knew I would never to be the same. The experience of falling in love with Jesus has never waned since that night. It was as if my heart was magnetized to his Sacred Heart. I understood that He loved me. I would return His love in service of the Church as He willed. I would love all people and all things in and through His heart.

This grace has been so deeply imprinted upon my soul that it is as fresh today as the day it occurred. I did not speak about this night of grace for a long time. I wanted to test it by its fruit. Twenty-one years later, my heart is still in union with Christ's heart, manifested by my zeal for the things of God. That this occurred on my pilgrimage to Lourdes leaves no doubt that Mary, the Immaculate Conception, prepared the way that I would receive the grace of such conversion to love her Son. The Lord Jesus had captured me in totality.

Spiritual pilgrimages are opportunities for special grace. The last two popes have encouraged the faithful to plan time away from normal routines and make a spiritual journey to holy sites to pray and experience the Lord's presence. The grace given to me at Lourdes that night proved to be preparatory for what would happen later when a heavy cross came upon my family. The suffering in my family may have broken me completely if I had not been in close communion with the heart of my Redeemer.

The pilgrimage was an intense time of grace for all who participated. It had been two years since my first conversion back to the sacramental life, and for the first time I was experiencing the rich history of the Church, seeing the incorrupt bodies of saints—miracles that built up my faith. I was falling in love with the Lord and his Church. Prayer had become pure joy. This was the first of many such experiences. The experiences of annual pilgrimages with the prayer group and the daily discipline of liturgical prayer prepared me for the future trauma that would shatter the easy existence of our family life.

When I first left for Lourdes, I put what Lorraine said about Magnificat in the back of my mind, until Fr. Raymond brought it up while we were in Lourdes. He implored me to consider being on the founding service team. This team of four ladies was looking for one more person to begin the ministry. Since a priest was inviting me, I was open to exploring the possibility, but first I needed to experience Magnificat.

Upon returning home from Lourdes, Fr. Raymond took me to my first Magnificat prayer breakfast, hosted by the "mother chapter" in California, the San Fernando Valley chapter. I learned that Magnificat is based on the visitation scene in Luke's Gospel. My first Magnificat experience was truly like a "visitation" scene—women full of joy, rejoicing in God and imitating Mary in service to one another. The highlight was the inspiring testimony of the speaker. I felt the stirring of my heart that day and said "yes" to Father and to the four women who awaited me so we could start the Orange County Magnificat chapter.

Following the Lourdes pilgrimage, our prayer group attended the Southern California Renewal Communities conference. I had no prior exposure to the Catholic Charismatic Renewal before entering the conference with 10,000 Catholic charismatics! My first concern was whether this was authentically Catholic.

Fr. Robert Faricy, S.J., from Rome, led the first conference session I attended. He was praying for a gift called the Baptism or Renewal in the Spirit. I was skeptical. When he walked down the aisle, he stopped and prayed over me for the grace of a personal Pentecost.

I received a new prayer language initially, but I did not understand and doubted the whole experience. It was only afterward, when I returned home and continued praying, that I noticed a big difference in my interior life. It was as if a light switch was turned on from within, illuminating my mind and heart with God's light.

For example, I had an affinity for reading books about the lives of the saints and was prompted by the Holy Spirit to have an increased desire to become holy, to make Jesus Christ the only Lord of my life, to read Scripture, and to pray more. The Mass came alive for me in a new way. The things of this world no longer attracted me. The Holy Spirit had truly captured my life for Christ.

When I read a spiritual classic by Archbishop Martinez, *The Sanctifier*, I understood the grace of Baptism in the Holy Spirit to be a marvelous awakening to the Third Person of the Holy Trinity. So moved was I by this experience and by the writings of Archbishop Martinez, that at the end of the book I knelt down and prayed that I could always spread true devotion to the Holy Spirit just as Archbishop Martinez did in his life.

The grace of Baptism in the Holy Spirit is real, lasting, and life changing! This grace prepared me for what was to come. My conversion occurred in three stages: 1) Mary, when I took up the holy rosary, 2) Jesus, when I experienced Him at Lourdes, and 3) the grace of Baptism in the Holy Spirit, which animated my interior life.

I began going for spiritual direction to Father Raymond Skonezny in 1992. He was a Trappist monk who had studied in Rome. A Trappist monk knows about prayer and sacrifice, and I learned a lot from the stories he told about his seventeen years in Our Lady of the Most Holy Trinity Monastery in Utah. When Fr. Ray discovered that I was attending daily Mass, he urged me to do two things:

1. Let the liturgy of the Church fashion your prayer life. Let the Church be a spiritual mother guiding you by her liturgical worship. In this way the liturgy will animate your interior life and anchor you in Christ. Be mindful of the Church's liturgy and draw from it. It will be a fountain of grace for your soul. God will speak to you through the Church's liturgy. Listen for the Lord's voice after Holy Communion.

2. Pray every day for a minimum of one hour before the tabernacle. I do not care if you squirm in the pew. Do not leave until one hour passes. If your mind wanders and you are thinking a myriad of other things, stay with the Lord in front of the Blessed Sacrament. If you experience no consolation or perceive nothing but distraction, persevere to show up for prayer and the Lord will do everything for you.

Father Raymond's words settled into my heart like graced arrows of wisdom. I have done what he advised me to do for twenty years. I pay attention to the liturgical life of the Church. Grace streams into my soul in a synchronized rhythm with the liturgical seasons: Advent, Christmas, Lent, Easter, and ordinary time.

Father's advice to pray before the Blessed Sacrament sounded familiar. I recalled that my mother took my brothers and me to make visits to the Blessed Sacrament. Often during the week, especially on Fridays and always during Lent, we walked a mile and a half to St. Pancratius Church to "make a visit," as she would say. My mother appeared to be talking to God as if she were talking to her close friend. She sat us in the pew and then she went before the tabernacle to pray. As a child this seemed natural. I noticed that my mother was more peaceful and joyful after those visits to the tabernacle. It was time for me to resume those visits to the tabernacle.

One of the first signs of authentic conversion is repentance. After Lourdes, I returned to the Sacrament of Reconciliation on a weekly basis. The words of absolution prayed by the priest were a healing balm. My conversion moved me to desire the purification of the capital sins of pride, anger, envy, lust, gluttony, sloth, and avarice. The quote below reflects what was happening in my interior life:

"The Christian way is different, harder and easier. Christ says: Give me all. I do not want so much of your time, and so much of your money, and so much of your work: I want you. I have not come to torment your natural self, but to kill it. No half measures are any good. I do not want to cut off a branch here and a branch there, I want to have the whole tree cut down. I do not want to drill a tooth, or crown it, or stop it, but to have it out. Hand over the whole natural self, all the desires which you think innocent as well as the ones you think wicked—the whole outfit, and I will give you a new self instead. In fact, I will give you my self: my own will shall become yours." (C.S. Lewis, *Mere Christianity*)

At the start of my conversion, I had a dream where I saw a white sphere covered by many cancerous growths. As a trained medical assistant, I knew what cancerous growth looked like. What God was showing me was a representation of my soul sickened by the spirit of the world. I had a strong urge to hide myself from the Lord, not wanting Him to behold such a wretched thing. In the dream I turned away from Him and ran in the opposite direction. Then I seemingly bumped into the Blessed Mother, who said, "Ask for Divine Mercy."

I turned back to God and prayed, "Lord, have mercy on me, a sinner." The image of my soul began to clear up. Jesus provided the grace of true repentance; I no longer wanted to offend the Lord. The world and its allurements no longer captured my heart. Following every confession, I feel so much lighter spiritually. I am convinced we are created with the need to confess our sins, to unburden ourselves to the Lord in the confessional.

On the Feast of Our Lady of Lourdes, 2008, Cardinal Javier Lozano Barragan celebrated Mass for the sick and for pilgrims at the 16th World Day of the Sick. During his homily, the cardinal recalled that it was the 150th anniversary of the apparition of the Virgin Mary to Bernadette Soubirous in the grotto of Massabielle in Lourdes.

He posed the question, "Is it possible to experience the suffering of Christ in our own suffering, to find therein happiness and joy?" Then he said, "The answer can only come from the Holy Spirit, fusing our suffering with that of Christ through His infinite love. The Eucharist is the memorial of Christ's suffering. The reality of the mystery of suffering, which in Christ becomes positive, creative, redeeming, happiness and joy, while not ceasing to be extremely painful, is the Eucharist. Participation in the Eucharist is the authentic way to make our own suffering part of Christ's suffering. This is the Eucharistic communion. The Eucharist is thus our cross and our resurrection. It is the only true remedy to pain. It is the medicine of immortality."

The cardinal added that responding to the love of the cross implies pronouncing an unreserved "yes" to the mysterious plan of the Redeemer. This complete "yes" of love is the Immaculate Conception of our dear Mother, Mary, who participated "… on Calvary as the co-redeemer of the Savior … Christ on the cross suffered all the pains that his most holy Mother suffered. And she in Christ suffers all our pains; she assumes them and knows how to commiserate with us. Our suffering is also her suffering. Suffering has value inasmuch as the death of Christ inherently comprehends His resurrection."

God's grace is extremely practical and His timing perfect to prepare us for what is coming. The intensity of my conversion corresponded to the intensity of what was to come. My prayer life was progressing so that I recognized the voice of the Good Shepherd when He spoke through the liturgy or during times of prayer. Time spent in His Eucharistic Presence brought deep spiritual consolation.

In adoration, Jesus gave me an attraction to his Passion. I meditated on the sorrowful mysteries of the rosary as if I was the only person for whom He was dying. I would contemplate the crucifix for long periods of time; hours could pass and I never grew weary of thinking about the

Lord's Passion. I received consolation as the Lord taught me to place my suffering with His suffering on the cross. When I did so my suffering always seemed small compared to His. The contemplation of Christ's Passion was becoming incredibly personal.

Our family life was going well. Joy and prosperity abounded. Then suddenly, our comfortable family life was shattered.

It was a beautiful spring day, a Saturday morning when the boys had their sport games, which we enjoyed as a family. A phone call came, advising us to go immediately to St. Mary's Hospital. My father-in-law had been admitted. Two women driving by the front of our family lumber business had found Dad lying on the sidewalk in a pool of blood. They covered him with a blanket and called the paramedics.

At the hospital we discovered that Dad had been brutally beaten about the head with a piece of timber. When we saw him in the emergency room he was unrecognizable. It was shocking to see the sheer brutality of the violence against him. He needed brain surgery to save his life.

Dad underwent a surgical procedure called a frontal lobectomy, wherein the front lobe of the brain is removed to allow for the swelling from blunt-force trauma. Surgery did not save him. He died that day at the hands of two thieves. The case aired on the television program, *America's Most Wanted*. To this day, it is an unsolved crime.

To be at the bedside of a dying loved one is a special blessing, and a sorrow. To observe a person you love take his last breath and the body rendered lifeless is incredibly painful. One moment there is life, and the next moment it is rendered back to God. Gloriously, our faith entered to help reconcile the whole dying process, bringing much needed consolation. I kept reminding myself, "He lives. His life is not over, it is just changed."

After our family's trauma, I struggled to reconcile the reality of this violent murder with the permissive will of God, Who is love. How cheap life has become in a culture where a person kills an innocent man to steal a few things like a microwave and office equipment! I felt the horror of disrespect for life to the core of my being. There was a loss of innocence in my heart, and in the family. I experienced the culture of death that day and felt vulnerable for the first time in my sheltered life. I had always associated the culture of death with contraception, abortion, and euthanasia. This cold-blooded murder seemed the result of a culture turned away from protecting human life. This dark reality entered my family and was terribly personal.

On the day of the funeral the church overflowed its capacity. My father-in-law was a well-known, beloved pillar in the business community. Every face seemed to radiate a mystified sorrow. In a way, each person there had been violated. For me, I could only reconcile such pain by contemplating, Jesus, the Man of Sorrows.

Sadly, our family has never fully recovered from this violent loss. There has not been a cohesive unity in the extended family since that time. Our grief was too quickly pushed aside in an effort to return to normalcy. The copious tears shed in the hospital room and at the funeral were the last of them. We could not talk about the situation; it was too hard to articulate our grief and loss.

The family dug in to keep the business going. Our pain was repressed in an effort to cope with the traumatic loss of the father who was the glue that kept the family united. I could not repress the pain of this trauma. After my husband left for work, I would cry each day for months following the murder. I ran to the Blessed Sacrament, bringing my pain to Jesus, expressing my bewilderment. Not only was I grieving the loss of a father whom I loved as my own, but also the loss of innocence, the reality that horrible things happen in the world. Only Jesus could bring solace to my wounded heart. In the silence and solitude of those holy hours, I felt Jesus healing me.

Providentially, I was reading the diary of St. Faustina, secretary of Divine Mercy, when the murder occurred. At a later time, while I was trying to make sense of this tragedy, a grace came through the message of Divine Mercy. I felt the Lord asking me to pray for the eternal salvation of the murderer. At first, I was taken aback and put aside the inspiration. Daily before the Blessed Sacrament I sensed this call to intercession from Jesus, inviting me to ask for mercy so the murderer would not be eternally lost. During holy hours following the murder, the Lord taught me that He alone knows the disposition of a person's heart. He made me understand that no one gets away with murder. I could count on Divine Justice. Would I intercede for Divine Mercy?

I began to realize the magnanimity of Divine Mercy. God so loves the sinner He does not want anyone to be lost eternally. Grace made my heart docile and I did not refuse the Lord. I was able to pray for the soul of the murderer. In this sacrifice of intercession, I could fully appreciate the words of Jesus from the cross, "Father, forgive them, for they know not what they do."

Jesus desired me to echo His forgiving plea of forgiveness. I offered daily intercession for the murderer, and my heart grew in its capacity to forgive. This would be the first of many lessons on becoming a vessel of mercy for others. God granted me awareness that I have been the recipient of His mercy; therefore, I must extend mercy to others.

This trauma deepened my reliance on God and confirmed the efficacious power of praying before the Blessed Sacrament. I found great solace in the Eucharist. I could run to Christ, talk to Him, listen to Him, hear Him, and simply rest in Him. Never did I leave the tabernacle without having been enriched for being there. The more often suffering bore down on the family and me, the more I relied on those holy hours with God. The Lord never disappointed. He gave me precisely what I needed, when I needed it. He brings good out of every trial and temptation.

As a medical assistant I saw patients in terrible pain due to sickness. All medical resources were utilized to alleviate suffering and restore wellness. Medical science teaches that the human body is in a perennial process of purification and regeneration. There is also a consistent process of degeneration called the aging process that ultimately leads to physical death. This is one type of human suffering.

Another type of suffering is invisible, occurring in the soul of the person. My suffering is hidden in the depths of my heart. No one can see the insult and injury that caused my wounds, yet I know the reality of an interior torment that is as all-consuming as any physical pain in the body. These interior wounds are real, painful, and beg the attentive mercy of Jesus the Healer.

In my opinion, the science of the cross parallels the science of medicine. The body's process of purification and regeneration is at once life and death. It is the same for the soul who yields to the Divine Physician. In the Sacrament of Baptism, we enter mystically into the death and resurrection of the Lord and are born into the mystical body of Christ. So begins an interior life of grace that suffers a process of death and life toward transformation into Christ. As I struggled to discern the truth about the meaning and value of suffering in marriage and family life, the Saint Ignatius principle of discernment of spirits was a vital tool in helping me respond to suffering.

At thirteen years old, I met the man I would someday marry. We went through grade school, high school, and college together. We were best friends through those years, and our families socialized together. I was twenty years old when we married in the Church with the blessing of our parents. I had no doubt this was a match made in heaven. It was the fulfillment of a dream to marry a prince among men and begin a family. I knew my husband was a good Catholic and a righteous person. We desired to create the same loving Catholic family environment in which we had been nurtured.

Our married life was blessed, although we were not always faithful to the practice of our faith. We were blessed with two sons, and I was able to stay home to raise the children after twelve years of working as a medical assistant. My husband was a good father to our sons and devoted to me. Our lumber business prospered, and we lived a comfortable, if not extravagant, lifestyle. We were living the American dream.

My husband suffered with chronic, serious medical conditions from as early as his thirties. I became concerned about his health when he lost forty pounds in two months. One day when he was sick and resting in our bedroom, I entered to see if he needed anything. His words would pierce my heart like a thousand swords. Nothing prepared me to hear these words: "I do not love you. We should never have gotten married. It was a mistake."

After twenty-two years of what I perceived to be a good marriage, this rejection was sudden and unexpected. Utterly shocked, God flooded me with grace in that moment. My husband was emotionally distraught after sharing his feelings, so I moved to comfort him. I became forgetful of myself and concentrated on consoling him. Though I could not process what I had just heard, I was filled with love (from the Lord) and began to thank my husband for allowing me to feel that I was loved for the past twenty-two years. He seemed in agony. Before me was a broken person who needed help, and his needs were more important than mine. My response to this trauma was truly the grace of God.

In the dark days and nights that followed this revelation, I was thrust from a position of security into an uncertain future. My husband wanted to separate. We agreed that it might be good to get away to consider the situation. We planned that he would take an apartment by our business for one month and then return. I prayed this would be a time for him to come to his senses. Then everything would return to normal.

The months passed into years.

My husband changed into a person I scarcely recognized because of his sudden indifference to the family and me—so unlike his former self. These are matters of the heart that cut to the core. Suffice to say that I struggled daily for the sake of holding our family together.

The rupture of this sacramental union felt like I was cut in two. Scripture states: "Two shall become one" in the covenant of marriage. Little did I realize how much my identity was interwoven with my husband! The Lord would teach me now the true power of sacramental grace of Catholic marriage.

Daily Mass and Holy Hour enabled me to carry on for our eleven-year-old son. In the area of my personal dignity, the evil one toyed with me, presenting an image of myself as one spurned because of my own faults and imperfections. I began to perceive myself as one worthy of rejection and shouldered all the blame. The battleground of my mind became a place of spiritual warfare. The spiritual battle was intense. It required constant discernment of spirits to distinguish the lie from the truth. In the discernment of spirits I relied on the help of my priest and spiritual advisor.

For years I resisted the reality of the separation and bore the weight of the cross with clenched fists, trying to hold it together until all would be normal again. I experienced the normal stages of denial, grief, anger, and then surrender. Each stage brought a corresponding grace. The Holy Spirit guarded my tongue from professing negativity about my husband's actions. Grace moved me to desire to forgive the one who caused the hurt, though there were terrible temptations to retaliate at first. The Holy Spirit taught me how to pray for my husband. The result was that even while separated we remained friends and business partners. He supported the family in the same manner as always. Nevertheless, when we went to our sons' football games together, spent holidays together, and went to family counseling, there was a painful division in our marriage.

The Eucharist and Holy Hour became my strength. I drove our son to school then went to Mass and remained in prayer for hours, desperately seeking God's will and some relief from the bleeding wounds of my heart. In the light of the tabernacle, I began to understand that God is so preoccupied with my salvation that He allowed my husband to become the instrument of my personal crucifixion. He allowed me to be broken open, to be brought low, to reestablish the proper hierarchy in my life. God would now move to the foremost place in my heart. The pride I took in my husband and family was a reflection of self-love. Our financial success gave me license to do whatever I wanted, so I felt that I was in control and the master of my life. God would now teach me the truth of my spiritual poverty.

The perfect family we once presented had become sick. Now, the light of truth was going to draw out the poison. As a wife and mother, there was unspeakable pain observing our close-knit family go into separate worlds of grief. Seemingly, only a thread held us together. The course ahead seemed obscured as we lived moment by moment in uncertainty. I had never before experienced such instability in my life.

But by uniting my suffering to Christ crucified, I felt myself become an intercessor for my family. I felt the Lord's invitation to lay down my life for the sake of the salvation of our family. I understood that even though physically separated, we were still spiritually bound by the sacramental grace of matrimony. The highest purpose of this union was each other's eternal salvation. I recall a priest once preached that God does not give us the spouse we desire, but rather the spouse we need to get to Heaven.

Our marriage is still in transition. The course was rockiest during the first seven years. The past several years have been a process of much healing. Each member of our family seems to have reconciled, at some level, with what happened. It is a testament to God's merciful fidelity that we are still together. My husband is returning to his true self and works long hours to support the family. The children have passed through various phases, growing in character and virtue. Because of the respect they see between their father and me, and because of the love I profess for my husband, they feel secure and are moving forward in their own lives. They understand how fragile the gift of family is. I believe they will take great care in their own families. What we have gone through has taught us the importance of fidelity to one another and reliance upon God.

Through my own experience and suffering, the Lord widened my scope of love to include prayer for all marriages and families. On a pilgrimage to the Shrine of Divine Mercy in Poland, I placed my head on the first class relic of St. Faustina—a large fragment of bone encased on the altar rail that is positioned in front of the miraculous image of the Divine Mercy. There I prayed, "Oh, Lord, I bring you my husband and children."

Immediately, I heard in my heart these words of Jesus: *"Would you bring me only your husband and children? Rather, bring all husbands and children!"*

The trials in our marriage helped me discover that it is possible to love without being loved in return. Is this not how God first loved me? Love is a decision of the will. I desired only the Lord's will for our marriage.

A Marian priest volunteered to lead me through a process of discernment through the St. Ignatius exercises to seek God's will for my marriage. After one year of weekly spiritual exercises and reading the writings of Pope John Paul II on marriage and the Theology of the Body, it was discerned that God was calling me to remain on the cross in my marriage. The Lord filled me with enough love to bless my husband. Eucharistic grace empowered me to be as Christ for my hurting family during these tumultuous years.

By looking at the lives of women saints who suffered marital discord, I found holy examples to follow during these years. There are many women saints, St. Monica and St. Rita for examples, who suffered in their marriages and were able to transcend the situation. I drew strength and encouragement from the examples of their lives. Even in our modern culture, God's proven way of sanctity still exists for those who persevere and believe in the saving power of the cross.

I also discovered that there are women saints who divorced because of marital oppression, such as St. Fabiola and Cornelia Connolly, whose cause for beatification is underway. As Rhonda Chervin states in her book, *A Kiss from the Cross*, the issue of whether to choose a path of outward resistance or inward self-offering will depend on the character of the husband, the circumstances, the needs of the children, and one's own emotional survival. In my case, when all illusion was stripped from me, I found refuge in the Sacred Heart of Jesus. The love of God captured me thoroughly and empowered me to embrace the cross in the knowledge that there was meaning and value to my suffering. My pain was intense and it was not taken away. The Lord provided a place for me to put it—namely in His pierced heart on the cross. He helped me understand that I could win grace for my husband's conversion and for the lives of the children if I would embrace the cross. "God works all things for good for those who love him, who are called according to his purpose" (Romans 8:28).

The Lord provided for our family's needs. Grace flooded each family member like a protective blanket so we would not self-destruct. In the midst of this trial, we entered into our true identity as dependent children of the eternal Father. We were not hopeless victims. There were years of confusion and sadness as we hung together by a thin, golden thread of grace. We each were being transfigured according to God's grace. The cross was the means of transformation for each of us. "He heals the broken hearted, and binds up their wounds" (Psalm 147:3).

One evening, in adoration of the Blessed Sacrament at St. Michael's Norbertine Abbey, I looked up at the large, detailed crucifix above the altar and prayed, "Oh, Lord, there is such disorder in my family. How can You be in this?"

In the depths of my heart, I heard the Lord say, "Look closely at the crucifix. Is there anything more disordered? I am here in the midst of disorder to restore creation."

I stood corrected. My Savior is compelled by His divine nature, which is all love, to enter into human disorder in order to bring forth the tranquility of order. His divine order does not necessarily look like our concept of order. "'I will restore you to health, and your wounds I will heal,' says the Lord" (Jeremiah 30:17).

The tragedy of this world is that so much pain is wasted. There is a bright jewel of merit for suffering united to Christ's passion, death, and resurrection. St. Paul teaches the truth of the disciples' mission to co-redeem with Christ. The call to co-redemptive suffering resounded in my heart, and I persevered by the grace of God. If my suffering had meaning and value, it was worth it. This truth kept me grounded and balanced in the midst of the tornado ripping through my household. I was fully engaged in a spiritual battle over the soul of our family. I clung to the following Scripture:

"Be sober and vigilant. For your adversary, the devil is like a roaring lion, traveling around and seeking those whom he might devour. Resist him by being strong in faith, being aware that the same passions afflict those who are your brothers in the world. But the God of all grace, who has called us to his eternal glory in Christ Jesus, will himself perfect, confirm and establish us, after a brief time of suffering." (1 Peter 5:8–10)

My vocation is wife and mother. But within this vocation is the deeper call to holiness. God gave me the bigger vision. A sacrifice now would procure a great reward eventually. My marriage situation continues to evolve in the Hands of the Almighty One through suffering, but I will not close off my heart or cease to love because of pain or fear.

My Eucharistic vocation proved to be a source of courage and hope. The Lord ministered to my broken-heartedness daily. My joy returned when I surrendered everything to God. Co-redemptive suffering proved to be the means by which God would increase and I would decrease.

Only an experience of God's ineffable love heals the human heart. There is no other method of healing that will last. All who suffer are in need of the delicate-yet-strong hand of Jesus, the Healer. He remains in our midst, accessible to each person in all the tabernacles of the world. Not only is He waiting there but He also longs for us to come to Him.

Did He not say, "Come to me, all you who are weary and I will give you rest" (Matt. 11:28)? Resting in the Eucharistic heart of Jesus brings revival and hope. Our family is together now in a whole new way. Our patience with one another has truly paid huge dividends toward healing each person and unifying us again.

In October 2005, I had the privilege of sharing my testimony at the National Assembly of the Council of Major Superiors of Women Religious at the Shrine of Our Lady of the Snows, Belleville, Illinois. The theme of the assembly was "Healing and the Mystery of Suffering."

The keynote speaker, George Weigel, presented "The Mystery of Suffering in the Teaching and Life of Pope John Paul II." As the biographer of the late pope, he relayed the martyrdom of love that John Paul II lived. The world could witness John Paul II's physical infirmities, and his spiritual radiance was easily perceived. His biographer had a more intimate perspective to share.

During the course of the long weekend, I gathered with many superiors of various women religious communities to worship the Lord at daily Mass. Different bishops, including Archbishop Raymond Burke, celebrated

Mass. The lectures included topics of human suffering, matters of life and death. Among the many religious orders represented in the CMSWR, it was edifying to see the multi-faceted services the various orders provide the Church in fields: medical care, healing arts, legal, teaching and prayer, and spiritual formation. I was encouraged to see so many vocations, and such profound depth of dedication to Christ. God is renewing the Church in this area. These spiritual brides of Christ are grace for the Church.

Mother Regina Marie, O.C.D., Carmelite Sisters of the Most Sacred Heart of Jesus, suggested my name as a speaker on suffering in the family. Mother assured me the committee would consider many other speakers as well. It seemed unlikely that my testimony would be selected. Approximately nine months passed when I received a phone call from the CMSWR in Washington D.C., inviting me to speak at the National Assembly. Then the letter of confirmation came with the list of speakers. They included Archbishop Raymond Burke, among other bishops, George Weigel, and various other doctors and lawyers. Then I saw my name.

I immediately went before the Blessed Sacrament, asking, "Lord, how can this be?" I prayed fervently to comprehend how I fit into such an esteemed assembly of consecrated people.

In the depths of my heart, the Lord said, "Ordinary! I chose an ordinary soul so I can manifest My Presence to the assembly by the example of your ordinary life. A life of prayer is a gift for the whole Church. I will be with you."

God was faithful to uphold me, an ordinary soul stepping out in faith, to give testimony at the CMSWR National Assembly.

The example of Mary's life taught me how to say "yes" to God so the Lord could reign in my heart and act in my life. The highest form of wisdom is surrender to God. If I did not give my "yes" to God in the midst of the great trials in my family, I may have reverted to the way of the world. Perhaps my family would have completely unraveled. My personal "yes" to God's plan, though painful for a time, was the key to allowing God to work things out in His way. By echoing the fiat of the Savior and the fiat of the Mother of the Savior, I discovered an empowerment of the Holy Spirit that brought forth a new life for my family and me.

As a disciple of Christ, I am mindful of the condition for discipleship given by the Lord in Mark's Gospel: "Whoever wishes to come after me must deny himself, take up his cross, and follow me" (Mk. 8:34). There is particular suffering unique to each person. But there is one, the Word Incarnate, who suffered all in His body, mind, heart and soul so as to heal me. "Upon him was the chastisement that makes us whole, by his stripes we are healed" (Isa.53:5). This truth became my consolation when I needed healing in all areas of my life. My daily Eucharist was the source of healing love applied directly to the wound caused by the murder of a loved one and strife in my marriage. I needed the daily healing salve of divine intimacy that is uniquely experienced in the Eucharist.

Sometimes in the midst of the most painful years, there were days when my feet seemingly did not touch the ground because I felt my heart inebriated with Divine Love. There were seasons when my joy was so complete I would have to remind myself, "I should be in pain, but I am not!" There were seasons when He took away sadness and preoccupied me with things of Heaven. The cross, at times so terrible, became sweet. How? It was terrible when I fought against it. It was sweet when I yielded my will in totality. The deprivation of human intimacy in a sacramental marriage is a sacrifice I offer God in reparation for the sins of my family. It is not ideal by any means, but it is the way it is for now. The Lord taught me to look at the cross in light of the resurrection, because resurrection is what Jesus is about!

Our family has been blessed with countless miracles over many years of restoration.

This past summer our eldest son married a beautiful lady from Berlin, Germany. As they stood at the altar of the Mission Basilica where, as a family, we attended Sunday Mass for ten years, I gazed at the beautiful young couple with so much love and hope for a future of marital joy. I was not afraid for them. My husband and I stood together praying for our son and new daughter. I harbored no more anger or anxiety over what transpired in our marriage.

As I listened to the Scripture reading of the Mass, I realized they had chosen the same verses my husband and I chose for our wedding thirty-three years ago. I cling to the truth and beauty of that Scripture. Thanks be to God, in 2014 we celebrated 40 years of marriage. The hills and valleys of the journey made it all the more amazing!

> "Love is patient; love is kind. It is not jealous, love is not pompous, it is not inflated, it is not rude, it does not seek its own interests, it is not quick-tempered, it does not brood over injury, it does not rejoice over wrongdoing but rejoices with the truth. It bears all things, believes all things, hopes all things, and endures all things. Love never fails. So faith, hope and love remain, these three, but the greatest of these is love." (1 Cor. 13:4–8, 13)

Bio–

Kathleen Beckman, L.H.S., has served in Magnificat since 1991 and is presently on the Magnificat CST Advisory Team and Leadership Formation Team. She is President and Co-founder of the Foundation of Prayer for Priests, an apostolate serving the Holy See. The author of several books on the spiritual life, her new book published by Sophia Institute Press is titled *Praying for Priests: A Mission for the New Evangelization.* She is also a writer for Catholic Exchange, and a retreat leader for priests, sisters, and laity. Since 2012, Kathleen hosts the *Living Eucharist* weekly program that airs internationally on Radio Maria, and is a frequent guest on EWTN TV and Radio. She is on faculty for the Pope Leo XIII Institute, a teaching apostolate for priests serving the Church's ministry of exorcism, healing, and deliverance. She and her husband are business owners and have two sons, one daughter-in-law, and one granddaughter.

Johnnette Benkovic

I had the great privilege and honor of being born into a Catholic home and spending the first twelve years of my education in parochial schools. The Vincentian Sisters of Charity taught me in elementary school, and the Dominican Sisters during my high school years. I remember with such fondness how the Sisters of St. Vincent DePaul taught us about the beautiful gift of faith, illustrating it in such a way that it became embedded in the very fabric of our hearts. And they did this so simply, so naturally!

For example, one winter's morning Sister was instructing us about grace and the quality of the soul in the state of grace. "Look out of the window, children," she instructed.

It was a sunny day, crisp and cool. A fresh snowfall from the night before blanketed our school lawn. The brilliance of the sunshine reflecting off the new-fallen snow glowed with a near-blinding radiance. All fifty-six of us oohed and ahhhed as our little eyes beheld the dazzling scene.

"This is what your soul looks like when you make a good confession," Sister said.

This comparison spoke to my little heart profoundly, and to this day that memory remains in my mind, un-dulled by the years. With it remains the desire planted there so many years ago—to be united to the One who can make us so radiantly pure.

Faith was the joy of my life at that time. I can still remember singing love songs to our Lord and writing poetry to Him. The saints were also a great love of mine, especially Saint Therese of Lisieux, more affectionately known as the Little Flower.

One day, at the age of eight, my mother was baking a French coffeecake in the kitchen and sat me up on the counter. She wanted to teach me how to measure, how to put this and that into the bowl, and how to use a mixer. But the truth is, I had no interest in baking back then—and still don't! So, there I sat on the counter-top, watching my mom prepare her recipe for French coffeecake and growing more bored by the minute. When I could stand it no longer, I picked up her recipe and wrote a prayer on the back to St. Theresa, the Little Flower.

It went like this: "St. Theresa, shower me with roses; shower me with roses of grace so that my soul might shine like white lace. St. Theresa, shower me with roses, shower me with roses until I die so that my soul to God may fly."

About fifteen years ago, I was looking through my mom's cookbooks, searching for a certain recipe, and there I found the French coffeecake recipe. On the back was the poem I had written. The print was big, and written in the perfect Palmer Method—two lines for the capital letters and one line for the small letters. What a joy to find!

However, when I entered high school, everything began to change. In the early 60s, a cultural revolution was already underway, and it moved inside the Church after the Second Vatican Council ended in 1965. I can still remember going home for summer break and waving goodbye to the sisters in their long habits and veils. When I saw them again, their habits were shorter and their hair was showing. It was all so bewildering—and would only become more so when I graduated from high school in 1968 and entered the Pennsylvania State University.

I was a typical college co-ed at first. But I wasn't at the University very long before I discovered there was something radical taking place, a new hip movement that I very much wanted to join. So I traded in my little plaid skirts for bell-bottom jeans, and those pretty fuzzy sweaters for army fatigue shirts. I put away my contact lenses and began sporting granny glasses. I even had the lenses tinted pink so that I could see the world through "rose-colored glasses."

And that's exactly what I did for the next two years of my college experience. I was having the time of my life—on the surface. But the more consumed I became by the rebellious culture of the time, the less I could reconcile my behavior with my Catholic beliefs. It was clear to me that something had to go, and unfortunately that something was my faith.

Looking back on it now, I realize that my slide into sin was a gradual process of sorts. Rare is the person who wakes up one morning and decides to become a great sinner. It happens more slowly and subtly, one small, sinful decision at a time, "little" sins at first, the venial variety, the kind the saints warn us not to commit because they chip away at the edifice of grace in our souls. As a result, those "little" sins soon give way to bigger and more serious sins, the kind we call "mortal sins" or "grave sins."

And so it was with me at Penn State. I didn't wake up one morning and say, "Today I am really going to become a big sinner." I did it gradually and slowly by making one poor decision after the other—a little sin here, a little sin there. One day I woke up and realized that now it was a big sin here and a big sin there.

I can still remember standing before the mirror on my twenty-first birthday and looking at myself. *Is that me?* I wondered. I barely recognized myself. How did I end up like this, so rebellious and faithless and sinful? I suddenly felt as if the whole facade I had fashioned for myself was crumbling to pieces. Perhaps I had internalized the prevailing cultural messages too much—the anger over the war, the many social injustices, the rush to become "liberated" from common-sense, moral constraints—because I had developed a deep sense of fatalism that robbed me of all passion for life. The resulting depression had become so profound I wondered if I would make it through the day. In that moment, I realized that my lifestyle in those last couple of years wasn't liberation—it was hell.

Isn't that how it often goes? We create our own hell by the choices we make—one poor choice after the other—choices that are so often centered on our own desires and selfish intents.

I remember feeling like I had to get out of my apartment. I felt claustrophobic. It was as if the world was closing in on me. I had to get outside. I needed a change of scenery. I needed to get away. Mostly, get away from *me!*

The weather at State College was beautiful that day, absolutely glorious. As I left my apartment, the brilliance of the day stood in sharp contrast to my own interior darkness. It was too bright outside, too lovely. The sun, the fresh air, the beauty of nature was painful. I couldn't stand it, not while I felt so dark and dirty and desperate. I decided to duck into a popular college hangout, a bar.

Funny to think about it now, but this bar was subterranean. It was located below street level. You had to walk down steps to enter through a basement door. In many ways that downward journey was metaphoric of the direction my life had taken.

When I sat down at a table, I asked for a glass of water. The waitress didn't seem too happy about that order because she realized there wouldn't be a tip. But I was too engrossed in my own misery to worry much about her disappointment. The darkness in the room was symbolic of my own interior depression, my emotional and spiritual state.

But there was something familiar about that darkness. It reminded me of the confessional. I like the traditional confessional. There is something about the darkness of the confessional box that aids me in getting in touch with myself.

As I sat in the bar that day and began to get in touch with myself again, it made me cry—and do something I hadn't done in a very long time.

Pray.

"Lord, I used to be so sure of You. The misery in my heart is so great, I am not even sure of You. But if You exist, and if You love me, could You show me? Because if You don't show me, Lord, I'm likely to do something very serious."

I remember getting up from the table with tears streaming down my cheeks. I walked back up those steps and out into the sunlight, and I remember throwing my head back and letting the sun dry the teardrops on my face. When I opened my eyes, there in the azure sky, with nary a cloud floating by, was a rainbow. A rainbow! In that instant, in the way only God can make you sure, I knew it was the sign I had asked for. God loved me, and He was showing me that love and proving to me He existed.

It was a turning point in my life, a beginning of a conversion, a return to what I had once cherished but had so foolishly left behind. I wish I could tell you the experience sent me right back into the arms of Holy Mother Church, but that wouldn't be true. Ten years would pass before I came all the way home to the Faith.

By then I was married with three children and had started to take an insurance class with a friend who was in the middle of a painful and difficult divorce. As we drove to and from class every weekday, she would share her grief with me, but also her confidence that Jesus had a plan for her even in the midst of the suffering she was experiencing. I was so touched by the depth of her faith. She believed God could work through her agony and bring good out of it for herself and her sons.

An amazing thing happened to me in the depths of my soul. I felt a stirring of grace in my heart. Perhaps it was the rekindling of the grace I received at my baptism as an infant. I don't know for sure.

One day I said to my friend, "It sounds like you have a personal relationship with the Lord."

She said, "Oh, I do!"

"It sounds like you talk to Him," I said.

"Yes, I do," she responded.

"Really? And you hear Him?"

"Yes, I do," she said.

"Do you think I could have a relationship with Him like that?"

"Oh, Johnnette, I am quite certain. I am quite certain that you could!" she replied with a bit more enthusiasm than I expected. With that she invited me to a prayer meeting the following Tuesday night.

As it turned out, the prayer meeting was at my own parish of Espiritu Santo (Holy Spirit), and it was a night I will never forget. It was August 25,

1981. We were late, but this didn't stop my friend from insisting we go inside anyway.

We walked into the church. The people were standing with their arms raised high and singing with gusto. However, I noticed they weren't singing in English or any other language I could identify. In fact, they weren't even singing in the same language. I didn't know what was going on and I wondered if it was "okay."

I asked my friend, "Do you think Father knows about this?"

She assured me, "Oh, I am very sure."

"Do you think this is really Catholic?" I queried.

"Oh, yes. It is really Catholic. Come on. Let's go up front to the first pew."

"To the first pew!" I exclaimed. I never sat in the first pew!

She urged, "Let's go, Johnnette." And off we went.

How do I describe what happened in that short walk? It was as if shackles were released from me with every step I took. Joy began to flood my soul, and hope began to fill my heart. By the time we made our way into the pew, I was experiencing the release of the Holy Spirit in me. I felt zapped by Him! I lifted my arms to the heavens, began to proclaim the glory of the Lord, and gave way to whatever song or utterance came from my tongue. It was glorious—heaven on earth.

I couldn't wait to get home to tell my husband, Anthony. As soon as I got home, I rushed through the door and excitedly announced, "Anthony, I went to a prayer meeting at our parish church, and you won't believe this but people were singing out loud, really singing—and loudly—in church and having a really good time. Did you know you can have fun in church? Can you believe that?"

He was surprised, to say the least, about the change that happened within his wife, but that's another story we'll save for another time. I had come back to the Church, and when I did, our Father God was as merciful and gracious to me as the father in Jesus' parable, who welcomed home his prodigal son.

God lavished His love upon me, and I lapped it up like a kitten laps up milk from a saucer. I was so hungry for Him; I couldn't get enough of Him. I couldn't get enough of prayer. I couldn't get enough of prayer meetings. I couldn't get enough of sacred Scripture. I read it every day and learned how to do Lectio Divina, holy reading, an ancient prayer tradition in the Church. Every word jumped off the page and seemed to be written just for me.

One passage in particular was most meaningful to me. It brought me wisdom and understanding, healing and hope, confidence and assurance. It became the rudder of my spiritual life. It is Ephesians 1:3–4.

This passage answered for me the three big existential questions I was asking at Penn State and in the subsequent years of my young adulthood. Who was I? Why was I? What was my purpose and mission in life? Perhaps you have asked these questions, too. Many have. I found the answers to them in Verse 4 of this passage. The Apostle Paul writes, "God chose us in Him before the world began to be holy and blameless in His sight, to be full of love." As I prayed through this passage, its meaning became stunningly clear. I "saw," as we can only see through the Holy Spirit, the reality of who I am and who every person is, why it is that we are, and what our purpose and mission in life is all about.

Each one of us has been especially selected by God—*chosen* by Him— to have life, that we might experience the fullness of His love, and be transformed by it. Thus do we grow in holiness and blamelessness, thus does divine love take up residence within us, and thus do we become conduits of His love in the history of man entrusted to us by virtue of the timing of our birth.

What healing this understanding brought me—I was intentioned by God from all eternity! What hope it gave me—I was called to know God and become like Him! What joy it ignited in me—my mission was to be His love in the world!

I realized still more—there is nothing that happens to us in life of which God is not aware and for which He does not provide the grace to get us through and use it for our best spiritual advantage. Whether it be accomplishment or disappointment, success or failure, suffering or joy, trial or pleasure, struggle or ease, God knows about it and He gives the grace to meet our need.

It is verse 3 of Ephesians 1 that tells us this. The verse says, "Praise be the God and Father of our Lord Jesus Christ who has bestowed on us in Christ every spiritual blessing in the heavens."

Notice the passage says God has bestowed on us in Christ Jesus every spiritual blessing in the heavens. This verb is in the present perfect tense. This tense indicates that an action which began in the past continues in the present and will continue also into the future. It is ongoing. Now, what past event in Christ has bestowed on us spiritual blessings? The answer, of course, is His redemptive act.

Through the Paschal Mystery, the passion and the death and the resurrection of Jesus Christ, redemptive grace is made available to us. This grace brings with it the promise of eternal salvation as well as the grace we need for every moment of our life. Objectively, redemptive grace exists, but to be efficacious, we must receive it.

The door that opens us up to receive redemptive grace and all of its spiritual blessings is baptism. The Sacrament of Baptism initiates us into the life of grace, and every sacrament thereafter fortifies, strengthens, nourishes and enriches God's grace within us as long as we remain in the state of grace. Actual grace, the "Johnny-on-the-spot" grace, is always available to us 24/7, in every circumstance, in every situation, in every trial, in every misgiving, in every doubt, in every state of confusion, in every struggle, in everything in all of our life.

No time in my life did the Ephesians passage serve me better than on the morning of March 20, 2004. At quarter to five that morning there was a knock on our door. I was instantly concerned because of the hour. For some reason, I immediately thought of a friend who had lost her son in a car accident. She had said this was how the police came to notify her.

As I walked to the door, I tried to talk down the panic rising up in me. "It can't be the police," I told myself. "They would never use the side door by the garage; they would come to the front door. Don't worry, Johnnette, everything is fine. It cannot be the police. It can't be. It just can't be the police. It cannot, it cannot, it cannot. But who else would come to our door at quarter to five in the morning?" The panic was winning out. My heart was beating wildly.

Two highway patrolmen were standing at the door when I opened it. I noticed the lights of their cruiser were not on and my son's truck wasn't in the driveway. I felt the life drain out of me. The officers asked me to identify who I was, and I gave them my name.

"May we come in, ma'am?"

"Yes, of course," I said.

They asked, "Are you alone, ma'am?"

I knew. Right then and there. "No, officers, my husband is with me."

"Go get him," they said.

I went to waken Anthony from a sound sleep, and when we walked back into the family room the police officers snapped to attention.

"Mr. and Mrs. Benkovic, on behalf of the Florida State Highway Patrol and the State of Florida, we regret to inform you that at 1:01 AM this morning your son, Simon, lost his life in a vehicular accident."

No words can describe what welled up in me as those words assaulted my ears and pierced my heart. The only thing I remember is doubling over in pain, a pain that was localized in my womb.

I asked the officers only two questions. "Was there anyone in the truck with my son?"

"No ma'am," they responded.

"Praise be to God."

"Yes, ma'am," said the officer.

Then I asked, "Officer, was there any other vehicle involved?"

"No, ma'am," he responded.

"Praise be to God," I said.

"Yes, ma'am," he responded again.

Where did those two questions come from? Looking back on it now, they were coming from the depths of the agony I was feeling in that moment, a searing, dark, abyss of anguish. I couldn't bear the thought of any other parent having to hear what I had just heard, or to know that another life had been lost in Simon's truck that night. Once I had those assurances, the pain of suffering overwhelmed me.

I fled to our bedroom and flung myself on the floor. The most dreadful sounds came out of me, uncontrollable, animal-like. I recalled the passage from Jeremiah 31:15, "Rachel mourns for her children, but they are no more, she refuses to be consoled because her children are no more."

I was wailing for my son … who was no more.

What pain! What devastation! I could not bear it and cried out to my God.

Scene after scene of Mel Gibson's movie, *The Passion of the Christ*, which I had recently seen twice, began playing in my head. The scenes were those of the Blessed Mother, one scene after the other of Our Lady. Somewhere in that dark and desperate moment I sensed the Lord was entrusting to me some kind of grief that was in association with Our Lady, but He was also telling me that Our Lady was there; that she was there for me. I didn't feel her. I didn't see her. But she was there nonetheless.

I reminded the Lord, "I have proclaimed Ephesians 1:3 from one end of this country to the other, from north to south, from east to west. I have proclaimed it on television. I have proclaimed it on the radio for seventeen years, and I believe it. Do You hear me, Lord? I believe it, and You tell us in Ephesians 1:3 that You give *us every spiritual blessing in the heavens*, and I am holding You to that. And I'm going to tell You which blessing I want.

"I want the very blessing that Our Lady received from You, that held her firm underneath the cross while her Son was being tortured to death. That is the blessing I want, Lord. Do You hear me, please, do You hear me?"

There was no sensible consolation. No interior consolation. No lifting of the weight of grief bearing down on me. No release from the pain in my womb. No surge of hope in my heart. Nothing, absolutely nothing, except for this: there was the light of grace, a grace that beckoned me to truth and decision. Am I going to trust in the Lord or am I not? Am I going to trust that, even though I don't feel it, the grace that sustained Our Lady under the cross of her Son is here for me now?

You see, faith is one of the theological virtues we receive at baptism and it resides in our intellect. We give a "yes," an intellectual assent, to that which we know to be true. In that moment of my deepest travail, I knew the Word of God was true. I knew that Ephesians 1:3 was true. I knew that the truth of it didn't depend on my feelings or my grief. It was *objectively* true.

If I relied only on what my feelings were telling me, I would cave. But I knew with the certainty of faith that God was giving me *every spiritual blessing in the heavens*—even in that horrible moment—most especially in that horrible moment, and I needed to act on that belief to receive and appropriate that grace. You see, though faith resides in the intellect it is exercised in the will; faith becomes operative through an act of the will. And as we act in faith, the grace is experienced.

So I pulled myself up from the floor, believing with all my broken, shattered might that the very blessing Our Lady received at the foot of the cross was available to me in that moment. I went back into the family room and thanked the officers for being there. I told them I would pray for them and that I knew this had to be the most difficult part of their job. They thanked me for my prayers and Anthony and I thanked them for their service to our State. When they left, my husband and I gave way to our grief as we informed family and friends and began the preparations necessary for laying our son to rest.

It is critical for us to understand that very often what we consider to be our biggest tragedy is really all about the mercy of God. I remembered that fifteen years prior to this, a priest friend of ours said, "Johnnette, when somebody dies tragically, it is an act of God's mercy."

I asked, "Father, what do you mean by that?"

He said, "You know God loves us so much that He created us to know Him, to love Him and to serve Him in this life, and to be happy with Him forever in heaven. Why did He create us? For an eternal destiny. It is the job of every parent to work for the eternal destiny of his or her children."

He continued, "God knows the precise moment when we are the closest to Him we will ever be in our entire lives. I have come to believe that tragic deaths are all about God's mercy. He takes that person from this life at the moment that is ripest for their eternal salvation." I held to that, believing it was a blessing, an insight that God had given to me through this priest all those years ago so that I would remember it at this most crucial moment in my life.

Simon, our son, was a child who always struggled. He was an A.D.D. (Attention Deficit Disorder) kid when A.D.D. was just being diagnosed. He had a tough time. He went to Iraq and came home with what I am certain was post-traumatic stress disorder. Was it possible that the tragedy of his death was his "ripe moment" to enter eternal life? Was this a case of Romans 8:28 being fulfilled in a life, "… for God works all things to the good for those who are called according to his purposes"?

One day soon after Si's death, I was praying the Rosary, the only prayer I could pray. As I prayed, I added my tears and my suffering to every bead. "Oh, Lord, all I wanted was one last hug. Lord, just one last hug."

I sensed the Lord say to me, "Johnnette, would one more hug have been enough?"

"No, Lord, not nearly enough. All I have ever wanted for Simon was healing."

He said, "My child, he is more healed in this moment with Me than he ever could have been with you."

I rejoiced! I rejoiced at the mercy of God! What mattered most to me for Simon, for each of my children, is eternal life. No! I would rather the sacrifice of the temporal for the benefit of the eternal.

Another day while praying the Rosary, it occurred to me how much I was suffering, how acutely, how profusely, how constantly. It suddenly hit me that if this pain was so difficult for me, a woman who is sinful, selfish, and only concerned about her own desires, how much more did the death of Jesus pierce the Blessed Mother?

I seemed to sense the Holy Spirit say, "Not only did she experience her maternal pain perfectly, but she was so conformed to the will of the Father that He, being pure Spirit, mourned His Son in her heart." Imagine that! Our Lady suffered maternally and paternally for our Lord's death.

I learned during my time of extreme pain and grief that we obtain immeasurable grace when we attach every suffering we have to the Cross, whether it be large or small—every contradiction, every betrayal, every reversal. I came to see in some mysterious way that if Simon's death in this manner and at this moment was beneficial for his eternal life, then so too was it beneficial for me and for my salvation. I wanted to "lean into the cross" as I had been advised, not run from it. I wanted to mine the treasure of grace that it contained.

People said, "Johnnette, you really should be taking anti-depressants."

"I'm not depressed," I would say. "I'm grieving. Do you know what God has entrusted to me? Do you know what He has given me? He has given me a share in His own passion. I don't want to miss one blessing, one grace, or one lesson in this. I want to remain fully alert to this mystery as it is being worked out in me."

We have a large crucifix in our bedroom leaning against the dresser. I remember one day I took that cross and I prostrated myself on it. I said, "Lord, immolate me. Burn this cross into my being. Let me embrace this fully, fully, fully because I trust in You. I trust in You!"

The power available to us in the midst of our suffering is incomprehensible. Think of it this way—it was through the suffering of our Lord Jesus Christ that salvation was won. His passion, death, and resurrection won eternal life for us. The greatest of all pain bought the greatest of all grace, a grace that continues to roll down Calvary's hill every day into the life of every person who is willing to receive it. When united to the cross, our suffering, our torment, our travail, our psychological disorder, our depression, our cancer, our loss, and our tragedies become conduits of redemptive grace that flows out to the world. (Colossians 1:24)

Less than a year after Simon died, Anthony and I were getting ready to attend the baptism of our first grandchild, when he suffered a grand mal seizure in our kitchen. He was rushed to the hospital and soon after diagnosed with terminal brain cancer.

There we were, still shallow-breathing from Simon's death, and now another major crisis faced us. My husband looked at me and he said, "You know, Johnnette, we can do this. We can do this. We know about God's sufficiency. We can get through this." And we did. Anthony offered every bit of his suffering for the sake of *Living His Life Abundantly*® and *Women of Grace*®.

I remember the day Sister Briege McKenna came to our home with a relic of Pope John Paul II and prayed over Anthony. "Oh, I see a beautiful road, a beautiful road," she told Anthony in her lilting Irish brogue. "Jesus is on this road. Tony, you are on this road. You are walking down this road. Jesus is with you on this road."

I thought to myself, *What she is gently telling us is that Anthony will not be healed.* My dear husband thought the same thing and voiced his thoughts. With tears in his eyes he turned to me and said, "I am giving you, Johnnette, all of my sufferings for the sake of *Living His Life Abundantly*® and *Women of Grace*®. Don't stop doing what you are doing or you will nullify the gift I am offering you." He was giving his very life.

At Anthony's insistence I remained active in apostolate until I was told he had about eight weeks to live. I wanted to be with him for as many moments as I could before he went on to eternal life. What grace transpired in that time! I watched the hand of God move so profoundly upon my husband. The Holy Spirit was palpable in him.

Fr. Benedict Groeschel has a little book that discusses questions and answers on the spiritual life. In his book I read something that I thought was so very appropriate to my situation. He said when somebody is terminally ill and he entrusts his suffering to the passion of Christ, God perfects that soul in a very short period of time. I am confident I saw that happen to Anthony.

I watched him travel with Our Lady through purgation to illumination, to what I believe was union with God. And so it seemed fitting that it was Easter Sunday morning, April 8, that he succumbed to the coma that heralded his passing. The Lord took him during the Easter Octave, the Wednesday prior to Divine Mercy Sunday.

I was at his side, as was a dear priest friend I worked with at the time and our children, son-in-law, and grandchildren. The Blessed Sacrament was reposed before him, and we had relics of many saints there, as well. As death approached, I was holding his hand and stroking his face, and telling him how much I loved him. Perhaps it was when he was struggling to take his last few breaths that I realized a profound truth but a stunning paradox—great sorrow and great joy can co-exist in the human heart. This is what I was experiencing.

"Anthony," I said, "I am weeping, but my heart is filled with so much joy because in a few short seconds you are going to behold Our Lord face to face. You are going to see Jesus, honey. I'm so excited for you! And I have to tell you I have spiritual envy. You get to go to heaven, and now I have to go to confession!"

Palm Sunday, the week prior to Anthony's slip into the coma, it was obvious the end was coming soon. I asked of Our Lord a favor. "I just want one blessing, Lord, when his time comes. Please send Your Mother and my son to get him."

In faith, I believe God heard my prayer and that He answered it. When he died, Anthony had a little smile on his face, the type of smile that signifies something very sweet had just happened.

The deathbed is such a sacred place. It is truly a place where eternity intersects time. I tasted that reality as I kept vigil with my husband. I was more aware of the spiritual realities than I was aware of what was taking place right in that room. It was like I had a foot in both worlds. Maybe a foot and a half in the eternal and half a foot in the temporal.

After Anthony had been dead for about a minute and a half, I turned to our priest friend and asked, "Father, do you think he has had his particular judgment yet?"

"Oh, Johnnette, I am quite certain he has," Father said.

"Oh," I replied, "I am so glad that is over for him."

I was totally caught up in the glory of what had happened. God had taken him home. After a twenty-five-month struggle with a fatal disease, Anthony was at peace. He was with God. And I was happy for him.

Now, don't get the wrong idea. I miss Anthony. I miss him terribly. I miss the solid assurance he brought to my life, the way he protected me and loved me. He was amazing! But would I want him back here? I don't think so. He is in eternal beatitude. It would be selfish to wish him back here in the natural sense. The reality is, I think he is here with me right now. There is no death in Christ, says St. Paul. Anthony and Simon are both with me still. We are united in the communion of saints. Pope John XXIII said it this way, "Our loved ones are not separated from us, only invisible to us." What consolation his statement has brought me!

Here is another question you might ask: "Johnnette, does it mean that if God calls you to His service, you have to lose a child or lose a husband? Because it scares me to think this might happen to me. If I say, 'Yes, I want to work for the Lord,' what will He require?"

This question lurks in the minds of many when they hear my story. Maybe it is on your mind too. So let's address it now.

I don't know what is in your future, but there is no correlation between actively engaging in apostolate and the death of loved ones. There is, however, a correlation between apostolate and seeing God at work in all things. God is going to ask you, and even expect you, to look at every circumstance in your life through the eyes of faith. I think He is going to ask you to take *every circumstance and trial* and unite it to His Son's cross; the joys as well as the sorrows, in union with Him.

Before His first creative act, He knew you already. He knew you by name, and He knew precisely the day and time in which He would give you life, because He knew He needed precisely you in that day and time. YOU, with your gifts, talents, and disposition, everything about you—He wants to use you as a conduit of His grace in the lives of others and in the world at large. And He wants to use the world at large and the lives of others to be instruments of grace who help you in your quest for holiness and blamelessness of life. Purification and sanctification in your life happen through the ordinary and the extraordinary events in your life, and through big sufferings and minor inconveniences.

You know that person who irritates you? Ask God to bless that person. God is working in that person through the irritation they cause you to perfect you—to give you patience, charity, perseverance, fortitude, long suffering, whatever virtue you may need. So when your husband or your children really drive you nuts, praise God! He is going to rain down grace and virtue upon you. Hug them and give them a big kiss. All He desires is the openness of your heart so He can come in.

I want to tell you about St. Louis de Montfort. I love St. Louis de Montfort's, *True Devotion to Mary*. St. Louis says that in the last days God is going to raise up greater saints than there have ever been in the times before. He tells us that He is going to do something terrific through these saints. In his book he states, "I said this would come to pass particularly at the end of the world and indeed presently."

He continues: "The Most High with His Holy Mother … must form for Himself great saints who shall surpass most of the other saints in sanctity."

God is looking at you today. You are the one He wants to make bigger than all of the other saints that have come before. He wants to suit you up in His armor. He even has a uniform with your name on it. My brothers and sisters in Christ, God has a mission for us today. God wants to use you powerfully and abundantly. All we need to do is say, "Come, Lord Jesus! Come! Come! Come! I will go with You. Take me, Lord Jesus. Take me and use me."

So, my question to you is simply this: Are you ready to go? Are you ready to suit up? Are you ready to be filled with the Holy Spirit? Are you ready to burn with the fire of divine love? Are you ready to go into the highways and byways? Are you willing to use the full measure of the gift of your authentic femininity, ladies? Gentlemen, are you willing to use the full measure of the gift of your authentic masculinity? Are you ready to go and to reclaim this world for Christ Jesus? If you are, now is the time to stand up and show Him that you mean it!

I pray this for you and ask that the power of the Holy Spirit would come down:

"We want a new infilling, Lord. We want an anointing, Lord. I ask You to send us the gift of fortitude, the gift of courage, the gift of perseverance. I ask You to send us in this moment a charity of heart the likes of which we have never known. I ask you, Lord God, to give us the desire to take every contradiction, every suffering, and every pain, and to put it into Your Most Sacred Heart for the good of the world. Lord Jesus, I ask You to use us to the full measure in which You have desired to use us. I thank You for the lives You have given. I ask You, Lord, to set us free, to send us out, to let us proclaim Your Word in Jesus' name."

Let us say along with all the saints of the latter times: "Amen!"

Bio–

What does it mean to be a Catholic woman in today's world? Well, to Johnnette, the answer is clear. When we look to the mission of the Catholic woman, we are called to participate in the spiritual motherhood of Mary. After years of being a non-practicing Catholic, Johnnette experienced a deep conversion back to her Catholic faith, and shortly thereafter began to discern a call to apostolate. In time, it became clear that her call was to proclaim the gospel message through the media. Founder and president of both *Living His Life Abundantly®* and *Women of Grace®*, Johnnette has been a prominent voice in Catholic radio and television through EWTN since 1987. Her television program, *Women of Grace*, and her radio program, *Women of Grace Live*, are aired Monday through Friday internationally. This is an adaptation of a talk she gave in Palm Desert, California, in October, 2007.

Babsie Bleasdell

I want to share a Scripture passage, Sirach 51, that has been woven into the fabric of my life since I was six years old:

"I give you thanks, O God of my Father; I praise you, O God my Savior. I will make known your name, refuge of my life; you have been my helper against my adversaries. You have saved me from death and kept back my body from the pit, from the clutches of the netherworld, you have snatched my feet; you have delivered me in your great mercy from the scourge of a slanderous tongue, and lips that went over to falsehood; from the snare of those who watched for my downfall, and from the power of those that sought my life.

From many a danger you have saved me, from flames that have hemmed me in on every side; from the midst of unremitting fire, from the belly of the nether world; from deceiving lips and painters of lies, and from the arrows of the dishonest tongues. I was at the point of death, my soul was nearing the depths of the nether world; I turned every way, but there was no one to help me, I looked for one to sustain me, but could find no one.

But then I remembered the mercies of the Lord, his kindness through ages past; for he saves those who take refuge in him, and rescues them from every evil. So I raised my voice from the very earth, from the gates of the nether world, my cry. I called out, 'O Lord, you are my father, you are my Champion and my Savior' … I bless the name of the Lord!"

This Scripture passage is a picture of my life in a nutshell, but I didn't understand it. I was about six years old when I had my first encounter with confusion, lies, and slander. I didn't understand then that it was a blessing. I am from Trinidad, the seventh child of a family of eight, a Catholic family.

My father would not let us mix with people who were not Catholic. However, he was a Catholic who only went to confession once a year, around Easter. He fulfilled the law. My mother, however, was a very devout woman.

She prayed on her knees. I never woke up so early in the morning that I didn't find her on her knees. And I didn't go to bed so late at night that I didn't leave her on her knees. She was a woman who believed in prayer.

My mother was married at a very young age, too young to understand what she was doing. She was told, for instance, that after she got married she would be able to go home, and she believed that, but she never did. She married my father, who was eleven years older than she was and the friend of her older brother.

My mother lived with a man who was what we would call today abusive, but I believed my father was a great man. He was full of joy and personality, but he was old-fashioned. My mother asked him once why he came home so late.

He said, "I am a man in my own house. I am lord of this manor; this is my domain and I am king. I am no boy. You can't ask me why I come home so late."

I remember going to Mass at 6 o'clock on a Sunday morning and seeing my father walking in for the first time since Saturday night. Nobody dared ask him any questions. He never allowed us to lock the door because he said, "No man has to knock at his own door when he comes home. He must be able to walk in."

Regardless of his attitude, he was an excellent provider, and he played with us. We knew him as "Papa." We had nicknames for him, and he had nicknames for us. He seldom called us by our real names, and when he did you knew you were in trouble. If he said, "Babsie," I would almost salute and click my heels, and shout, "Yes, sir!"

When I was three years old, I watched my father cut up hot peppers. I thought they were tomatoes and I demanded one. "No," he told me. "You can't have one. They are peppers and they will burn you." I did what every three-year-old would do. I screamed and shouted until Papa cut a sliver of the pepper and put it in my mouth. It was my first experience of "Don't doubt your father." Papa loves you, he knows you, and whatever he tells you is true. He will never lie. A foreshadow of God. Because I didn't believe my father, I had to "burn to learn" many times.

Thank God, I don't burn anymore. I know better now, but it took me a long time to believe him. I think back about what God has done and my memories rejoice. I am free, and what I can do now is help others realize that this God of ours is faithful. He is a good God. He never grows weary of you. He keeps on reaching out to help you. He is saying, "If only you would believe, you will see the glory of God. I cannot lie. I am constant in My love for you and I made a covenant with you and behold, I will never leave you.

I will rescue you from the lion's jaws wherever you are. If you believe, you will not get into the lion's jaws."

The first word I became conscious of—without knowing the meaning—was the word "bankruptcy." I heard my parents talking about being bankrupt, but I didn't know what it was. My father had a small business. He sold everything from aspirins to flour and sugar in a general store. We children were always in and out of the shop, stealing candy to take to our friends at school.

My mother was a seamstress. She sewed part-time. I learned to sew at a young age. We were always around my mother. I remember when I was six, she was making a bridal dress and putting beads on it. She had drawn the pattern, and I told her I wanted to help. She gave me the needle and showed me how to put the beads on, and I put the beads on with the pattern. I was so proud of myself. When the bride-to-be came in, she said, "Babsie, this is for you." She gave me thirteen cents. That was a lot of money for a little girl.

We lost the business and moved to our first house. On the way home from school one day, one of my classmates told me a story. It was not a nice story. She told me the story about a woman, whose house we passed every morning. In that house lived a little classmate of mine whom I liked very much. I knew the child was adopted. In our culture we don't legally adopt children. We just take them to live with us. Extended family is a very common thing. So, she lived with this lady, and when I heard what kind of a person the lady was, my first concern was for my friend.

The following morning I warned my friend that this lady was terrible. Perhaps she could return to her own mother and be saved. "Where is your mother?" I asked her.

She said, "My mother is in the country."

"You have a mother who is alive yet? Tell her you want to come home because the lady you live with is a vampire. You can't stay there."

It never occurred to me that the first thing this child would do was tell her adopted mother. That Saturday morning I was lying in my bed and heard someone calling. My father walked out, and I heard this lady complaining to my father about what I had done. I lay in my bed, shivering. I couldn't believe what was happening!

My father came to the door and called, "Babsie, come."

I went, and the lady told her story again. Papa asked me if this was true and I said, "Yes, Papa."

He told the lady, "This child would never say such a thing unless somebody told her."

I had to admit who told me the lie. Papa informed me he would have to spank me to teach me that you don't repeat what people say. This was the first time he ever spanked me. I couldn't believe my father would whip me. I believed I was his darling and that he loved me too much. I had not yet heard the Scripture, "What father does not discipline his child?" (Heb. 12:7)

For many years, that woman continued to curse my life and spread lies and slander about me. She stood out in front of our house, speaking about what I would become; how I would be dragged all over the street and nobody would respect me; and that she was going to see me destroyed.

I remember thinking that my father was so strict. He wasn't as strict to my sister, and she was two years younger than I. I decided that when I was big enough I would get married, and then I would escape my father's vigilant eyes. I couldn't wait to do that because I couldn't leave the house without somebody else being responsible for me.

As a child I thought, *The doctor is the only person in the parish who can go to the parish festival with all of his children and his wife and have lunch there.* I used to serve at the festival. My father could never have afforded to take all of us for lunch. I really envied this family and I told myself, "When I get married, I will marry a doctor so that our family can eat at the parish festival." Eventually, I did marry a doctor, but he hated the festival so he never went.

Eight years after I got married, I separated from my husband with two little girls—one almost seven years old and one almost six. This was not something I wanted. It was not something I ever dreamed would happen. In my heart there was a deep sadness and disappointment, and a lot of anger. "Why did I try so hard? Why did I save myself for so long? Perhaps, if I had run around it wouldn't happen to me." I didn't realize then that goodness is its own reward. To be in the right place with God is reward in itself, and you need no other reward.

After I got married, I soon found out that my husband was more vigilant than my father. I wanted to buy my own cloth and I couldn't. My father worked in a fabric department store and he knew cloth. He knew everything about good material. He bought me voiles and silks, and all I wanted was what my friends had, like how the children wear denim now, when you would like to buy them something else.

I married a doctor, just as I had hoped. He would have me go to the store and bring patterns home so he could choose which one he wanted me to have. Then I had to do the same with the material. He chose the fashion, and if I dared to vary from the fashion one inch, I would be in big trouble.

I remember when my daughter was five. She came into the room and saw me sewing some material, "Oh Mommy," she said. "What a beautiful piece of material!"

I said, "Do you like it?"

"I love it," she said. Then her brows furled and she said, "Does Daddy like it?"

"Well, I haven't showed him."

"Why, Mommy, why?" she asked. "Oh, I know. You are afraid. You are afraid you will quarrel and you won't go to the party tonight. Well, if you would have showed him, you would have quarreled already and tonight you would go to the party. Now, he is going to come home tonight, and you are going to quarrel, and you will stay home."

And that is exactly how it went.

I wanted to run away from this trap, for one thing, so I could buy my own material. Now I buy my own clothes and as soon as I walk out of my room, someone says, "Where do you think you are going with that?" Or I hear, "Auntie Babsie, where did you get that dress? Who made it?"

And I say, "Oh, Lord, it has caught up with me again!" The jealous love of Yahweh! At seventy-seven he still shelters me. And then I think how much like God my father was, striving to protect us, sheltering us, wrapping us up, not wanting us to get hurt, and we break all the bonds. We get hurt and then we blame God. Isn't that true? Now the Lord has allowed me to look into my soul under the Spirit and I realize how many times I could have been dead, and here I am: rejoicing in God my Savior and giving Him thanks for everything.

Bringing up my two daughters was difficult. I came under the malicious tongues and censure of almost the whole nation because my husband happened to be a doctor. In those days doctors were not so easily available for marriage. I couldn't find sympathy anywhere. Part of it was my own fault. Through this suffering of eight years I had never shared with anybody what I was going through. It was also partly pride.

During that time I had come to a place where I seriously considered suicide. I remember one morning after I got the children off to school and he was off to work, I lay on the bed just trying to pray. I told myself (or something told me), "You are alone. It would be so easy. Suicide is so simple. Take a razor blade and cut your wrist. You don't have any pain. You just slip away." And I considered it.

Then I thought, *But I am afraid to go to hell.* The Irish nuns who had taught me had warned me that hell was real and sin takes you to hell. I didn't want to go to hell. I was afraid of the Father God, Who would put me in hell. I was really struggling. I thought, *Maybe there is no hell. I will do it.* Then, *My father is such a proud man. How would he live after this? Oh, he will get over it. He has six other children who would help him. But my children! They are going to have to spend the rest of their lives, these two little girls, hearing that their mother killed herself.*

I jumped out of the bed and flew to the window. As I looked out the window, the sky was blue as only a tropical sky can be blue. The birds were singing, whistling from every tree, and a gentle breeze was blowing. I cried out to God, "Oh, God, where are You? The whole world is happy, the birds are singing, the clouds are floating happily across the sky. I alone am in turmoil. Have mercy on me and save me!"

I leaned over the window and wept. I don't know what happened, but somehow God strengthened me and I was able to carry on, still trying not to tell anyone what was going on. Finally, it ended and I came into a mass of distortion, lies, and confusion. I was on everybody's lips because the whole story hit the newspaper. I remember lying down in my bed one morning, and at four o'clock the scavengers sweeping the street were talking about me, and they didn't even know that they were outside of my home.

In the midst of all that, I knew one thing: I had to look after these children, and they needed my best. They became my life's vocation. It wasn't always easy, and I was so angry—angry at the world, angry at God, angry at everything. Finally, this God Who sought me continued to seek me. Eventually I discovered that I too could be a sign of God's mercy to anyone.

As we look back on our lives, we come to realize that in everything that God has allowed us to experience, He has implanted a priceless jewel. I think in many ways when our memories are healed, when we come to recognize that whatever He allowed us to go through, however bad it might seem to us, was the most merciful thing a loving God could do to bring us to our senses. I know now how hard God tried to get me to understand that my father loved me with a passion.

I look back now, and my spirit rejoices. I was subject to depression until this revelation of God came upon me by the power of His Spirit and the laying on of the hands of an Irish priest. I didn't ask for it. I didn't know you could ask for healing. I was confirmed and I used to ask myself, "How come, if you got the gifts of wisdom, understanding, and counsel, you can be so stupid?"

But now, my spirit rejoices in the God Who saved me. I know His saving power. I know His saving grace, and I know He will continue to rescue me over and over and over. I have good reason to rejoice.

In the morning I would walk with my cup of coffee and I would boldly say, "Lord, I have come for my peace." No one in the world gives peace, but the Lord gives it—and He gives it to you. You have to pick it up or it remains dormant. At last I understood peace is my portion. I say it aloud now so that my soul takes it in, and faith comes from hearing. If there is no one to preach to you early in the morning, you preach to yourself. But you have to know God's Word. You repeat God's Word to yourself. You hear it and you let it sink into the depth of your soul. Your understanding picks it up, and off you go again.

Vatican II came along, and I was very anxious about the Church. Where was the Church going? Because of my divorce and all it entailed, I felt less than whole. Some of you may have had that experience. It is like something inside you ceases to exist. In those days you were required to write a public apology for the scandal you caused the Church.

By then my father was an old man. One day when he went to Mass after I returned to live with him, he went to church and to confession. The priest told my father he should be excommunicated because he was harboring a divorcée.

My father had tremendous respect for the Church, and he had taught us as well. He was now going to Mass every Sunday. He came home and— half-smilingly—told us what happened. I felt so bad, but it was not in me with my upbringing to reel against the Church.

I used to say, "You can't go against the rules." If those are the Church rules then I have to do it—and so I did. I wrote the apology but still felt incredibly sad. So much so, that for a long time I didn't go to communion because I was afraid. I was very young, and I had this desire in my heart to prove that I was a good girl, to prove that I could live in a marriage. Somewhere deep down in my heart I was hoping that I could get a second chance at marriage.

I waited for a long time. The priest tried to encourage me to get an annulment but I said to him, "Father, I have no grounds. I married the person I wanted to marry. I have no excuse. If anybody had tried to stop me, I would not have listened. So in my willfulness, maybe I received what I deserved. I won't say anything except the truth. Just give me time."

At Mass, during the Consecration when the host was elevated we used to say, "Lord, I am not worthy to receive You, but say the word and my soul shall be healed," I would say, "Lord, I am not worthy to receive You. I don't know when I will be worthy to receive You. I know that someday You will make me worthy. Lord, have mercy on me." That was my prayer every day.

And then Vatican II approached, at which time I was already back in the Church. One day we began to read at Mass. I am a good reader and I like to read. We had a meeting every Tuesday to prepare the readings for Sunday, and that was a time of enjoyment for me.

One day, I received a letter when my cousin was sitting with me. "I don't like receiving local letters," I told her.

She said, "Why not?"

"Because I receive too many of these, and they are all filled with poison." I used to receive anonymous letters filled with evil intent. I would see a local post-office mark and say to myself, "Who wants to write to me? Anybody who wants to write me can telephone me. Why are they writing?"

"Do you want me to open this for you?" my cousin asked.

"Yes." I passed her the letter to read.

She began to get very serious and then very pale.

I burst out laughing. "It is one of them?"

"Babsie," she said. "I don't believe what I am reading."

I said, "I told you I have been plagued with this all of my life."

This letter accused me of all kinds of things, and finally it said, "And you dare to stand to read to us. Every time I see you there, I am so angry that I can't follow the Mass. I wish you would stop it because you have no shame."

The things she accused me of had no foundation whatsoever. I am sure it was because of my divorce and all the malicious talk that followed. I went to the priest. "I would like to be excused from reading," I told him.

"Why?" he asked.

"Father, because I disturb people," I said.

He said, "But you read so well."

"Father, there are many, many other people who will read as well, as you know."

"But how many people?"

I said, "Father, look," and I gave him the letter.

He was an Irishman, and by this time he looked like a neon light, flashing red and white. Then he said, "But, Babsie, it is only one person. We will miss you."

"Father," I said, "for one person Jesus would have died. So, for one person, I ask to be excused."

So he freed me. The irony of this situation is God is full of surprises! Years later, after the God of joy came into my life in such a powerful way, I was asked to lead the priest retreat in Rome in 1991. I read before 5,700 princes of the Church! I realized there is no way you can stop God. Those

He appoints, He anoints, and He is faithful to His call and to the gifts that He gives to us.

I began to realize how much joy there was in just being a Christian, but as Vatican II progressed, I was unhappy about where the Church was heading. So were many of my friends. However, I finally persuaded my friends to join me and to pray. I said, "If you are troubled and—believe me, I am troubled too—I can't help you and you can't help me. But perhaps it would help all of us if we told God what we are thinking. He knows what is in our hearts. God knows we are upset about the changes in the Church. We need to pray".

Thirty of us came together one night to pray. The Hound of Heaven was surely after me. A seminarian came to lead us because none of us had the guts to pray out loud in each other's presence. We always read our prayers, but now we were going to pray spontaneously. We were going to reveal our hearts to God in the presence of each other. Many of them couldn't do it and they didn't come back.

But it was so important to me that I pressed on. Six months after that night, an Irish priest came to the prayer meeting. I persuaded my sister to come. She came, but she was very sick. She'd had surgery but she had never healed. Three months had gone by and she was still in bed and unable to return to work or do anything. After she was there for an hour, Father still never said a word. He just sat in the background. I came to understand afterwards that he was discerning the Spirit.

I had to lead this meeting in the presence of a priest. I said to myself, "God, what else are you going to put me through?" All I knew about priests is that they pray and we say, "Amen." I had never done anything like this before in the presence of a priest, but I was going to press on because I was compelled. My sister told me she was very tired and in a lot of pain and had to go home. She said, "Father hasn't said anything yet."

I said, "But he will, that is why he is here."

"But look at him," she said.

I looked up and saw the priest with his lips moving. His eyes were shut and he didn't show any sign of moving from where he was or doing anything. I said, "Oh, Jesus!"

My sister said, "I want to go. I cannot stay here any longer."

I called my nephews. They lifted her up, and I think everybody in the room wanted to leave because many were not members of the prayer group. They left with her, and then Father spoke. He said, "There is a beautiful gift of prayer in this room."

I thought, *Gift of prayer? What is the gift of prayer?*

He continued, "And a lot of other gifts besides, but if you don't recognize them and use them, they will dry up." I got very excited!

"God wanted to heal that woman." He repeated it, "The united faith in this room will heal that woman. Who was she?"

I said, "My sister."

He said, "God wanted to heal her but you didn't pray. Would you allow me to use you to pray in proxy for her?"

I knew what proxy was. "Sure, Father, you can do anything." Besides, in those days what could you say to a priest? A royal invitation is a command. I fell on my knees right there.

He called everybody. "Let's make a cluster. Each of you reach out and make sure your hands are touching somebody. We are all going to pray for Babsie's sister's healing."

We just let our voices go in prayer. In the middle of this, I heard Father praying in a strange language. I thought to myself, *This is not Latin, I learned that at five. This is not French. It is in my culture and I studied it at school. This is certainly not English, and it is not Spanish. What on earth is this?*

I twisted my head to look up at the priest, and his eyes were still closed. The pores of his skin seemed to glow; a light was emanating from him and filling the whole place. I thought, "Babsie, how irreverent can you get? Duck!" So, I ducked with my head down and he continued to pray and prophesy over me. I learned all of this afterwards.

He began to prophesy over me, saying, "I called you. I formed you in your mother's womb and I have loved you with an everlasting love. I have reserved a work that you must do for Me, and I have called you now to come to the place where you can be My witness. But you must pray much. You must fast much and pray all the time. Have I not constantly delivered you from lying tongues and from tiger's teeth that would destroy you? Have I not continually rescued you from men who hated you and who would have torn you to pieces?"

My mind went back to when I was six years old and to all I had suffered in all those years. I was fifty-two years old, and now the Lord was talking to me through this priest, letting me know He had seen everything. I broke into tears and said, "Lord, You know everything. You know it all. I have nothing to be afraid of, Lord. You know they were lying. You understand all that has happened, so what do I have to care about? I don't care. You love me and that is all that matters." I wept and sobbed from the depth of my being.

Then the priest did something amazing. He prayed a prayer of peace over me. "My peace I impart to you, my daughter. Peace be with you. Receive my peace. It is my legacy to you." As he prayed, total peace came over me. And then he held me by my hand, lifted me up, and kissed me on my cheek. It seemed to be the seal of God's approval on my life.

But I had a real problem here. He said, "Fast much. And pray all the time." I knew many prayers. The nuns had groomed me well, along with my mother, who taught me to recite the Psalms against the bad things that happened throughout my life.

But fasting? I had tried. As a good Catholic, on days of fast, like Ash Wednesday or Good Friday, I followed the rules of eating one full meal and two small ones. We were allowed to drink between the meals but not eat. And me? If I could convince myself that ice cream was a liquid, I would drink it.

This was my predicament. How was I going to respond to this call? The following day, I went to look for the priest. I went to the rectory to talk to him, but when I pulled the car up I began to panic. I couldn't barge in and disturb a priest and ask him to explain what happened the previous night. There was a difference in me—there was a certain joy in my heart. Everything looked beautiful, and I was so full of excitement about life.

Except for the fact that I was required to fast and I didn't know how I could do it. I spun the car around, put it back into gear, and went to my sister's house. It reminded me of Mary visiting Elizabeth. When I pushed open the door, she was there working. I stopped with my hand on the door handle and said, "How are you?"

She said, "Good, but I am afraid." I asked her why she was afraid. "Well, you know how sick I have been. This morning I woke up without pain and thought I would get the children ready for school and then go back to bed." Then she said, "Babsie, it is ten o'clock and I have not gone back to bed. I have no pain and I don't know if I am sick or well."

I began reciting the Psalms and the Magnificat and "The Lord is my shepherd, I shall not want." All of the prayers that the nuns had taught me began rolling out of my mouth. "Son of the living God, be merciful to me a sinner. Jesus, meek and humble of heart, make my heart unto thine. Jesus, Mary, and Joseph, I love you." Everything just flooded my mind. Spiritual things I had given up on years ago began to come alive in me again.

And something completely new happened. I was a completely changed person. People began realizing it and said, "You look so different. You are always smiling." Yes, it was like a secret inside of me. Before this happened I would encourage people to pray by leaving little pamphlets on their desks as I felt the need, but I never had the courage to tell them to pray. But now I was able to talk to them about Jesus and about commitment to Jesus. Things changed completely!

Very soon, I realized my job had lost its luster. I knew I wasn't going to stay, and yet I had previously thought it a fantastic job and loved it. I worked for the doctors and the medical faculty. My children were grown and I had nothing else to do. I thought I would stay there until I was too old to work. This was the most perfect place I have ever worked in my life.

But all of a sudden I was so busy. People were calling me from everywhere. Priests were calling me to come to their parish to begin prayer meetings. I said to a priest, "But Father, there are many people who come to my prayer group." At that time there were 500 coming to the prayer group. Many times I could not say "no" and I was so busy. At times I was at the far end of the island of Trinidad, and I would not get back home until two or three o'clock in the morning.

I was being questioned everywhere. Some people believed, while others laughed at me. One day, I was walking along the street and somebody asked a nun who was standing on the side of the road, "Who is that woman?"

The nun answered, "Oh, that is the pope of the Charismatic Renewal."

In the midst of crying, I continued because I couldn't stop. Propelled and impelled by God and the Holy Spirit, I could not stop.

One priest said, "Please come and start a prayer meeting in my area."

I said to this priest, "Father, there are many people in my prayer group who belong to your parish."

He said, "Babsie, I will not entrust my people, my flock, to anyone but you because I know you love the Church." It was a most amazing statement: *You love the Church*. Was this a special love that I had for the Church? When I began to realize it, he was right. I did.

In the midst of this growth of the prayer groups, I began to be invited outside of the country to speak in other countries. I went every time with trepidation. *What can I do? What can I say?* I prayed to the Holy Spirit continually, "Tell me what to say. Tell me what to do. Command me to do it. I promise to be submissive in everything that Thou should ask of me, and I accept all that You permit to happen to me. Only show me what is Your will."

I promised God I would never say "no" to Him. I had wasted fifty-two years of my life trying to walk in my own understanding and on my own, seeking what I thought was the pursuit of happiness, and I ended up at a dead end. Now, the Lord had opened the way and I said, "Never will I say 'no' to You again."

One night, I was invited to speak and I was filled with trepidation. I thought *My God!* as I looked at 25,000 people. Do I really have to speak here? But it was worse than that. The master of ceremonies left the microphone and came to me and said, "Babsie, do you know the words to the song, "The Old Rugged Cross"?

"Yes." I had sung it with others many times.

He ran back to the microphone. "Are you ready to sing it then?"

I was in shock!

"Aren't you going to sing it for us?" he asked.

I answered, "Since you have spoken to me, I have forgotten every word of it."

He said, "I will pray for you," and then he ran back to the microphone. He came back and said, "Are you ready now?"

"No."

"Please, Babsie, will you do it for me?"

I mumbled to myself that I had promised God never to say "no" to Him again.

The MC then announced, "Our beautiful, black sister from Trinidad will now sing, 'The Old Rugged Cross.'"

I couldn't believe it. I told God, "I promised You I would never say 'no' to you again, but I never thought You could be so stupid! You know I can't sing! How could You do this to me?"

But here I was ready to make a fool of myself. The musicians picked up their instruments and tried to support me, but when I opened my mouth the key that came out had never been heard before in Heaven or on earth. Desperation covered their faces. They put their instruments down, but I held on doggedly and sang it. I half spoke it and half cried it. Some people tried to help me, but they couldn't pursue it.

I ended up singing this tremendous solo by myself. I was covered with confusion. I cannot tell you how horrible I felt. But the people kindly applauded afterwards. I sat down and said, "I don't want to hear anything about this again!" I was consumed with shame. I kept telling God, "Lord, you took the mess of the cross and You did something with it. Now, take this mess and see what You can do with it! Just do something with it—*anything* for Your honor and glory. I know it is impossible, but You are the God of the impossible."

The following day I avoided everybody. I tried to walk by myself to escape the crowd, but I heard someone calling me from the back. I looked and there was Sister Ann Shields. She came and fell into step with me. "Babsie, about last night," she began.

"Sister … nothing about last night. Nothing ever again. I don't want to remember that last night even happened."

"No, but you must listen," she said. "You need to hear what happened to me."

"Something happened to you? Well, I begged God to use it. Let me hear what happened to you."

She said, "As you struggled with that song before 25,000 people, I just thought, I have been a nun for twenty years and I have never fully surrendered. Babsie, as I watched you labor I thought, I have got to make a new commitment for Christ right now."

I said, "Thank you, Lord."

That was the way I came to discover God's gifts, by many such experiences that seemed to be experiences of near death for me. I came to realize the cross is an intrinsic part of the Christian life. Each of us is called in some way to share the suffering of Jesus Christ. My way was the slander that was poured upon me. I had to put up with it until the present day, but I have learned to accept it and laugh at it.

When somebody now says, "Listen, Babsie, somebody said ..." I say, "Let them tell me themselves."

I don't want to hear it from anybody else. When I come to hear something, sometimes by these poison pen letters, I am amazed that people can still say those things about me after all that has happened in my life.

The Lord told me he was going to teach me so I could teach others. I try my best to be available to him as He teaches me. I have shared what He has taught me. I have gone to Nigeria, Canada, Europe, Singapore, Holland, Ireland, and many more places. Again and again, thrown to the wolves by the Lord and then redeemed by the same Lord.

I have traveled in many of the states in the United States. I have had to depend entirely on the Lord and the strength of His presence to open my mouth to say anything. I have come to know now that whatever pain we have, the cross is the only key with which God can open the tortured hearts of men and bring them into the peace and joy that He has planned for them. The Lord has worked away at me many times, opening my heart larger by the suffering I have endured. But now it is okay. It is a way of life. I have seen the glory of God and His power to rescue us from the dung hill and bring us together.

At present I have no children living with me, and no grandchildren. But I am surrounded by orphan children I have rescued. Thanks to many Americans we have been able to buy a house for them. Many of these friends have come to Trinidad to see what I am doing, and they have seen these children and have fallen in love with them. They know many of them by name and they send gifts. I never beg. I never ask for anything, but the Lord in his graciousness unexpectedly sends us gifts.

I wanted to rent a house for the children but learned I couldn't pay the rent, and I couldn't find anything suitable for which I could pay. But a man kept ringing me at five o'clock in the morning. He had a house he wanted to sell me. One morning I finally broke down and said, "If you ring me at five o'clock tomorrow morning I will kill you." (I am not holy enough yet not to say that to someone.) But the minute I said it, I begged God for forgiveness and I said, "Lord, I am supposed to be gentle like Jesus."

The next morning he called and said, "Auntie Babsie," (everybody calls me Auntie Babsie), "This house is ideal for a prayer meeting."

My heart about stopped. "If only I could rent it and be able to look after the children, it might work. How much?"

"A hundred thousand dollars."

"I cannot afford it," I said. "I have no money. No, no forget it."

Then a friend sent me a note that said, "Please tell me what you are doing."

I wrote back and told her about the house and the outrageous cost (I put a few exclamation points at the end).

She received the letter and immediately called me. "I have ended up with a lot more money than I know what to do with." She sent me the one hundred thousand dollars to pay for the place, and she didn't write the check to me under the Word of Life, the ministry. She sent me the check under my name. I could keep it! It was mine!

But God knows He could trust me. There was a time when, if I had a hundred thousand dollars, I would have spent it all on me instead of giving it to God. As soon as the check arrived I had a picture taken with me holding the check, because nobody would believe me otherwise. I was able to buy the house with cash.

God is at work in all the trials of our lives to make us whole. God wants to heal us. He doesn't want us to live in the past. He wants us to live in His living presence and to enjoy His love. I trust as you read this message it continues in your own life.

Recently, I have suffered through an unbelievable amount of slander. As I hear it I turn to the Lord and say, "I bear the cross of Jesus Christ." Each of you will have to bear that cross in a different way. We cannot avoid the cross. We must go through it in order to enjoy the resurrection. The way I go through it is not your way. I have had a myriad of ways, but always it ends up the same—unbelievable slander—but the Lord has been my champion. The Lord has been my shield. "Blessed are you when men revile you and send all manner of evil against you. Rejoice and be glad for such is the kingdom of God" (Matt. 5:11).

In this particular time in the history of the Church and the world, I think we are going to behold the kingdom in a brand-new way. I think we are going to behold again a Church filled with the glory of God. A Church where men and women will come in and be healed. A Church that, when the people enter, the power of God will be so strong they will fall down in adoration because of the reinstitution of perpetual adoration and the new devotion to Mary. I know Don Bosco's prophecy is coming to pass: "When the reigning pontiff manages to establish perpetual adoration and a true devotion to Mary, we will see the glory of God in His church on earth."

I am looking forward with excitement. It seems with all the turmoil in nature that God is trying to remove every distraction. In a moment the wind can come and blow out every house, but He takes a minimum of life because Scripture says that God does not rejoice in the death of a man, but God hopes that every man will live and be saved. It is a time of salvation.

Let us listen to the pope, and even now let us pray that the Lord will do in each of our hearts the miracle He did in the heart of Mary. That as women He will fill our hearts with gratitude for the function that He has given to us, and we will nurture and bring life into the world and seek life for all. That we will be so filled with gratitude and the awareness of the deep dignity of womanhood that He has symbolized in Mary, a young woman, and Elizabeth, an old woman who was not afraid of the challenge to bring forth a child in her old age. And Mary, who was not afraid in her youth and her meekness, to bring forth Jesus, the Prince of Peace, the Lord of Lords, the Holy One of God, the Messiah, the mighty Deliverer, the faithful God, and the great Physician.

God is asking us to harbor in our hearts this Jesus and show Him off wherever we are. God is asking us as women to cover the children and cause each of them to know that each bears within them a promise of God and the gift of Christ, that none of them is an accident but each of them was called and chosen to do a work to make the kingdom visible in a world that is filled with darkness.

According to Pope John Paul, living in a culture of death, women are supposed to bring life. The old adage remains then, that the hand that rocks the cradle is the hand that moves the world. Yet, this work cannot be done in the flesh. It cannot be done by university degrees. It can only be done by the anointing of the Holy Spirit.

To give our lives to Jesus is to publicly renew the promise we made at Confirmation with a fresh consciousness. It is to let it come from the depth of our hearts, not just from our lips or intellectually from our minds. We invite Jesus into our hearts and lives and say, "I renounce the devil and all his works and all his pomp, and I give my soul to Jesus Christ."

When we do this from the depth of our hearts, God does a miracle. A new life breaks forth within us. A man is born again! If we will do what God asks, if we would just believe Him and respond to His invitations, we would realize that everything that is allowed to happen is the best thing He could do for us.

I want to end by saying that Mary, a woman, reestablished us in the favor of God. Through her obedience and through her response of giving praise to Him, we have come into the whole inheritance. I don't think it is by mistake that the meeting of women—this cooperation of women—is called Magnificat. I think we are called to praise God, to worship Him, and to allow the Holy Spirit to do in us what He did in Mary.

The people who are going to lead the world and the Church, especially, into the new millennium are going to have to be a people who believe God! A people who agree that God is God and that He can help us. People who can say, "Fiat. Let it be done unto me according to Your will. I am not afraid. I am not dismayed because You are with me. Where You lead, I will follow."

Bio –

Born June 15, 1921, the Lord lovingly called Ursula Marie-Crescence Bleasdell home on July 22, 2013. Known to many as "Auntie Babsie," she is remembered as a beautiful vessel brimming over with joy and confidence in her Savior. This extra-ordinary woman from Trinidad had been a dynamic speaker at many conferences and retreats both in this country and abroad. She was an inspiring witness to God's mercy and power, which led her through many trials to the joy of the Baptism in the Holy Spirit.

In Trinidad, Babsie founded the prayer community called The Word of Life. Because of her devotion to Mary and the objectives of Magnificat, Babsie became a Magnificat ambassador to the people of the Caribbean. She and her Magnificat committee began many Magnificat chapters in Trinidad, St. Thomas, Barbados, and St. Croix. She even introduced Magnificat to the people of Providence, Rhode Island. It would be difficult to find a more powerful witness to the outpouring of the Holy Spirit than Babsie. Since the early 70s when she began ministering in her native Trinidad, she preached God's Word around the world. She was mum to Erica Mapp and Paula Owolabi and has four grandchildren and two great-grandchildren. May her soul, and the souls of all the faithful departed, through the mercy of God, rest in peace.

Dorinda Chiappetta Bordlee

L uke 6:38 speaks of the law of the gift: "Give and it shall be given to you; good measure, pressed down, shaken together, running over, will be poured into your lap." These are the words of Jesus near the end of His Sermon on the Mount. His love as a model of self-giving was the recurrent theme of my hero, now Saint, Pope John Paul II, whose words continue to inspire and guide the mission entrusted to me and my law partner to put law in the service of life.

Years ago when I gave my first testimony at a Magnificat breakfast in my home town of New Orleans, Louisiana, I was the mother of four children under twelve, and I thought that was challenging. Then, having four teenagers at once taught me a whole new level of surrender. Our children are now thriving young adults whose talents and virtues continue to beautifully unfold in the midst of the challenges of this world. The experience that my husband and I had of being the parents of four growing children taught us the true meaning of the Church's teaching on love as finding yourself through a sincere gift of self. Pope Saint John Paul II referred to this as the "law of the gift." He focused on this law that governs a core aspect of the human person by repeatedly emphasizing an insight from Vatican II: that the human being, "who is the only creature on earth that God willed for itself, cannot fully find himself except through a sincere gift of self" (*Gaudium et Spes* 24).

My story recounts how the Lord gave me the grace to find myself and His plan for my life—both through my gift of self to Him and His precious unborn children, and through the gift that many generous people have made of themselves to me. I do not want to focus on what I have done, but rather to recount what the Lord and the Blessed Mother have done for me and through me.

In so many ways the story of my conversion, where I came to know Jesus and Mary, starts with Magnificat Women's Ministry, through its mother chapter in New Orleans, Louisiana. Marilyn Quirk was the founding coordinator of Magnificat, with the spiritual direction of Fr. Harold Cohen, S.J. and at the direction of then Archbishop Philip M. Hannan. It was a great blessing to later benefit from the friendship of these two extraordinary men. Fr. Cohen was a Jesuit priest filled with the Holy Spirit. There was a Magnificat breakfast in New Orleans that my mother brought me to in December of 1993. I had just graduated from law school in 1990, and that Magnificat breakfast turned out to be an important turning point in my life.

I grew up as the oldest of three daughters. Because my father, Guy Chiappetta, was the last of eight children, born of an Italian immigrant family, I enjoyed being raised in the midst of many cousins. My mother, Theresa "Nell" Oge Chiappetta, was Dad's high-school sweetheart. She is from a Cajun French family. My sisters Shelly and Dawn would agree that the food in our home was always delicious.

My parents were faithful Catholics. They sacrificed greatly to take me out of a failing public school when I was in the third grade so that I could benefit from the spiritual and intellectual excellence of our local Catholic school, Resurrection of Our Lord, under the guiding influence of Msgr. Francis Boeshans. My parents also guided and encouraged me to attend Saint Mary's Dominican High School in New Orleans, an all-girl's college prep high school. Sister Delia and Sister Henry were key influences in teaching me to strive for excellence both in academics and in my interior life.

I had a solid Catholic upbringing. Then I went into the world. Once I was out of my parent's protective Catholic cradle, I started to become more and more of the world. I went into college, got married, and went to law school. By the time I graduated with an undergraduate degree in Finance, I had serious doubts about the reality of God and about the teachings of the Church. I had become, in essence, a secular humanist. I had concern for humanity but not for the soul. I stopped going to Mass, and I focused on the goals of making money and attaining social status.

While I left Mary and Jesus, they apparently had not left me. When I was in my third year of law school, I noticed an unusual newsletter that someone had placed on the front desk of the law school library that reported on apparitions of the Blessed Virgin Mary in a place called Medjugorje. At that moment I was more than ready to take a break from reading about contract law, so I casually picked up the newsletter and started reading about the Blessed Mother appearing to a group of children in Medjugorje. I wondered if there was any truth to this fantastic story that reminded me of a movie that I loved as a child called *The Miracle of Our Lady of Fatima*. When I went to my parents' home to visit, I found the rosary I had received at my eighth-grade Confirmation—a crystal rosary that had pewter links— and I began to pray.

As you may know, many people who pilgrimage to Medjugorje have their rosaries turn to gold, and they see the miracle of the sun, where the sun's center is blacked out and it pulses out concentric circles of many vibrant colors. Law school was a very toxic place for my soul, very power oriented, and fraught with temptations.

But the stories of Medjugorje caught my interest and raised my curiosity, so one day I decided to just pray the rosary as an experiment. To my surprise, the pewter links of my rosary turned to a golden hue before my eyes. This beautiful, mystical gift is experienced by many Medjugorje pilgrims, but here I was, experiencing this wonder as I sat on a levee in New Orleans next to the Mississippi River. I began to question my prior conclusion that religion was simply the opiate of the masses. I said to myself, "Maybe there is something to these Marian apparition stories, or perhaps it is simply that my rosary is getting rusty. I am not sure which."

I went home and found some Brasso to clean the rosary, but the links remained that golden hue instead of the prior pewter color. I was amazed and filled with a tentative hope from this encounter with the infinite mystery of the world that exists beyond our physical senses.

I began to experience an intense spiritual battle that my return to the rosary seemed to precipitate. Despite the fear induced by these interior battles, I remember feeling very grateful that Our Lady would make her presence known to me as she taught me to call out for her assistance in her role as the woman who crushes the head of the serpent.

Soon after my conversion experience, we decided to start a family. I had been using the contraceptive pill since the beginning of my marriage in 1985. No one had given us any coherent explanation of the Church's teachings on fertility regulation. It was completely unforeseen that the government's contraceptive mandate was later to be at the heart of the battle against religious liberty, so it is interesting that this topic is the one Mary chose to bring me back into the Church and then later into the pro-life movement, as I will soon explain.

In my senior year of law school, my father, who I absolutely adored, had a heart problem. He was in the hospital. His heart was racing. We rushed to the hospital because we thought my father was going to die. Thank God they stabilized him and everything was okay. But that experience made me realize that my father was not immortal, and that I should probably give him some grandchildren before he died. I had been married for five years when I decided to start having children. In 1990, I gave birth to my oldest daughter, Rachelle, who was smart and beautiful, and then in 1993 we welcomed our son, Michael. I believed two children were enough. After all, I was a career lawyer with big plans.

I had clerked for the Chief Justice of the Louisiana Supreme Court, and I had later worked for the general counsel of the Louisiana Sheriff's Association, specializing in civil rights defense law. I said to myself, "I am a lawyer, and I have a girl and a boy. Life is good. I'm done, and so now it's time to get back on the pill." Even though I considered myself pro-life, I was afraid to admit it to my friends and colleagues. As I clerked at the Louisiana Supreme Court, I remember praying that no abortion cases would come to the court because I was embarrassed of my pro-life views. I did not want to have to talk about that controversial issue.

After a few years, I had an interesting experience during a dentist appointment. I am constantly amazed at how God works. I would never have imagined that while having my teeth cleaned I would end up getting my soul cleaned. God has such a sense of humor: He knows that to keep Dorinda quiet long enough for her to hear a message, He would have to wait until this big-mouth lawyer was lying in a dentist chair with fluoride receptacles in her mouth. Sure enough, that did the trick in keeping me quiet enough to listen to someone else. It was August 1993, and I had just given birth to my second child, Michael. As I was lying there totally helpless, the dental hygienist shared with me about her prayer life and her relationship with Jesus and Mary while she was cleaning my teeth.

A couple of days later I received a book in the mail from her, entitled *The Apostolate of Holy Motherhood*. The messages in that book really spoke to me. This book, which has the imprimatur of the Church, is a collection of revelations to a busy, young mother with small children. She doesn't even know if praying her rosary is valid because she can't get it finished without one of her children interrupting her. The revelations are from the Blessed Mother and Jesus Christ as a child. These messages share insights about how motherhood is a vocation; it is a very beautiful calling for a spiritual movement of mothers. As I held my infant son, Michael, I began reading *The Apostolate of Holy Motherhood*, and the Lord used that book to begin speaking to me in the depths of my heart and soul.

One Sunday in August of 1993, I took my son to Mass. I must admit that I took him to Mass because he was dressed in beautiful new baby clothes that day. Because we had been to a baby shower for a friend, Michael was wearing a precious blue outfit, and I thought I looked pretty good myself. You see, that is why I went to Mass occasionally—to see and be seen, and to show off my well-dressed children.

On this particular day, the Mass was being celebrated by an outstanding young priest who was just out of the seminary, Father David Dufour. His homily focused on Humane Vitae because it was the anniversary of that encyclical, which is at the heart of the Church's teaching on artificial contraception as a disruption of marital union. Fr. Dufour preached on how contraception interferes with the unitive and pro-creative aspect of sexuality; facilitates the objectification of the woman; and degrades the act of self-giving love into an act of using the other to satisfy oneself.

I had never heard this kind of homily before. That evening when I went home, I read my book and was really feeling this urge, this call to do pro-life legal work. I had these two beautiful babies that I was totally in love with, and I wanted to be able to use my gifts in the pro-life movement. I began to pray and ask the Lord to let me use my legal talents to defend the sanctity of human life.

I had this desire because one of my close friends had shared with me that she'd had an abortion when she was eighteen years old, and that the abortionist had torn a hole in her uterus using the sharp instruments that are used to scrape the baby out of the womb. She was now thirty years old and still suffering the physical and emotional consequences of that abortion. My friend's experience shattered the myth that abortion helps women and gave me a strong, personal motive to use my law degree to expose what abortion does to women, children, and their families.

I had recently written several letters offering legal assistance to Right to Life groups on the national and local level, but I never got any response. All of a sudden, I had this powerful experience. I can only say that with the "eyes of my soul," as I was sitting in my bed, I saw the Blessed Mother at the foot of my bed. She was in her blue mantle and was looking right at me. She said, and I will never forget these words, "If you wish to speak for life, you must follow the teachings of my Son's church and throw away your pills."

I did not understand what the Pill had to do with the pro-life movement, but I knew that to do otherwise than what she had asked me to do would be in direct defiance of Heaven. So, I got out of my bed, got my pills, threw them in the trash can, and got back into bed.

At this point, I realized that I would have to explain this decision to my husband. I wondered what we would do for contraception now. Then I remembered that when I was at Loyola, we had a required course on vocations, with marriage being one of the vocations; they brought in a woman who talked about natural family planning. Because of this woman planting a seed, because I knew natural family planning existed, I went to

St. Paul's bookstore the next day and got the little books and the charts, and I began learning how to use this natural method of fertility regulation.

No one tells you about all the health risks of oral contraceptives. As we recently outlined in an HHS Mandate amicus brief that summarized scores of scientific studies, there is a four-times rate increase of cervical cancer and a tripled risk of breast cancer. Perhaps, even knowing the facts might not stop us. I did not stop using contraception because of increased health risk, I did it because Our Lady asked me to do this, and I had no idea why. It made no sense to me at the time, but with the grace of God I did what she asked me to do.

A few months later, my mother invited me to a Magnificat breakfast and I accepted, after having refused her many times. It was in December of 1993, and Fr. Cohen gave a Scripture teaching on the angels that really intrigued me. He was so full of the peace of the Holy Spirit, and he talked about the supernatural world in a way that made it seem real. Jesuits are very intellectual. And here was a man using his intellect and reason to talk about the supernatural world in a way that appealed to me as a lawyer.

I started realizing these mystical experiences I had been having might be valid. Fr. Cohen was a Catholic priest, and he was talking about the angels, and I was drawn to him. I began stalking him a little bit, tracking him down! I found that he was celebrating the First Friday masses at the St. Paul bookstore where I had bought my NFP (Natural Family Planning) materials. I went to the First Friday Mass, and he had confessions available afterwards.

I went to confession, the Sacrament of Reconciliation, for the first time in ten years. I told him how I had strayed away from the Church, and I shared how in law school I had become personally pro-life but not opposed to a woman's right to choose. I had no children for the first five years of my marriage, so this worldly position made sense to me. I had watched from afar as my mother had lobbied on the steps of the Louisiana Capital for an abortion ban that was passed and was later struck down in the courts. I remember being proud of her for using her civic voice, but her witness at that time didn't impact me. Now, it was all coming back to me, and I began to understand why she was so passionate about these "least amongst us." It was because of her love for her own children, and her heart for all of God's children.

Now, years later, I was with Fr. Cohen in the St. Paul chapel, giving a confession of ten, long, sinful years. He not only absolved me from my sins in the name of Jesus, but he also did something that I did not understand at the time. I was seeing a pattern here—I was always confused. He laid his hands softly and gently on my head and prayed the Spirit down upon me. He baptized me in the Spirit right there in the confessional. He gave me a copy of the "Divine Mercy" book, and he taught me about the author, Sister Faustina and her motto, "Jesus, I Trust in You." Jesus revealed nuggets of wisdom that her confessor asked her to write down in her diary. It later became the book, *Divine Mercy in my Soul*.

I went home not understanding what transpired. All I knew for certain was that I was transformed—a completely new and different person. To my surprise, my husband didn't notice. My parents came over that evening to see the babies and they didn't notice. I kept waiting for someone to say, "Hey, what's different about you? You have changed." Because I was different. I knew I was, but no one noticed. I didn't know about interior rebirth.

I had been self-employed for about a year at this point. I was the publisher of a monthly legal journal that I founded called *Louisiana Supreme Court Reports*. The journal itself was a gift from God that He gave me when I prayed for a way to stay home with my two children. He showed me this journal and the business plan in one glance, after I had been praying every day for about two weeks: "Lord, show me how I can serve You and stay home with my children."

God gave me the idea for this journal while I was working in a private law firm. As I mentioned earlier, I had previously clerked for the Chief Justice of the Louisiana Supreme Court. I had written drafts of the decisions under his direction. I knew that the decisions that the justices wrote went into the vast void of the law library with all of these other books. This was before computer research was really available, so it was difficult to find the decisions that you needed. Every six weeks when opinions came out, I compiled a little, six-page summary of each case that was made available— that I could mail out to all the attorneys in the state—all while I stayed home. The vision of the journal and business plan hit me so suddenly that I sat up really quickly and completely threw out my back (allowing me to stay in bed that New Year's Eve to sketch out the business plan)! Over the next few months, with the help of my parents and sisters, we stuffed and stamped 7,000 newsletters and sent them out in the mail to every attorney in Louisiana. I was so excited when the subscriptions began to roll in! I was then able to leave the private firm and work on my journal from home.

Being a business owner of the law journal enabled me to speak out for life, boldly and without apology. If I had continued to work for a law firm, I would have been discouraged from speaking publicly about anything controversial. Now I was not only able to stay home with my children, but in addition provide some income. After attending another Magnificat meal,

I heard about the Life in the Spirit seminars. My mom and I attended one, and I fell in love with the Scriptures. I continued to read the Scriptures voraciously for almost a year. I had been Catholic my whole life and I would hear the readings at Mass, but I never really sat down with the Bible to read it. I could not get enough! I kept turning page after page. It was so beautiful, and the words seemed so alive as they spoke to my heart. As I continued to read Scripture, I had an intense and growing desire to dedicate my legal services to the pro-life movement, but again, no opportunities surfaced.

I volunteered to write Fr. Cohen's newsletter. It was a Divine Mercy newsletter I created using a desktop publishing program that I knew how to use from my college job of working with IBM. This was the early 1990s, when personal computers were just coming onto the market. His secretary gave me a gift of thanks, a pro-life rosary. The rosary was made out of little baby beads, where you could have your baby's name spelled out with the little baby blocks. Each of the beads was a block. Since "Choose Life" had ten letters, every decade of baby beads spelled out, "Choose Life."

I would pray on my pro-life rosary, "Put me in, put me in, put me in." Just like I was talking to the coach: "Put me on the field, give me the ball. Come on, come on, coach, I can do this." God made it very clear to me that I was not ready to go out yet. I had to really steep myself in His word and the teachings of the Church. I watched EWTN and Mother Angelica to learn the beautiful teachings of the Church as I rocked my babies. I went to conferences for the Catholic Charismatic Renewal and learned about receiving and using the gifts of the Spirit.

One day, a woman at the Charismatic Renewal asked me, "What is your apostolate?"

I was an educated lawyer but I didn't know what the word "apostolate" meant. But I knew it had to be something about what you do for Jesus. So I said, "I give out books about motherhood." The book is *The Apostolate of Holy Motherhood*. Ah, there's that word, "apostolate." It must mean telling people about it. That was my calling, I suddenly realized. I promoted motherhood! Since the time I had received the book from my dental hygienist, I had bought about a dozen copies and had given them out to my friends and family, and I would talk about it to anybody who would stop and listen to me. I would tell them about this beautiful apostolate of holy motherhood. And I was still begging the Lord to use me.

I consecrated myself to Jesus through Mary, according to St. Louis De Montfort, which can be found in a beautiful book you can buy at any Catholic bookstore: *Consecration to Jesus through Mary*. Another way to do this consecration is presented in an outstanding book, but I not only consecrated *my* life but also my children's lives. Mary was my best friend. As a young mother, like her, I could feel her presence with me, leading me to her Son.

Following Holy Motherhood's example, I adored Jesus as the infant Jesus, as the baby Jesus. And so my next two children came along, not planned by me but planned by God. My son was only ten months old, and I was reading my *Apostolate of Holy Motherhood* book in bed, when the birth of my daughter, Gabrielle, was announced to me through that book. It was April 29, 1994. I read this: "Even as the Angel Gabriel announced to my mother the coming of my incarnation, so we announce to you the beginning of a new work of the Lord on the same day."

I suddenly had a deep interior understanding of the importance of these words for me. I reached into my nightstand and took out one of those little pregnancy wheels, where you put in the date when your last period was and it can tell you when the baby is due. If I was indeed pregnant, this baby was due December 25th. I took the pregnancy test without having any idea I was pregnant. Indeed I was, and I was due on Christmas Day. The spiritual depth of my little Gabrielle has been from the beginning—and to this day— an extraordinary gift to me. She is now seventeen, and I remember when she was eight years old, she asked me, "Exactly what is the Immaculate Conception? And if God created everything, then who created God?"

I sat there amazed and amused, saying, "Umm ... I'm going to get back to you on this. Mommy has to do a little research." Gabrielle also helped me with her little sister, Mia. Her full name is Maria Teresa.

When Mia was acting up once as a baby, little Gabrielle said to her, "Now, Mia stop crying. Remember what Mary said to Bernadette? 'I cannot make you happy in this world but only in the next.'" I was simultaneously stifling a laugh and wondering at this child's wisdom. Gabrielle was just confirmed a few months before, and I was delighted when she chose Bernadette as her saint's name (without any prompting from me).

I also read about St. Therese of Lisieux's "little way" that she recounted in her diary, *Story of a Soul*. The little way that St. Therese teaches us is that we achieve holiness not by achieving great things but by offering little things with great love to Jesus. And so, as I changed my children's diapers it was Jesus' diapers I was changing. When I fed them in the middle of the night or carried them when they were crying, it wasn't a burden because it was Jesus that I was feeding and it was Jesus that I was holding. This made the mundane tasks of doing the dishes for the 800th time that day okay because I was doing the dishes for the King. Now, don't get me wrong, I hate and still hate doing the dishes! But when I offer it as a little sacrifice to God, as if I'm doing the dishes in the palace of the King of Creation, it transforms that little act into a great honor and a great joy.

I later learned about Mother Teresa, who had served the poorest of the poor. She would serve people living in horrible, squalid conditions and she would say, "I get to touch Jesus every day." She wasn't in misery. She used these small acts of kindness as if she was serving Jesus. That was quite a consolation to me and made my motherhood of my small children a joy. With Fr. Cohen's guidance as my spiritual director, my relationship was very much with Mary because I could relate to her as a young mother. Fr. Cohen would also bless my tummy with his St. Faustina relic when I was pregnant: for Gabrielle, and later for Mia.

Then something happened that I call "The Grand Inquisitor." This was in early 1994. Perhaps you've heard the hymn that says, "I Have Heard You Calling in the Night"? I had a different calling every night for three weeks. Every night, I would wake up and there was a voice of an accuser, and he would advocate for abortion. He would give all of these really great arguments for abortion, and I would debate him in my mind and in my heart. It was as if I was being given a great gift of understanding and ability to debate this issue.

I had not previously studied, I didn't have books with great answers for abortion arguments, but I was given the truth to combat the enemy. As I received this training for three weeks, I wasn't sleeping well. I literally could not sleep through the night for three weeks. "Lord, I have got to get some rest. I have little children to take care of."

Finally, one night at three o'clock in the morning, I got out of bed and went to my personal computer and wrote an opinion piece for my local newspaper. I titled it, "In Defense of Women and Unborn Children." I wrote how people in the pro-life movement were advocates who love all children, as well as their mothers. I explained how women were being harmed and exploited by the violence of abortion, often coerced into abortion by men who use them as sex objects instead of loving them as women equal in dignity. It was a pro-life, pro-woman argument in response to news articles claiming that people who protested in front of abortion clinics were filled with hate.

After I wrote this letter—a very short, pro-woman, pro-life piece—and I was headed back to bed, I heard another voice that was not the accuser. Instead, I heard very close to my ear, "Your life will never be the same again." Perhaps it was my guardian angel, and it turns out she was right. That Monday morning the piece was printed. A half hour after I had read it in the paper, I received a phone call from Carlton Guillot, one of the board members of New Orleans Right to Life, inviting me to their monthly meeting that was being held that evening in order to discuss an important subject.

It was amazing because when I went to this meeting I was still pregnant with Gabrielle. I had recently had an ultrasound. Back in the day, they were the old, fuzzy black-and-white kind, but this one was extraordinarily clear. When Gabrielle was two years old, she said she wanted to grow up to be a princess, and she did, indeed, turn out to be a graceful princess—she was a Mardi Gras princess when she was in high school! As a precursor, here she was in her ultrasound picture, posing as if she was waving to the camera, and the camera caught her in this awesome position. I was amazed at this twelve-week-old unborn baby posing with one hand perched on her hip and the other waving at the camera.

My bank was right across the street from the abortion clinic. My plan was to show this ultrasound picture whenever I would see a woman going into the clinic. But every time I drove by, I never saw anyone ever go into the clinic. I later learned that they're admitted through the back door. They have bouncers who tell people to drive around to the back because out front there are people praying, counseling, and giving out pro-life information about alternatives to abortion.

At the New Orleans Right to Life board meeting they asked me to go to Baton Rouge, the state capital, and lobby what is called the "Woman's Right to Know Law." I immediately agreed. It was 1995, and the Supreme Court had recently upheld *Roe v. Wade* in a case called *Planned Parenthood v. Casey*. Sadly, the Court upheld the central, so-called "right" for a woman to choose an abortion, but they also held that they had undervalued the interest of the state in protecting the unborn children.

The Casey court upheld a Pennsylvania law that required a booklet be created by the Department of Health to be given to each woman that went into an abortion clinic for an appointment. That booklet shows—at two-week increments—a colored picture of the development of the unborn child, with a little information like: the heart is fully formed, the fingers and toes are present—easy-to-understand facts that show the humanity of the unborn child.

The booklet also included a description of the various abortion methods, so that the woman could understand what these vacuuming sounds are, what is happening as the fetus is dismembered, and emotional risks they are going to face after the abortion. The booklet lists the medical risks, both the short-term and long-term. Also required in this law is a separate booklet (or website) with public and private agencies that are willing to help bring a child to term, parenting resources, health care, and state and federal programs to help a young woman find health care—everything needed to promote the choice for life.

The leadership of the New Orleans Right to Life board, Sharon Rodi and Robert E. Winn (whose deep experience has shaped me throughout the years), asked me to assist veteran pro-life advocate Peg Kenny in bringing this Pennsylvania law to the Louisiana legislature so women could see colored pictures of their unborn children. Once a woman receives a booklet at the abortion clinic, the law requires a twenty-four-hour reflection period. No abortion can be done for at least twenty-four hours so that she can consider this information.

I then recalled that my idea was to use one black-and-white, fuzzy picture, but God thinks much bigger than I do. Peg and I embarked on my first adventure of bringing a pro-life bill into the legislative process. It was challenging yet rewarding as I met the amazing men and women who serve in the legislative body and governor's office to make Louisiana one of the most pro-life states in the nation. Since 1995, every woman in the State of Louisiana (and about twenty-five other states) now see color photographs of their developing unborn children. This is God's big idea. I was honored to have a small part in its enactment by helping with the drafting, testifying in legislative committee hearings, and serving with Peg on the taskforce appointed by the governor to create the content for the booklets.

In 2010, we were able to amend this law in Louisiana based on several other states that now require ultrasound examinations to be offered. After forty years of the social experiment in legalized abortion, we have thousands of post-abortive women who are bravely seeking reconciliation with organizations like "Silent No More" and "Project Rachel." Some of the women are willing to testify to the state legislatures about what the abortion lie did to their lives. My law partner and I also drafted a law that was enacted in 2011, something we call "Signs of Hope" that requires an eighteen-by-twenty-inch sign be posted in the waiting room of abortion clinics. The sign reads:

Pregnancy Resources.

You are not alone. There are many public and private agencies that are willing to help you bring your child to term, and to assist after your child's birth.

You and Adoption. The law allows adoptive parents to pay for the cost of prenatal care, childbirth, and newborn care.

You and the father. The father of your child must provide support of the child even if he has offered to pay for an abortion.

You can't be forced. It is unlawful for anyone to make you have an abortion against your will, even if you are a minor.

As I consult with other state legislatures now, I am no longer afraid. However, when I first started in 1994 (now twenty years ago), I was very fearful. My friend Peg Kenny, who was an experienced veteran, was an outstanding teacher. But even with Peg at my side, I was still scared to death. What I decided to do after much prayer was to ask Mary to lead the way and to hide me under her veil. So in my mind's eye, I would hide behind Mary's veil, clinging to her skirt like a little girl. I would hide my way into the legislature. Here I was, as prideful as any lawyer can be. Yet, Mary covered me with her mantle of humility, and I soon found that I was accepted by these legislators and consulted by them. The lawyers in the Louisiana Attorney General's office would soon allow me to assist in defending the laws in court. The governor's office appointed me to be on the task force. It was all happening so quickly.

One evening I was up late. I was alone at my kitchen table. I was finishing my briefs to the U.S. District Court on a parental consent case. Parental consent is also about the "law of the gift," reincorporating the family back into the abortion decision. Minor girls were being taken by school counselors into abortion clinics. You would think that a law about parental consent or parental notification would be something we could all agree on, but the abortion industry lawyers from New York City filed a legal challenge. I was given that case to defend the law in the U.S District Court. I had my briefs written. There was a stack of them, and I remember thinking to myself, while looking at my picture of baby Jesus, "You know, there probably isn't even a God. I am probably doing this just to make myself feel better, but it is probably just for nothing. I am wasting my time. It is just about me."

I had attended a Medjugorje prayer meeting earlier that day with a group of twelve good women and friends. Standing in a field, we all witnessed the miracle of the sun. It was incredible. There was the sun with a black disc in the center and it would pulsate, spinning off colors of red, blue, and green. It was the most extraordinary thing. I couldn't believe what I was seeing. I would look down and think, *I'm losing my mind.* Then I would look up, and there was this beautiful miracle of the sun. I had a gold rosary, and I had seen the miracle of the sun! People would ask, "Have you been to Medjugorje?" and I reply, "No, but Medjugorje has come to me."

Yet, despite these signs and wonders, that evening as I was praying, I was still thinking, *I'm such a skeptic. I have been given all of these gifts and I still have doubt that there is a God at all.* Then, I started to read my apostolate book, where the Christ Child is speaking:

"Be prepared for extraordinary circumstances to begin to occur in you and others who have been likewise chosen to fulfill My will in an extraordinary fashion. My mother's plan to accomplish 'The Triumph of her Immaculate Heart' has been underway now for me for some time. It continues to gain momentum as more souls consecrated to her are called forth to begin their particular mission for which they are picked. This is why it is of the utmost importance that you do all that is asked of you, down to the letter so as not to leave any part of her plan not accomplished through your own negligence. Reverence for the person of Christ and all persons, and particularly for children, is the reason for this."

After reading this, and with my rosary in hand—looking at the stack of legal briefs in front of me that I had to file the next morning—I thought, *I might be talking to the air, but I am going to say a prayer.* I began praying over these briefs. When I opened up my hand, the crucifix was in the palm of my hand, and all of a sudden Jesus on the cross—not the cross, but the corpus—began to turn red! I witnessed a light, a red light hovering. It went all the way down His legs, and then the red light went all the way up to His head and arms.

The cross was still a pewter color; the chains had previously turned to gold, but the cross was still pewter. A glowing red light hovered over the crucifix. Jesus, on the cross, now completely red, looked to me like a tiny, aborted fetus on the cross. I examined it under a bright light, thinking perhaps it was reflecting light somehow. Everywhere I went to look at it, it remained just as red as could be!

The next day I brought it to Fr. Cohen to show it to him, and he saw it as well. Everyone I showed it to could see this red, little, aborted fetus on the cross. I understood that this was Jesus saying to the skeptic, "You are not doing this for yourself. You are doing this for Me." I still struggle with questions about whether my intentions are well placed, but this sign from the Lord has been a great consolation to me as I strive to persevere with my colleagues to do all that we can to build a culture of life.

This amazing sign was yet another gift from God to give me the resolve over and over again to become convicted that the hard things I have to do I am doing for Him. Each of you reading this book would move heaven and earth for your children, right? For those of you who do not have babies, think of a good friend and what you would do to help another who is in need.

That is the Law of the Gift: that each of us finds the most joy when we forget about our own problems by focusing on the needs of others—by dropping everything and being there to stand by someone you love. That is what the Lord did for me to help me find the meaning and purpose of my life. Although it is incredibly difficult to engage in litigation and legislative battles against the abortion industry, the pharmaceutical and fertility industries, and the government agencies that do not respect our rights of conscience, the grace that is continually given to me to advocate for His children—as if each of them were my own—makes my problems seem small and insignificant.

I could do none of this alone, which is why I am deeply grateful for the gift of self that so many have made to me, especially my parents and sisters, my husband, my four beautiful children, and my friends who are so important to the deepening of my spiritual life, especially Shannon Driscoll Adams and Monique Colon Toso (who also works with BDF to defend life). I am especially grateful for my law partner and co-founder of Bioethics Defense Fund, Nikolas T. Nikas.

I first met Nik during the first round of litigation on the state partial-birth abortion bans (a practice that is now banned under a federal law that was upheld as constitutional in 2007). In 1997 President Clinton twice vetoed a federal ban of partial-birth abortion, a horrible "procedure" used by late-term abortionists to deliver babies feet first, leaving only the head inside of the women as they pierce the skull and suction out the child's brains (or, as they would later explain in depositions, "reduce the cranial contents").

This practice that they characterized as a constitutional right is a brutal, violent crime, and because a ban had been twice vetoed in the federal legislative process, pro-life organizations were now focusing on passing partial-birth abortion bans in the states. In 1999, it had passed in Louisiana and about thirty other states. I was asked by the Department of Justice in Louisiana to defend this law in court because the abortion industry had come in and challenged this law, claiming that this brutal practice was a constitutional right. I could not understand how anyone could look in the mirror and believe that this is a right—and not a brutal act of violence.

I tend to believe that it is a spiritual blindness. I pity those who advocate for the violence of abortion. They are blind to the humanity of the child as they fight to defend empty sex under the guise of "women's autonomy." Love looks toward the good of the other, while "autonomy" looks only to one's self as it aggressively objectifies and destroys those who stand in the way.

The partial-birth abortion litigation was one of the first cases I was asked to handle as counsel outside of a firm. I was scared because I had to defend this law alone in a federal court. I had grown to be reasonably comfortable drafting legislation and testifying in legislative committees, but now I was being asked to go into federal court to defend a high-profile, pro-life law. I am not ashamed to share that I was frightened to my very core.

I started praying and begging for help. My prayers were answered when the general counsel of a Chicago-based, pro-life organization gave me a call out of the blue. He had been litigating partial-birth abortion bans in about a dozen other states. When he heard the news of the Louisiana case, he contacted the Louisiana Department of Justice to offer to litigate it himself or to assist me as special assistant attorney general. His name was Nikolas Nikas, and he is now my law partner and co-founder of Bioethics Defense Fund.

As an experienced litigator, Nik's assistance was invaluable in developing the legal strategy and in obtaining the statements of abortionists. Imagine reading the depositions of abortionists as they boldly describe in cold medical terminology how they dismember another human being. They used terms like "disarticulate the limbs," and "remove the fetal tissue." Nik took the live depositions, and I used the transcripts to write the briefs. Frequently, as I was looking through the depositions and writing the briefs, I would find myself crying at the computer. As time passed, I no longer cried on the outside, but I don't think I'll ever stop crying on the inside.

After having worked with Nik for about six months on that trial, he offered to hire me as the national legislative director for that Chicago-based, pro-life organization. Because my children were young, we agreed that I would work from my home office in New Orleans and travel to legislatures or courts as needed. Sometimes, there was a conflict between work and events for my children. Nik consistently acted as a model of a boss who respects women and families, saying, "Dorinda, if we are going to build a culture of life, it has to start in our own families. So, if there is a conflict with your duties as a mother versus being a lawyer, pick the one as a mother. The kindergarten play never comes again."

Nik worked with me to reschedule work events, or he would step in for me. It was a great witness as an employer to recognize the value of women and to recognize we don't have to abort our children to have a voice in society. We put our children first, we don't apologize for it, and that is okay. And guess what? People respect our calling as mothers first because they instinctively know that this is what a culture of life and family looks like.

As an example, I was on playground duty when my cell phone rang. It was a U.S. Senator whom I had been trying to get in touch with, and I knew that I could not let this opportunity go. So, here I was on a noisy playground shouting, "Hello, Senator. If you hear kick balls and children yelling it's because I am on playground duty for my nine-year-old today."

He replied, "Oh, let me tell you about my grandchild." He talked on and on about his children's children. This conversation taught me that even when we are in the work world, we are human beings; we have families and we don't have to apologize. When I say this to law students during a presentation on "How Roe Ruined Romance," you can see their eyes light up. If you have a vocation to be in a profession or because of circumstances in your life you need to work, you don't have to deny your first vocation and your most important vocation as a mother. Is it easy? No. It is difficult to find the balance, but it can be done with the grace of God, and lots of help from family and friends. It might look like a mess, but your children will know that you are trying to put them first. Having a spouse who supports this vocation is key, of course, and I am blessed in that area as well thanks to the support of my husband, Tony Bordlee.

Mother Teresa used to say she experienced spiritual dryness for forty years after she answered her call within the call. She had been a Loreto nun and then she was called by Jesus to serve the poorest of the poor. After she said "yes" to that, her spiritual dryness began.

My mystical experiences now are of a very different kind. Rather than experiencing ecstasy in union, He is teaching me the mystery of the cross in and through the writings of Saint John Paul II and Mother Teresa's teachings on love as giving until it hurts. He is teaching me the meaning of a motto that I have come to accept and adopt. That maxim in Latin is *via cruces ad vita*, "through the cross to life." He has taught me now that crosses are a portal, a doorway, a passageway to life. Our crosses and our sufferings lead to resurrection if we go through them instead of running away, going around, or numbing ourselves to them.

There is life after the cross and in the midst of the cross. Our experiences in life teach us the mystery of the cross. I call it the "secret of the pearl." As a Louisiana girl, I love oysters, and I have had the experience of finding a small pearl on occasion. I learned that a pearl is formed when a piece of sand or other foreign body enters the soft body within the shell. The sand irritates the oyster—the sand seems to be a problem. The oyster responds by secreting something called "nacre" from its inner shell. This "gift of self" of the oyster coats the irritating sand, transforming it into a beautiful pearl.

The secret of the pearl is that it was once an irritant and a problem, but it is now a valued thing of beauty. When we place our trust in God and give of ourselves to the apparent problems in our lives, His grace is the nacre that can transform the problem into a pearl of wisdom. This requires one to strive to trust in the Lord with peaceful patience.

If I had to summarize the small amount of wisdom I have gained from giving my legal talents to the pro-life movement, I would point to the words of Pope Saint John Paul II when he said "faith and reason are like two wings on which the human spirit rises to the contemplation of the truth" (from the Encyclical, *Fides et Ratio*, 1998). I have come to understand that right and wrong are not arbitrary standards that we must adhere to "because God said so." Rather, "right" is what is good for the human person and the common good, and "wrong" is what harms the human person and the common good. I have learned through the "law of the gift," that we find ourselves when we make sincere gifts of ourselves—in our families, our work and our recreation.

I have come to understand that abortion is wrong not because it "offends" God, but rather because it saddens God as our Father, Who sees the woman whom He created robbed of an incredible gift of love that could free her from the shackles of her own self-sufficiency. Abortion is wrong because it denies the woman the opportunity to make a gift of herself to her child and to the child's father, and thus find the meaning of her life. Abortion is wrong because it facilitates the sexual exploitation of women by men, who are likewise robbed of their vocation as protector and provider. Abortion is wrong because it distorts the beauty of sexual intimacy from an act expressing our calling to love and be loved to a meaningless act that says we should just use and be used.

Abortion is wrong because it robs women of their dignity, it robs men of their vocation, and it destroys a unique and unrepeatable human life. A civilized society cannot sanction this act of violence as a constitutional right without grave consequences to our law and policy, and to our concrete human relationships. The culture-of-death ethic has spread also to the world of science, with the use of human embryos as raw material for science experimentation, and even to the fertility industry, where human embryos are created and destroyed in labs, and where women are used as commodities to provide ova to create children they will never raise and to act as wombs for rent in a form of reproductive trafficking called gestational surrogacy. It is a huge challenge to fight these forces via law, policy and education, but it has also been a great honor that teaches me humility, due to the difficulty of promoting what I like to call a "holistic feminism."

I would like to share a quote from the encyclical *Evangelium Vitae*, the Gospel of Life, which embodies the vision of a holistic feminism:

"In transforming the culture so that it supports life, women occupy a place in thought and action, which is unique and decisive. It depends on [women] to promote a "new feminism," which rejects the temptation of imitating models of "male domination," in order to acknowledge and affirm the true genius of women in every aspect of the life of society, and overcome all discrimination, violence and exploitation."

I am well aware that in this cause for life, I stand on the shoulders of giants—men and women with far greater talent and far greater virtue than I will ever know. There are too many veterans to name, and the next generation is yet to be named. So to conclude, I ask you to pray for our common mission to be a voice for the least amongst us, and to join me in praying for the Lord's guidance as we collaborate with leaders across the globe to restore law in the service of human life.

Bio–
Dorinda Bordlee was led on a spiritual journey back into the heart of Our Lord's Divine Mercy after attending a Magnificat breakfast at the invitation of her mother in 1993. Dorinda's prayer life was nurtured by Father Harold Cohen, S.J., the spiritual advisor of the Magnificat Central Service Team. A series of mystical experiences soon overflowed from her heart as a mission to dedicate her legal talents to the service of unborn children and their mothers. Dorinda is now chief counsel of Bioethics Defense Fund, a national pro-life legal and educational organization that she co-founded. Dorinda has consulted with lawmakers across the United States and abroad on strategic model legislation, has filed strategic amicus briefs in key U.S. Supreme Court cases, and has lectured around the world, including addresses in the Vatican City to Catholic medical groups.

Kitty Cleveland

"My grace is sufficient for you, for power is made perfect in weakness."
(2 Cor. 12:9)

I was raised in the vibrant city of New Orleans, LA, the first of six daughters born to Carl and Joey Cleveland over the course of twenty-three years. Surely, the grace and mercy of God will speed them to heaven for what they endured during our teen years!

There was nothing extraordinary about my simple Catholic childhood. I was a plumpish sanguine student who daydreamed a lot and didn't particularly excel at anything until the sixth grade. It was then that we discovered—much to my surprise and delight—that I had a certain amount of artistic and musical ability.

In the seventh grade, my parents moved us to the suburbs and into a new school with a wonderful music program. The pivotal moment for me came when I was given my first vocal solo, a terrified version of "You Light Up My Life." Notwithstanding my shaky knees and dry mouth, I had found my passion. I would go on to sing in the choir at Archbishop Chapelle High School and in musicals at the boys' high schools.

My dream was to move to New York and pursue a musical theater career on Broadway. It had not occurred to me to ask God what plans *He* might have for my life and my talents. I only wanted to sing, act, have fun, and have my dad take care of me for the rest of my life.

In addition to opening up my musical horizons, our move to the suburbs also brought us to a new church parish. It was here that my parents were introduced to Cursillo, a weekend encounter with the Lord Jesus that had a profound impact on them. My mother Joey, a Methodist convert, started devoting much of her time to pro-life apostolates and to being the church choir director, as well as meeting weekly with her friends from the retreat. Thirty years later, they still meet almost every week.

My dad's Cursillo was his first encounter with the living God, and he came home a changed man. Up until this point he had achieved great success as an aggressive trial lawyer, always representing (as he would tell it)

"David against Goliath." He had perfected a certain amount of confident, in-your-face swagger that suited him well in the courtroom but did not always translate well in a house full of sensitive women. After Cursillo, my father was still larger than life, enthusiastic, and strong-willed, but his explosive temper softened a great deal. His Cursillo experience also led to his eventual ordination as a permanent Roman Catholic deacon.

A profound spiritual awakening also came for me when I was sixteen, the summer before my senior year in high school. I had just returned from an exhausting, seven-countries-in-two-weeks trip to Europe, which included a stop in Rome. Since it was during an extraordinary jubilee year in the Catholic Church, we had been given the special grace of walking through the Holy Door at St. Peter's Basilica only opened every twenty-five years. It must have affected me because back home I found myself praying, *God, if You really exist, I want to know.*

In that instant, it was as if a lightning bolt of intense joy shot through my body and totally filled my spirit. I had never felt so loved, so safe, so *joyful*—and I wept off and on throughout the night. As of this writing, it remains the most intense experience of the presence of God I have ever felt.

For the first time in my life, I knew God was real, that He loved me and was *living inside of me*, and that even if I died the next day, I would be okay because God would be there to meet me. At the same time, I received the gift of tongues. While I didn't understand most of what I was saying, one thing I consistently repeated was (phonetically) "Kreest-ee-ar-ee-uh," which would later have great significance for me. I returned home transformed, telling my family that I was sorry for all of the mean and selfish things I'd done over the years. They knew I was different because I told my sisters that I loved them, for the first time *ever*.

Not only did I love them, but I had fallen in love with the Holy Spirit. I devoured everything I could read about the spiritual gifts, and the Bible became alive and relevant for me. My new prayer life also led me to ask Jesus what He wanted me to do with my life. I sensed that He was calling me to sing for Him, proclaiming the great truth that I had discovered: *God is alive, really loves you, and is living in you!*

Not long after this my mom invited me to my first Magnificat breakfast—the mother chapter founded by Marilyn Quirk—where my mom helped lead the praise and worship music. Fr. Harold Cohen was there, and I approached him with great anticipation to ask if he might want me to sing for his television program, *A Closer Walk*. He thanked me but added that he already had someone to do that (he certainly did—Dana Scallon). Still, I knew that somehow, someday, I would find a place to channel this passion. And it was truly a passion—a painful longing that would not leave me.

Tulane University became my new home after high school graduation, and I continued to have this desire to glorify God through music. But my prayer life was dismal. It gradually became more important for me to fit in on this secular campus than to be an evangelist. I sang for the nine o'clock "last-chance Mass" on Sunday evenings, but I was also absorbed in the campus sorority and fraternity party culture, where I drank heavily, smoked, and hung out with friends until the wee hours of the morning.

I was very much influenced by the religion of secular humanism on campus, so that my feelings and my poorly-formed conscience—formed more by false compassion and by some wacky college professors than by the authentic teachings of the Catholic Church—dictated what was right and wrong. It was also *verboten* for me to speak of moral absolutes, else I be branded close-minded or—even worse—judgmental. It was so much easier to go with the flow and stay numb.

Though my passions in college were singing and musical theater, I ended up graduating from Tulane four years later as a sociology major due to my aversion to music theory. The reality was that I had no plan and was terrified of what lay ahead for me. I had hoped to meet my future husband on campus, but he never showed up. What was I going to do with my life? How would I survive?

Since working in my dad's law office was my only work experience, I took a job as a paralegal in a large defense firm. After a year, and in search of new direction, I attended my own Cursillo. At the closing, I was the first one to get up, telling everyone with new-found conviction and joy that I was going to spend my life singing for and about the Lord. When the high from the retreat wore off and the reality of a dearth of opportunities for Catholic singers set in, I slipped into the next-easiest alternative, doing what many people do when they don't know what to do with their lives and would prefer to delay adulthood for a few more years: I enrolled in law school.

My dad was thrilled, since his dream was for all of his girls to practice law with him, a firm he would playfully call Carl's Angels. Unfortunately for me, law school was like being right-handed but having to write with your left hand for three years. I could do it, but it took twice as much effort as those more naturally inclined to left-brain thinking. I knew God wasn't calling me to be a lawyer, but a lukewarm prayer life and fear of the unknown kept me paralyzed.

Summer school in the south of France the following year eased the pain a bit, but—just to show you where I was spiritually—I passed up

Lourdes on the train so that I could go to Pamplona for the running of the bulls. No longer did I sing in the choir at Mass or participate in any kind of apostolate, but the small ember still flickering in my heart led me to pen the lyric, "Lord, You know my heart, Your wings en-shadow me, You'll never leave. And if I only let go of the chains that bind my soul, I'll be free— through the strength of my surrender." This foreshadowed the first song I would write and record years later—a song for my dad that would change the course of my life, called "Surrender."

After passing the bar exam there were very few jobs available, so I begged my father to give me a "daddy job" until I could find suitable employment with another firm. Plus, it would give me plenty of opportunities to join him for fancy three-hour lunches in the French Quarter. I really didn't think like a lawyer, though. "Why can't people just get along and treat each other fairly?" I would wonder, disdaining the all-or-nothing, combative world of litigation.

To appease my growing discontent, I decided to get trained as a mediator and to participate in musical theater again in order to have a little fun. It was there that I met my future husband, Mel Rogers, a gentle giant of a woodwind player and the orchestra contractor who hired the musicians. He caught my eye with his tall physique and good looks, but he won my heart when he corrected the strings who were playing a wrong note on one of my songs.

Mel did not exactly fit my pre-conceived idea what my husband would be like. He was divorced with two children; was not a practicing Catholic; and was sixteen years my senior. He also didn't want to get married again and had ensured through a vasectomy that he would not father any more children. But he was lots of fun, was willing to have a wardrobe make-over, and did an excellent job of distracting me from my unhappiness at work.

After a few months I was completely smitten and couldn't imagine my life without him. The feeling was clearly mutual when he offered to have the vasectomy reversed so that we could have children together. We were engaged less than three months after our first date and married the following year—after Mel's annulment—in the beautiful St. Louis Cathedral in the heart of New Orleans. I instantly became a stepmother to two young teenagers, Karl and Kiersten. And while the step parenting classes I took before we married were helpful, there was only so much a class could teach. The next several years "grew me up" as I learned what real love required. All these years later they are both kind, gentle adults whom I dearly love.

Sadly, the vasectomy reversal was a failure, and a second truly heroic reversal was also unsuccessful. I was heartbroken. When I learned that sperm aspiration and *in vitro* fertilization (IVF) might work for us, I received a phone call from a nun (tipped off by my concerned sister) who informed me that to do IVF would be immoral.

"How can bringing new life into a loving marriage be wrong?" I asked incredulously. After all, I knew beautiful families who had children conceived in this way, and I didn't understand why we couldn't be one of them. She mentioned something about the moral necessity of both the unitive (physically joining man and woman) and pro-creative (being open to life) aspects of the marital act being present when new life is conceived, but this meant nothing to me. All I heard was that the Catholic Church was telling me that I would never have a baby, and I was indignant.

I finally took my anger with the Church to a priest in confession. After I told him the whole story he said, "You have nothing to confess here. Of course you can do *in vitro*—you're married. Go forth, be fruitful and multiply," he continued, "and call me when you get pregnant."

I was relieved, but at the center of my spirit I still didn't have peace. How could I be getting two different answers on this? Confused, I consulted another priest about it who said that IVF was in fact immoral for reasons outlined in the church document *Donum Vitae*. So just to be sure, I decided to ask a third priest—the tie-breaker. Bachelor priest number three said that since procreation is one of the purposes of marriage, it might be immoral for me not to do IVF!

Up to that point, it had never occurred to me that there was even an issue here, or that there was this kind of chaos in the Catholic Church. My conscience now mandated that I find out what the Church really taught, not because Church teaching makes it true, but that the Church teaches it *because* it is true.

When I consulted the Catechism and *Donum Vitae* they both confirmed that IVF was indeed contrary to God's plan for procreation. I came to understand that not only does it separate the unitive and pro-creative aspects of the conjugal act, it reduces human life to a product manufactured by third parties, opening up a whole Pandora's Box of unintended consequences: hundreds of thousands of frozen and abandoned embryos; selective reduction, i.e. abortion, when too many babies start to develop; sex and health selection that results in the destruction of "less desirable" children; the necessary death of untold embryos in the process of IVF; and severe financial and emotional strain that often results in divorce.

Regardless of how children are conceived, they are all precious and beloved children of God. Occasionally, there are consequences that need to be reckoned with and confessed, trusting always in the goodness and mercy of the One who made us.

I sat on my sofa and sobbed, "Lord Jesus, if this is really what You are asking of me—to sacrifice my unborn children—then I trust You. But please let me know if this is not Your will!" Notwithstanding the anguish and the lack of understanding, there was now a supernatural peace in the middle of it that confirmed my decision. Surprisingly, my love for the Lord grew exponentially as this cross helped me to grow in intimacy with Him.

Some may think it quite naïve of me to allow the Magisterium to direct me in such a personal matter, but this guidance was ultimately a great gift that brought me true freedom. My former pick-and-choose Catholicism according to the Church of Me had only brought confusion and lukewarmness of heart. And while this choice to follow authentic Church teaching was initially painful, I was ultimately given the grace I needed to accept with joy and gratitude this renunciation of my own will out of obedience, trust and love.

Mel and I would eventually decide to pursue adoption, but for now I continued to practice law with my father and dig in as a wife and stepmother. After spending three long and restless years practicing law, I finally got the courage and the clarity on a retreat to make a big change. I knew God was calling me to trust in Him alone and to start doing work that was healing and life-giving. So in the fall of 1995—six years after my Cursillo—I returned to school to get a master's degree in counseling and finally start writing, singing, and recording music for the Lord.

Before school started, I visited my sister Connie for a few days at the Franciscan University of Steubenville, where she was studying for a master's degree in theology. This visit would change my life in two profound ways. The first happened when a copy of Scott and Kimberly Hahn's conversion story, *Rome, Sweet Home*, was casually put into my hands. It was a summer of record heat in Ohio, with temperatures close to 110 degrees. Since Connie's old house was without air conditioning, I couldn't sleep a wink. In exasperation, I picked up the book and didn't put it down until I had read it from cover to cover. It was now four o'clock in the morning. For the first time in my life, I understood what a treasure I had in the Roman Catholic Church. God bless Scott and Kimberly Hahn!

The second profound event happened when Connie took me at twilight to visit a stone replica of the Portiuncula, the chapel restored and beloved by St. Francis of Assisi in Italy. This was the first Eucharistic adoration chapel I had ever been to, and it was packed. Students filled the pews and sat on the floor—some writing in their journals, others staring intently at

Jesus-in-hiding, others praying quietly with heads bowed and eyes closed. The small, darkened chapel had only one spotlight, which was focused on a gold monstrance containing the Eucharist.

A welcome, cool breeze wafted through the open doors. The only sounds I heard were coming from outside as the winds bent over the cedar trees with a *swish* and the locusts announced the coming night. And then came the fireflies. One by one they lit up the chapel like little stars announcing the presence of the Savior. It was breathtaking. *Jesus was there!* It was nothing short of a mystical experience of the real presence of Christ in the Eucharist.

It was by divine providence that I began to find my home again in the Catholic Church that weekend because just a month later—the very same day I left my dad's law firm to register for my master's degree—my world as I knew it was shattered. When I called in to get my messages, one of the paralegals picked up. "The FBI is here, and they won't let anyone leave," she said fearfully. "And they want to talk to you, too." Thus began a nightmare for my father and our family that would only end years later, after many tears and much heartache.

The FBI agents seized all our files, announcing to us and to the media that the law firm was implicated in their investigation into political corruption in Louisiana. If you know anything about Louisiana politics, corruption is nothing new, but it was certainly new to us. Our firm was pulled into the fray because one of our clients was being charged with selling shares of his business to Louisiana politicians in the hopes that they would protect their interests with favorable legislation. The law partners had loaned the client money and helped him to get licensed. Though I was doing the vast majority of the work for this client when this happened and was threatened with indictment, I was miraculously spared.

Instead, the prosecutors set their sights on my father, making it clear that they would destroy his life if he did not give them information—*true or not*—that would help them convict the politicians they were really after. As a highly regarded trial lawyer and Catholic deacon, the feds knew Dad would make a good witness and that he had a lot to lose if he didn't cooperate. Having no knowledge of any wrongdoing, and being unwilling to fabricate information to save himself, my father was indicted on multiple, groundless charges that held penalties as severe as those for murder.

We were all terrified, but my dad seemed confident that it would all be straightened out once the facts were known and he was able to testify. After all, he had spent his life in the courtroom and was comfortable in front of a jury. But this was his first criminal case, and this was the first time he was the defendant.

The trial started almost two years later and involved six defendants, including two state senators. It lasted for weeks and led the news every night. Fear and anxiety brought me to my knees, causing me to pray with much more frequency and fervor than I had in years. I also started reading the diary of St. Faustina about the Divine Mercy of Jesus, which I found deeply consoling.

A few weeks before the trial began, my parents went up to Steubenville for my sister Connie's graduation. While there, they ran into their friends Patti and Al Mansfield who offered to pray with my dad. Patti felt led to open the Bible to 2 Cor. 12:1–10. In this passage St. Paul begs God to remove the "thorn in the flesh" that tormented him. But God answers, "My grace is sufficient for you, for power is made perfect in weakness."

This was not the warm-and-fuzzy Scripture passage my father was hoping for. It was instead about the anguish and personal weakness God allowed St. Paul to experience so that God could be his only strength. As providence would have it, this passage turned out to be the reading at Mass on the day the trial began.

Everything was going remarkably well for my father, as the evidence clearly showed his innocence of any wrongdoing. Even the IRS testified on his behalf when the prosecutors accused him of tax fraud. Once my dad took the stand and explained every remaining question, we all breathed a sigh of relief. The reporters congratulated him as he left the courtroom, and we celebrated that night with our extended family and friends.

After a week of deliberations, we were called in to hear the jury's verdict. Our stomachs were in knots as we walked in, and my dad said quietly to me, "Kitty, if there is even one guilty verdict against me, my life is over." He knew the importance of his reputation in the legal community and to his future service as a deacon.

My father was the first defendant to hear his fate: "Guilty." There was an audible gasp in the courtroom. My heart raced in panic, and I began sobbing in disbelief as they continued to read more and more guilty verdicts against him. I clung to my mother and my sister, who were inconsolable. My father—several feet in front of us—simply sat down and hung his head.

My eyes searched the faces of the jurors, trying to find some kind of explanation, but they just stared straight ahead. *"We believe in you, Dad!"* I yelled across the courtroom. In desperation, I closed my eyes in prayer, crying out to God. And then I received a special grace. Rather than seeing darkness as I buried my face in my hands, I clearly saw the Divine Mercy image of Jesus given to St. Faustina. Over and over I prayed, "Jesus, I trust in You!"

I later remembered that St. Faustina wrote in her diary, "If God sends such great suffering to a soul, He upholds it with an even greater grace, although we are not aware of it. One act of trust at such moments gives greater glory to God than whole hours passed in prayer filled with consolations." I must qualify this by saying that I know many people have suffered much more injustice in life than my family or I ever have—unspeakable horrors. But for us, this was the scariest, darkest hour of our lives. My dad was our rock, and he was being crushed. How would he survive? What was going to happen to my mom, to my little sisters, to our family, to me?

My father was eventually sentenced to ten years in federal prison (serving a minimum of eight-and-a-half years) on convictions of tax fraud— yes, even though the IRS testified on his behalf—and of having a hidden ownership interest in the client's business. Not only did he not have such an interest, this charge was not even considered a crime in most states. He was also ordered to forfeit more than $1.5 million in assets to the government— assets he had never received from this client—which meant that my parents would lose everything they had, and my mother and youngest sisters would lose our family home.

As he went to sleep that night I heard him crying in despair, "My God, my God! Why have You forsaken me?" Truly, he was suffering the agony of the cross, a feeling of total abandonment by God. This was 1997, the Year of Jesus Christ instituted by John Paul II, in preparation for the Great Jubilee in 2000. We all came to know the suffering, persecuted Christ more intimately. All requests that my dad be allowed to stay home pending the appeal were denied by the judge. She ordered him to report immediately to a federal prison in Pensacola, Florida. The first letter he received came from a priest friend who quoted 2 Cor. 12:7–10, including "My grace is sufficient for you, for power is made perfect in weakness."

We learned at our first prison visit that we would need to wait in a long line before submitting our clear, gallon-size, Ziploc bag "purses" for inspection. The rules were arbitrary and tedious: playing cards and cigars were permitted, medicine and fresh food were not—but you could buy junk food from the machines. It was not unlike the maddening, changeable rules at airport security, where even pregnant mothers and old ladies can be treated with suspicion.

My father came in to meet us wearing a green jumpsuit with the number 25306-034 on his chest pocket. He looked tired and haggard, and we all fought unsuccessfully to hold back the tears. A migraine headache started blinding my vision, which was actually a welcome relief from seeing my father like this. When it was time to go, my dad hugged us all tightly and then exited by a separate door. My stoic baby sister—only eight years old—collapsed outside of the doors and sobbed, *"I'm not leaving my daddy!"* This was the darkest hour for my dad. He could hear her plaintive cries as he was being subjected to a full body cavity search by the prison guards, the first of many.

Once we returned home, all of our family celebrations and usual festive gatherings after Mass abruptly ended. My father had been the chief cook and organizer of all of our fun adventures—he was truly the life of the party. We deeply mourned the loss of his infectious energy and generous spirit, and a pall of grief now blanketed everything we did. Unlike a death, where you move through the various stages of grief to healing and closure, our hearts were in open-ended, profound sadness.

We regularly drove the six hours from New Orleans to Pensacola and back to visit, though there was little we could do to console my dad other than to sing and provide music for the prison Mass. My Methodist grandmother would sit at the piano; my husband would play flute and clarinet; sometimes our friend Debbie would bring her guitar; and my mom, sisters, and I would harmonize. They put up signs on the prison grounds that the *von Cleveland Family Singers* were coming, and Mass attendance would surge. We suddenly found ourselves with a prison ministry, and one old man told me after Mass that for the first time in eight years he had just cried tears of joy.

In the meantime, I had gotten my master's degree and was offered a job teaching—and I do appreciate the irony of this—*Career Planning* at a nearby university. I was also singing with the New Orleans Opera Chorus and planning to audition for the Metropolitan Opera since this was my last year of eligibility; however, I still had not written any songs for the Lord as I had promised—mostly out of fear, I think. What if my songs weren't any good? What if all of this longing was really for naught? These weren't conscious thoughts, but in retrospect I think this is why I struggled so much to follow through with my aspirations time after time.

A few weeks after taking my dad to prison, I read Sr. Briege McKenna's book *Miracles Do Happen* in preparation for a retreat I would be attending with her in January of 1998. Sr. Briege, who has the gift of healing, writes about her deep love for and relationship with Christ that has developed out of her devotion to doing three hours of Eucharistic adoration daily no matter where she is in the world. This intrigued me since I'd had that powerful experience at Steubenville and since I had a perpetual adoration chapel only ten minutes from my new home.

The first time I went to my local chapel, as I was writing in my journal about my dad's trial and imprisonment, I was transported by a powerful daydream. I suddenly saw myself sitting with Jesus on a hill under a beautiful tree surrounded by spring green grass. I watched as He carved our initials in the bark: "JC + KC." Then He put a big heart around it and said,

> *Fall in love with Me. I have always loved you, and I want you to love Me, too. Rejoice, My beloved! Know that I have called you very personally by name. You are Mine, Kitty. You have given part of your life to Me. Now, let Me have all of it so that you might live more fully in and through Me, and I in you.*

I was profoundly moved. Just days later, my brokenhearted mother and I were on retreat with Sr. Briege, joining a large group of women at a retreat center on the Gulf Coast of Mississippi. The first thing she did was tell us about her conversation with Jesus in adoration that morning. I recall her telling us in her wonderful Irish brogue, "'Lord, what can I do fer ya today?' And He said, 'Briege, I want ya ta pray with the women.' So I said, 'All 900 of them, Lord?' And He said, 'Yes.'" She then heroically invited us to come down row by row in front of the exposed Blessed Sacrament, encouraging us to give Jesus our hearts while she and Fr. Kevin Scallon prayed over us individually.

As I stood there in front of the monstrance, arms outstretched in total abandonment, the sobs burst forth from my soul. Sr. Briege put her hand over my tears, and gently said, "Ohhh." As she held her hand there with such tenderness and love, something deep within me was healed. It felt as though Jesus himself had put His hand on my face that night. And through copious tears I gave Him my heart again, rededicating myself to writing and singing music for His glory (for the umpteenth time).

Also that night, I heard myself praying a new phrase in tongues. The Latin translation I later came to find out is: "Ah! Joy! You have appointed me to be a singer! Oh, unless I sing Your praise, I sing noise." Wow. The next day in adoration on the retreat, I started writing a song for my dad called "Surrender." I also understood for the first time the translation of the words I'd prayed in tongues in high school: "Kreest-ee-ar-ee-uh," was "Christi aria"—"Song of Christ." Truly, miracles do happen! I left that weekend on fire for pursuing music ministry—not the opera—and a newfound devotion to Eucharistic adoration. This was the year John Paul II declared to be the Year of the Holy Spirit, and it certainly was for me.

Some weeks later I watched a program on EWTN, the Catholic cable network, called *Life on the Rock*. I had never watched EWTN before, but my sister Connie called from Atlanta to tell me that she was in the opening credits, and I needed to check it out. She didn't know when the show came on, so I started channel surfing while we spoke. Not only did I find EWTN, but as soon as I did, I saw her face on my TV!

What I continued to watch would have a profound impact on the course of my life. Jeff Cavins, the host, had invited a young singer to witness about the miraculous healing she had received of an eating disorder in high school. She thereafter started keeping a daily holy hour, praying the rosary, going to daily Mass, and going biweekly to confession. What really convicted me was the fact that she was singing and recording music that lifted up the Lord, and she was only nineteen years old!

I went to the adoration chapel in tears, once again ashamed that I had not kept my promises to Christ that I had made on my retreat. It happened to be the first day of Lent and I vowed that day—*in writing*—that I would keep a daily holy hour to pray and write music until Good Friday. I also thought that maybe I could go on *Life on the Rock* one day to sing since there weren't any other performance options that I knew of for Catholics.

Once the daily adoration began, I simply fell in love with Jesus. I looked forward to our special time together each day, and I marveled at the stream of people that regularly came in to see Him. As I learned how to listen to the Lord's voice, I clearly heard Him calling me to be a "music missionary." I wasn't sure what that entailed, exactly. "What am I to do, Lord? Knock on people's doors like a Jehovah's Witness and ask if I can sing for them?" I asked, only half-kidding. But the call was clear, and I trusted that the details would come later.

On one Lenten night, I was simply exhausted after a long day. I did not want to go to the chapel and finally dragged myself there around 11:00 P.M. When I could no longer hold my head up I prayed, "Lord, can't we just call it a fifty-minute hour like they do in therapy?"

"Just open the Bible before you go," He replied in my heart.

I did as I was told, and my eyes fell on Matthew 26:40: "Could you not keep watch with me for one hour?"

I was stunned, and tears of joy and sorrow streamed down my face. What's so beautiful about the Lord is that He doesn't condemn us. He simply invites us into deeper relationship with Him. This taught me that my promises really do matter to Him, and He shares His heart with those who love Him. In this case, I was showing my love and my trustworthiness by giving Him my time. A wise priest once told me, it's important for us to "waste time" with God.

The time spent in adoration helped ground me in prayer as we waited for my dad's appeal to be heard by the Fifth Circuit Court of Appeals. My mother grew increasingly anxious as the hearing grew closer. One evening she said fearfully, "Kitty, if we lose this appeal I'm not going to make it. I can't keep living like this!" It was taking a toll on her not just as a wife but also as the mother of six grieving daughters.

"We don't have the grace for that yet, Mom," I responded, surprising myself. "We only have the grace for today, and today we're okay."

We can all become overwhelmed by our projections into the future, can't we? Perhaps we can live with the heavy cross we are carrying for the next minute, but we can't imagine carrying it for years on end. This is when people despair, when they take their lives or give themselves to the slavery of addiction. But God promises us only the grace for the day, which requires radical dependence and trust on our part that He is with us and will personally care for us in the future.

One-and-a-half years after my father left for prison, *we lost* the appeal on all counts. As far as I knew, it was our last hope. While we were profoundly disappointed, everyone—my mom included—had the grace for the day to get through it. My father, surprisingly, found his greatest serenity at this point. Knowing that he had many years of prison still ahead of him, he surrendered to his fate and simply asked God to give him the gift of peace. Immediately *the peace that surpasses all human understanding enveloped him* (cf. Phil. 4:7), and he walked around in a "grace bubble" that protected him from the violence, profanity, noise, and filth all around him. Dad lived alone with Jesus in the midst of hell.

He chronicled his prison experiences in monthly newsletters that he typed on an old typewriter, and they became a source of inspiration to hundreds, if not thousands, of people every month. My mom emailed them to her whole list of contacts, and the recipients invariably passed them on to others. The newsletters were filled with great humor; terrible sadness; interesting anecdotes; and always spiritual lessons in faith, hope, and love. His ministry as a deacon had never been more powerful.

As I tried to make sense out of why God had not answered our prayers, I was inspired to finish writing the song "Surrender" that I had begun on that retreat with Sr. Briege eighteen months earlier. The lyrics summed up everything I had learned from my father since his convictions, and it allowed me to proclaim the full truth to those who has written him off as a common criminal. Now that I actually had some material and a little fire in my belly, I finally found the courage to start working on my first CD.

My dad published the lyrics in his prison newsletter and, upon my request, invited his readers to financially sponsor the project in some way if they were interested. It was terrifying to make myself so vulnerable, but I had no money to pay for it due to my multiple misguided post-secondary degrees. Deep down in my heart, I was surrendering to Divine Providence and feeling immense joy. The first week passed without any donations, but I took heart knowing that these things take time. Then the second week passed. Nothing—not even five bucks from my mother.

I went to the chapel and sobbed, "Jesus, I thought You wanted me to do this, and no one believes in me! What was I thinking? I've made a complete fool of myself." I stopped crying long enough to hear a whisper in my heart say, "Just wait. Great things are coming." The next day I got two checks for $5,000 each (one was from my mom). I cried so hard that my husband thought someone had died.

That seed money became the foundation for my first CD, *Surrender*. As I needed more money, it just seemed to show up as I stepped out in faith. My husband and I also decided it would be a good idea for me to use my maiden name on the CD, both as a way to show solidarity with my dad and as a way to get a little more use out of a pretty fun stage name. Not long after I started recording in the studio, a chance encounter with Jeff Cavins led to him inviting me to speak about career planning as a guest on *Life on the Rock*. "Would it be okay if I sang a song while I'm there?" I asked. He said that would be great. I couldn't believe that this was all happening just as I had envisioned in the chapel.

Shortly thereafter my mother got a mysterious phone call. A woman on the other end said, "You don't know me, but the Lord told me to tell you that He is going to 'restore what the locusts have eaten.'" To our utter astonishment, we were later informed that the U.S. Supreme Court had agreed to hear my father's appeal. They can receive over 80,000 applications a year for a criminal hearing and accept fewer than sixty. That's less than a fraction of one-percent—a statistical miracle for us! And then a priest with many mystical gifts who didn't know our story told my mother, "You know, they thought that Jesus was a common criminal, too. But don't worry—great joy is coming to your family, and incomprehensible doors will be opening."

As a matter of procedure my dad's lawyers petitioned the trial judge to let him come home while we waited for the hearing, though no one expected her to grant the request. When I learned that she would hear arguments on the Thursday between Easter Sunday and the first official Feast of Divine

Mercy the following Sunday (when Blessed Faustina would be canonized!), my heart quickened. I decided to do my first novena—a joint novena to Blessed Faustina and to St. Joseph, restorer of families, with the specific intention that my dad would be with me on Divine Mercy Sunday. On Easter Thursday my sister Beth called me after the hearing, but I couldn't understand her. Finally she said through sobs, *"Dad's coming home!"* It was three o'clock—the hour of mercy. We brought him home with great joy, and my dad was with me at St. Joseph's Church that Sunday, where I sang through tears of gratitude for the miracle of mercy we had been given.

Only weeks later we were all on the set of *Life on the Rock*, and I was singing "Surrender" for the first time—on live television and in front of my dad and a potential audience of over 80 million households around the world (not that they were all watching). Coincidentally, that same day the first 2,000 copies of the *Surrender* CD I had been working on for almost a year—after many bizarre and frustrating mechanical setbacks—finally arrived. So began my career as a music missionary, only thirteen years after first hearing the call. I imagine my guardian angel breathed a huge sigh of relief that day.

When we got back home we had a grand party to celebrate Dad's release from prison and, in a smaller way, the release of my new CD—a "joint release" party, if you will—where all of the friends and family who had faithfully stood by us during the hard times came to share in our joy. Life and love and laughter filled our home once again.

We knew, of course, that he may have to go back to prison. But in the fall of 2000 the U.S. Supreme Court *unanimously reversed* my father's convictions, holding that what he had been convicted of wasn't even a crime. This was the year of the Great Jubilee, a tradition going back to the Jewish roots of Catholicism when debts are forgiven and prisoners are set free! He was home for good, the government could no longer demand that he pay money he didn't owe, and we could all begin the process of healing.

Sadly, my dad was still considered a convicted felon due to the two tax fraud charges that didn't involve constitutional law and so couldn't be appealed to the U.S. Supreme Court. Though he was entitled to a new trial on those convictions, the prosecutors told my dad that if he didn't waive that right—and his right to sue them for wrongful prosecution—they would continue to pursue him relentlessly.

For the sake of peace he reluctantly signed away those rights, but the legal hearings and red tape with the Bar Association dragged on for years. This kept him from being reinstated both as a lawyer and as a deacon, the latter being dependent upon the former, and the one he cared about most.

It was a thorn that God allowed to remain. So he put his energies instead into getting his fishing captain's license, a large commercial fishing boat, and a camp down in Venice, Louisiana, where he could house and cook for his large parties of deep-sea fishing enthusiasts. His trusty black Lab was always at his side, and he was having the time of his life.

My dad and I also started working together again, only this time it was divinely ordered. We traveled to several churches and radio stations around the country—even down to the island of St. Vincent—where he shared his story and I sang. It was healing for both for us and for those to whom we ministered.

While I found this work with my dad deeply fulfilling, my heart still longed—*ached*—for motherhood. My hopes were suddenly rekindled when Mel and I were presented with the opportunity to adopt three frozen embryos from an acquaintance named Cecilia, a beautiful young mother of triplets and identical twins who had done IVF and was now dying of pancreatic cancer at the age of thirty-eight.

While the magisterial teaching on IVF was clear, I discovered there was a split among respected and orthodox moral theologians on the legitimacy of embryo adoption. After much prayer and spiritual direction, in which we were told that to do so was not only licit but also heroic, we formally adopted these three little ones with the intent of implanting them in my womb and raising them as our own children. This gave Cecilia a great deal of peace as she prepared for her imminent death, and it gave me tremendous joy to collaborate with her in this unexpected way. I planned, God willing, to name one of my future daughters after her and St. Cecilia, patron saint of musicians.

During that time, I received a letter in the mail from a prominent member of the Catholic clergy predicting that embryo adoption would be the key to reversing *Roe v. Wade*. Imagine my surprise when, after months of taking ridiculous amounts of hormones, my implantation day landed on January 22, 2003—the 30th anniversary of *Roe v. Wade!* I went into the clinic only to be told that my body wasn't ready yet. My next implantation date fell on the feast of the Annunciation, when the Blessed Virgin Mary found herself pregnant in a most unexpected way. Again, my body wasn't ready.

When the day finally arrived for implantation, all three of the embryos died in the prerequisite thaw. I was crushed and felt tricked by God. "Did I misunderstand you, Lord?" I sobbed. "Why did you let this happen?" Clearly, God's ways are not our ways. One day I will understand fully, but for now I know that I can count on the intercession of my three adopted babies and their mother. As it turned out, in 2008 the Magisterium issued a document called *Dignitas Personae* which addresses embryo adoption and offers cautions, but it offers no definitive moral judgment on the practice. If and when the Church does speak clearly on this issue, I will submit to her guidance with docility and peace.

Some months after Cecilia and the embryos died, I was praying in the adoration chapel when a woman approached and asked to speak to me outside. She wanted me to pray for her sixteen-year-old niece, who was pregnant and in a home for unwed mothers. "Does she have an adoptive family yet?" I asked tentatively. She did not, but she was interviewing them now. My heart began to pound when she introduced herself: "My name is Cecilia."

I rambled out the story about my friend and the frozen embryos, and how I wanted to name my little girl Cecilia. Her eyes widened as she said, "You won't believe it, but my niece has already named the baby Cecilia, after me." We both teared up as I thought, *This is my baby!*

Arrangements were made for my mom and me to drive up to Alabama to meet with the young mother and anxious grandmother. We spent hours with them, and I shared with the teenage mother my deep longing for a child. She shared her hopes for little Cecilia's future, and my mother reassured the grandmother that all would be well. Mom and I returned home with great anticipation.

A few weeks later I got the grandmother's phone call: Her daughter had chosen another family. My heart broke again and—though I knew God would never trick or abandon me—it certainly felt that way. I have since come to understand that our sufferings are often an atonement for the sins of others—a participation in the priesthood of Christ conferred upon us in baptism. This gives a meaning to the crosses we carry that I find deeply consoling.

After two more years—and a full twelve years after Mel and I married—God led us to adopt a beautiful baby girl from China, a precious sixteen-month-old whom we named, of course, Cecilia. After so many disappointments, God had at last granted me my heart's desire. I had become a mother—and to a child who would bring more love and joy to our family than I could have ever hoped for. It was a true match made in Heaven.

My dad delighted in her and his ever-expanding family of women: a wife, six daughters, and now *five granddaughters!* Prison had purified him of his pride and rough edges, making him the humble, gentle, interested father and husband we had always hoped for. And then on his 60th birthday—at long last—my father was finally rewarded with his first grandson. It was a true honeymoon period for all of us that lasted until 2003, when my dad was diagnosed with an aggressive form of prostate cancer and given only months to live. With God's grace he miraculously beat the odds and was still with us three years later.

On Divine Mercy Sunday in 2006 we were once again at St. Joseph Church in New Orleans, but this time my father was thin, frail, and confined to a wheelchair. Sr. Briege McKenna happened to be at that Mass, and she generously offered to pray over him. His face was radiant afterwards, but his body continued to decline rapidly.

A few months later, Dad was sent home from the hospital to die in hospice care. A therapist, who had come over to help us through the transition and had just come from the vigil Mass, said that the reading made her think of my dad. It was 2 Cor. 12:7–10, the "thorn in the flesh" reading. We were dumbfounded and could only marvel at the perfect timing of God as He reminded my father—and us—that His grace was all we really needed.

The hospice nurse expected him to die that day, but four days later he was still alive. He whispered to me, *"Kitty, why am I still here?"* We didn't know that God had one more special gift for him. Later that day my sister went into premature labor with her first child, so my mom rushed with her to the hospital. As Caroline was preparing to give birth and my mom was preparing the death certificate for my father's imminent death, the cell phone rang. A jubilant voice on the other end proclaimed, "The archbishop has just reinstated Carl as a deacon!" When I told my father, he responded with a whispered "Wow! God is good!" Yes, God had indeed restored what the locusts had eaten.

We continued to hold a prayerful vigil, singing and praying him into Heaven. He died peacefully nine days later in our living room, surrounded by his family and faithful black Labrador retriever. Carl Cleveland was just sixty-three years old.

Hundreds of people came to pay their respects at the wake, where my father was laid out in his diaconate vestments. Priests and deacons filled the sanctuary to overflowing for the Mass, during which my sister Connie read 2 Cor. 12:7–10 and the seven Cleveland women sang "Press On" at Communion. It was truly a celebration of his life and the goodness and mercy of God.

I miss Dad terribly. But in some ways I feel even closer to him now, especially when I receive the Eucharist. I know that he is accompanying me in spirit as I go about my travels and share through music and testimony what God has done for us, all in the hopes that it will encourage others in their own struggles. As to the future and what it holds for us, I can only say, "Jesus, I trust in You!"

Bio–

Singer/songwriter and inspirational speaker Kitty Cleveland has been delighting audiences around the world, having appeared on television, radio, in concert, and as a keynote speaker throughout North America and in Europe. Though she put her singing on hold after college to pursue careers as a lawyer, university instructor, and career counselor, Kitty's life as a recording artist began in earnest after launching her first CD in 2000. She has since released eleven CDs, including two popular CDs with Lighthouse Catholic Media. She has been seen many times as a guest on EWTN's *Women of Grace*, *Life on the Rock*, and *Backstage* television series, as well as singing on the EWTN broadcast of the Mass on Divine Mercy Sunday in 2013 from the National Shrine of Divine Mercy. Kitty makes her home in the New Orleans area with her musician husband and daughter, whom they adopted from China in 2005.

Sharon Lee Giganti

This is a message of hope, repentance, and triumph over tragedy. It demonstrates what I've learned about God's authentic love as I experienced the nightmare of the mental and emotional collapse of my brother, whom I love dearly. These lessons were painfully learned from tragic loss of life, but the Good News miraculously came about from this painful experience. My hope is that my message can help other families and prevent them from enduring the same heartache. As I share the lessons about God's love that I learned, I hope they can help steer you in the right direction, if you seem to be looking for love in all the wrong places.

My story begins with one heart-breaking night of my brother's life—a night that would forever change my life. The events of that evening would make headlines and be relayed in horrifying detail on the daily news for a long time. One media source reported that in the chill of that cold winter night, my brother left his girlfriend screaming in a parking lot as he sped off into the darkness with their four-month-old son. Later that same evening, he was seen coming out of the bushes with an empty baby stroller and a shovel.

The inevitable phone call came: the baby was dead, my brother was arrested for the alleged murder of his own infant son, and nothing would ever be the same again. My sister called and said, "Shar, get over to Mom and Dad's right away."

I will never forget those first moments with my parents. There's no way to describe how much it hurts to see your mom and dad in so much pain. I rushed into their arms, and we just clung to each other. Through his tears, Dad kept repeating the same four words over and over: "The worst possible thing … the worst possible thing … " All my Mom could do was sob. Her heart was broken not only for her son and her precious grandson but also for the baby's mother. Being a mother herself, she was feeling the pain doubly.

I tried desperately to rescue them from this crushing grief. "We all know how much you tried, Dad."

"He wouldn't listen," Dad said. "He just wouldn't listen."

"You prayed, Mom," I said to my mother, although at that time I didn't believe in prayer the same way she did. But I knew how much it meant to her. "We all know how much you prayed."

"My prayers weren't answered this time," she cried softly. "Not this time!"

Soon, media headlines blared: "Baby's body found in shallow grave. Four-month-old suffocated. Father held as suspect."

It appeared to be an act of revenge fueled by the loss of custody of his son. But appearances can be deceiving. Anyone aware of my brother's longstanding pain, anxiety, and addiction would know he was not in his right mind when he committed this horrible crime.

Admittedly, he seemed to be harboring horrible feelings of rage, but there was so much more to it than that. For example, it came up in court that my brother had been overheard saying, "If my baby and I can't be together, if we can't be a family with his mother, then I wish I could just give my baby back to God. Then he'd be with Jesus, and he wouldn't have to live in this horrible world." So apparently, in the loss of his mind, mingling with feelings of rage and revenge, he was also feeling a very deep and sorrowful anguish.

My brother may have been suffering for years with the serious neurological conditions of manic depression and obsessive/compulsive disorders, which were not understood at the time. So, my brother had not been diagnosed or treated. This illness invisibly aggravated the moral and spiritual disintegration that was already going on within him.

After an excruciating trial, my brother was found guilty of the murder of his infant son and was sentenced to life in prison with no possibility of parole. And our families were plunged into a nightmare that we could not seem to awaken from.

What no one heard then was the history of my brother's slow and torturous mental, emotional, and spiritual collapse. This was the tragic end result of my brother's sorrow, frustration, and rage over the hopeless wreck his life had become, after living recklessly for a very long time.

He had experienced many years of severe alcohol and drug abuse with *crystal meth*, one of the most damaging drugs, which certainly wrecked his mind, his judgment, and eventually his very soul. All those years of suffering and struggle leading up to this tragedy flashed before my eyes when I stood there, phone in hand, hearing the terrible news of what my Dad so accurately called "the worst possible thing."

I couldn't have known at the time, but I was about to receive a great gift that would miraculously come out of this tragedy. In that moment of acknowledging those years for what they truly were, I began to experience an authentic Christian conversion.

I could suddenly see that all those years of my brother's anguish—the endless cycle of depression, violence, lawlessness, and jail sentences—had been a window of opportunity. I could have reached out more to help him get the help he needed. Sadly, I have to report that aside from a few limp efforts, I simply had not. In this fallen world, results are never guaranteed, but I'm talking about making the effort, and that I did not do.

I knew in that clear moment of revelation that the New Age ideas I'd been embracing at the time had crippled my ability and my desire to help him. During those crucial years for him and my family, my New Age influence had negatively affected history. I had unwittingly played a part in the loss of two lives and in the most searing heartbreak a mother can endure. That night, two mothers lost their children—one to death and the other to a living hell. And I had played a part in it.

Some may say my New Age influence didn't play a part. I can't agree, and only God knows for sure. But *I* knew two things for certain when I got that horrible call telling me that my baby nephew was dead, and most likely I'd never see my brother again in the outside world. I knew that most of what I'd been taught in the New Age was a lie, and that everything I'd just started reading in my Bible was true.

In that moment, hearing that terrible news, I understood that we must never underestimate how much we influence one another through what we believe and what we live. If what we believe is a lie, it can be deadly. You see, during the last few years of my brother's struggle, just as he was approaching rock bottom and it became obvious that a crisis was looming, several loved ones called and asked me for help in helping him. Their concern had grown from an anxious worry to a sickening fear, and they wanted to know what to do.

During those crucial years, I constantly counseled them as to how we should respond to the destructive behavior they described. But my advice was based on the New Age spirituality and secular philosophy I was so heavily involved in back then. I wish I could have known how detrimental my New Age answers and directives were—and how utterly useless.

It went something like this: They would say, "We've got to do something! What do you think we should do?" I'd answer with the faulty premise I'd learned from these definitely un-Christian philosophies: there is no such thing as good or bad, right or wrong. There is only that which you personally find desirable and that which you don't. Also, sin and guilt are not real. They are either illusions, effects of our own mental projections, or just inventions of the human mind—ideas created by men that are used to control other men.

Through all of my brother's years of lawlessness—and not just his, but my other younger brother, as well, who was almost lost to the same downward spiral of apathy, afflictions, addiction, and law breaking—I advised those closest to them in this way: if we really loved them, we would not make either of them feel guilty, or that they were doing anything wrong. In fact, we were not to focus on their dire situation at all.

My New Age teachers claimed that we all create our own reality with our thoughts, and we attract more of whatever we focus upon. So, to face this ugly reality would only make the situation worse. I also advised these loved ones that we were never to deter my brother from the supposed wrongdoing he was committing. His free will had to be honored at all costs. In the New Age circles I traveled in, free will is elevated to such a degree that if you truly love someone you honor them best by honoring their free will—no matter how dangerous their choices might be.

I was taught that as "extensions of God," our will was *God's* will. This cleared up any issues of right or wrong in my mind, because if my brother willed to do what he was doing, then surely it was God's will too. And the addiction problems? Well, I enlightened my concerned loved ones that in "true spiritual reality," all drugs and chemicals were harmless. We didn't really live in bodies anyway—that was just an illusion.

When my sister came to me for advice about our youngest brother, he had spiraled so far out of control that he was homeless and looked like he weighed only a hundred pounds.

"We've got to reach him somehow," my sister said in anguish. "We've got to help him."

I said, "Oh, no! Don't even look in his direction if it causes your vibration to plummet."

"But Sharon," she said. "He has no shoes. Our brother has no shoes!"

"Try daydreaming how you would like it to be," I replied.

The solution I was being taught, in a thousand ways, was to deny the reality I saw right before me and simply envision them all being happy, healthy, and whole—while doing nothing.

Even before the tragedy with my brother, there had been (among other horrors too many to mention) the devastating crisis with someone I'll call Jane. This tragedy, in my opinion, was also part of the horrible aftermath that can result from New Age teaching. It marked the point in my life when the New Age "mask" began to slip. Later, my brother's tragedy would be the final blow and the main catalyst that sparked my conversion (re-version) back to Christianity.

But my experience with Jane was the first "chipping away" at my hardened heart and the New Age's façade. With Jane, I had to acknowledge—even if only for a moment—what was actually happening when I applied New Age fallacy to real people with real problems. The promised happy endings never materialized. In the end, my journey brought me crawling back to the Catholic Church on my hands and knees. So even before my brother's crisis, that journey home had already begun with Jane.

I was one of the last people Jane spoke to the night before she disappeared. Jane knew me as an "Abraham ambassador," and she knew I was into the *Course in Miracles*. She attended several of my workshops and often asked me about these spiritual teachings and the Law of Attraction. The last few times I saw her, her questions were all about end-of-life issues—especially the subject of taking one's own life. She asked me if suicide was morally wrong or hurtful. If she took her own life, would her family be devastated? Was it really a sin? Would God be displeased with her? Would she wind up in hell?

During Jane's last visit, I answered her questions about suicide, as I had already done so often, by repeating the teachings of a channeled spirit that I followed named, Abraham; suicide was only "wrong" if she *thought* it was wrong, there's no such thing as "sin" or "hell", her family would only be devastated if she *envisioned* them that way, and finally, I told her, "That which you refer to as 'God', is nothing more than the Law of Attraction and the Universe that responds to it, and you are free to attract *anything* that you desire—*even death.*" Because it was late, Jane spent the night at my house. The next morning she left my home, checked herself into a hotel, and drank poison until she died.

When I heard the news, I was not happy for Jane. I was horrified! It was God's grace that hit me momentarily with the reality that this was very wrong. She was so sad! Why had I not seen that? If the New Age "way" was right, then why wasn't I happy for her in her decision and new transition? I had the fleeting thought that maybe it's true that God really does write His laws on our hearts, as I had heard so long ago as a child.

Someone asked me later, "When Jane was asking you all those questions about taking her own life, why didn't you hug her, tell her that you loved her, and that you'd miss her if she was gone?" I didn't know how to explain that I no longer saw Jane as a person. Thanks to my New Age spirituality, I saw everything only in terms of "energy" to be manipulated, or vibrations to be "attuned."

I wish I could say that Jane's suicide woke me up completely to the dangers of New Age, but unfortunately it didn't. After that fleeting moment—when I had felt God's grace and the veil of deceit was lifted—just that quickly it came down again. I decided that I was just having trouble adjusting to my new orientation. This feeling of sorrow and regret was just that old conditioning playing on my emotions. This is what I told myself, and this is how blind we can become when we embrace diabolical belief systems. Sadly, I began to apply the same New Age principles to my own flesh and blood—my brother.

Many Christians don't know the Bible very well, so they don't have God's Word for comparison. They are especially vulnerable to New Age ideas because we Christians are all about love and wanting to relieve suffering when and where we can. To relieve our suffering—that's all I had wanted!

It had been so painful to watch my loved ones tortured and self-destructing before my eyes. You can imagine how relieved I was to hear in my New Age spirituality, "We've all lived a thousand lifetimes, and we're going to live a thousand more, so don't worry. His one wrecked life right now isn't such a heartbreak because he'll have a thousand more lifetimes to get it right. And since there's no such thing as sin or hell, no matter what he's doing right now, all of his experiences on this long journey will eventually lead him to God, and nowhere else." So, there was really nothing for me to worry about. I had been taught New Age ideas like this incessantly, especially by the channeled spirit, "Abraham".

I remember something not very funny from those days, right when the worst was happening and I was completely immersed in and spreading these false teachings. One of my little nephews was just learning how to talk. He couldn't say my name very well, so every time he tried to say, "Aunt Sharon," it came out "Aunt Dead-end." That's who I was for a whole year to my little nephews: Aunt Dead-end. Out of the mouths of babes! One of the triggers for my Christian conversion was when I suddenly realized that with my New Age ideology, all I had wound up being for my brother when he needed my help the most was just another "dead end."

I didn't know back then that our faith has taught for centuries that we're not to seek guidance from spirits that are channeled through a medium because of the danger of interacting with evil spirits (not to mention the fact that it is idolatry and leads us away from God). I know now that it's *not* true there's no evil, and that there's only good in the spiritual realm. There are real, demonic beings that too often disguise themselves as "angels of light." That's one of the reasons why consulting a medium with their "familiar spirits"—and other forms of divination—are so dangerous, just as the Bible and the Church has always warned us. But I didn't realize that at the time, so I devoutly listened to channeled spirits like "Abraham."

After my family's tragedy, I can't tell you how many New Age friends rushed in to reassure me that it was still all good. My brother had to have that experience for his growth. Oh, and the baby volunteered to participate in that experience—for his growth. "Really," I said. "And when was that agreement made?"

"Well, in one of their previous lifetimes together, of course!"

Just a few months before the crisis, I had been riding the fence between which "truth" was true—New Age spirituality or the authentic Christianity I had started reading about in the Bible. When the tragedy struck, I was pushed off the fence and came down with both feet firmly planted on the side of Christ.

One of the first things I did as a new Christian was grab my Bible and call a family meeting. Together, with love and compassion, we supported my youngest brother through rehabilitation. I told him I loved him but the things he was doing were *wrong*. Because I loved him I was no longer going to look the other way and do nothing. We let him know we were committed to supporting him in his recovery. I'll never forget the look of relief on his face. This one act of love helped to turn his life around. His final week of rehab, we spent Easter Sunday at the center with him—the perfect place to celebrate his life restored, along with the resurrection of Jesus Christ.

We have good intentions, but without guidance from the right authority, too often they're followed by a faulty approach. We need God's approach; no one else's will work. To learn how to love authentically, I needed to seek the highest instruction through the Word of God in holy Scripture, through the only Son of God, Jesus Christ—our model for love through the Holy Spirit—the power of love, and through His holy, apostolic Church, which He founded for our continued guidance. I thank God now for the teaching Magisterium of our Catholic Church. My story demonstrates that our love must be guided by God's righteousness and truth, or we can wind up hurting ourselves and the ones we care about the most.

I had been baptized and had Christian faith formation growing up. I believe this is partly what rescued me from spiritual darkness. I am forever grateful to my parents for having me and my siblings baptized in the Catholic faith, and for all of the sacrifices they made to send us to Catholic school. Thanks to my loving parents, I was blessed to receive a Catholic education from first to eighth grade.

Unfortunately, by the time of my brother's crisis—in my late thirties—I had long since wandered far from the sacraments and the Catholic faith I'd been taught in my youth. I wound up trading Christian truth for the New Age lie. I am convinced, however, that my baptismal seal and all the grace from the sacraments I received growing up had planted the life-giving (and life-restoring) seeds in my heart and soul, which I think helped me to finally recognize "a great light shining in the darkness."

I found my way back to Jesus and the Bible right in the middle of my New Age mentality. I believe that my much-needed turnaround came about through an actual intervention of Jesus Christ Himself, and the Holy Spirit's assistance in helping me to see clearly—by the light of holy Scripture—the real consequences of sin, the fallacy of New Age ideas, and the true teachings of the Bible, all playing out right before my eyes, amid the tragic events surrounding me.

Two things began to happen simultaneously. Before my conversion, I read Scripture through the lens of New Age Ideology. As I began to doubt and reject some of the lies I had been fed, I began to see Scripture through the eyes of its authors—the Holy Spirit and the apostles. The more I read, the more confused I became, and the more I doubted various false teachings I had previously embraced. At the same time, I had reached a point in my New Age "spiritual" development where they say you can make contact with your own spirit guide, by going into a deep state of "meditation" (which I realize now was equivalent to putting myself into a light trance) and then requesting the spirit appear to you. I didn't realize this was dangerous at the time!

Holy Scripture and the Church warn us not to deliberately seek this kind of altered state of consciousness, and we're especially not to seek to make contact with spirits in the metaphysical realm, except to ask the angels and saints to pray and intercede for us. There is a real possibility that we can open a door to the influence of evil spirits. But I didn't know that back then, and I had not read Leviticus or Deuteronomy yet. So, I went into this deep meditative state and "invited" a spirit guide to approach me.

Given all that I had been studying, I was so excited to find out who my spirit guide might be. I was thinking maybe a beautiful goddess or a fascinating alien. Just to cover all the bases, I asked for the highest wisdom, the highest truth, and the very essence of love. I wanted only the best.

Well, in this trance state, in my mind's eye I saw a figure walking toward me dressed all in white. When He came closer, I recognized it was Jesus. Of all people! My eyes shot open. I know this sounds bad, but please remember that I didn't believe in Jesus at the time, except as a concept or energy. I remember thinking, *Oh, great. Is that all my imagination could come up with? Who's next, the Easter bunny?*

Again, I warn people *not* to practice this occult exercise to "find a spirit guide." I truly believe the only reason Jesus showed up for me—right in the middle of my performing this forbidden and sinful act—is because it was an intervention. I believe Jesus appeared to turn me back to Him and away from all of my occult and New Age seeking—to save me from the demonic darkness I was dabbling in.

So, there He was. I started off by scoffing, but the truth is, by this point I was tired. I was exhausted by all that I had tried and all that had failed me in the New Age. I had seen so much darkness and pain and terribly wrecked lives. I was depressed. I was close to breaking down. I said to myself, "I've tried everything else, and He's already here. If He has something that can help me, then I'm going to give this Jesus a chance."

I closed my eyes again, and Jesus reached out His arms to me and held me in this wonderful embrace. He said that He loved me. Then He said the most amazing thing. He said, "You're doing just fine." Even to my New Age mind, I knew He didn't mean that "everything is just fine," but in His arms I could finally face the truth: I had committed grave wrongs. I understood immediately that He simply meant that now that He was here, I was going to be okay.

I couldn't believe it. I said, "Oh, right! After all the mistakes and bad choices I've made." I sobbed, "I'm just stupid ... stupid ... *stupid!*"

He said, "No, honey, no matter what's coming out of your mouth— and yes, I've seen all the wrong turns you've taken—but I know your heart. I know what you've been seeking after this whole time. What did you say you wanted just now? 'The highest wisdom, the highest truth, the very essence of love,' and I Am Who showed up. I Am the One you've been looking for. I Am the answer that you have been wanting. I have what you need, and I'm going to be right here for you."

I had never felt such love before in my life. This Jesus was so much more than the "energy" or "vibration" they told me He was; much more than a mind-set or "Christ consciousness." If you think that's all Jesus is, you're missing a lot, because a vibration is not going to die on a cross for you and cannot love you the way I felt this Jesus loving me.

Jesus is not just some spirit guide or angel. He is the only Son of God—fully human and fully divine. How can I be sure that my encounter was really with Jesus and not some evil spirit guide posing as Jesus? For one thing, during this interaction, I felt it very strongly impressed upon me, that I should *stop* the occult activity I was involved in. An evil spirit would not have led me away from New Age. During this experience, I went from mockery to an acknowledgment of my own poverty, misery, and need for

God, to faith—openness to God's grace and wanting it—to experiencing God's love, and finally to a complete change of life.

I knew that on some level what happened was very real. From that moment on I was hungry for anything I could find out about this awesome "spirit guide" I had. I wanted to know everything I could about Jesus, my Lord and Savior. I couldn't put the Bible down. Once I rejected the New Age teaching about Scripture, I was open to the truth, and the Holy Spirit gave me understanding. I continued to read about all that He said and did, and when that fateful phone call came—the last piece fell into place.

It was undeniable to me how true Christ's teachings are. I had seen with my own eyes both ways being lived: the lies and the truth. I knew that Jesus was the only way. Now I knew that the gospel of Jesus is where we go to truly learn how to love—not to the latest secular trend of thought, not to New Age channeled spirits, and not to any private humanistic interpretation of what "God" is, or what "truth" or "love" is.

Some of the saddest times for me during this ordeal were when I visited my brother in prison and he'd talk about coming home. He talked about how happy we all would be when he came home. But my brother can't come home. He's serving a life sentence with no possibility of parole. Yet in his mind, he thinks there's hope that he can, if he can somehow just convince someone that he had such good intentions.

We need something more than human good intentions. It took tragedy, heartbreak, and death to wake me up to this fact. God's Word has always taught that true love entails giving, service, and self-sacrifice—putting someone else's needs ahead of our own. But that's not what I was taught in New Age. New Age not only teaches relativism and narcissism, but also pleasure seeking—hedonism. I think it was probably *that* lie that crippled my ability to love the most.

Believing that pursuing my own delight was my number one priority, I wasted years sleepwalking through my brother's endless cycle of depression, addiction, and emotional anguish. I shielded myself from the pain of it, from the mess of it, and from the maddening inconvenience of it. I didn't want to be anywhere near that suffering, and I certainly wasn't going to sacrifice.

I had been taught that to love my brother required that I look the other way—and to do right in his situation meant that I had to remove myself from it. But the moment it was too late to do anything, I wished with all my heart that I had been right there in the middle of it, helping him and going through it with him. With that thought, I got in touch with a love much higher than what was passing for love in the New Age and in the world. I got in touch with the love Who is God.

Did you know the original root meaning of the word "suffering" is simply "to undergo" or "to go through"? Jesus never taught us to escape from this world. He wanted to equip us to go through it together and with Him. He prayed to the Father, "I do not ask that you take them out of the world but that you keep them from the evil one" (John 17:15). The human tendency is to pull away from pain and suffering. But the Bible tells us that we're called to take up our cross and follow Jesus, and that we are to help widows and orphans in their affliction.

True love carries burdens. It can withstand the presence of pain and suffering. It must because that's when love is needed most, not when everything is pleasant and rosy, but when things get downright ugly. Love can bear sadness. It doesn't banish you outside for fear that you'll track mud all over its precious happiness.

My New Age teachers taught me that my life was my creation, and the purpose of my life was to fill it with as many personal pleasures and delights as I could conjure and create. I'd done just that, and then I had guarded that creation viciously. I'd done it in the name of love because my New Age teachers said that the best way to love others was to make your own self happy, make "feeling good" the only goal in any situation, and love your own life more than anything.

But that's not what Jesus taught. True love is willing to be uncomfortable for someone else. Jesus says, "No one has greater love than this, to lay down one's life for one's friends" (John. 15:13). Jesus gave His life for us because contrary to what the world would have us believe, we do need a Savior. We need to be redeemed.

I realized three things with blinding clarity the moment I heard the news that the baby was dead at the hands of my brother. First of all, I realized how desperately he had needed hands-on—drop-whatever-you're-doing, nothing-is-more-important-or-more-valuable-to-me-than-his—loving intervention. He needed to experience the love of Jesus through me. He needed someone to "lay down their life" in an effort to save his. The second thing I realized was just how much I had *not* been willing to do that. And the third thing I realized was "why." It was terribly simple: I had grown to prize feeling good above anything or anyone else. It was these realizations that brought me to a total repentance and completed my conversion, or re-conversion. That repentance now affects every choice I make.

I'm haunted to this day by a story my parents told me. I didn't know it at the time, but my parents told the police. You see, from the time my brother took the baby, three days passed before the police caught up with him. Around the second night, he suddenly appeared on their doorstep. He had come home one last time to say good-bye. He was sobbing.

They pleaded with him, "Just bring the baby back, son!"

And he said, "I can't. I can't bring him back."

"Why?" my mom cried. "Why don't you just bring him back?"

In total despair, my brother said these chilling words: "No, you don't understand. I … can't … bring … him … back."

In that horrifying moment, my parents were afraid they knew what he meant. Before they could restrain him, he was gone. In the end, their worst fears were realized.

Our choices affect our lives and the lives of others forever. I said earlier that my brother speaks with the hope of coming home. In those moments, my heart breaks for him. He's in a miserable, dark, and frightening place, and he's so lonely. He just wants to come home. But, he can't—not ever.

Knowing this, the only thing that gets me through a day, or even an hour, is the good news of Jesus Christ. If my brother confesses and repents, which I believe he has done the best he can, then in a short time (it may not seem short to us, but in the grand scheme of things it is very short) he will be home—truly home with God, forever. We have that hope in Jesus Christ through confession and repentance and God's forgiveness. My brother has that hope, and so do we.

But what about all of my other brothers and sisters—all of God's children with whom I share this planet? They are my brothers and sisters too. If there's one thing this experience has shown me, it's broadened my idea of family. What if one of them lives their whole life without knowing the one, true God? They can't ever get home because they don't know the way! What my brother has to go through for his remaining fifty or so years is hard enough to endure here in this physical world, but I'm talking about life in the world to come, which lasts for eternity! What if you wind up in a place that's miserable, dark, and frightening, and you're so lonely, and you just want to come home, but you can't … *forever!*

I've already lost one brother; do you think I'm going to let that happen to another? Not on my watch! Jesus asked, "Could you not keep watch for one hour?" (Mark 14:37) Well, this is my watch. My whole life is my watch. That is the miracle that came out of this tragedy, that my life has this beautiful, new mission now, to "keep watch with Jesus"; to warn others of demonic deception; to share and safeguard our saving faith; to bring as many as I can to the true love of the real Jesus; and thereby help all of my brothers and sisters find their way home.

While I cannot go back in time, I don't let the fact that I can't do it all stop me from doing my share. Well, this is my share. This is my hour. When I spend it sharing God's Word through my testimony and leading others to Christ, it is my finest hour. And, dear reader, if during our brief time together I have unlocked a prison gate that would let any one of you come home to God, then it has been time very well spent.

Bio -

Sharon Lee Giganti, a former runner-up to Miss California USA, left Hollywood at the height of her success (guest-starring in over twenty television shows and several films) to pursue a "Higher Purpose." Raised in a Catholic family, Sharon Lee wound up exchanging the truth of Jesus Christ for the deceptive lie of the New Age ideologies. After tragedy struck her family in 2000, Sharon's search for the truth began to lead her back to the Catholic Church. Her conversion was not complete until she experienced an "intervention" by Jesus Christ. Her desire to know as much as she could about Jesus led her to the Bible. The Holy Spirit gave her understanding and enabled her to recognize in Scripture the truth. Now a national speaker and a professed member of The Holy Family Institute, Sharon Lee has spoken at many Magnificat chapters throughout the U.S. She has also been a regular guest on *Catholic Answers Live Radio*, heard world-wide via EWTN, since 2008.

Marilyn Heap

I am delighted, honored, and truly blessed to share how God has been faithful to me. I want to shout, "Sing joyfully to the Lord, all you lands; serve the Lord with gladness; come before him with joyful song ... Enter his gates with thanksgiving, his courts with praise; Give thanks to him, bless his name, for he is good; the Lord, whose kindness endures forever and his faithfulness, to all generations" (Ps.100).

There are numerous places in sacred Scripture where it states that God is faithful—forever faithful. This underlying message of God's faithfulness has a strong impact upon me. It is as if He says, "I am faithful, even when you are not aware of My faithfulness, even when you are angry with Me or unfaithful to Me. My faithfulness and mercy are for real. *They are never exhausted.*"

The more I take time to ponder my life's journey, the more I see His Hand in my life. I love to recount my story! Each time I do I am more and more convinced of His faithfulness, and for that I'm eternally thankful.

I have no dramatic conversion to relate. My story is simply about a cradle Catholic who never had a problem believing in God, trusting His Word or His actions, or desiring to please Him. I am an only child born in New Orleans, Louisiana, and have lived in that area most of my life. God gave me two parents who loved me, were upright, God-fearing, practicing Catholics who helped shape and strengthen my character with traditional moral values. They set high standards for me and had high expectations of me.

My mother was a Sicilian, not overtly affectionate, and she expected much from me. I now realize her determined way caused me to constantly stretch higher and—as a result—ultimately helped push me in the right direction. She had a great devotion to Our Lady of Perpetual Help and started her day praying the rosary. I believe I have been the beneficiary of this devotion. My daddy was a Scotch-Irish, English, Georgia native, who was a convert to the Catholic faith. He was not talkative, but he was a good provider with a kind and gentle spirit that let my mother "run the show."

Although as an only child I could be lonely at times, I have beautiful recollections of growing up close to an extended family—the family of my mother's two brothers and four sisters. Two of my cousins, who are about my age, have been close like sisters. I only knew one grandparent, my mother's father. Perhaps one of the most significant recollections I have of him is being seated in his rocking chair during WWII, listening to the radio and praying his rosary. I believe he always prayed for his grandchildren, and the many rosaries he must have said for us brought me to Jesus through Mary.

My parents lived their lives around mine. They saw to it that I received sixteen years of Catholic education. I was given clarinet lessons and spent nine years involved in school bands, and they sent me to dancing school. This developed a desire in me to make a career of being a dancing teacher, which in turn led to my teaching dancing in high school and college.

Both the elementary and high school I attended had us start the day with daily Mass. I not only received a premium parochial education, but most of all I learned to value my Catholic faith. This foundation helped me center my religion as an important part of my life. Being a receptive child and one who liked to please, it came easy for me to love and appreciate anything religious and to participate in religious functions.

I believed in God at a very young age and sought to live God's Word, "But seek first the kingdom [of God] and his righteousness, and all these things will be given you besides" (Mt. 6:33). I thank God for my Catholic education, which constantly reinforced the truth of this Scripture passage.

One particular way in which this came about became a pivotal point in my life. I was a cheerleader during high school until at one point the band began playing at athletic games. I could no longer be a cheerleader, but was required to play with the band instead. Cheerleading is *very* important to a teenage girl today, and I felt the same way back then. I was distraught and on the brink of rebellion, when a wonderful priest-moderator of the cheerleaders convinced me to assume the position of a "non-participating captain" of the cheerleading team, creating routines for them.

He asked, "Isn't it better to be a creator rather than a creature?" His question opened up the understanding that surrendering to something difficult and not to my liking—in direct obedience to a higher authority—brought forth a new dimension, one that had greater value than whatever I was giving up. I believe this was the beginning of my tendency to look for meaning in undesirable situations in life by flipping the coin to see the other side.

The desire to serve the Lord and to live what I believed never left me. As I grew into young adulthood, God granted me my heart's desire—to someday marry a man who loved the Lord and His Church as I did. My husband, Raymond, came into my life in my junior year of college at

Loyola University in New Orleans. I had my eyes on him to ask him to be my date for a "backwards" dance, but his athletic involvement on campus appeared to allow no time for such activities. In addition, he, his father, and his two brothers commuted sixty-five miles each weekday to and from New Orleans for work and college, and they always spent weekends at home.

One day shortly after school began in September, a good friend of mine remarked that she noticed Ray Heap watching me "more than a new mother watches her first baby." I shared with her my desire to date him but felt it was hopeless because he lived out of town.

In response to my desperation, she introduced me to a fifty-four-day rosary novena, suggesting that I say it for this "date" to happen, if it was God's will. A novena is a prayer said nine consecutive days. This novena was six novenas in one, which included twenty-seven days of prayer in petition, followed by twenty-seven days in thanksgiving, whether or not the request was granted.

On the twenty-seventh day of petition, on their commuter drive to New Orleans, the Heaps met with an automobile accident that totaled their only car but caused only minor injuries. The good news was that the three brothers had to stay with friends in New Orleans until arrangements could be made for them to board at Loyola. That very night, the twenty-seventh day of petition, Raymond called me for the first time, and I seized the opportunity to ask him to the "backwards" dance.

He accepted without hesitation. We knew on our second date that we wanted to be married. During our courtship, we began the practice of saying the rosary novena together. In 1956, almost two years after our first date, we began our married life, ending a fifty-four-day rosary novena on the night of our wedding. We continued to pray rosary novenas together well into our marriage.

The rosary was our prayer lifeline in those early years of our marriage. I am reminded of a particular outcome that I believe was due to the Blessed Mother's intercession for us. As an ROTC commissioned officer, Raymond was required to serve two years in the army when he finished Loyola. Upon completion of his basic training at Fort Benning, Georgia, he decided to attend paratrooper school. However, he was late in registering and not accepted. As it turned out, all those who had been accepted went to Korea, as the war was winding down. We were blessed to stay at Fort Benning for the remainder of his time in the army.

Ray, Jr. was born in Georgia fourteen months after our wedding. Contraception was not part of our thought process or vocabulary. We would never in any way impede God's desire to gift us with children, but it was not His will that I should ever conceive again. How I struggled with this! Being mindful of lonely moments as an only child, my greatest desire was to have a large family … like ten children. Raymond was one of ten, and my beloved in-laws have fifty-six grandchildren.

The Heap women always seemed to get pregnant in three's. I always cringed when his family members looked at me, expecting me to be one of the "three." Every month when I discovered I wasn't pregnant, I cried out to the Lord in pain and distress.

Then one day the promise of Scripture came alive for me: "They cried to the Lord in their distress; from their straits he rescued them. He changed the desert into pools of water, waterless land into water springs. He blessed them and they became very many" (Ps. 107:28, 35, 38). God is faithful, and in His great mercy He answered my prayer and lifted me out of my misery in a marvelous way.

When we registered our son for kindergarten at our parish school, the principal, a commanding and persuasive nun, discovered I had a college degree. It made no difference to her that the degree was in Business Administration and not Elementary Education. She insisted it was my responsibility as a parishioner to join her staff as a teacher. God was revealing His plan to me, but I resisted for a time, being blind to what He was trying to do for me.

In the end, Ray, Jr. went to kindergarten and I became a teacher at the fifth-grade level. I was mother hen to forty-five children and loved every minute of it except, of course, grading papers. Seven years later, I was asked to become the assistant principal at the school of our newly created parish, which had become our church parish when our existing parish was divided. The Father in His great generosity gave me 1,000 children to tend! He had turned the *desert into pools of water, blessed me, and gave me many.*

It was the early 1970's. Various changes in the Church, brought on by some of the misinterpretations of Vatican II, were creating chaos within my inner being. Like storm winds that shook me to the core, they troubled me deeply. As assistant principal, I also taught three seventh-grade religion classes. Religious education workshops I attended—and the new textbooks being published to conform to what was then perceived as Vatican II directives—caused upheaval for me in many ways. I noticed that:

1) Catholic devotions seemed to be considered taboo, thus ignoring the need for intercession from saints in Heaven and on Earth.

2) The oneness of mind about the tenets of our faith that had united us and given us such strength and security was being eroded away.

3) Obedience to God's laws was becoming subject to our feelings and convenience. For example, it was commonplace to hear high school students being taught, "If you don't feel like going to church on Sunday, it does no good to go."

4) Faith and trust in God wavered, being discouraged and challenged with questions like, "Do you really think God is up there paying attention to the requests of everyone?"

5) Devotions to our Mother Mary, especially the rosary, were considered immature and meaningless.

6) Satan ... well ... he did not exist.

I hesitated to express my true sentiments, fearful of being an out-of-date obstructionist bucking God's will. I could find no one with whom I could share my deep faith and trust in God, not even my husband. I felt like an alien in a strange land, where a violent storm was raging. Unfortunately, Raymond and I no longer regularly prayed the rosary together—or alone, for that matter. Although we never stopped attending Sunday Mass, life was too hectic for me to give any thought or time to prayer.

But God was faithful! In His great compassion and mercy, He saw me and the confusion eating away deep within my heart. To paraphrase Ps. 107:28–29, *He rescued me from my straits, hushed the storm within and without seeking to swallow me up, sent a gentle breeze, and the billows of the sea were stilled.*

Through providential circumstances involving our parish, Raymond began attending the large Catholic charismatic prayer meeting that had begun in our area. He begged me each week to come with him, but I resisted the Father's plan. Finally, during Lent, I agreed to go as a Lenten penance.

Hesitant at first, I came along, gradually sensing that this place was a safe haven, where I could find the faith expressed to my heart's satisfaction. I attended a Life in the Spirit seminar and my baptism as an infant was revitalized, refreshed by the Baptism in the Holy Spirit. Ever so gradually, I began to learn how to tap into the power that flows from God's living water, His Holy Spirit. I began learning how to turn the spigot of that fountain to allow His waters to flow into all areas of my life.

As a result of my becoming involved in the Charismatic Renewal, I found brothers and sisters who spoke freely of Jesus and how He is alive and active, healing and setting captives free from outer and inner, deep-seated bondages. Their stories built up my faith and strengthened my trust in God.

Through my involvement, I became equipped with the tools I needed to grow in this new life in the Spirit. Daily prayer was given top priority in my life, bringing inner healing and releasing me from inner bondages. Scripture came alive and began speaking to me—feeding, convicting, strengthening, consoling, and comforting me. Fellowship with a community of worshipers who were free to express their devotion to God publicly became an essential part of life for Raymond and me. The rosary resurfaced and became part of our regular routine during our forty-minute drive every week to our weekend house. To fast forward a bit, in 1989 we started gathering our large, extended Heap family together to pray the rosary once a month. That practice is still going after twenty-five years.

Through our involvement in the Charismatic Renewal, Raymond was attuned to hear God's call to become a permanent deacon and was ordained in 1976. Thirty-eight years later, he continues to serve as a chaplain at a local community hospital and as a deacon in our parish church.

About six months before Raymond's ordination, I felt the Lord calling me away from teaching. God seemed to be saying, "Raymond must increase, and you must decrease." I took this to heart. As assistant principal in our parish school, I was well known in church circles, while Raymond was not.

At the time, our son, Ray, was in his freshman year at Southeastern Louisiana University in Hammond, Louisiana. Mark, a twelve-year-old foster child who stayed with us for three years, was still with us. Suddenly, my heart's deepest desire was to be a better wife and mother. I decided to quit teaching, not knowing how I would handle so much time and space in my life.

It took about a year before I began to feel restless and unproductive, like I was wasting my time. On the other hand, I sensed that God had me in a holding pattern, waiting on Him. One day when I cried out to the Lord about all this confusion, I sensed Him saying, "Marilyn, you and your whole house will be My witnesses to the ends of the earth." With that word, I knew the Father had His plan, and I must simply wait upon Him to act. The loving Father was preparing me for what was to come.

Before returning to college in January 1978 for his junior year, Ray announced that he and his girlfriend, whom we admired a lot, had mutually agreed to split up until they were sure they were meant for one another. I knew how hard this was for him.

Then one day out of the blue, I had this conversation with the Lord. *Lord, have You allowed this breakup because you want Ray for your priesthood? Will there never be anyone else for him, and he will be a late vocation? But, Lord! What about grandchildren? If Ray becomes a priest, I'll have none. You can't do that to me, Lord!*

The Lord responded, "Marilyn, someone needs to give their son for a priest. Would you deny Me that?" Of course I wouldn't, Lord!

That ended the conversation.

At spring break in March of that same year, Ray almost lost his life on an Arkansas river during a flash flood, while he and some friends were camping. His first words to me upon returning home from this near-fatal camping trip were: "Ma, God saved my life!" At that point in Ray's life (I was told later), he began attending Mass daily. God had convinced him—and me—that indeed His eyes and hands were upon Ray.

One month later, my husband, Raymond, went on his annual retreat. Ray decided to come home to keep me company that weekend, knowing that Mark, our foster child, would be visiting his dad, and I would be lonely.

Ray was in the habit of challenging me by picking my brain about controversial questions, particularly about morals and religion. Later on, I would often overhear him sharing my ideas as his own with his friends. He was very troubled that weekend about the state of affairs among his peers. He shared at length with me, but he never revealed their specific problems.

He summarized his feelings of utter desperation saying, "God better do something or send someone to straighten out this mess. A strong leader is needed because no one listens!"

I responded by saying that God had already sent Someone—a "suffering Servant," His Son, Jesus. I suggested that what was needed was for those of us who call ourselves Christian to listen to the Word of God, where He says, " … if my people, upon whom my name has been pronounced, humble themselves and pray, and seek my presence and turn from their evil ways, I will hear from heaven and pardon their sins and revive their land" (2 Chronicles 7:14).

I explained that if we do what God tells us in this passage, God will do what He says. He will hear us from heaven, pardon our sins, and heal our land. I wrote down this passage for Ray on an index card, numbering it as a seven-point plan, and sent it with him back to college that night so he would remember what to do. Weeks later, this card was found being used as a marker in the book he had been reading titled *I Am Third*, meaning God is first, others second, and self is third.

The next day, Monday, the Lord placed on my heart another passage from Scripture, which lingered with me all that day: "Glorify the Lord, Jerusalem; praise your God, O Zion. For he has strengthened the bars of your gates; he has blessed your children within you. He has granted peace in your borders; with the best of wheat he fills you" (Ps. 147:12–14). This passage became a source of much consolation for me in the weeks and years ahead.

The following day, God showed me that He desired my faith in Him to be based on conviction—conviction about His faithfulness to me—and not based on emotions, which can run the gamut from high to low at different times.

At college, Ray boarded in what was then the Catholic dorm at Southeastern. This dorm was adjacent to the Catholic Church and the student center that housed the rectory on the third floor. It was customary for the boys to meet in the rectory with the priest every Monday night for the game of the night. At that time, baseball was also a Monday night attraction as the game of the week.

On occasion, one of the boys would slip away to the balcony of the rectory, jump into a tree that reached up from the courtyard below, slide down the tree, then ring the bell to the rectory. "Surprise!" he'd yell to the one who had hurried down the three flights of stairs to open the door. It is believed this is what Ray did that Monday night when he was found unconscious at the base of the tree.

It was 3 a.m. when we received the call that Ray had an accident, had serious head injuries, and was being transferred to a hospital in New Orleans. My first instinct was to cry out, *"My Lord and my God! What is it that you want of me?"*

My mind flashed with thoughts of how this accident would change my life. It could mean tending a brain-injured child perhaps in a vegetative state; or it could be proclaiming God's miraculous power through a dramatic healing; or it could be walking in faith in the face of death. My mind swept from one end of the spectrum to the other.

The response to my question came instantly. "This is a test of your faith, not meant to end in death but to bring glory to God!" (Later, I recalled that Jesus had used a phrase similar to this when speaking of his friend Lazarus's death in Jn. 11:4.) I immediately felt a perfect sense of peace—the peace that is beyond all understanding—descend upon me, although my stomach was still tied in knots. I knew without a shadow of a doubt that whichever way this injury went—be it paralysis of body or mind, a sovereign healing, or physical death—God's hand was upon Ray, and no *eternal* harm would come to him.

As we made our way to the hospital in New Orleans, my spirit was compelled to sing songs of praise as the three men did in the fiery-furnace story from the third chapter of the book of Daniel. I knew this story well because I had made it a practice to read it to all my seventh-grade classes.

The story tells how three faithful Jews, who refused to submit to practices against their faith, were thrown into a white-hot furnace, where they never ceased praising God. They came out of the fire unharmed and did not even smell of smoke. Their words to God, saying, "all your deeds are faultless, all your ways right and all your judgments proper" (Dn. 3:27) and their canticle in which they recited how all God's creations "bless the Lord, praise, and exalt Him above all forever" (Dn. 3:58) flooded my mind and sent my confidence in God as high as the sky.

As I praised Him, I became utterly convinced of God's love for me and knew with certainty that He would never permit any circumstance to happen in my life that would be harmful or destructive. As I exercised my deep convictions about God's love for me, the Spirit of God took control and total reign over my emotions. He directed my mind into a safe and secure place, just like a boat being steered into a safe harbor at the height of a storm.

When I stood at Ray's bedside, my mind was being guided to see the hidden, unseen dimensions present … the other side of the coin. I sensed that Ray was very tired. Our conversation two nights prior had impressed me that he was working hard to convince his peers of God's way. I didn't know exactly what he was referring to at the time, but later I learned that one did not bring up abortion, homosexual behavior, or premarital sex if they did not want Ray to teach and preach into the wee hours of the morning.

I sensed birth occurring, not death. I felt like I was holding Ray's hand as he was being born. There were others on the other side of the veil extending their hands toward him. My mind was beseeching all our deceased relatives and all the patron saints of all our family members to pray for him and to pray for us. I perceived that these were the people present there, taking him by the hand.

All grace comes from God, but those who are in heaven can bring our prayer and petition to the Lord, and I believe they did. Ray was being born anew, and my sick stomach, with all its piercing pain, revealed that once again I was experiencing labor pains, the labor pains of his *eternal* birth.

I believe God gave us a glimpse of Ray's spirit—very much alive—while he lay in an unconscious state with his flesh on the brink of death. At one point, I whispered in his ear, "Praise the Lord, son." Immediately, his breathing through the tracheotomy breathed out a rhythm duplicating my words.

I said, "Son, thank the Lord," and again the cadence of these words came with his breathing. Fr. Hal Cohen, a Jesuit who began the Catholic Charismatic Renewal in New Orleans, and who was the first spiritual advisor of the mother chapter of Magnificat, was with us at Ray's bedside that early morning. Confirming my experience, Fr. Cohen shared with me that in spite of Ray's condition, there was response from him, and this seemed most unusual.

I sensed Ray laying down a challenge for me, saying, "Ma, this is an opportunity for you to put your money where your mouth is." In other words, now was the time to pray and have faith like never before.

Immediately afterwards, a doctor who had been standing in the room beckoned us to come into the hall. "There will be no heroic acts around here," he said. "This boy is neurologically dead."

My mouth was silenced at his statement, but my mind shouted, *Mister, his brain may be dead, but there's something here that is quite alive!*

Sometime later, I stood in the hall outside the room where Ray lay, and a lady came from a housekeeping closet and asked, "Who is that in there?"

"It's my son," I said. "He is dying, but I must praise the Lord."

With that, the woman grabbed my hand and we began praying together. We began to pray in tongues and praise God. Moments later, they called me to come into Ray's room. He was breathing his last. God had sent an angel to pray with me immediately before the end. Through this prayer, my spirit was joined with Ray's spirit as he was ushered into eternity.

Death came at 8:30 that late April morning, but I knew Ray's spirit had walked home with Jesus to the Father. On a normal day, I would have been at my parish church for 8:30 Mass. I sensed my own Mass had begun. My body was shocked and numbed, but my thoughts were of Mother Mary, who lost her only Child.

Who am I that I cannot lose mine?

Standing at the wake, greeting those who had come to express their sympathy, was to me more like a wedding receiving line. I recall Raymond saying over and over again, "Everyone wants the best for their child. God has given us the best." As we prepared the liturgy for his funeral Mass, I sensed that I would be attending Ray's wedding. For me, his funeral was a marriage of his spirit to the Spirit of God, and my heart experienced joy instead of sorrow.

Oh, how I thank God for my baptism, for being raised to know God as Father, Son, and Holy Spirit; to believe that Jesus was raised from the dead, and that my body will be immortal one day, like His resurrected body; that He is my Savior, the Truth who lights the way for me.

I praise and thank God that I know Mother Mary as my mother, interceding for me, and for brothers and sisters everywhere, whose prayers for me absorbed much of my pain. God's peace and joy flooded my heart as I exercised a steadfast faith in Him, so much so that there were some who expressed deep concern that I was in denial and headed for a breakdown. But God was granting me the privilege of tasting the "sweet wood of the cross."

Adjusting to being childless has been painful. I have wept often, and I still experience moments of deep hurt from the void. However, in the days, months, weeks, and years that followed, God consoled my grieving heart with many signs to confirm my faith that Ray is alive and well. I remember several instances of how He did this right from the outset.

The night of Ray's death, as I tried to sleep, I kept hearing over and over again, "Your lamb of God." I felt this was referring to Ray. The next morning at Mass, a dear friend told me that as she was praying the rosary for me, God had given her a word for me as she was saying the fourth joyful mystery—the presentation of Jesus. He told her, "She has presented me the choicest of lambs." In His mercy, God confirmed for me what I had been hearing all night long.

The morning after the funeral when I went to pray, I opened the Bible at random. My eyes fell on John 14, Jesus' last discourse, where He said to the apostles, "Do not let your hearts be troubled. Have faith in God and faith in me. In My Father's house there are many dwelling places … I am indeed going to prepare a place for you" (Jn. 14:1–3).

As I read those words, my thoughts turned immediately to Mary Magdalene at the tomb of Jesus. She thought she was talking to the gardener, but it was Jesus! I began shouting inside myself "He is risen! He is risen!" as I became convinced that God was allowing Ray to speak these words to me through John's gospel. I realized at that moment that this experience was similar to Mary Magdalene's, when the man she thought to be the gardener turned out to be the One for whom she was grieving.

For several days after Ray's death, another dear friend had visions of him as she prayed each morning. The morning of his wake, she saw Ray in a green suit, walking toward a bright light. She was shocked at the wake to see him in a dark-green suit.

The next day at prayer she saw him still in the green suit, getting closer to the bright light, with her grandmother facing him, standing in the light. Finally, on the third day, she saw him beaming, wearing cut-offs, standing in the light with her grandmother. Both were facing outward with the light at their backs. All this occurred before there was any publicity about reported instances of life-after-death experiences.

A couple weeks after Ray's death, a niece called me, all excited. Her faith was really being tested over Ray's death, and she began desiring a sign from the Lord. She could hardly contain her excitement as she related how God had confirmed for her that Ray was alive and well. She'd opened the Bible at random that morning and began to read Acts 20:7–12. It is the story about a lad who had fallen from a third-story window. To the great comfort of the people, he was taken away alive. Praise God that my niece recognized that God was comforting her and she had courage enough to share her experience with me so it might comfort me, as well.

Although I could relate many more similar stories, the last one I will share concerns my conversation with the Lord about Ray being a late-priestly vocation. The August following his death, on the feast of St. John Vianney, the patron saint of the priesthood, I was at daily Mass. As the homily was being preached, I began to hear the Lord speaking to me in my spirit. "Marilyn, your son is a priest."

I questioned, "O Lord, what is a priest? What does he do?" Then I answered my own question. "O Lord, I know. A priest brings you to people, and people to you."

He responded, "That's right. And your son is a greater priest than had he been one in the flesh."

God can break any barrier and scale any wall. This conversation consoled my heart and convinced me that Ray had a function in his eternal home. Through intercession, he is to bring people to God, and God to people.

Sometime later, a dear friend's mother, Dottie, whose birthday happens to fall on the feast of St. John Vianney, shared with me that while at Mass at St. Joseph's Abbey in Covington, LA, seminarians were gathered around the altar, and she saw Ray among them. She said emphatically, "I've never seen Ray, but I know it was Ray. He was there among the seminarians." She was absolutely convinced of this fact and was totally flabbergasted when I shared the priest-story of my conversation with the Lord on the feast of St. John Vianney.

God constantly sends confirmation and consolation, even after thirty-six years. There is a sequel to the "Dottie" story that adds further to God's mighty ways and faithfulness. Several years ago, when Dottie went home to the Father, I was praying the breviary on the morning of her funeral. As I was praying and thinking about her, my son's picture holy card fell out of my breviary. How it was in the breviary is a mystery, since it is always in my Bible. I sensed that Ray, with a whimsical smile on his face, was present with Dottie and wanted me to know that he finally had met her: the lady who confirmed for me what it is that he is busy doing now.

Rarely does a holiday or a meaningful occasion occur without us attending some special celebration, or we receive a special "surprise package" of some sort, like flowers, a letter, a call, a meaningful word or boiled crabs (which I love). I consider these things reminders of our son's love for us, and I like to call them gifts from him.

I am confirmed in this belief by the "Prayer over the Gifts" in the Mass of All Saints Day, the Roman Missal, November 1973. It says, "May we always be aware of their concern to help and save us." I believe that God allows Ray to have a hand in sending gifts that speak of his aliveness to us. Through all of this I have learned that I must be open to receive gifts from my son in an indirect way, like when one person sends flowers to another by the hand of a third party, not by the one who sent them.

About three years after Ray's death, in 1981, God raised up Magnificat through a group of women involved in the Charismatic Renewal in the New Orleans area. A year or so later, I was asked to join the mother chapter service team. Six years later, we formed the central service team, the national board of Magnificat, and I served as treasurer of this body for thirty years. It has been, and still is, exciting and rewarding to meet and relate with sisters in chapters that have formed in numerous states in the United States and all over the world. In a way, serving these chapters on the central service team gave me many spiritual children. God's plans are far superior to mine. He has continually blessed me with many children.

It also happened, three years after Ray's death, that we were asked to take in a Vietnamese girl, who was a boat refugee. I resisted at first. It was a struggle to give up Ray's room, but God won out. His plans, as usual, proved to be for my good. She came to live with us for three years; addressed us as Mother and Father from the very beginning; met and married a super Catholic boy; moved to California; and became the mother of two girls, our precious grandchildren. During their early years, the little girls spent from four to six weeks with us for seven summers. I recall my conversation with the Lord about grandchildren. "For nothing is impossible with God" (Lk. 1:37).

When Raymond and I reached our sixties, we began having a few health problems. Raymond has had heart bypass surgery twice, prostate surgery due to a microscopic-size cancer, and has lost his sight in one eye.

I have had two breast surgeries for cancer, including a mastectomy, radiation, and chemotherapy, and later, a thyroidectomy. Periodically, God seems to allow little interludes to occur in our lives. Through all these adverse circumstances, I have learned to trust Him more and have come to know without a doubt, that as I surrender myself to His will and His graces to carry out His will, the crosses that befall me only make me more aware of His Presence and strengthen my understanding of how much He loves and cares for me. I know too that it is through the prayer support we have from many communities of brothers and sisters that Jesus seems to march us through our trials quickly and with ease.

I am no one special, singled-out for special treatment, nor have I done anything to deserve all the concern, consolation, and comfort that the Lord has poured out on me. What I do know for certain is that I am one of the Father's beloved daughters. The kind of love I have experienced from the Father is for each of us—His beloved children.

Our Father's greatest desire is for us to see His hand in our lives as He allows only what is best for us, according to *His* plans, designed by His magnificent, eternal wisdom. He tells us "Fear is useless. What is needed is trust" (Mk. 5:36).

May God grant us the desire to surrender more and more to His plans for our lives and help us put aside whatever prevents us from surrendering to Him so we can receive the joy this will bring.

Let us pray:

"Father God, I give my life to you. Take possession of me. I am Yours. I want whatever You want for me. That is what I choose. Send forth Your Holy Spirit upon me. I want to trust You with all my heart; to rely not on my own intelligence; to be mindful of You in all my ways; and to know with confidence that You will make straight my paths. (Prov. 3:5–6) Help me surrender to You in all things and to trust You as Jesus, Your Son, trusted You. Amen."

We have asked, and we will receive because God is faithful in all His words and loving in all His deeds! He is an awesome God, forever faithful and worthy of all praise!

Bio–

Marilyn Heap has been multitasking for Magnificat from the beginning! She scrambled eggs for the historic first breakfast in New Orleans on October 7, 1981. By 1987, the Metairie Mother Chapter service team had become the Central Service Team for the expanding ministry. Her business degree from Loyola University of the South suited her perfectly to assume the office of Treasurer. A former teacher and assistant principal, she found her duties escalating and added International Conference Chairperson to the growing list. A daily communicant and an extraordinary minister of Holy Communion, she has long been devoted to the Liturgy of the Hours and assists her husband, Deacon Raymond Heap, in his chaplain's duties at a nearby hospital. Her life has not been without the cross. However, she and Raymond heroically faced the tragic death of their only child, Ray, Jr. Marilyn embodies the characteristics expressed in Sirach 6:14–15— a sturdy shelter, a treasure beyond price.

Elizabeth Kim

I t is with great joy, gratitude, and humility that I attempt to glorify the Father by sharing with you how loving our Father is. I owe my Abba an immense debt of gratitude. I want to sing the song of my salvation and to give our Father and our Lady a hymn of praise for Magnificat, in the words of our Lady: "My soul proclaims the greatness of the Lord; my spirit rejoices in God my savior. For he has looked upon his handmaid's lowliness; behold, from now on all ages will call me blessed. The Mighty One has done great things for me [and you] and holy is his name" (Luke 1:46–49).

As I reflect upon my conversion, I cannot help but recall the words of St. Paul:

"God chose the foolish of the world to shame the wise, and God chose the weak of the world to shame the strong, and God chose the lowly and despised of the world, those who count for nothing, to reduce to nothing those who are something, so that no human being might boast before God" (1 Cor. 1:27–29). Verse 31 says, "Whoever boasts, should boast in the Lord." I am here to boast of my Abba Father, my Daddy, my super Father, and how good He is.

I was born into the Kim family, which includes my parents, Angela and Paul, and two brothers, Peter and Alex. I am the middle child and the only girl. Among Koreans, the Kim name is like the American name "Smith."

The country of Korea is located in Asia and lies between China and Japan. The Korean Catholic Church was founded in the eighteenth century by brilliant, esteemed scholars. They studied to discover the truth and concluded that the supreme truth is found in Catholicism.

Catholicism soon began to spread. However, the Korean government saw this as a dangerous threat to the social order and the corporate structure of their society. The Korean people used to worship ancestor spirits, but Catholicism taught that there is only one God. The government tried to suppress and persecute the Catholic Church for over a hundred years. This resulted in more than 10,000 laity being martyred, as well as ten clergy. They were not just killed. They were tortured.

When St. Pope John Paul II visited Korea in 1984, he canonized 103 saints. I am sure the spirit of those Korean martyrs is here with us today. Presently, about ten percent of the population in Korea—over one million people—are Catholics. The good news is that the vocations to the priesthood and religious life in the country continue to grow. Praise God!

Both of my parents are converts. When I was little, I went to church every morning, and I also loved Sunday school. I was naïve and happy about all of those things. But when I entered adolescence, I began to have a lot of confusion about my faith. I developed a self-identity crisis, as well as a faith crisis. With a child's faith, I knew God was present and that He loved me. However, I had not experienced the love of God in my personal life.

After reading many different books and being exposed to other philosophies of faith, I began to doubt the existence of God. Also, when I was very young, I became sick. As the result of a high fever, I was left with a disability in my right leg. I was not really self-conscious as a child, but as I grew up, I noticed people treating me differently and making comments here and there. The accumulation of these experiences began to influence me more as I entered puberty.

These two dynamics played a role in not knowing who I was and not having a sense of really being loved by God. Having doubts about His existence continued to make me feel depressed and despised, even to the point of being suicidal. I knew my parents dearly loved me, and overall I thought I had good self-esteem. However, Korean society is a homogeneous society—they have rigid norms. To be accepted, you have to fit into the norm. If you are too tall or too short or too this or too that, you are an outcast.

Because of my physical differences, I felt rejected, despised, and isolated. I cried every night, thinking how I could complete my suicide plan. The world appeared very cruel to me, and I began to hate myself. Not only did I doubt the existence of God, but I also thought that if He was really there, He wouldn't treat me this way. He wouldn't allow this difficult, unreasonable suffering.

I had so much hurt and shame—shame about who I was. I struggled a lot. Psychologists would say my shame was not just a sense of embarrassment. Toxic shame is different from guilt. Toxic shame says something is wrong with you at a deep, profound level, the level of your state of being. Guilt is an advanced emotion, where we say, "I *did* something wrong." Shame is the feeling that "*I am* something wrong."

Around 1976, my mother, Angela, attended a New Life in the Spirit seminar. It is an eight-week course that teaches people to deepen their faith. People learn more about the Holy Trinity and the work of the Holy Spirit.

After my mother completed the course, she looked really different and very happy. She prayed more and listened to more praise music.

Mother said there was going to be another New Life in the Spirit seminar and asked my two brothers and me to go. The three of us were the only children there. The rest were adults. Before I went, I prayed. I thought this might be some kind of new hope for me. I prayed, "Lord, if You are really living and alive, please show this to me through this seminar. If You are, I will dedicate myself to You and follow You. But if I can't find You there, I am going to renounce my faith and end my life."

When I attended the seminar, I didn't understand everything they were talking about, but they gave us an assignment: daily prayer with the Scriptures and read their booklets. I did my assignments faithfully and wrote a letter to the Father each day: "Dear Father, this is what I am feeling today. I am kind of downhearted but Your Word says, "Come and I will fulfill your thirst." This is what was happening at home after attending the retreat.

The fifth week was on the Baptism in the Holy Spirit, and they asked us to gather together to receive that prayer. I asked for all the Charismatic gifts from 1 Corinthians 12, except for the gift of tongues and the interpretation of tongues. I was afraid of praying in tongues. At the time, I didn't understand how precious this gift was to my spiritual growth. Unlike other people, I did not experience a huge healing or a sense of warmth; no warm, fuzzy feelings. There was nothing like that, but little by little after the seminar, I became convinced that God exists, and that He is worthy to be studied and learned about further.

After the seminar, I never missed the Friday weekly prayer meeting. May 17, 18, and 19 of 1978 were very special to me. On the 17th I finished a fifty-four-day rosary novena to Our Lady. The first twenty-seven days I offered up petitions. The second twenty-seven days I offered thanksgiving in advance. I attribute my miraculous healing to our Lady's intercession for her little daughter. Mary is our Mother, our model of faith, intercessor, protector, and advocate. I believe that our Lady is the Mediatrix of all graces. St. Louis Marie de Montfort said, "The quickest way to be a saint is to be like Mary."

A prayer from St. Pope John Paul II to our Lady says it well: "Totus Tuus, Totally yours, Immaculate Conception, Mary, my Mother. Live in me. Act in me. Speak in me and through me. Think your thoughts in my mind. Love through my heart. Give me your own dispositions and feelings. Teach, lead me and guide me to Jesus. Correct, enlighten, and expand my thoughts and behavior. Possess my soul. Take over my entire personality and life. Replace it with yourself. Incline me to constant adoration. Pray in me and through me. Let me live in you and keep me in this union always."

The next day, May 18th, my mother attended a healing service for the leaders of the Charismatic Renewal, and she asked me to join her. I didn't know what it was about, but out of obedience to her I showed up. When I walked into the auditorium, they were praying for the healing of memories. Dr. Francis MacNutt and his team from the United States conducted this service. I sat there as a teenage girl, receiving the prayer.

That prayer was so powerful! He led us from the moment of conception through different stages of life: childhood, elementary school years, and junior high school. At some point during the prayer, I was overwhelmed for the first time in my life—overwhelmed with the presence of God and the love of God. I had never felt that God loved me that much.

When he read Jeremiah 1:5 from the Scriptures, "Before I formed you in the womb I knew you, before you were born I dedicated you." the living Word of God began to minister to me. I sobbed. I couldn't control my tears. The Word goes on, "I have loved you with an everlasting love."

My heart was so wounded and broken before because I didn't know God loved me that much. Before this experience, I knew intellectually that God is love; but it was just intellectual information. The knowledge never traveled from my mind to my heart. It was during this healing prayer that I experienced the tremendous love of God for the first time.

Psalm 139:13–14 states: "You formed my inmost being; you knit me in my mother's womb. I praise you, so wonderfully you made me." On that day as I was coming home in the car, and that night when I took a shower, I was just sobbing. The Holy Spirit was healing me from past wounds I was not even aware I had hidden deep within me. I had felt trapped like a little bird by a hunter's snare. The lies and false beliefs had trapped me. The world said I was "this" and I was "that," but the Holy Spirit wiped out all the lies by His power of love. Where the Holy Spirit is there is freedom. When the Son of God frees you, you are truly free.

For the first time in my life I really felt free. That healing prayer did more for me in one moment than five years of psychotherapy. Praise God!

The next day, May 19th, another healing service took place in a huge auditorium. Over 50,000 people from all over the country attended. Some people sat in wheelchairs, others lay on mats or had canes. Some were lame or blind. So many physically challenged people came.

While we were praising God and singing "I've Got Peace Like a River," I really felt that peace. I was so happy. I felt like jumping all over. Somehow, the Holy Spirit led me to open the Scriptures. Matthew 7:7 jumped out at me: "Ask and it will be given to you; seek and you will find; knock and the door will be opened to you."

With the Word of God, I prayed, "God, I know you are here. I know you can hear all of these people, but this is my very first time asking you to heal my leg." Somehow, the prayer came to me, and the Lord graced me with expectant faith. I really expected something to happen.

After the teaching and everything else that was part of the service, Dr. Francis MacNutt sent out the prayer ministers among the people. All of the sick were receiving prayer. I stood at the back because others needed prayer more than I did. I didn't want to move forward, but somehow my mother brought a precious priest, Fr. Xavier Bongdo Choi, over to me. He was the president of a Korean Charismatic Renewal at the time.

My mother, my brother Alex, and two other friends were there. The priest let me sit on the chair and asked about my condition, so I shared. Fr. Xavier Bongdo Choi then said, "Elizabeth, your condition is so chronic that it is going to take a long time for your healing, but I will try." I sat still while he placed his two hands on my leg, especially my right leg. I closed my eyes.

After a few minutes, Fr. Xavier Bongdo Choi woke me. He said, "Elizabeth, Elizabeth, open your eyes."

Before I opened my eyes, I thought, *How come Fr. Choi only prayed for me such a short time?* I thought he was going to pray with me for hours and hours until I felt something. I opened my eyes and immediately jumped out of the chair. I saw that my legs were even! I walked back and forth, jumping around.

Later, Fr. Xavier Bongdo Choi told me, "When I placed my hands upon you, I saw my hands moving forward, three times, like this." He demonstrated. "Then I thought, 'I have to stop now.'"

That's when he shook me.

My prayer experience was just like the story in the Acts of the Apostles. When Peter and John went to the Beautiful Gate, a beggar lay there begging for money. Peter said, "I don't have silver or gold, but in the name of Jesus Christ I ask that you rise and walk!" The beggar rose, walked, jumped, and was praising God. I was like the beggar, and this priest had asked me to get up and walk. The priest also asked me how I felt. I normally had a lot of pain when I walked, but now I had no pain. I was walking lightly and freely.

I saw my doctor a few days later. Earlier, he had recommended surgery. I was getting taller, but my leg was getting weaker. After he examined me, he said my leg had grown about two inches and he did not know what had happened to me. It could not be explained medically. Praise God!

Before Father asked me to open my eyes, my mother saw Jesus come to me in a white robe and kneel down before me. He put His finger on my ankle and pulled. Jesus indeed was pulling on my leg!

Father Xavier Bongdo Choi was persecuted and misunderstood by so many people during the beginning of the Charismatic Renewal. He continued to be anointed by the Lord with the gift of healing, both physical and inner healing. Even at the age of eighty he continued to teach about this gift of healing and "prayers of hope" to seminarians, religious, priests, and all Catholic people in Korea.

My brother Alex, who happened to be there, witnessed God's extraordinary miracle for his sister. He experienced it with me. He wept and rejoiced with me. Later, after we came to the United States, he received a calling to the priesthood and is now a priest in the Diocese of Orange, California.

Looking back, the physical healing in itself is not that important. The most important thing is that my heart was converted. My heart was healed and connected with the Father, the Son, and the Holy Spirit. That was the awesome blessing. I also asked the Lord in prayer, "Why did You give me this incredible miracle?"

The Lord said, "Elizabeth, the miracle I gave you is not for you to keep. I gave it to you for the Body of Christ. I gave it for people to believe that I am well and alive, now and forever."

Many people have incredible crosses and sufferings to bear. There is consolation in knowing that suffering—if united with Jesus' suffering—becomes a gift. It can be a source of blessing, a source of conversion, and a source of purification. Even if we suffer for a while now, we must always have hope. The fire of hope will melt all the struggles, sufferings, pain, and confusion.

Our family immigrated to the U.S. in August 1978. When I came to the U.S., I immediately wanted to find a prayer group. Eventually, I had the privilege of attending SCRC (Southern California Renewal Communities), as well as serving on the board of directors. I witnessed many committed and faithful priests, religious, and lay people serving at SCRC. I prayed, "Lord, let me be committed like they are, whether I am healthy or sick. I want to live my life for You like these people, your faithful servants."

God blesses all of us with faithfulness whether we recognize it or not.

I would like to share some thoughts about the day of Pentecost. In Acts 2:1–4, 120 disciples gathered together with Mother Mary in the upper room. They were praying as Jesus instructed before He ascended into Heaven. Suddenly, the rush of a mighty wind was heard, tongues of fire came upon them all, and they began to speak in different languages.

Before this experience, the disciples were afraid of persecution from the Jews, but they received empowerment from the Holy Spirit and went out to proclaim the good news. On the same day, Peter, who had denied Jesus three times, stood up and boldly proclaimed who Jesus was: "Jesus, Whom you crucified, is alive! He has risen!" When he preached this, many people were converted.

Like Peter, we all need power from on high. Our human effort is not enough. We need to cooperate with the Holy Spirit. We need the power of the Holy Spirit.

Many popes have written about a new Pentecost. St. Pope John XXIII prayed, "Renew your wonders in this our day as by a new Pentecost." Pope Paul VI said, "The very greatest question we are supposed to ask is, 'What is our greatest need in our Churches today?' The Church needs an eternal Pentecost."

Not just as in Chapter 2 of the Acts of the Apostles, not just on the day of Pentecost, but Pentecost is supposed to be eternal. Pentecost is for every single day in the hearts of believers. St. Pope John Paul II said, "The Church needs a new Pentecost." With this in mind, we ought to be convinced of how important it is for our prayer life to receive the fullness of the Holy Spirit.

Consider the prophet Ezekiel (Ezek. 47:1–12). Ezekiel entered the waters. At first it was ankle deep, then knee deep, then waist deep. Later, the water was so deep he had to swim. Likewise, as Catholics we all have unique backgrounds and different spiritual places. Some new believers experience the Holy Spirit at ankle deep, some of us feel the Holy Spirit to the waist, and some of us experience the fullness of the Spirit so much that we can only swim.

As the Psalmist says, some of us are "like a tree planted near running waters," and we receive our life-giving spirit. We have life-sustaining power through the Holy Spirit by being deeply rooted in God. The tree we become will bear abundant fruit, the fruit of the Holy Spirit. The fruit of the Holy Spirit is love, joy, peace, patience, kindness, generosity, faithfulness, gentleness, and self-control (Gal. 5:22–23). Our leaves will be medicine for others.

I believe God is calling holy women through the beautiful ministry of Magnificat to be trees, not withered but tall and strong, bearing all kinds of beautiful fruit so that they will be able to share this fruit with others. This is "evangelization."

People may look at you and wonder why—in the midst of the turmoil of this world—you have such joy and peace. They wonder how you can be faithful even when you are sick or are suffering through trials such as financial troubles or unemployment; or when you have problems in your marriages or in your families. How is it possible that you have such joy and peace? Because you are like that tree rooted in the living water.

One day when I was praying, the Lord said, "Elizabeth, look into My heart."

I said, "Okay, I can look at Your heart." As soon as I looked into His heart, I saw a river flowing out of His heart, and the river was flowing to my heart.

"I want you to be a river through which My love will flow out, My good news, My life—to my children," He said.

We are all called to that. All of us have the obligation and responsibility as baptized, beautiful Catholics, with the help of Our Lady, to open up to receive the fullness of the Spirit and to share the overflowing, life-giving Spirit with others.

What about praying in tongues? Worldwide, over 120 million Catholics are baptized in the Holy Spirit. The Catholic Charismatic Renewal started in America in 1967. However, many Catholics are not adequately taught about the gift of praying in tongues. Praying in tongues is nothing more than the Holy Spirit praying in you.

Father Robert Faricy said, "Praying in tongues is a vocalized, non-conceptual, contemplative prayer." Vocalized means we have to make sounds using our tongue, lips, and voice box. Non-conceptual means there is no particular meaning. You don't even know what you are saying. It is a contemplative prayer because it directly focuses on God. This prayer never offends God. This prayer is always according to the will of God because the Holy Spirit is praying through us.

Praying in tongues is an opening to all the other gifts of the Holy Spirit, such as healing, miracles, prophecy, and discernment. I have used the gift of tongues ever since I received it. I have never stopped using the gift of tongues. I pray in tongues every day. I pray in tongues when I am driving, and especially when I am praying for other people, discerning the will of God, or when I don't know how to pray for my situation or the situation of others. This is an incredible gift. I want all of you to receive it from the Lord.

As time went on, I began to learn about St. Therese's "Little Way of Spiritual Childhood," from Fr. David Carvalho, a Benedictine monk priest from Oceanside. From his teaching I came to understand that we always stand before God as a child, as His child. That is what the Little Flower taught us. Children are free, joyful, trusting, weak, dependent, and vulnerable. Before Jesus we are like little children; like beggars, blind, deaf, and helpless. There is nothing we can do without His grace. Fr. Carvalho taught total dependence upon God.

Father used to say, "Don't be mistaken, Elizabeth. Everything you receive from God is not yours."

I asked, "Then, Father, what is mine?"

He said, "Yours is your weaknesses and your sinfulness. The rest belongs to God."

Because I received so much healing through the love of God, I decided to study and pursue psychology. I went to USC for graduate study. I didn't know it, but the enemy was trying to get me out of the program. I met the criteria for admission and all the other requirements.

But the first day during my interview with the dean of the department, he asked, "Elizabeth, why do you want to study counseling psychology?"

"I want to help people through counseling."

"Foreign-born students usually don't do well in our department because of the cultural differences," he said. Counseling is usually defined as a middle-class, white, verbally orientated activity. So, he discouraged me from entering the program.

I was so discouraged. When I went home and opened up Scripture, the Lord was right. He encouraged me with Psalm 27: "The Lord is my light and my salvation; whom do I fear? The Lord is my life's refuge, of whom am I afraid?" So I knew the Lord wanted me to be there.

I started the program and obtained the degree. My Ph.D. is not merely a scholarly degree. For me, Ph.D. stands for prophet, healer, and deliverer. That's who I aspire to be—a prophet not because I know what is going to happen, but because I am sharing the Word of God with my brothers and sisters; a healer because I am praying for other people's healing in mind, body, and spirit through the love of God; and a deliverer because with Jesus I am praying for freedom from bondage. Some people are bound in affliction by the enemy. The power of darkness is rampant.

The Church is the mystical Body of Christ, but the world is being seduced by Satan. We need to be aware of the existence of Satan. We need to be aware of what is going on with our young people—the occultism and New Age practices and beliefs even in our Catholic Church. We need to deliver people in the name of Jesus with the power and authority given to us.

In the year 2000, I had an opportunity to go to the famous Medjugorje. I received a lot of graces at Medjugorje. Mother Mary taught me to pray not only for myself but for the world, for the needs of all people, for our Catholic family, and even for non-believers.

Every day, I place certain people I am praying for, including myself and my family, at the foot of the cross and ask the blood and water from the side of Christ to wash away our sinfulness and protect us from the enemy. Mother Mary quickly comes and wraps her mantle around us. Then I ask for the grace of the evangelical counsels of spiritual poverty, chastity, and obedience; for St. Paul's zeal for the salvation of souls; for docility to the promptings of the Holy Spirit; and for the charismatic gifts and fruits of the Holy Spirit, as well as the armor of God.

Chapter 6 of St. Paul's letter to the Ephesians says, "Draw your strength from the Lord and from his mighty power." The battle belongs to God, not to us. We are not fighting against human power but we are fighting against evil in Jesus' Name. Jesus' Name has power to save and power to overcome evil.

I sensed that God said with a smile, "You ask me a lot," with my daily intentions. I said, "Okay, Abba, but I know you can handle that."

I pray that our past, present, future, time, talent, treasure, body, mind, and spirit glorify and honor God. I offer all these things for the salvation of souls and holy souls in Purgatory.

Those familiar with the Prayer of St. Gertrude know that whenever the prayer is prayed, 1,000 souls are released from Purgatory. It says, "Eternal Father, I offer you the most precious blood of your Divine Son, Jesus, in union with the Masses said today, for all the holy souls in Purgatory, for sinners everywhere, for sinners in the universal church, those in my home and within my family. Amen."

We are all covered! Then I pray for salvation, purification, sanctification, healing, and deliverance; for the Baptism in the Holy Spirit and protection and grace over our clergy, religious, seminarians, all lay leaders, and Magnificat chapters. I pray that the same grace would come to my family, relatives, and family tree; to all my spiritual family and their relatives and family trees. I don't know where I would be without my spiritual family and my Magnificat family. I also pray that the same grace would come to my patients of the past, present, and future, and their families and relatives, and their family trees. I pray that the same grace would also come to pro-life, marriages, family, and children. This is the daily offering Our Lady taught me.

Some years ago, I went to a huge conference. Someone prophesied, "As I have touched you, touch my people." When I heard that word, I knew it was spoken for me. I try to touch the lives of God's people any way I can. The Lord gave me Isaiah 61:1–2, the mission to the afflicted: "The Spirit of the Lord God is upon me, because the Lord has anointed me; He has sent me to bring good tidings to the lowly, to heal the broken hearted, To proclaim liberty to captives and release to prisoners, To announce a year of favor from the Lord."

What is the difference between psychology and inner healing? Psychology is a science that studies the human mind and behavior. Inner healing is using the principles of psychology with the inspiration of the Holy Spirit to heal our inner self, starting from the moment of conception in the womb.

We all need to be healed in our family tree. Our ancestors had certain traits going down generations after generations. The negative traits and behavior patterns need to be healed. We receive lots of love, grace, and blessings from our ancestors—thanks be to God—but we also receive negative traits like certain physical problems or certain dysfunctional patterns. For these reasons, we need to offer our prayer for the healing of our family tree.

While in the womb, some of us were blessed and well protected. But some of us were not. The little infant in the womb has not developed cognitive function to understand, to reason why he or she feels the way they do. There is a close connection between mother and infant in whatever the mother went through. For instance, if the mother had a huge trauma while she was pregnant, the child can be impacted by it.

There are so many teenagers who have an addiction to porn. When they develop this addiction, especially to internet porn, the brain chemistry becomes changed. It is a difficult addiction to break. I know this issue is partly a chemical issue of the human brain, but it can also be a spiritual one. Whether we are praying for someone with marriage and family problems or homosexuality, we pray that God would restore their wholeness using the holy sacrament of Eucharist and Reconciliation, Mass, spiritual direction, counseling, and Scripture, etc.

What about the spirit of suicide? If you know anyone, or perhaps yourself, who has ever thought about suicide, please renounce the spirit of suicide three times in order to honor the Holy Trinity. Even after I was converted and received a lot of healing, I realized I had suicidal thoughts out of nowhere. I learned that I needed to renounce the spirit of suicide. When I did, I no longer experienced those reoccurring thoughts.

We all need healing. Nobody is exempt. We are born into an imperfect world with imperfect parents. We love our children, but inevitability we make mistakes and hurt our children and ourselves. We need to build a strong self-identity as a child of God. So, who am I? The Trinitarian union is the key. For myself, I can tell you I am a beautiful, precious child of God. So are you. Never forget that! This is the relationship we have with the Father, our Abba.

To Jesus, both men and women are the Bride of Christ. We have a spousal relationship with Christ. The Lord calls me in prayer, "Hey,

Darling." So I call Him Darling too. He calls me, "My Lovely Lily." After He called me Lovely Lily, I went to the church. They had lilies everywhere, so God was confirming it. As for the Holy Spirit, you and I are partners and instruments. To me, the Holy Spirit is my soul mate. I am loved; I am lovable; I am loving.

We need to be loved by God first, in the depth of our being, then we are able to be transformed. With His love, no matter what you are going through—if people reject you, abandon you, misunderstand you, persecute you—you know in your heart who you are: loved by the Holy Trinity. You are very loveable. Since you are lovable, you can act more lovingly.

Say it to yourself right now: "I am loved, lovable, and loving." The Lord wants to restore our inner child as well as our femininity as women and masculinity for men.

To sum up: Once I was confused and didn't know His love, to the point of being suicidal. But He brought me from the power of darkness and the power of the enemy, who was trying to destroy me, into His marvelous light. Thanks be to God. He delivered me from despair to hope, from sadness to joy, from bondage to His freedom, and from all kinds of negativity to His positive affirmation and His truth.

The grace I boast about is this: when I was little and the Father took me to the foot of the cross of Calvary and laid me there to participate in Christ's redemptive suffering in my little suffering, He gave me grace to be an intercessor. This is why I boast of my Abba Father. How privileged I am.

Finally, consider Romans 8:31–33, 35 and 37–39. Nothing will take us away from God, Who is our life's goal. Jesus is our life's meaning and goal. He is everything for us:

"If God is for us, who can be against us? He who did not spare his own Son but handed him over for us all, how will he not also give us everything else along with him? Who will bring a charge against God's chosen ones? What will separate us from the love of Christ? Will anguish, or distress, or persecution, or famine, or nakedness, or peril, or the sword? No, in all these things, we conquer overwhelmingly through him who loved us. For I am convinced that neither death, nor life, nor angels, nor principalities, nor present things, nor future things, nor powers, nor height, nor depth, nor any other creature will be able to separate us from the love of God in Christ Jesus, our Lord."

Alleluia! Amen! May God bless you!

Bio–

As a director of the Brain Fitness Center in LA and Orange County, Dr. Elizabeth Kim's multi-ethnic, dynamic practice is the perfect setting for her vast experience in the healing arts, which she places under the Lordship of Jesus, the Healer. This distinguished USC graduate is a licensed psychologist, marriage and family therapist, and board-certified Neurofeedback practitioner whose practice integrates the Catholic faith with psychology in the treatment of children, adolescents, and adults with childhood trauma, abuse, depression, anxiety, ADHD, marriage, and family issues. The Divine Physician has truly helped countless numbers of people through this humble servant. She received a miraculous healing at the Korean National Charismatic Healing Service in 1978 and immigrated to the US with her family the same year. She has served the Church in various positions including Youth and Healing ministry, speaker at international conferences, and on the Board of Directors for Southern California Renewal Communities.

Kathy MacInnis

T hanksgiving is the theme of my life as I strive to give thanks to God for everything. In 1 Thessalonians 5:18, St. Paul says, "In all circumstances give thanks, for this is the will of God for you in Christ Jesus." He also writes, "We know that all things work for good for those who love God" (Rom. 8:28).

Growing older has its advantages. As I look back on my life I can clearly see that with every cross I carried and with every suffering I had to endure, God supplied all the graces I needed to get through. He has given me blessings and spiritual growth, as well, in the midst of these trials.

Not all of my life has been filled with crosses or trials. But like everyone else, I have crosses to endure as best I can. Through it all, I echo the words of our Blessed Mother in her Magnificat: "The Lord has done great things for me and holy is His name."

I have come to see the Lord working in my life. It has been a process, but I can now truly thank God in all circumstances. Some years ago this was not the case. I would not have thanked God for my life circumstances. Back then my prayer would have sounded more like "*my* will be done" rather than "*Thy* will be done."

I have to admit that at one time the idea of giving thanks in *all* circumstances was a foreign concept. This wasn't because of my upbringing. I was born into a devout Catholic family and had a good Catholic education. In elementary school the nuns inspired us with stories of the saints and the martyrs. I wanted to be a saint. More particularly, I wanted to be a martyr. "Kill me! I won't give up my faith in Jesus Christ!" The stories were so beautiful and inspiring that I wanted to follow in their footsteps.

I grew up in New Orleans, a very Catholic town. I was confident I would marry a Catholic. I rarely dated a non-Catholic. But when Ron MacInnis, a non-Catholic, came to town from Boston to attend Tulane University and we had our first date ... wow! I forgot all about my vow. We soon realized ours was a very special relationship and that one day we would marry. We had to wait three and a half years, however. Ron's father was paying for his college education. If Ron married before he graduated, his college funds would be cut off.

This was an incentive to wait.

Ron and I went to Pre-Cana, marriage-preparation classes, and the priest explained to my husband-to-be the implications of marrying a Catholic. He explained that birth control wasn't permitted; however, natural family planning was. In addition, we were to baptize and raise our children to be Catholic. I had already indoctrinated Ron beforehand, because I didn't want to marry anyone who wouldn't agree to do these things.

Ron must have thought the priest was trying to convert him. "I don't ever plan to become a Catholic," he said.

"What would make you think we would want you to?" the priest replied.

That put Ron at ease. He had a great sense of humor and so did the priest.

We were married three days after Ron's graduation from Tulane University, and within the first five years of our marriage we had two sons. Life was hectic, and I was planning for life after my kids were in school. I wanted to join a tennis league and go to lunch with my friends. My plans were not lofty, holy, or spiritual.

But God had a different plan. The same day both of my sons were in school was the day my father-in-law came to live with us. Ron's father had a debilitating stroke, and the doctor said he probably wouldn't live very long. We were advised to begin making funeral arrangements for him. We didn't do that, but when my father-in-law was scheduled to be released from the rehab hospital, the doctor prevailed upon us to take him into our home rather than put him into a nursing home. He said Ron's dad would be better off being cared for in our home for the short time he had to live, and we agreed. He was still mentally sharp and relatively young, just seventy.

He had a hospital bed, a wheelchair, and a leg brace—he was paralyzed on the left side. Professional therapists came to our home, and nurses and nurses' aides helped until the Medicare payments ran out. After that, we were on our own, and I cared for him. For the next fourteen years my father-in-law and I were constant companions. My lofty plans of joining a tennis league and going out to lunch with my friends didn't materialize. I sometimes wonder where I would be now if my "lofty goals" had materialized.

During the time we cared for my father-in-law we were very blessed. One of the blessings was attending a Marriage Encounter weekend. We didn't go happily at first but went "kicking and screaming." We were a mixed marriage (I was Catholic, and Ron practiced no religion), and I didn't want to subject my husband to something spiritual and Catholic. However, our friends wouldn't take no for an answer. We agreed to attend for their sakes.

The weekend was *very* difficult for Ron and me. It showed how different we were in the ways we thought about things. Afterwards, upon arriving home, we discussed the events of the weekend for over two hours. In the midst of sharing, Ron began talking about what a positive experience it was. He was amazed and touched that the three team couples, who came from New Jersey to New Orleans, would actually give up a whole weekend just for us. I was shocked to hear Ron say, "This is the most positive weekend I have ever spent. Whatever they have, that's what I want."

They had Jesus in their marriages. What we thought was going to be a terrible weekend turned out to be a life-changing weekend. Two weeks later Ron decided he wanted to become a Catholic. Two months after that he was brought into the Church. He received a conditional Baptism, was confirmed, and received his First Communion.

The Marriage Encounter weekend changed our lives as a married couple. This proves that you never know what the Lord has in store. Even uncomfortable situations may turn out to be extraordinary sources of grace. In all these things, I learned to give thanks and to trust the Lord.

For the next ten years Ron and I worked together in Marriage Encounter programs: Evenings for Engaged, Evenings for Couples, and Evenings for Families. We volunteered in our parish; we helped with Marriage Encounter community nights; and we met a lot of great people. It was a very exciting time. But after about ten years of being involved in Marriage Encounter, my spirit was starving. I needed something more spiritual—something deeper—but I didn't know what it was or where I could find it.

Thanksgiving Day in our home includes about a thousand football games (slight exaggeration here), and the guys watch them all. I am the only female in the house (even the cat is a male), so I have no control over the TV. One particular Thanksgiving weekend I was fed up with football. I told all the men in the family, "I'm leaving. I'm going to the mall." I don't think they cared or noticed.

Once there, I had no idea what I would do at the mall. I don't particularly like to shop, but I had no other place to go that day. I walked into a secular bookstore and browsed the shelves, finally ending up at the section labeled "Inspirational." I bought a book that seemed to jump off the shelf, titled *Inner Healing*. That book really ministered to me. It helped me better understand the working of the Holy Spirit in my life, and I wanted more. The longing for a deeper relationship with the Holy Spirit was what I wanted, without putting a name to it.

I learned about a charismatic prayer group in our parish church, but the Marriage Encounter people warned me not to go there. Half-jokingly, they said, "You don't want to have anything to do with those people. They're very strange." They called them "Holy Rollers." But the people I knew who were in that group were the pillars of faith in the church community, so I reasoned they couldn't be all that bad.

I went to the prayer group, and they welcomed me with open arms. I loved the prayer group. It ministered to me and was just what I was looking for in my life—more of the Lord and more of the Holy Spirit. They encouraged me to attend a Life in the Spirit seminar and to be baptized in the Holy Spirit. I had never heard anything about this before, but since I felt they were credible people, I decided to proceed.

It was a seven-week program, which included six weeks of teaching and one night dedicated to the Baptism in the Holy Spirit. The teachings were on how the Holy Spirit works in our lives, the gifts of the Holy Spirit, the fruit of the Holy Spirit, and an emphasis to keep God in the center of your life. And, of course, the Baptism in the Holy Spirit. I'd call it a crash course on Holy Spirit theology.

I went through the whole course, and on the seventh week the leaders prayed over me (and each person who attended) for a greater outpouring of the Holy Spirit. There was such hype about it during the previous weeks leading up to this day that I thought I was going to be zapped and *poof*, my whole life would change.

After they prayed for me, it appeared as though nothing had happened. I thought maybe I missed something, like I'd received a vaccination and it didn't take. But as I look back now, I can see that my spiritual life changed from that moment on.

It was imperceptible at the time, but eventually I realized that deep, spiritual changes were taking place in me. My entire spiritual life went from black and white to living color. I started reading the Bible, and the Scriptures came alive for me. It was as though they were written yesterday and were written just for me. I started watching EWTN on TV and began learning more about the Church.

I couldn't get enough of reading the Scriptures and learning more about the Church's teachings. It was a hunger, an absolute hunger, and it was extraordinary. It was as if a faucet had been turned on and it couldn't be turned off. It was a very grace-filled time. The Lord was feeding me and bringing me to a new depth of spirituality, a new depth of trusting Him and living in the Holy Spirit, while allowing the Spirit to guide my life.

Still caring for my father-in-law (a full-time job), it was always a blessing to have time away. The blessing came in the form of a retreat I attended. On this retreat the priest gave us a prayer to pray, "The Prayer of Abandonment."

"What I am going to ask you to do," the priest said, "is to silently pray this prayer to yourself for ten minutes. After that we will all say the prayer together, but those parts of the prayer that you can't agree with or can't live with now, don't say those words. Only say the words you can agree with now."

This is what happened when I started silently reflecting on the Prayer of Abandonment:

"Father, I abandon myself to You." I stopped. *I don't think I can do that,* I thought. *What if He asks me to do something I don't want to do?*

"Do with me whatever You will." I thought, *I can never agree with that! It has to be "let my will be done."* This is where I was!

"Whatever You do, I will always thank You." *There is no way!* I thought. There are things that happen in my life that I am not going to thank God for!

"I am ready for all, I accept all." I couldn't agree with this either.

And on and on it went as I prayed through the prayer. My thoughts were the same. I finally thought, *I don't like this prayer! I don't think I can accept this prayer.*

Ten minutes is a long time when one is going through a short prayer like the Prayer of Abandonment. I had time to go through this prayer many more times. At the beginning, my thoughts were negative. I couldn't let God rule my life! I had plans for my life.

Then I thought, *You know, that is pretty arrogant. That's a bad place to be. God certainly knows what is best for me. I am going to have to let go and let God take it over. After all, He is God, I'm not.*

I realized after a while that while I thought I had control of my life, I really didn't. I was fooling myself. God should have control over my life, and I might as well give it to Him and say, "Lord, whatever You want in my life is fine with me because You know better than I do. I am going to let it go; I'm going to let it go and let You take care of it."

By the end of the ten minutes, when the priest called us back to pray together, I had received an extraordinary grace, enough grace to pray every word of this prayer and to make it my own! I realized by that time that God knows what is best for me and that He loves me and that I can trust Him. After all, He is God!

The Lord gave me true grace that day to pray this prayer with honesty and mean every word. "Okay, Lord, I will do this," I said. "I may not understand or totally put everything into practice right now, but I am going to try my best."

From that time on, it has been my prayer every day. It is not a prayer that can change a person instantly into saying, "I've got it! From now on I am going to thank God for everything that happens in my life." No, that's not how it works. For me it was one step at a time. I can practice it every day. And with purpose I can make a habit of thanking God for everything in my life.

I cared for my father-in-law for fourteen years in our home. When he needed more care than I could give, we had to place him in a nursing home. We selected a Catholic nursing home even though he was neither Catholic nor religious.

One day when I visited him, he said, "The sister said I should have someone pray over my hand." He had carpal tunnel syndrome. I asked him if he would like the priest to pray over his hand.

"I can't ask the priest to pray," he replied. "I'm not a Catholic … yet."

My ears picked up the word "yet," and I wondered what he meant. I assured him he didn't have to be Catholic to have a priest pray.

When I returned home, I asked my husband, "Do you know what your father said today? He said, 'I'm not a Catholic … yet.' I wonder what he meant by that."

Ron said, "I know you are not going to be satisfied until you find out."

I went to visit him the next time. "Dad," I said. "Last week you said, 'I'm not a Catholic … yet.' What did you mean by that?"

He responded, "Well, I think I am too old to become a Catholic."

"Oh, Dad, I don't think you are ever too old to become a Catholic! Let's talk to the priest and see what he thinks."

The priest agreed. "Mr. MacInnis, you are never too old to become a Catholic."

So, after five years of living in a Catholic nursing home, Dad decided to became a Catholic.

On the day of his Baptism, First Communion, and Confirmation he was dressed with a bow tie and a jacket and a flower in his lapel. He looked great! The nurse's aides gathered around him. "Oh, Mr. MacInnis! You look like you are going to a wedding."

"I am going to a wedding," he answered. "I'm marrying Jesus today."

No one had told him that, but it was his heartfelt reply. He was marrying Jesus that day.

My father-in-law was eighty-nine years old at the time. During the last five years of his life, he went to Mass and Communion every day, and it was the joy of his life. God is so good!

By this time I was suffering from severe intestinal problems, and had been for many years, but the doctors couldn't find anything wrong. I began to develop a variety of symptoms that didn't seem related to each other, and my condition worsened.

Someone recommended a doctor who finally discovered my problem. I was diagnosed with candida, an overabundance of yeast in my colon, an overtaxed immune system, and many food and chemical allergies. These culprits had caused my mysterious symptoms. After six weeks of medication and a drastic change in my diet, I found I could control the adverse reactions.

However, there was no cure. I could have no sugar, no fruit, no salt, no dairy products, no yeast, no alcohol, no vinegar, no white flour, and no soy sauce. I lost my taste for meat of any kind and could no longer swallow it. Because I was allergic to many individual foods and many categories of foods, the list of what I could eat was a short one. I lost thirty-eight pounds in eight weeks.

For the next eight years I existed on oatmeal for breakfast, with no salt and a few raw almonds added for calcium and flavor. For lunch I'd have a salad with raw vegetables, with a dressing made from a small amount of fresh lemon juice and olive oil. I ate steamed, fresh vegetables with olive oil for supper. I baked "bread" made from oats, whole-wheat flour, a small amount of salt-free butter, and water.

As long as I stayed on this strict diet I had a lot of energy and few symptoms, but if I deviated at all I suffered the consequences: severe intestinal distress, hives, hay fever, sinus, aches in my joints and muscles, and swelling and splitting of my eyelids. If I had any salt at all, my eyelids would puff and split and take a week to heal. While they were healing the skin would become so taut that my eyelids couldn't close all the way when I slept. If I tried to close them tightly they'd split, and it took another week to heal.

The first Thanksgiving I was on this restricted diet, I prepared a complete turkey dinner for the family. When I set it on the table, I realized I couldn't eat anything I'd cooked. It was a very sad moment in my life, especially since I hadn't prepared anything for myself.

Whenever Ron and I were invited out to dinner it was hard to find anything on the menu I could eat. So, I'd eat at home and order something "special." Unfortunately, many times when it was served, I found I couldn't eat it.

I never prayed for healing, and I don't know why. It wasn't until eight years later, when I heard that Sr. Briege McKenna was coming to New Orleans for the Charismatic Conference, that I decided I would attend and ask her to pray for healing. I signed up and then realized I had to be in Memphis for a dear friend's wedding. I was crushed; there went my big chance to be healed. Then I recalled my daily prayer, "Give thanks in all circumstances."

The Lord had another plan. The day I got home from the wedding I got a call from a friend, Marilyn Quirk, to ask if I was available to drive some of the conference speakers from their hotel to a special Mass being said for them at Loyola University in New Orleans. Of course I could! The next morning when I arrived at the hotel, Marilyn asked me to drive Sr. Briege McKenna. I couldn't believe it! Sr. Briege is world-renown for her healing ministry. She prays, and in many cases God heals.

So, while driving along the interstate in New Orleans, Sr. Briege asked if she could pray for healing of my food allergies. Someone had told her about my symptoms, and she'd been praying for me. She had heard of only one case of a person whose allergies were worse than mine. This person was even allergic to his own clothing.

I was delighted that she would pray for me and said, "Yes!"

Sr. Briege said a simple prayer, asking Jesus to heal me. Right then and there, a heat went through my whole body and I knew I was being healed. Praise God! Can you imagine that? Healed instantly! And I was. I can now eat and drink anything, and I praise God. He is amazing! I am so grateful to God for His mercy and healing!

Some years later I had another opportunity to thank God in a most unusual circumstance. A dear friend invited me to go on a pilgrimage to the Holy Land with her. It had been a lifelong dream to walk in the footsteps of Jesus. I asked my husband about the trip, and he responded with his usual brand of humor saying it was a great idea as long as he didn't have to go. I assured him he didn't have to go and then quickly signed up for the trip.

In preparation for the pilgrimage, I had two prayers: first, I wanted to come to know what Jesus had suffered for me. What better way than to experience and see the places where He had lived and suffered and died for us. My second prayer was that I wanted to offer up my pilgrimage for the Jewish people to come to know their Messiah.

God answered both prayers.

Just before boarding the plane to Israel, I began to feel weak. I told my friend I didn't know if I could get on the plane. This was a strange, sudden illness. I am not afraid to fly and I don't get airsick. My friend asked me to sit down. Soon, the weakness passed and we boarded the plane.

The plane trip was miserable. I was ill the whole time. After we landed in Tel Aviv, Israel, we took a long bus ride to our hotel. Once in the hotel, I went to bed and languished there for the next two days. Nothing stayed in my stomach, but I had no fever. After two days, my roommate called the house doctor. He diagnosed me with an intestinal obstruction. I had to go to the hospital and would probably have to have emergency surgery to eliminate the obstruction. The hotel called their favorite taxi driver, Egal, to take me to the hospital in Tiberius. Egal became one of my angels in Israel—my Jewish angel.

In the emergency room, I found myself praising and thanking God, but silently. If anyone had known about this they would have thought I was crazy. But by this time, it came naturally to me. "Give thanks in all circumstances for this is the will of God for you in Christ Jesus" (1 Thess. 5:18). I had the opportunity to put this verse into action, not yet knowing why I was thanking God.

X-rays confirmed there was indeed an intestinal obstruction (actually, a kink in my intestine) and I would undergo surgery the next day. After I was assigned a hospital room, I encouraged my friend to continue the pilgrimage. I would be well taken care of. She left reluctantly and in tears. Egal, the taxi driver, picked her up and took her back to the hotel. It was midnight by that time.

The first day in the hospital the doctors tried to clear up the blockage with chemicals. That failed, so surgery was scheduled for the next morning. I had no family members with me and no one to talk to, since I did not speak the language.

However, the Lord sent many loving and caring people to comfort me. First, the social worker came. She was concerned for me because I was alone. I told her I was not alone, that God was with me, and that He knew exactly where I was. And He was allowing this to happen in my life at this time, so I was not concerned. She was surprised at my sense of calm. Frankly, so was I. But God was truly with me. His grace and the prayers of my Magnificat sisters all over the world were with me, giving me supernatural strength.

Then another visitor came, an eighty-two-year-old Franciscan friar from the Holy Land, who took public transportation to reach me. He came to my hospital room to administer the Sacrament of the Sick and to bring me Jesus in the Eucharist. Since I was NPO (nothing by mouth), I received just a tiny piece of the host, but it was the whole Jesus! He told me that

Denise from California, who was working to form a Magnificat chapter in the Holy Land, had called him to request that he come see me in the hospital. What a special gift from God!

Next, there was the beautiful Israeli woman doctor. She showed up in my room and assured me that she would be with me before, during, and after my surgery so I would not be alone. She spoke perfect English. I asked her if she was a pediatrician (she had a Tweedy Bird sticker on the stethoscope around her neck).

"No," she answered.

"Are you my surgeon?" I asked.

"No. You will have the head of the surgery department as your surgeon," she said.

I suspect she was really an angel sent by God to comfort me. How would a doctor have time to spend most of a day just keeping me company?

The next person God sent to comfort and care for me was Muhammad. He was a male nurse—Arab Palestinian—and he was a Muslim. He couldn't do enough for me. I spent nine days in the hospital, and Muhammad came to my room several times a day. Even when he was not working on my floor, he visited to see if I was okay and if I needed anything.

Muhammad arranged for my husband, miles away at home in the States, to call his cell phone so that Ron could talk to me after the surgery was over (there was no phone in my room). Because Muhammad was not pleased with the room they gave me, he had me moved to a new room, "a room with a view" as he called it. I was surprised by his kindness. We became good friends in those nine days and for some time afterwards.

I once asked Muhammad why he was so kind to me. I was obviously a Catholic and had my crucifix on almost all the time. He explained that his father raised his children to make a difference for the good in people's lives. He told me stories of his father's generosity, how he left figs and olives on the trees on the perimeter of his orchard so that the poor could have fruit to eat.

"The next time you come to Israel," Muhammad said, "come as a tourist and not a patient. You and your husband can stay at my home with my wife and me. We will show you all around Israel."

My son Ronnie came to Israel a day and a half after my surgery and stayed a whole week. What a blessing! He left his business, his wife, and his two sons to sit in my room, help me, and often times just watch me sleep. He was there for me the many times I was in extreme pain and sick to my stomach after my surgery. He was always there to help me and comfort me.

One day Ronnie came around my bed to hold the bowl so I could be sick (I was in such agony). He patted me on the side and said, "It's all right. I'm here with you." It was as though God the Father was saying those words. I was deeply touched and grateful. Not once did he make me feel that he wished he were somewhere else. It was truly the love of God made manifest to me.

Pope John Paul II said, "Much of the reason for suffering is for the sake of compassion." My illness certainly did bring out compassion in my son. He took such good care of me. Because of my experience of such pain, I now have a better understanding of the pain others suffer. I have more compassion for others.

I spent nine days in that hospital, and each moment of each day I offered up my sufferings for the Jewish people, the chosen people of God, to come to know their Messiah. Viktor Frankel, a Holocaust survivor, said, "Suffering ceases to be suffering when we find meaning in it." The meaning I found for my pain made my pain not only bearable but acceptable.

I identified many times with Our Blessed Savior. I felt His pain and experienced his Passion in a number of ways. On my bed (a very hard bed in a cold room) at night, I would often wake up in severe pain. I thought of Jesus on that cold stone floor of the pit where he was thrown after He was scourged, awaiting His crucifixion. I knew I was suffering just a little of His pain, but I would combine my suffering with His. I could have called for a nurse and received pain killers for my pain, but Jesus could not do that. For nine days I had no food or drink, not even ice chips. Nothing! I now know the meaning of "I thirst" on a physical level.

My Jewish roommates were wonderful. Though we did not speak each other's languages, we communicated in the language of love. Leah would come and sit at the foot of my bed and rub my ankle, and would raise her hands to heaven as if to say she was praying for me. I would place my hands together to let her know I was praying for her. Those visiting my roommates shared food with my son Ronnie who, though he is slim, eats a lot. There was no cafeteria in the hospital. One Jewish lady, who was visiting her husband in the room near mine, brought me her laptop computer and played a DVD movie for me to help pass the time. Amazing!

When it came time for me to leave the hospital, my roommates and I hugged each other, cried, and promised that we would pray for each other. My son left the day I was released from the hospital, so my husband came. Ron and I spent five days at a hotel as I continued to gain my strength for the trip home. The hotel was across the street from the Sea of Galilee. We could look out over the sea from our ground-floor, wooden deck. It was the only holy site I saw while in Israel.

Egal, my Jewish taxi driver, was invaluable in getting needed supplies for us and taking Ron to bank and to the drug store and then returning our rental car. He was our translator, advisor, guide, and friend. He wanted to take us to some of the holy sites, but I was still too sick. The day we left Israel, Egal drove us three hours to the Tel Aviv airport, then he turned around and returned home before sundown because it was the Feast of Passover (everything in Israel closes down at sunset). Muhammad, my Muslim nurse, had all of the hospital records translated for us and visited us at the hotel several times.

My pilgrimage was not the pilgrimage I had imagined, and it was certainly not the pilgrimage my fellow pilgrims had in mind. However, I would not trade this journey for anything. It was the pilgrimage Jesus chose for me. I had the opportunity to better understand what Jesus suffered for me, and I had ample opportunity to offer up my sufferings for the Jewish people, God's chosen people, and to pray they come to know their Messiah in a closer and more intimate way. I had to abandon my expectations and my will to the will of God. It was a journey of a lifetime.

If I had not received the grace to give thanks to God in all circumstances, I would have surely been a bitter person after this trip. I would have complained loudly to the Lord, "Why did you bring me to the Holy Land to let me suffer and not see any of the places I wanted to visit?"

Instead, God gave me the grace to see through His Eyes the blessings He provided for me while in Israel. The prayers of my Magnificat sisters gave me the strength to recognize and accept the will of God and to embrace it. I couldn't have done this without that grace.

The two prayers I prayed before my pilgrimage were answered. I received so much love and care from the Lord! It overwhelmed me then, and it overwhelms me now to think about it. He provided for me just when I needed it.

I share this story so that you can also realize how wonderful our God is and so you can see how I have grown in my relationship with the Lord. I have learned to thank God in all circumstances and to trust that His plan is the best plan for our salvation. He is the Father who loves us and only wants the best for each of His children. I invite you to abandon your life to God, and to realize as I have learned that He has a plan for your life and it is the *best* plan, because it is *His plan!*

I'd like to present you with an opportunity to read over the "Prayer of Abandonment" and make it your own. As you read it over, ask God to give you the grace to accept this prayer. It is only with the grace of God that we can give our lives to Him fully.

I pray God's blessing upon you.

Prayer of Abandonment
Written by Blessed Charles de Foucauld

"Father, I abandon myself to You,
Do with me whatever You will.
Whatever You may do I shall always thank You.
I am ready for all. I accept all.
Let only Your will be done in me
And in all Your creatures.
No more do I wish than this, O Lord.

Into Your hands I commend my soul.
I offer it to You with all the love of my heart.
For I love You, Lord,
And so need to give myself into Your hands
Without reserve
And with boundless confidence,
For You are my Father."

Bio–
Kathy MacInnis is Coordinator of the Magnificat Central Service Team (CST), which oversees the international workings of the Ministry and its 80+ Chapters in twelve countries. Kathy served for fifteen years on the CST with Marilyn Quirk, the founding Coordinator. Kathy has directed the formation of more than fifty new Chapters around the world and sees first-hand how the Holy Spirit works in women from all walks of life. She is a wife, mother, grandmother and has been a caregiver to both her mother and father-in-law. In 1999, she was miraculously healed of severe food and chemical related allergies. Painfully shy for many years, the Lord brought her to a place of freedom and abandonment to His Holy Will. This included being interviewed with Marilyn Quirk by Fr. Mitch Pacwa on *EWTN Live* in 2008, founding a chapter in West St. Tammany in the Archdiocese of New Orleans, and speaking to chapters spreading the word of God's love.

Patti Mansfield

I begin my testimony with a prayer for my reader:

"Dear Father in Jesus' name, I ask Your richest blessing on each person reading this today. Grant that this would be a time of refreshment and opportunity to experience Your presence, hear Your Word, and be set free by Your truth. Lord, You know the circumstances in the lives of the hands that hold this book. I pray that in Your own wonderful way You will speak to each heart, and following Mary's example, we will give our wholehearted "yes" to whatever You are asking. We thank You and praise You for the peace that surpasses all understanding, the peace of Christ that guards our hearts. And I ask Mary, our Mother: Daughter of the Father, Mother of the Son, Spouse of the Holy Spirit, to pray for us. We are totally yours. Totus Tuus. Amen."

I grew up in Irvington, New Jersey, Archdiocese of Newark, about forty-five minutes from New York City. I am the first of four children of two marvelous people: Peter Gallagher, a real Irishman with a beautiful Irish tenor voice and a wonderful sense of humor; and my mother, a pure Italian, Netta Scarfone. Her family was from Calabria, Italy.

At the age of fourteen, both of my parents had to help support their respective immigrant families, so they went to work at Purolator Oil Filters on a factory line. They met, fell in love, and had a beautiful marriage. My parents' love for one another and for us four children gave me a strong foundation in life. It also inspired me to be a wife and mother as my vocation.

We were a Catholic family, but my parents didn't have the money to send any of us to Catholic school. I went to a public grade school and a public high school, Irvington High. There were 2,400 kids at Irvington High, with 660 in my class alone. I was elected class president four years in a row. This gave me a great deal of experience with public speaking and leadership. I didn't realize then that this experience was preparing me for a life of evangelization. The Lord knew way back then that He would use me in this way.

The high school I attended had a large Jewish population. I had one Catholic girlfriend and two Protestant girlfriends. Everybody else I knew and loved was Jewish. In fact, the young man I was interested in was a fervent Jew. His parents wouldn't let him date me because I was a Gentile. I didn't know I was a Gentile; I didn't even know what a Gentile was!

This boy later grew up and became a famous Jewish rabbi. Being in that Jewish environment when I was about sixteen or seventeen caused me to want to learn more about my Catholic faith. It was the first time I was discriminated against for my faith. This influenced my decision about attending college. I knew I wanted a Catholic university. I loved French and wanted to become a French teacher. I was looking for a Catholic school in a big city with a strong foreign language department. I also wanted that all-important good ratio—not professors to students, but men to women!

In September 1964 I began my studies at Duquesne University in Pittsburgh, Pennsylvania. While there I became friends with another New Jersey girl. She was part of a small Scripture study group that met once a week to read the Bible and pray a short form of the Divine Office. My friend invited me to this group and although I felt attracted, I was also afraid.

As much as I wanted to learn more about my Catholic faith and the Scriptures, I was afraid that if I got too close to God He would ask something of me that I didn't want to give Him. I was young and naïve. I thought that if I kept God at a distance, I could avoid suffering. In my mind I believed that anyone who got too close to God would suffer. That may sound familiar to some readers.

For one year my friend kept inviting me to join this Scripture group called *Chi Rho*. For one year I found every creative way of refusing to come without offending her. Finally, at the end of the year, I accepted her invitation to go to a picnic with these people. The students were so welcoming and kind to me that my fears disappeared. When I met the young man who was president and saw how handsome he was, I decided to join *Chi Rho*, after all. We would chant with a simple psalm tone the Psalms of the Divine Office and discuss the Scriptures.

Chi Rho planned a retreat in February of 1967. As a public school girl, I had never gone on a retreat in my life. I didn't know what to expect. We were told to prepare for the retreat by reading the first four chapters of the Acts of the Apostles in the Bible.

I was so ignorant of the Bible that I didn't know where to find the Acts of the Apostles. I figured it must be in the New Testament but I didn't know where to look. I had to look it up on the contents page. I didn't just read it once. I read it over and over again before the retreat. Why? Because even though I had confidence in some aspects of my life, when it came to the faith, I felt ignorant. I was sure all the other young people in the *Chi Rho* Scripture study grasped the meaning of the Acts of the Apostles in a way I did not.

The other way we were asked to prepare was to obtain a little paperback book called *The Cross and the Switchblade*. The book told the story of a Pentecostal minister who was dramatically led from his small town in Pennsylvania into the streets of New York City to work with drug addicts.

As I read that book, all references to the Baptism in the Holy Spirit and charismatic gifts, like speaking in tongues, went right over my head. What captivated me was that someone living in modern times actually knew God in that way. The minister in this story, David Wilkerson, seemed to have a great intimacy with God and received His guidance in extraordinary ways.

After reading the Pentecost account in the Acts of the Apostles and then reading a modern-day story about the activity of the Holy Spirit, I found myself thinking, *Wouldn't it be wonderful if an ordinary person like me could actually know God ... could actually receive guidance from the Holy Spirit? Wouldn't it be wonderful if what the apostles and disciples experienced at Pentecost, and what this minister experienced, could be true in my life?*

I share this question I pondered to help you get in touch with that same question in your own life. I pray this is the day you can say, "I know Jesus Christ in a personal way. I have given my life to Him. I know the Holy Spirit." Perhaps you are uncertain about the commitment, or maybe you do feel that hunger, thirst, and longing in your heart as I did. I didn't just want to know *about* God; I wanted to *know* God.

About a week before the retreat, I began reflecting. On the one hand I said, "Wouldn't it be wonderful if I could actually know God?" On the other hand I said, "No, it is impossible. That kind of intimate knowledge of God, of Jesus, and of the Holy Spirit is only for priests or nuns. I don't want to be one of them. An ordinary person like me wants to get married and have a family. That kind of a person can't know God intimately."

Even though I was studying the *Documents of Vatican II* in class as a university student, I didn't grasp what the council fathers were saying to us when they said that everyone is called to holiness. The mission of the Church to evangelize belongs to the whole people of God. It didn't sink in at the time.

One night before the retreat, while all this was stirring in my heart, I was alone in my dormitory room. I knelt down and prayed, "Lord, as a Catholic, I believe I have already received your Spirit in Baptism and in Confirmation. But if it is possible for your Spirit to do more in my life than

He has done up until now, I want it." When I said those words, I really expected something. As I prayed that prayer, my eyes were closed. I opened my eyes and looked around the room.

I would have been happy to see an angel, an apparition, or at least have some kind of warm feeling—like a glow. After reading the dramatic story of Pentecost with the fire and wind and shaking in the Acts of the Apostles, and then reading in *The Cross and The Switchblade* about the Spirit's dynamic interventions and guidance, I was looking for *something*. What I felt that moment after that prayer was … *nada*. I felt nothing! I said, "I will never tell anybody about this prayer because I guess it didn't work. I guess I am too ordinary. I can't expect God to intervene in my life."

But the truth is God *did hear* and God *did answer* that prayer in a way infinitely greater than I could ask or imagine (cf. Eph. 3:20). What I was praying for without realizing it was the Baptism in the Holy Spirit, a life immersed in the grace of the Holy Spirit. God always hears that prayer. God always answers that prayer. Perhaps He was waiting for the key that I had not yet turned. I had not yet completely surrendered control of my life to the Lordship of Jesus Christ.

Off we went the weekend of February 17–19, 1967—about twenty-five students. We stayed in a beautiful, three-story, wood-frame retreat house run by an order of nuns. Each time we gathered in the upper-room chapel, we sang an ancient hymn called the *"Veni Creator Spiritus"*, the *"Come, Creator Spirit."* We sang it in the Gregorian chant melody, but we also sang it in English.

The song begins like this: "Come, O Creator Spirit, blest and in our hearts take up Thy rest. Come with Thy grace and heavenly aid to fill the hearts which Thou hast made." In the United States we know this hymn in this version: "Come, Holy Ghost, Creator blest, and in our hearts take up Thy rest. Come with Thy grace and heavenly aid to fill the hearts which Thou hast made, to fill the hearts which Thou hast made."

This is the first hymn I learned as a little girl preparing for Confirmation, and I always loved it. It's significant that the Catholic Charismatic Renewal was born in the midst of this hymn. The *"Veni Creator Spiritus"* was written in the ninth century and it is the hymn used in the Church to invoke the Spirit. It is sung at ordinations and religious professions. It is sung at the beginning of conclaves, synods, and important events. It has been sung by all the saints since the ninth century.

When St. Claire was received by St. Francis, I understand that *"Veni Creator Spiritus"* was being sung. When St. Teresa of Avila, the great mystic and doctor of the Church, was at an impasse in her prayer and she went to her spiritual father, he told her to get on her knees and sing *"Veni Creator Spiritus."* When she did, for the first time in her life, she experienced a rapture in prayer. This song can be dynamite in your life!

St. Louis de Montfort in his beautiful classic, *True Devotion to Mary*, says if you want to grasp the mystery of Our Lady, prepare by praying the *"Veni Creator Spiritus"*. This hymn, as Dr. Bert Ghezzi writes, is like a mysterious thread woven in the lives of the saints. I didn't know that. I was twenty years old and attending the first retreat of my life. But when the director of that retreat said we were going to sing and sing and sing again, "Come, Creator Spirit," it was as if he was saying, "We are going to keep invoking the Holy Spirit until we know He has come."

The first presentation Friday night was a meditation on Our Lady. She was presented to us as a model of faith, humility, prayer, and praise. The next activity was a communal penance service. Jesus said, "When the Holy Spirit comes he will convict the world of sin" (John 16:8). He doesn't mean the world in Los Angeles or New Orleans or New York City. He means the world right in our hearts—the world in you and the world in me. Jesus said, "Repent, for the kingdom of heaven is at hand" (Mt. 4:17). If you want more of God in your life today, if you want more of the Holy Spirit in your life, if you want more peace, love, and joy, you must repent.

I had never taken part in a communal penance service before, and the people were praying spontaneously. I had heard rote prayer and liturgical prayer but never spontaneous prayer. Students were praying like this, "Lord, forgive me for my jealousy. Lord, forgive me for my hard-heartedness. Jesus, forgive me for my greed. Forgive me for my lust. Lord, forgive me for my pride and my arrogance." Wow! As I listened to them confess in prayer that way, I thought, "Their sins sound like my sins".

There is a certain solidarity in sin that we read about in Scripture: "All have sinned and are deprived of the glory of God" (Rom. 3:23). All have sinned. After the spontaneous prayer, we were given an opportunity to make an individual confession and receive absolution from the priest.

There is something of a pattern to the way God worked among us that night to prepare us for the sovereign outpouring of the Holy Spirit. We were all together in prayer in an upper room. We began with an invocation of the Holy Spirit, then we turned our eyes toward Mary to strengthen us, and finally we repented. If you want more of the Holy Spirit in your life today, repent and avail yourself to the sacrament of Reconciliation. It has fallen into such disuse in the modern church.

I remember visiting a cathedral in an Austrian town, and the handles of the confessional door were bright and shiny. Do you know why? Nobody uses it! It doesn't matter that the murals were restored. It doesn't matter that the confessionals have new kneelers. That didn't matter at all. No one avails himself or herself of the sacrament. What a grace is being neglected!

If you haven't been to confession recently, make a decision today: "I am going to go to confession at the first opportunity." Get before that representative of Jesus, the priest. It doesn't matter what you have done. Jesus is so merciful. One drop of His blood is enough to cover the sins of the whole world. If you saw the movie, *The Passion of the Christ*, how could you walk away from that depiction of the sufferings of Jesus without saying, "The blood! The blood!" The blood of Jesus was shed for the forgiveness of our sins—for yours and for mine.

The next day, Saturday of the retreat, a Protestant woman came to speak to us. She was probably middle-aged—the very age I am now—and I thought she was an old lady. I was totally turned off by this woman, not because she was a Protestant but because I thought she was simplistic. She stood up and said, "Well, I don't know what I am going to say, but I've prayed and asked the Holy Spirit to guide me."

I thought, *Hmm, what a poor excuse for not preparing a talk. Here she is, a Protestant coming to speak to us Catholic students, and she doesn't take the time to prepare a talk. She thinks the Holy Spirit is going to fly down from Heaven and save her out of her mess.* So I crossed my arms and said to myself, *So, impress me. Impress me with your Holy Spirit.*

And guess what? She impressed me!

She only spoke about twenty minutes, but those twenty minutes changed my life. I began with a closed attitude toward her, but as she spoke about her relationship with Jesus, I was moved. She spoke about Jesus with such intimacy. It was as if she had just had her morning coffee with Him.

What was most striking was her relationship with the Holy Spirit. It was apparent that for her He was not simply a heavenly dove flying around somewhere. He was not simply a tongue of fire as seen in some stained-glass window. She knew the Person. She knew the Holy Spirit. He empowered her. He consoled her.

I found out many years later that she had mentioned charismatic gifts, like praying in tongues. That went right over my head on the retreat. I thought maybe it meant praying in English with greater fervor. What captivated me and melted my resistance was that this woman had something I didn't have, and I wanted it. In my little, inexpensive notebook, I wrote these words: *Jesus, be real for me!*

We got into discussion groups of four or five people, and the discussion was focused on the question, "How are we Catholics to understand a term like 'receiving Jesus'?" We asked the faculty member who was in our group, "Didn't we receive Jesus when we were baptized?"

"Yes," he replied.

"But didn't we receive the Holy Spirit when we were confirmed?"

"Yes."

"Don't we receive Jesus every time we go to confession or receive communion?"

"Yes."

"Well, why should we talk about 'receiving Jesus and receiving the Holy Spirit'?"

The professor said our questions were good Catholic questions. He explained that for most of us these sacraments of initiation took place when we were infants or young children. I was confirmed around the age of twelve, and I admit I wasn't focused on the spiritual aspects of the day. I was thinking more about whether I was going to get the gold charm bracelet I wanted. I was wondering how hard the bishop was going to slap me across the cheek, and if I could wear lipstick to Confirmation.

The professor explained that now, as young adults, we needed to ratify those sacraments. We needed to say our "yes, amen" wholeheartedly.

The professor asked, "Who is Jesus in your life right now?"

It was as if the living Lord was standing in front of me. I didn't see Him, but I sensed He was there asking me the question He asked of His disciples: "Who do you say that I am?" (Mark 8:29). Not who do your brothers and sisters say that I am. Not who do your husband or children say that I am. Not who does your parish priest say that I am, but *You*, Patti, "Who do you say that I am?"

Although I did love Him, although I went to church every Sunday, although I chose a Catholic university to learn more about my faith, although it was important to me to do the right thing, although I had joined the *Chi Rho* Scripture study group and had begun attending daily Mass, I was attending this retreat and yet … I couldn't say that Jesus was the center of my life. My prayer life was something like this, "Dear Lord, bless my plans and do my will, according to my time table. Amen." It was basically *me* telling Him what to do and usually how to do it and when to do it.

Is that prayer? It is *something*. At least I was speaking to God. But that day, when I was asked the question, "Who do you say that I am?", I realized I had never made an unconditional surrender to Jesus as the Lord of my life. One of the young men in the discussion group, David Mangan, said, "Maybe one of the things we should do to close this retreat is to have a renewal of our Confirmation."

The rest of the students didn't seem too interested in this idea, but I thought it was brilliant. David and I looked at each other, linked arms, and said, "Even if no one else at this retreat wants to renew Confirmation, we do and we will." The Lord was listening!

Saturday night there was supposed to be a birthday party for some of the students. We had a birthday cake, but the party never got off the ground. People were listless and wandering around. Although I was shy about prayer and spiritual things, I was an organizer. I said to myself, *Well, the problem here is that we are all scattered. We need to get everybody together in the same room, where we can cut the cake and start the birthday party.*

I took it upon myself to gather the people from the retreat house. I started out on the second floor where the chapel was. I entered the chapel with no intention of praying. I simply planned to tell those at prayer to come down to the birthday party.

When I entered the chapel that night and knelt in front of Jesus in the tabernacle, I knew in a way I had never experienced before what we Catholics mean when we say, "The Real Presence." By faith I had always genuflected in front of the tabernacle. I never doubted that Jesus was present in the Blessed Sacrament.

But that night, February 18, 1967, as I knelt in front of the tabernacle, I felt His awesome presence, and it made me tremble. My whole body was trembling. I thought, *God is here. He is King of kings. He is Lord of lords. He is holy, and I am not holy. If I stay in the presence of this holy God, something is going to happen to me. Maybe He is going to ask something of me, something I don't want to give Him.*

Yes, there was fear, but greater than my fear was my need. I needed to give myself unconditionally to Him. We all have that need. God made us for Himself. St. Augustine said, "You have made us for Yourself, O God, and our hearts are restless until they rest in You."

In that moment in that little chapel on my knees, I quieted my heart and prayed, "Father, I give my life to You. Whatever You ask of me, I accept it. If it means suffering, I accept that too. Just teach me to follow Your Son, Jesus, and to love the way Jesus loves."

When I finished that prayer, I found myself prostrate, flat on my face before Jesus in the tabernacle. Somehow in the process my shoes had come off. Like Moses, I was on holy ground. I felt filled with the love of God … immersed in the mercy of God. This love is totally gratuitous.

God is love! That is who God is. God made each one of us, we belong to Him, and He loves us. He can't help Himself. He is in love with us. St. Catherine of Siena has said, "He is like a mad lover. He is crazy, mad with love for every one of us." No matter who we are. No matter what we have done. There is nothing we can do to merit or earn the love of God. Here is the Good News! There is nothing you or I can ever do, no sins so great that we could ever commit, that will make Him stop loving us. God is love.

That's what Baptism in the Spirit is all about: the love of God. St. Paul proclaims it this way: "The love of God has been poured out into our hearts through the Holy Spirit that has been given to us" (Romans 5:5).

As soon as I experienced this overwhelming love of God, as much as I wanted to stay, to bask in His Presence, I knew I had to leave. I had to tell others what I had just experienced that day, February 18, 1967, and what I still know today: that this grace of encountering the love of the Father made flesh in Jesus, poured out into our hearts through the Holy Spirit, is a gift for everybody! If I, with all my misgivings and all my own plans, who didn't even go into the chapel to pray, could experience this love of God, then anybody on the face of the earth could experience this grace as well.

I ran and told the priest what happened. Father told me that David Mangan (the young man who agreed with me to renew our Confirmation) had been in the chapel a few hours before and had an identical experience. He had walked in, and the next thing he knew he was flat on his face. He said the Presence of God was so thick one could cut it with a knife.

"Well, Father," I asked. "Whom should I tell?"

His reply has echoed in my heart over all these years: "The Lord will show you."

Almost immediately, two girls from another school came up to me. "Your face looks different," they said. "What has happened to you?"

I didn't know the Scriptures well enough at the time to know that when Moses was in the presence of God, he came back with such a glow that he had to put a veil over his face. St. Paul says in 2 Corinthians, chapter 3 that all of us—not just special people—all the people of the New Covenant, "beholding the beauty of our Lord, Jesus, are transformed from one glory to another." Then St. Paul says, "This is the work of the Holy Spirit."

I took these two young women by their hands and told them I had just experienced what we had been talking about all weekend. I brought them into the chapel and we knelt in front of Jesus. For someone who had never prayed out loud before, prayers were pouring out of me. Not fancy prayers, but prayers from my heart. "Oh, Lord, whatever you just did for me, do it for them. Whatever you just did for me, do it for them."

This was the shortest *Life in the Spirit* seminar on record!

As we were kneeling there, other students began to enter the chapel. No one rang a bell and said, "Everyone come to the chapel." No, it was a sovereign outpouring of the Holy Spirit. There before Jesus some people were weeping, others were laughing. Others, like me, were feeling our bodies on fire. You may have experienced the tingling feeling when your hand or foot falls asleep; I felt like my hands and arms were on fire. Some students were holding their hands and arms up. It's not unusual today in charismatic renewal circles to pray with raised hands, but in 1967 you would never see any Catholic lay person pray like that.

One of the people said he wanted to pray and praise God but knew it wasn't going to come out in English. We didn't know how to yield to the gifts of the Spirit. We could all have prayed in tongues right then, but we didn't know how to begin. In walked one of our professors and he said, "What is the bishop going to say when he hears all of these kids have been baptized in the Holy Spirit?"

None of us dreamed that what began that weekend—which has now been dubbed "The Duquesne Weekend"—would spark a move of the Holy Spirit that has traveled around the world. Today there are an estimated 120 million Catholics in over 230 countries around the world who have experienced the grace of being baptized in the Holy Spirit. The ministry of Magnificat grew out of this grace of the Baptism in the Holy Spirit.

The words of Psalm 126 best describes our experience when we got back to the campus of Duquesne University: "When the Lord brought Zion's captives back, we were like men in a dream. Our mouths were filled with laughter and our lips with shouts of joy. Even the pagans began talking about the great things the Lord had done. What marvels God did and we are glad indeed."

We were like people in a dream. We were stumbling into the gifts of the Holy Spirit. For example, when I returned to my dorm room, I saw a note that our dorm director was in Mercy Hospital with phlebitis and would be out for a long time.

A thought came into my mind: *Go, lay your hands on her and she will be healed.* I panicked. I was thinking about some television evangelists with their dramatic healing ministry. I didn't want to go and pray for her in the manner I saw on television, but I decided to put a fleece before the Lord. I prayed, "Jesus, if this is really You, and if You want me to go and pray for her, let me wake up really early tomorrow morning." This was a safe prayer since I am notorious for sleeping late. However, early the next morning I was wide awake and still had the thought, *Go, lay your hands on her and she will be healed.*

I went to the hospital, but I didn't know how to lay hands on somebody or how to pray. Then I remembered that my Italian mother would make a little sign of the cross on our foreheads and bless us before we went to bed. Before I left Mrs. Jones's hospital room, I said, "Mrs. Jones, I know you will be fine." Then I made the sign of the cross on her forehead. To my utter amazement, she was released from the hospital the next day. All the swelling had disappeared and she was healed. Praise God!

It was the same for the other students. We literally stumbled into the gifts of the Holy Spirit. At one of our first prayer meetings, David Mangan began to pray in perfect French.

"I didn't know you spoke French," I told him afterwards.

"I *don't* speak French," he replied. "I've only studied Latin and German."

That got my attention! Up until that day I didn't really understand the gift of tongues or desire it. I was working so hard to learn French that it almost offended me to think that someone else could come into another language with no personal effort.

When I heard David praying in a language he had never learned, I was convinced this gift was authentic and I began to ask the Lord to give it to me. "Lord," I prayed, "if the gift of tongues can help me praise You when I don't have the words, please give it to me." But I didn't know how to yield. I somehow expected that it would just force its way out of my lips with no effort on my part.

One morning I awakened with a clicking in my throat. *What if this is the gift of tongues?* I thought. *I'd better cut my classes so it doesn't come out of me during class.*

I hurried to an oratory above the chapel at Duquesne University, where I could be alone. I knelt before a crucifix above an altar and said to the Lord, "I am not getting up off my knees until I pray in tongues."

I opened my mouth and waited. I waited for quite some time. Then it began in my throat. It sounded like grunts. I was dismayed. "I majored in French because of the beauty of the language. What if I receive an ugly, guttural tongue?"

When I finally yielded to the gift, I was singing a beautiful, lilting melody in an equally beautiful language. My hands were raised high to the Lord. In my heart I understood exactly what I was singing. I was singing Mary's Magnificat, "My soul magnifies the Lord!" I felt as if I had somehow entered into Mary's own person and that in some mysterious way, in my littleness, I had entered into her greatness in proclaiming that God, Who is mighty, has done great things and holy is His name.

My gift of tongues was enabling me to proclaim the mysteries of God's love and mercy for the little ones, the humble ones. I was so filled with exaltation and joy that I didn't want to stop. I was also afraid I wouldn't be able to begin again. I rushed downstairs to the chaplain's office and spoke in tongues into the ear of the secretary. Imagine what she must have thought of me!

If only we'd had someone to explain to us that anyone can receive this gift by asking for it in faith and then beginning the process of speaking. The only requirement is that you don't use English or any other language you have learned. Baby sounds are all you need to make, and the Holy Spirit will quickly take over and form a new language of praise. How beautiful it is to know that this is a language in which you have never said anything evil. How beautiful to know that the Spirit is providing exactly the right thing in your prayer. It is a most valuable and powerful charismatic gift.

Within one or two weeks of the Duquesne Weekend, we had a visit from Cursillo leaders Ralph Martin and Steve Clark. I didn't know who they were or what the Cursillo movement was. I didn't even know their last names. In my little notebook, I wrote these words: "Lord, leaders of Cursillo are coming tomorrow, Ralph and Steve. When You come to them, You will come to the States and to the world."

This was a prophetic intuition since these two men were extremely influential in the spread of the grace of Baptism in the Spirit around the world. They were among the first to organize conferences and seminars to teach people about Baptism in the Spirit.

I never did teach French. After I was baptized in the Spirit, all I wanted to do was talk about Jesus. I couldn't focus my mind on anything. I remember in one of my French classes, I was looking out the window thinking about God. I guess I was lost in contemplative prayer. I heard my classmates laughing, and the French professor repeated in French, "We are awaiting the awakening of Mademoiselle Gallagher."

I *was* awake. I was more awake, more alive, than I had ever been before.

My life since then has been an ongoing discovery of the love and providence of God. Early on I discovered a wonderful promise in Psalm 37:4: "Take delight in the Lord and He will give you the desires of your heart."

I desired to be married to a man who had a vocation to serve the Lord in the Charismatic Renewal. I wanted a "Spirit-filled saint as a husband." Fr. Harold Cohen, S.J., teased me and asked if I was open to having one with a Southern drawl. In 1971, Fr. Cohen invited Al Mansfield and me to New Orleans to serve in the Charismatic Renewal, which was booming at the time. Al and I worked together in ministry and were good friends for a few years. In 1973 we fell in love and married. The Lord blessed us with four children and at this writing, seven grandchildren with another one in heaven.

God has given me the desires of my heart in the wonderful, Spirit-filled husband He sent me and the life we share as a family. Yes, there have been sufferings, like the loss of our home, office, and retreat facility in Hurricane Katrina. But His providence has cared for us beyond our wildest dreams.

After the hurricane we were recalling the readings we chose for our wedding. They were prophetic. The first was from Isaiah 43: "When you pass through the waters you will not drown and the floods will not overwhelm you." The second, Romans 8:28, has become the banner over our lives: "God makes all things work together for the good in the lives of those who love Him." It is true!

Our gospel was John 2, the wedding feast of Cana: "There was a wedding in Cana of Galilee and the mother of Jesus was there." When we were displaced for five months after the hurricane, we felt the tender care of Our Lady of Guadalupe, whose image greeted us each place we stayed. Truly, the Lord cannot be outdone in generosity. He will provide our every need according to His riches and glory in Christ. (cf. Phil. 4:19)

Don't be afraid to surrender unconditionally to God. The Father Himself loves you. Don't be afraid to ask Jesus to be your personal Lord and Savior. He died for you. Don't be afraid to open yourself completely to the Holy Spirit and His gifts. He is the sweet guest of the soul. The love of God is poured into our hearts through the Holy Spirit who has been given to us. (cf. Rm. 5:5)

Since 1973, my husband and I have been privileged to serve the Lord full time in the Catholic Charismatic Renewal of New Orleans. We have witnessed conversions, healings, and blessings beyond measure in the many thousands of people who have passed through this ministry. In addition, Al has served the national renewal for many years on the advisory council and as a Traveling Timothy.

After the children were in school, the Lord began to call me to a broader ministry, first through a monthly column in *New Covenant* magazine, then in writing four books, and then for the past twenty-five years through an extensive traveling ministry. By His grace I have been to five continents to proclaim the gospel and the gift of being baptized in the Spirit. What a joy to follow Christ and be used to spread the kingdom of God!

One of the questions I have been asked the most over these years of the Charismatic Renewal is this: How does it feel to have been there in the beginning and see how many millions of Catholics are now involved in this movement? My answer is this: In some small way I feel like Mary. When she said "yes" to the will of the Father, the Holy Spirit overshadowed her and Jesus took on flesh in her. From then on, her mission has been to bring Him forth to the world.

When I said my "yes" to the will of the Father during the Duquesne Weekend, the Holy Spirit overshadowed me. I never dreamed that my personal surrender to God would have had an impact on anyone else's life. But it has. This is a mystery. Each of us is called to be like Mary ... to let Jesus take on flesh in us and to bring Him forth to the world.

I want to echo Mary's Magnificat, which I have made my own since the night I was baptized in the Spirit. After my experience in the chapel I returned to my room, too excited to sleep. I opened the Bible at random and my eyes fell upon her words in Luke 1. When I prayed in tongues the first time, I knew I was singing her words again. It is Mary, my Mother and Queen who has kept me faithful to the grace of God over all these years.

With her and in her I want to proclaim: "My soul magnifies the Lord and my spirit exalts in God my Savior. For He has looked upon his servant in her nothingness. Henceforth all generations will call me blessed. God who is mighty has done great things for me and holy is His name!"

Bio–
Patti Mansfield is a wife, mother, grandmother, speaker, writer, and teacher. She was baptized in the Holy Spirit in 1967 at the famous Duquesne Weekend, which marked the beginning of the Charismatic Renewal in the Catholic Church, and has traveled the world witnessing to the New Pentecost. Patti has authored several books, including *Proclaim the Joy of the Gospel: Spirit-filled Evangelizers* and *Everyday Holiness: Bringing the Holy Spirit Home* (both by Amor Deus Publishing) and has over fifty teaching CDs. Patti and her husband, Al, received the Papal Medal, Pro Ecclesia et Pontifice, for outstanding service to the Catholic Church. Patti spoke before 400,000 people in St. Peter's Square when she was chosen to thank the Holy Father, Pope Benedict XVI, in 2006 on behalf of ecclesial movements and new communities. She was acknowledged by name by Pope Francis in June, 2014, as being "one of the first to experience the Spirit in an intense way." Patti is married to Al Mansfield and they have four adult children, seven grandchildren on earth, and one in heaven.

Sr. Briege McKenna, O.S.C.

I would like to begin my testimony with a prayer.

"Lord, I thank You and I praise You with my sisters and brothers. I thank You that You have heard my cry. I thank You, Lord, that You have invited each one of us to follow You, to allow You to take possession of our lives, of our marriages, of our homes, of our children. Send Your Holy Spirit upon me. Help me to only share what will magnify You, Jesus, with Mary. Help me, Lord, that what I speak to my sisters and brothers will help them to see that You do not ask us to do great things. You just ask us to say 'yes.' And Mary, intercede for all of us that we may, like you, be open to whatever Jesus' plan, whatever the Father's plan, is for each of us. Amen."

As I went to adoration this morning, I received a passage from Scripture. It is the passage where Jesus said,

"I am the vine, you are the branches; he who abides in Me and I in him, he bears much fruit, for apart from Me you can do nothing. If anyone does not abide in Me, he is thrown away as a branch and dries up; and they gather them, and cast them into the fire and they are burned. If you abide in Me, and My words abide in you, ask whatever you wish, and it will be done for you. My Father is glorified by this, that you bear much fruit, and so prove to be My disciples. Just as the Father has loved Me, I have also loved you; abide in My love. If you keep My commandments, you will abide in My love; just as I have kept My Father's commandments and abide in His love. These things I have spoken to you so that My joy may be in you, and that your joy may be made full." (John 15: 5–11)

As you look at this tree with all its branches, that is Magnificat. The vine is Jesus, and the branches are Magnificat chapters, with each individual woman a small part of each branch. As the branches are nurtured by the vine, extraordinary things happen. Jesus said that if we are grafted onto Him, or connected to Him, we will "bear much fruit."

If we are connected to Jesus, He can do great marvels. God has worked great marvels in my life. As I look back on what the Lord has done through me, I can say, "For a human it is impossible, but with God all things are possible."

My mother died when I was a child, on Christmas Day. In one way, death seems very tragic, and it was very tragic because my father was left with a young family. I was only thirteen. I felt really desperate, being the only girl in our family, and I remember crying and thinking, "What am I going to do?" That Christmas night the Lord spoke to me. I heard a voice: "Briege, don't worry. I will take care of you."

So began my journey. I never thought about becoming a nun before that night. That was the furthest thing from my mind. I had beautiful long hair and the only thing I knew about nuns was that they had to have all of their hair cut off. But after I heard that message, I woke up saying, "I am going to be a sister. I am going to be a nun." I told my first cousin, and she said, "Oh that is just because you are sad and your mother is dead."

I lived with my grandmother for some time, but every day, like a little plant, the desire to become a nun continued to grow. At that time, it was not hard for families to accept religious vocations among young people. I lived in a faith-filled culture where everybody went to Mass and everybody made retreats, so I did not have any opposition. I pray for the young people of today because our culture is an obstacle to vocations.

When I was about fourteen, I decided that it was time for me to enter the convent. I could not get it out of my mind, so I went to the Poor Clare's. I wanted to go right to the top, not to any "second in command." I wanted the highest authority, so I asked to see Mother General. I was brought before this "big" nun. What a sight I was with my long ponytail and wearing my school uniform.

She asked, "What do you want, child?"

"I want to be a nun," I said.

"Hmm, how old are you?"

"Fourteen and a bit."

"Oh, come back later," she said.

So two weeks later I went back. It seemed to me long enough for her to make up her mind.

She said, "I meant later."

So I went back three weeks later, and I kept at her. She took me in when I was a little bit over fourteen and a half. I became an aspirant then and started my journey. I loved it. Nothing they asked me to do bothered me.

At fifteen and a half, I was given away at the altar by my father. I was dressed as a bride and presented to the bishop, who represented the Church. Everything was going fine. I made my first vows when I was sixteen.

Now I explain about my experience in this way: Did I know I took a vow of poverty, chastity and obedience? Did I know what I was doing? I definitely did not. For one thing, I had never been in love. I had no crisis to go through. And obedience? I had only been to school, and it was a way of life. Now over fifty years later, I can tell you that I do know what it means.

At seventeen, I had to have my appendix removed, and it was after this surgery that my feet and hands began to bother me. Some thought it must be a symptom of unhappiness because they could not see anything wrong with me. I kept getting worse, and finally I was diagnosed with crippling rheumatoid arthritis. My feet and hands were becoming deformed. I spent a year in and out of the hospital with casts on my feet. Eventually, the doctor told me that there was nothing they could do with the exception of trying to ease the pain.

I had made my first vows in 1962 at the age of sixteen before I became ill. If I had been diagnosed with a crippling disease then, I would not have been professed in the Order. I believe that is why God orchestrated my entering the convent while I was still very young.

After my final vows, I volunteered to go to America. At that time, Florida was a mission territory, and I was going to the missions. I came to Florida thinking, "This is going to be the answer to my prayers." Everybody told me that Florida's climate was beautiful and that it would be a great place for my health. So I came to Florida all dressed up in black, completely covered in heavy serge, a big petticoat, and all the trimmings of a nun. I had a priest tell me, "All the nuns are gift-wrapped for Jesus." Times have really changed since then. When the mother general sent me from Ireland, I came with five shillings, which was probably worth about five dollars or so, and I was told to bring the change home to the mother superior. Imagine that.

After I arrived I went to college, taught little ones, and was a cook for the nuns. I had never cooked in my life. Those poor nuns had to eat what I made. All the while, my arthritis got worse in the humid Florida climate. But I was happy. I loved people and I never had any doubt about my vocation. In all these fifty-plus years, I know I am where God wants me to be. But did I know the Lord? That is a different story.

Coming to America was all so new for me. I cried for two weeks, day and night, and thought, "I will never get used to this country." The first day I taught school, a little boy with a Cuban accent started shrieking and crying. The mother came and said, "Oh Sister, he does not want to come to school anymore because he says the new nun speaks Japanese." I had a terrible time. I called one poor little boy "Josie" for a week, when his name was really José. He cried continuously. I told another little boy he had to wear a jumper to school.

"I'm not going to wear a jumper," he kept telling me.

In Ireland, a jumper is a sweater. I finally discovered that in America a jumper is a dress.

The arthritis progressed to a point where medical intervention was the only thing that helped. After a year, I was on about thirty pills a day and taking a lot of cortisone. I struggled with my memory. I was frustrated. Even with rheumatoid arthritis I still looked healthy. People looked at me, expecting me to be full of energy, and yet I was in such pain. Then I got gout, which gave me acid sores on my elbows. I was in a pretty miserable state, not to mention my big moon face from the cortisone.

Then something happened. I was twenty-three years old and young mothers started coming to me with their children saying, "Sister Delphina, would you pray for me?" That was my name at the time. They would tell me all about their marriage problems.

Of course, I always said, "I will pray for you." I got up early in the mornings in order to get all my prayers in so that I could be free to do other things throughout the rest of the day. I was always looking at my watch, only to find out I had ten more minutes in my hour of prayer. I said my prayers and did everything that legitimately made me a good nun.

Think about it: if after you got married you said to your husband, "Listen, I am giving you one hour a day and that is it," how long would your marriage last?

That was the way I was treating Jesus.

Then one day when I was sitting in front of the Blessed Sacrament, I realized that many priests and sisters were leaving their religious life. There was a crisis coming. They were professed, they had given their lives to Jesus and the Church, but now they were changing their minds?

I was astounded. I began to question and doubt. I remember one day sitting in front of the Blessed Sacrament and saying, "I wonder what will happen to me?" It was as if the Lord opened a passage of Scripture for me. It was where Jesus had called the Pharisees and Sadducees "whitewashed sepulchers" (Mt. 23:27) because they were keeping their man-made laws and performing all their rituals for everyone to see. They did everything right. They looked good.

I realized that I was also going through a crisis. My crisis was not about leaving the convent; mine was a crisis of faith. I had never gone through it as a teenager. I never doubted Him. If Mother Superior said to me, "Stand on your head," I would have stood on my head. I always went to Mass. I never questioned anything. But I also never asked myself, "What do you believe?"

Suddenly, at the age of twenty-three, I asked myself, "Do I really believe in Jesus?" I was not sure. Would I die for Him? At that time, I doubted it. I was even ashamed to pray out loud. I met people and blessed them. This seemed to really impress people. "Oh, look at this lovely young nun," they said, "You must love Jesus a lot to give up all you give up."

I looked at them and thought, *I do not love Him that much.* They were all excited, but I was not that excited. *I must be missing something,* I thought. *Wouldn't I be a fool to live a lukewarm life, to live a life that I was not convinced of?* And I remember thinking, *I gave my life to Jesus. There must be more, but what is it?*

One day, Mother Superior asked, "Would you like to go to a prayer meeting?"

I answered, "I don't know. It sounds very Protestant to me. I am from Northern Ireland, and we do not go to prayer meetings. So, you will have to excuse me." She said, "Well, I am going to go see what it is like." She was gone four and a half hours. How could anyone pray for four and a half hours? She came home and told me all about it.

I thought, *Oh no, I would not go to anything like that.*

Then a good friend, a Franciscan sister, called me up and said, "Briege, there is going to be a prayer meeting for sisters. Why don't you come?"

I thought, *Sisters? That would be very good.*

It was the most inhibited group of nuns I had ever seen. These nuns had all kinds of degrees—theology, you name it—and many were lecturers at colleges. They sat there with their arms folded. We all sat there, afraid of each other.

I soon received a second invitation to a Mexican prayer meeting; so I went. I could not understand them, but I knew they loved the Lord. They were singing and praising God and talking to Him. *Now, they have something,* I thought. *Either I need it, or I have it and I am not using it.*

I attended this little prayer meeting every Monday night because this nun kept pestering me, and I did not want to say no to her. She was an old saint in her late seventies, and she would call me up to say, "Come on, Sister Delphina, you will love this prayer meeting."

Every Monday night I went there. I would gaze at a big picture of the Sacred Heart and say, "You know Jesus I love You, but I can't pray here. But I am here. I could be watching television, but instead I am here wasting my time."

It was during this time that the doctors told me, "Within a couple of months, you are going to be in a wheelchair." There was not much they could do for a young person with crippling rheumatoid arthritis. But still, I attended this prayer meeting, all the while thinking, "It is not my way of praying, but I am here."

I am sure Jesus was looking at me and asking, "What is your way of praying?" And He was right. These people were praising Jesus, and I was the one who was supposed to have given my life to Him. Instead, I was confused and felt something was lacking in my prayer life.

After about two months of attending, my friend the nun said, "There is going to be a retreat in Miami and you are going. It is a charismatic retreat."

What is that? I thought. I had no idea what I would be attending, but my superior and I went. I kept thinking, *I hope this retreat is worth this long journey.*

We traveled from Tampa to Miami, and it turned out to be a beautiful retreat center. On one of the doors, there was a big sign posted that read: "Gifts of the Spirit."

I thought to myself, *I need them all because I have lots of first-graders now.* I went into the room, where a lady was there ready to pray for me. "And what would you like me to pray for?" she asked.

I told her I wanted peace, some courage and patience, and a whole list of other things.

She sat down and asked, "Would you like to pray in tongues?"

"No, English is fine," I said.

She began to pray for me, and what happened next baffled me. I got mad. I got so mad that I started to laugh.

Her reaction was equally surprising. "Sister, go and sit in the corner."

She then prayed over Mother Superior. She was not getting anywhere with her either, and proceeded to ask us, "Is there anything between you and God?"

I believe this lady gave up on us. She could not seem to help either of us, despite the fact that we were both nuns.

When we returned home after the retreat, I thought that the charismatic form of prayer was not for me. However, the Lord kept tugging at my heart, and I am glad that He did. Even though I felt this way about charismatic prayer, I kept attending the little prayer meeting every Monday night.

Finally in December of 1970, I went to a retreat in Orlando. During this retreat, Father Ed O'Connor gave a beautiful talk which made a lot of sense to me.

"You are all Catholics here," he said, "And you are all talking about how wonderful the sacraments are, and they are wonderful. So why are you so powerless?" He continued, "If you had a birthday gift and you never opened it because you got totally overwhelmed with the wrappings, what good would the gift be to you? What we all need to do is pray that the Holy Spirit will come upon us, that He will give us an understanding of all His gifts, and that we will be open to receive the Holy Spirit and all His gifts. We need to pray to the Holy Spirit."

When he said this, I realized this was exactly what I needed, but I was afraid. I was worried about my vocation and the future. I was not full of zeal. I was not what I should be for the Lord.

When Father said this, I thought, "If only he would pray with me."

Then a voice within me said, "No Briege, seek Me."

Here I was going through this terrible disease that was about to completely cripple me, but I was not thinking about the physical sickness. By this time, I had such a hunger, as though my soul was thirsting for God. I knew then, without a doubt, that if I was going to be a cripple, I could be a cripple and a saint. I knew that if I did not experience or find this relationship with Jesus, I would never last as a nun, or if I did, I would be a phony.

I closed my eyes and pleaded, "Jesus, please come."

A voice said, "Seek Me."

I had no idea what would happen, but never did it occur to me that what would happen would be miraculous. I said, "Please Jesus, help me."

At that moment, I felt a hand touch my head. This power went through my body. Suddenly, my whole body received strength and I was healed of the rheumatoid arthritis. But that was not the greatest thing that happened. It was then that my eyes were opened with the ability to really see Jesus for who He is. I jumped up shouting, "Oh Jesus, I love you!" I began singing and praising the Lord.

This poor man beside me said, "Are you all right, Sister?"

That day I met Jesus. I met the living Jesus. I remember having an overwhelming sense like Thomas and proclaimed, "Jesus, you are really a living person. You are really here. You are alive."

Three things happened to me that day. One, I fell in love with a person. I realized my commitment was to a person, Jesus. The second was I fell in love with the Church. I realized the Church is the Bride of Christ. I would never, with the grace of God, leave or turn away from the Church. It was my home. And the third was that I discovered that my vocation was not mine. Jesus revealed to me that my vocation was not my gift to Him, but His gift to me.

I had received the graces from the three vows I took, even though I did not understand them at the time. When you face the world, the world confuses you. The vows were not given to bind me. I did not take the vows of poverty, chastity, and obedience to inhibit or bind me; I took them to liberate me. Their graces were to liberate me, to leave me totally free to serve Jesus. When I saw the vows in that light, it changed everything. My prayer life, the Eucharist, and everything else changed. Now I love to pray. Do I get distracted? Of course, we all get distracted, but I could sit in front of Jesus all day.

People often ask me, "What do you say to Him?"

My answer is: "You do not have to say anything to a person when you love them." I often ask those who are married the same question: "Do you have to talk to your husband all the time?" Of course, the answer is no. You can just be with your husband without talking. You can enjoy his company. The same holds true with Jesus. You do not have to talk to Him; you just have to be with Him. He knows what is in your heart.

At this point everything in my religious life changed. In the Gospel of John, Jesus says, "You have to be born again" (John 3:7). I was reborn in the Spirit. My whole life with Jesus had led me to that very moment. I learned that the Baptism in the Holy Spirit is a powerful experience that changes lives. It is truly powerful. After you have received it, you will never be the same. Some people think you have to jump up and down, and do all sorts of strange things. But no, not at all.

Afterwards I went back to see my doctor. He cried. He said he would love to take the credit for my healing, but he had nothing to do with it.

Little did I know what the Lord planned for me or what lay ahead. At that time, I was a happy first-grade teacher, and I taught my little students to pray powerfully. I soon found myself involved in a prison ministry and doing many different things for Jesus.

Everything was going wonderfully until one night on the eve of Pentecost.

In the silence of my chapel in Tampa, Jesus spoke to me. "Briege, you have My gift of healing. Go and use it."

"I don't want any gift of healing Jesus," I said. "Please keep it to Yourself." After all, I was happy here, and I was already doing many things for Jesus: I was working in the prison; I had a youth prayer group; I was teaching, and I was cooking. I told Him, "Jesus, You should be really happy with me. I am doing a lot for You."

Unbelievably I said that to the Lord; that was my answer. I finally realized the error in my thoughts. This was pride on my part. It was a terrible way to think. Who did I think I was? I knew there was absolutely no way I would tell my sisters what had happened to me that evening in the chapel. They would have me committed to a psychiatric hospital for hearing voices.

Sometime later I attended a prayer meeting in California, where a gaunt, holy-looking man turned to me and said, "I have never spoken to a Roman Catholic nun, but you have the gift of healing. Jesus spoke to you in your chapel. When are you going to use it?"

I looked at him and thought, *He is a Protestant and I am a Catholic. How would he know?* Then I realized who needed the healing. "Oh, I could never accept that," I said. "I belong to a very strict order. My mother general and the bishop and"—I listed everyone but the pope—"would never allow me to be a healer."

"I am not one bit interested in that," he said. "Tell me what happened to you in your chapel."

Is he a mind reader? I wondered. Then I went on to tell him what had transpired that evening.

He looked at me with his elderly gray eyes and said, "God will never force you. He has revealed His will."

I never saw that man again.

I am very stubborn, and I resisted the idea. I did not want the gift of healing.

I was soon sent away to college, where I attended classes with many long-haired hippies. I did not know if they believed in God or not. However, they did say strange things to me such as, "There is something about your hands" and "You have a gift."

When I returned home to Florida, I made a deal with Jesus. "Look, Jesus," I said. "I am telling nobody about this gift of healing, but if You want to, You do the telling and I will do the praying."

God is so patient with us, and He can do the impossible. Such was the case with me. One day I visited the Franciscan Retreat Center to give a talk. I planned to stand up and give my talk without mentioning anything about healing.

During my talk, a woman stood up and said, "Excuse me. Excuse me."
Who is this rude woman interrupting my talk? I thought.

"You have the gift of healing," she said. "You know you have it, but you are more interested in what people think about you than about doing God's will."

I was amazed. Thoughts ran through my mind. *Who is she? It's hard to believe that she knows. I have never seen this woman before in my life.* "Who are you?" I asked.

"Sister, I came here tonight looking for the young Irish nun with the gift of healing."

"Did the Holy Spirit tell you I am Irish?" I asked.

What she said next astounded me. "I am a freelance writer from Quebec, Canada. Two weeks ago I saw your picture on a wall. The Lord revealed to me that you live in Florida and that I was to go there."

"How did you know it was me?"

"I was there when you were healed," she answered.

She had been at that retreat and witnessed my song and praise to Jesus. This freelance writer wanted to write an article in a magazine about my gift of healing, and I panicked. I had to go to my mother superior and I hoped she would say "no."

When I arrived home, I told her the entire story. She also happened to be the principal of the school where I taught. "Have nothing to do with this," she said. "You will ruin the reputation of the school." I was delighted with her answer. It was not my responsibility now. If anyone said anything to me, I could say, "Oh no, my mother superior will not give me permission."

This is an example of using obedience to suit yourself. Forget about God, whether He agrees or not.

About two weeks later, I was in the convent and full of delight. I was going to live my life and forget all about this healing stuff. I kept thinking, "It would be terrible to be called a 'faith healer' or get some other name tagged onto me."

Then one night a priest called. "Briege," he said. "I have a small group of ladies, and I would like you to give them a little talk on prayer. Would you?" He told me about ten ladies would be attending.

Who's afraid to talk to ten ladies? "Okay, Father," I told him. "I will talk to your ladies."

When I arrived, there were at least sixty ladies from the women's guild. I began my talk about prayer. I definitely planned on saying nothing about healing. Mother Superior had said "no," and I had said "no."

I am not sure what I said or how my talk about prayer (no mention of healing) sounded, but in the middle of my talk a woman stood up, walked out, and slammed the door.

I thought, "What is wrong with her?"

Two days later the parish priest phoned me. "There is a crazy woman in my parish. She called me at four o'clock the other morning and told me you were in her room. She has called several times. Please go see her, Sister Briege, and get her off my back."

I went to see the woman.

"Sister," she said when I arrived. "I heard you speak the other day. I left the Catholic Church fifteen years ago. My husband is a devout Baptist and we have one child. I lost four children at birth. I have had a tumor on the brain, and I live with migraine headaches. I have a terrible life. My poor husband is suffering with me and so is my little girl. I decided I would take my life."

She planned to commit suicide while her husband was away on a business trip, and when her child was at her sister's. She had it all planned. But her child came home from Catholic school with a notice that read Briege McKenna (no mention of "Sister") was speaking—not in a church, but in the social hall. She wondered if Briege was a man or a woman.

So, the woman decided at the last minute to attend. She came to the social hall and sat in the back row. "You made me so mad," she said, "because you are very young. You talked about prayer, and it looked like you had lipstick on. You really could not be a nun."

During my talk, she had all these things on her mind in order to reject me. She was so bothered that she got up and left. The next night she had prepared to commit suicide. She placed a letter in her child's bag and sent her off to her sister's.

She went on to tell me, "Sister, you came into my room and said, 'Beverly, why do you not believe in Jesus? Have you lost hope in Jesus?' I told you to get out. But walls did not bother you. Every direction I turned, you were there. I could not get rid of you. So, I called the parish priest at four o'clock in the morning."

I was petrified. Oh, dear Jesus, I prayed silently, "Don't have me roaming homes at night. I will do whatever You want." "Beverly," I said aloud. "I will say a prayer with you."

I was scared, but I put my hand out, and an amazing thing happened. The moment I touched her, she was filled with hope. "Do you think it is possible, Sister Briege, that I could get healed?" she asked.

I never realized that one of the greatest gifts needed today is hope. What is the opposite of hope? Despair. Two days later, I came down with the flu. When she heard I had the flu, she phoned me. "Don't worry," she said. "Put your trust in Jesus."

This woman was completely transformed. And that was just the beginning. Mother Superior or no Mother Superior, I realized that all Jesus wanted from me was my "yes." I said, "yes" that day.

During the first year in this ministry, I saw cancer, leukemia, and many other diseases healed. I was the biggest skeptic. Thanks be to God, the Holy Spirit does not depend on me. Sometimes people think that if you are close to the Lord or aiming to be close to the Lord, you will be different from everyone else. They are afraid to be friends with you because they think you are too holy. They think you are going to lose your sense of humor. Instead, Jesus embellishes your natural gifts. He makes you happier. He gives you more joy.

In that first year, some people said to me, "I don't really believe in you."

"You don't have to believe in me," I always answered. "I am not in the Bible. But do you believe in Jesus?"

A year later the Lord led me into a ministry for priests. He gave me a five-hour vision of the ordination of the priesthood. I wept. He revealed to me that a great crisis was going to come to the priesthood and a great shortage of vocations.

"Oh, this is terrible," I remember thinking when I recalled the things the Lord had showed me that would take place. The Lord placed a love in my heart for the priesthood. "Oh, my God," I cried. "I can't believe these things would happen to a priest or a bishop."

This was at the end of 1971 or the beginning of 1972. I was overwhelmed by it all. I went to my bishop and told him about the vision. Thankfully, he seemed open to what I was saying.

He got up and walked over to the window to look out. Then he turned around and said, "I see on the horizon a great crisis, but God always prepares His people. He raises up instruments in His church, men and women, to counteract or to stand up at the time of crisis, to be able to hold before the Lord these crises and to plead. I believe a time will come when God will use you in the Church."

Around the same time I had received this vision, I met Vinson Synan, a great Pentecostal and a man of the gospel. Noticing that I was dressed as a nun, he sat down next to me and began to tell me about himself.

I thought, "This is really a man of God." He prayed with me and shared a beautiful prophecy: "Sister, a day will come—I see mitered men and clergymen—when God will use you to encourage them and call them to holiness."

I still had a stubborn heart, as my response revealed. "Well, that's for the birds. I am scared stiff even to talk to priests. It will never happen."

After the prophetic words of both my bishop and Vinson Synan, I shared my experience with dear Father Harold Cohen who I had met at a prayer meeting. I also told him how I had started a ministry of praying for priests with my students.

There was a priest who was going through a crisis. I remember saying to him, "Father, I will have my first-graders pray for you."

I did not tell the children what was wrong. I just told them that Father was not well, which was true. So they prayed for a man they did not even know. "Can we draw pictures and send letters to Father?" they asked.

I had his address, so I allowed them to do this.

One student drew Father with his leg up and plaster on his arm. They wrote letters to him. Three months later, this same priest came to my classroom with a big bag of candy to visit the little ones who had been praying for him. He read me one of the letters that had transformed his priestly life.

The letter was from a six-year-old, who told him that Father Cohen had come to their classroom and explained that priests are very special, that Jesus really needed them, and that they could make Jesus come down on earth like nobody else.

It was a beautifully inspired letter from this little child. When Father had read this letter, his whole priesthood was renewed. It was the prayers of all the children behind the letter that were successful.

From my classroom, a ministry to priests spread. One day Father Cohen called and said, "The Bishop has asked me to give a retreat in Minnesota, and I would like you to come along and give the retreat with me."

"Father," I said. "You are a Jesuit, and I am a first-grade teacher. No, no, no. I am just a teacher; there is no way."

In Father Cohen's beautiful, convincing way he said, "Sister Briege, it will not do them any harm that you are a first-grade teacher. Do not worry about the priests. You do not need to know anything about theology. You only need to know Jesus. That is it."

I was scared. I hoped Mother Superior would say, "No, you can not get out of school."

Instead, she said, "That is wonderful. Take the week off."

Reluctantly, I went.

We arrived, and that first night Father Cohen became ill and was rushed off to the hospital. However, God taught me a lesson. In the Bible, there is an account of Peter, when he got out of the boat to follow Jesus (Mt. 14:22–33). Peter saw Jesus, and Jesus said, "Well, come on, Peter. Come."

All excited, Peter jumped out of the boat and headed toward Jesus. In my mind, I could just see the other disciples back in the boat. "Peter, what are you doing? Get back in the boat. You're going to drown."

Sometimes we discourage each other from taking the leap. We say, "Oh, you can't do that." However this time that was not the case. God bless those priests. They kept saying, "You can do it. The Lord is going to use you."

While it was unplanned I took a step of faith and gave the retreat to the priests in attendance. It was a powerful retreat. It launched a worldwide ministry to priests.

A short time later, when I was at Mother Angelica's monastery, the Lord showed me a vision of a priest. He told me I was going to meet him, that he was going to teach me much, and that we would travel the world together. I told my friend Marilyn Quirk, who was involved in the charismatic renewal, that I did not want to work with a priest. I was all right on my own.

Marilyn's words to me were, "Briege, you need somebody. You need protection. You should not be going out on your own. God wants you to work as a team."

When Marilyn met Father Kevin Scallon, she knew he was the priest God chose for me to work alongside. Father Kevin did not want to meet me, and I did not want to meet him, but we met. He, of course, has his own version of this story.

Today, Father Kevin and I travel the world. After forty years of doing so, I marvel at the work God has done in our lives and in the lives of others. We have been invited to give many retreats for bishops and priests. Often I feel nervous and empty. Then I think that maybe it is good to be empty. If we are always full, there would be no room for Jesus. Before these retreats, I go before the Blessed Sacrament and plead, "Lord, I do not have anything to say. Please help me." This prayer is so important. It keeps me totally dependent on the Lord.

Before this testimony, I prayed as well. I received a word from the Lord, and I believe it is a word for us all. It is the story of the wise virgins and the foolish virgins from Matthew 25:1–13.

In this parable, Jesus spoke about ten virgins. Five were wise and five were foolish. The five wise virgins had flasks of oil with their lamps. The five foolish ones did not take any oil with them, and their lamps went out.

The bridegroom was coming, and the virgins were to go out to meet him. The foolish virgins wanted some oil from the wise virgins, but the wise virgins explained they only had enough for what they needed. So the foolish virgins went off to buy more oil. While the foolish virgins were out seeking oil, the bridegroom came. The door was opened, and the bridegroom invited the wise virgins inside. The foolish ones were nowhere to be found. When they returned, the door had already shut. They asked to be let in, but the bridegroom said, "I do not know you."

One day not too long ago, I was thinking about this story, and the Lord said, "Now I will teach you what this means in your life and Mine."

At baptism, we receive a candle that symbolizes the light. The lamp is our souls. And all of us at baptism receive oil for our souls; it is poured into us. Our lamp is filled with oil. This is why we tell parents at baptism that they must nurture their children in the faith; they must help their children grow in their relationship with Jesus—to keep the oil in their lamps. Eventually, the time comes when we are all responsible to keep our lamp continuously filled with oil. That is why we have sacraments in our Church. Jesus said, "You are the light."

The wise virgins replenished the oil for their lamps continuously because it burns. I believe that oil is grace. It is receiving the sacraments. It is prayer. It is in reading the scriptures. It is the infilling of the Holy Spirit.

People today have tried everything to fill their lamps. We see it in the feminist movement, with women trying to fill their lamps with success, with power, with whatever they can find to try to fill their lamps. The soul really is the lamp, with a hunger and a desire, but nothing can fill it except God.

I believe God is calling us today to stop and think for a moment. If the Bridegroom came today, is your lamp full of oil? Do you take care to nurture the lamp? Do you replenish your oil? Or do you think other things can fill your lamp? If you put water in your car, it won't go. If you put water in one of those lamps, they won't burn.

I see the ministry of Magnificat as a tremendous dynamo of light around the world. You have discovered the oil. You have replenished your lamp, and your light is burning bright. This is why others are drawn to you. They see this light and they want it, but there is a price to be paid. We have to submit and surrender our lives to Jesus.

I will conclude with a prayer. If you have not given your life to Jesus, ask for the release of the Holy Spirit. Maybe you are saying to yourself, "I would just love to know Jesus." He wants you to know Him. If you feel your lamp is empty, that you are not what you should be, it only takes an open heart. He will flood it with His living oil.

Picture yourself standing in front of Jesus: Jesus, who loves you; Jesus, who died for you; Jesus, who said, "I have come that you may have life and have it in abundance."

He is looking at you and saying, "I love you. I don't need much from you. I just need your heart. I just need your 'yes,' and I will do the rest."

"Lord, Jesus, I adore You and I praise You. I pray for my sisters and brothers. Jesus, I invite You again into my soul. I invite You to take possession of my life. I ask You, Jesus, to forgive me for choosing other things and substituting them for the oil in my lamp, things of the world, things that do not satisfy. I pray today,

Jesus, that you fill me with Your Holy Spirit. Come, Jesus, and baptize me in Your own Spirit. Release in me the power of Your Holy Spirit. Give me, Lord, oil in this lamp. I pray for all of those who have committed their lives to you.

Sometimes, Lord, the light grows dim. We become lazy. We become satisfied. Lord, rekindle the fire in our hearts today. Fill our lamps again, Lord, with Your oil. Fill us again, Lord, with Your Holy Spirit. Give us again, Lord, an anointing of Your Holy Spirit. Take away from us any lukewarmness. Anoint us with the gift of prayer. Anoint us with the charism of Your own Holy Spirit. Jesus, take us and mold us, form us and shape us. Praise You, Jesus."

I have this beautiful image of Jesus with his arms spread out and a sense of Him looking at you, smiling and saying these words:

"My daughters, I called you here today to let you know the depth of My love for you. Many of you have walked with Me for a long time and I rejoice, but I have a greater work for you to do. In your midst today, I have placed sisters. Sisters whom I desire to touch and renew and to show My love in a new way. I call you, My daughters, to be that lamp, to let My light shine.

Do not be afraid. Do not worry about the past. Look at your children. Do not worry about them. I will hold them in the palm of My hand when you give them to Me. I will press them to My own heart, and I will love them into holiness and wholeness.

What I ask of you, My daughters and My sons, is your "yes," so you can continue to magnify Me. I call you to intercede for this world. I call you to intercede for your sisters who walk in darkness—who sit in the darkness of ignorance and blindness. I call you to intercede for My children. Many have lost their way, but you are the light that I have chosen.

I call you because I desire, in and through you, to be the light and the power in this nation. I call you to raise your hands in intercession. I call you. Do not be afraid to speak about Me. Do not be ashamed of My name. Too few people use My name to worship. Too few people witness to Me, the Lord of life. I call you as My sons and daughters. I call you to speak about Me. Put My name on your lips. Praise Me. Call others to praise Me."

I see this huge image of the *name Jesus*. It is as if the Lord is saying to us, "My name today, the name of Jesus, is being blasphemed and misused in many ways."

I have this beautiful image of Magnificat. I see it with candles and big, bright lights and the name of Jesus all lit up. From the name of Jesus, I see streams of water flowing into the world, and gardens growing.

I sense the Lord saying, "Just as my Mother not only had the name of Jesus on her lips, she had Me, Jesus, in her very body, in her womb, in her spirit. Take My name. Say it often in love. Use My name to praise Me. I love you to say it. Every time you say it, the power of My name will liberate you and set you free from those things that harass you. When you are confronted with any harassments and worries and anxieties, whisper My name and I will pour My Spirit upon you."

Praise You, Jesus. Praise You, Jesus.

Bio–

Sr. Briege McKenna, O.S.C. was born in County Armagh, Ireland. She has an international ministry of healing and evangelization that has taken her to many countries of the world. Since 1985, she has been ministering to bishops and priests in collaboration with Fr. Kevin Scallon, C.M. Sister is the author of two books, *Miracles Do Happen*, where she tells the story of her encounter with the healing power of God, and *The Power of the Sacraments*, where she explains how nothing can substitute for the power of the sacraments. For over forty years, since she was healed of crippling arthritis, Sr. Briege has ministered hope and healing to countless people. She is the 1988 recipient of the Poverello Award from the Franciscan University, and the 2009 recipient of the Award for Outstanding Catholic Leadership from the Catholic Leadership Institute.

Rosalind Moss

Shalom! Sometimes people ask, "What is a nice Jewish girl like you doing in a place like this?" The fact is, the Church *is* Jewish. Jesus, Mary, Joseph, all the apostles, and the first Christians were all Jewish. So the question is not, "What is a nice Jewish girl like you doing in a place like this?" The question is, "What are *you* doing in a nice *Jewish* place like this?" But I know what you are doing here.

I wear a cross with the Star of David and could write a book about what happens as I go through life wearing this cross. It was a gift from a dear family and is very special to me. A while ago I was in a supermarket and wasn't looking where I was going. The fellow who crashed into my basket wasn't looking either. Both of us looked up. If you look at me, you would not be certain that I am Jewish, but if you looked at *him*, you knew.

He saw the cross and Star of David and said, "Don't you have a couple of conflicting things going on?"

I responded to him as I do with every Jewish person who asks: "I am Jewish and I am Catholic because I believe that Jesus Christ is the Jewish Messiah—God, in fact—Who came to earth, died for our sins, and rose from the dead to give us life. He established His Church, the Catholic Church, and I am in it. And so the most Jewish thing a person can do is to be Catholic."

Apparently, this gentleman had not heard such a thing before. Although he was Jewish, he was a young man who had lost his faith. I pray our conversation was the beginning of his coming to know the very reason for his existence through the God of Abraham, Isaac, and Jacob who became Man for us.

Once, when I attended a Magnificat meal, one of the organizers said, "Ros, we've got a tent, a very Jewish tent."

I quickly responded, "I love tents!"

For forty years in the wilderness we Jews lived in tents. Someone wrote, "Everywhere Abraham traveled, he pitched his tent and built an altar. When it came time to leave, he packed up the tent but the altar remained. The tent told people that Abraham was not a citizen of Earth, but a pilgrim. The altar told everyone that he was a citizen of Heaven.

Who knew, growing up in my Jewish home, that this, the Catholic Church, would be the most Jewish place on Earth and the fulfillment of all that God promised to Abraham through Isaac and Jacob. *Who knew?* My mother, my father, my grandparents ... everyone was Jewish. As conservative Jews, we followed all the traditions of Judaism: Shabbos candles, Schule, the celebration of every major feast, and the knowledge that we were God's people, that nothing could change that.

Every Passover we sat down to the Passover table with our extended family and hoped for Messiah's coming. We had a chair for Elijah, who would precede the Messiah. Everything was ready for the Passover Seder, but we would not eat for a couple of hours yet. That did not bother us even as children. We loved it, because it told us *who we were.* We would recount the entire story of God's deliverance of our people from Egypt. Each year it was someone's turn to go to the door—left ajar for Messiah—to see if Elijah or the Messiah (who, we hoped, would not be far behind) had come.

When I was eleven, my brother, David, two years older than I, had his Bar Mitzvah (that is, he became a "son of the Law"). That year it was my turn to go to the door. I was so nervous. What if the Messiah was out there—on the twelfth floor of our apartment building in Brooklyn? What would I do? I was shaking from fright as I approached the door and hallway which, alas, was empty. And so, somewhat relieved though disappointed, I turned back to the waiting family and announced that the Messiah hadn't come.

We continued with the Seder, knowing that when Messiah finally came, He would gather the Jewish people from the four corners of the Earth and put us back in Jerusalem, where we belong. He would set up His kingdom, a literal kingdom in which He would reign, and there would be peace. Life would make sense when Messiah came. We would sing as we left the Passover table, "Next year in Jerusalem," so hopeful that it was just where we were going to be when Messiah comes.

I remember going to bed as that little eleven-year-old thinking, *Well, He didn't come this year, so He'll come next year. Next year we will be in Jerusalem.* And yet, I wondered at the same time, *Is there really a Messiah? Is He really going to come?* But I believed. It was the only hope the world had.

As we (David, my sister, Susan, and I) grew into our teens, David began searching for *truth* in life, to see if there was such a thing as truth, and to know if one could find it. He wanted to know if you could really know that God exists. We never claimed that God did *not* exist, but how do you know that He does exist? Is it just by faith? Can you *know?* Can you find truth?

David, yet in his teens, came to the conclusion there was no God. He declared himself an atheist.

Oy veh! I thought, *an atheist!*

"David," I exclaimed, "do you know what you would have to know to know there is no God? How could anyone *know* that?" But inwardly I wondered: If it were possible to know, could knowing make a difference in one's life?

David was married in his early twenties to a lovely woman who was brought up in a nominal Protestant home and who also had declared herself an agnostic, if not an atheist. They figured that when their children were old enough they would simply choose their own religion. However, when their oldest son began elementary school, he came home with questions that caused David to resume his search for truth, for answers to life, reading through more books than I might read in a lifetime.

David's wife chose instead to visit various churches near their home in upstate New York. Through the grace of God and the love of the people at a small Baptist church, she gave her life to Christ. She came home, it seemed to David, an instant fanatic.

All of this was unknown to me at the time, until David phoned one night to tell me that his wife had given her life to Christ. Until he came to his own conclusion, their children would be raised to believe in Christ at that Baptist church. When David came to his truth, he would deal with it then. Until then, the children would have something to follow.

I loved David with all my heart; there was nothing he could do that I would not support him in. But now, for the first time, I did not understand my brother, nor could I muster any support for what, to me, was *unthinkable*. I hung up the phone and thought, *How could you love your children and let them be raised to believe in a man, a prophet, teacher, or whoever Christ is. We are Jews, and if there is a God, we have a direct connection.*

During my visit that summer, David's wife invited me to accompany them to church Sunday morning. I wanted to go. I wanted to see and hear what David was allowing his children to believe. I could hardly fathom it. I sat through that Baptist service of about a hundred people and listened to the choir, which was singing a hymn I had never heard before: "Grace Greater Than All Your Sin."

For some unknown and utterly unexpected reason, those words penetrated straight through my heart. I sat there trying to breathe and reason silently: Grace that is greater than all my sin. How can anything be greater than my sin? And then the thought, *What sin?* Sin had nothing to do with me, so I thought. I wasn't sure myself at that point that God existed. Who would I sin against … mankind?

I was hit that day with a sin that was mine and with a love that was not. I knew for the first time in my life that there was not simply an *amount* of love that existed in this world, but a kind of love that was foreign to my life. I tried to hold back the tears that welled up inside me, but I could not. My sister-in-law, smiling from ear to ear, began telling me about Christ.

"Get away from me with those words!" I quickly interrupted. "I know what I am feeling. Don't tell me Christ is the reason for it." I would not listen.

Months later, preparing to move to California, I visited David and his family again. David, still searching, had come across an article that was about to change the course of our lives. The article stated that there was such a thing as Jewish people, alive on the face of the Earth, who believed that Jesus Christ (a name I had never pronounced and that was not allowed in our home) was the Jewish Messiah the rest of us were waiting for. I was thirty-two years old and had never heard such a thing.

"David," I said, still in shock, "I don't care who believes what, in this world. Everyone can do his or her own thing. But Jewish people believe this? Jewish people believe that the only hope the world has, the Messiah, came already—two thousand years ago? He was here on Earth already, and nobody knows He came? He didn't make an impact? We are not back in Jerusalem? There is no peace. And then He left? That's insane!"

"Ros," David responded, "I didn't say it was true. That is what the article said."

The article also reported that these Jews who believed this were out in California and were called by all sorts of names: Hebrew Christians, Messianic Jews, Jews for Jesus.

There are all kinds of troubled people in the world, I thought. *Jews are just as entitled to be as troubled as everyone else. You cannot be Jewish and believe in Jesus, but you could be Jewish and have problems. So, if there are Jews who are troubled, that has nothing to do with me, and nothing to do with truth.*

I moved to California (in no relation to that article). A few months later, while walking through an arts and crafts festival on a Sunday afternoon in Westwood near UCLA, I saw, off in the distance, a young, hippy-looking fellow in his twenties. He had a beard, wore a T-shirt that read, "Jews for Jesus," and was handing out flyers.

I could hardly believe my eyes and that these people actually existed. As I approached him, the young man explained that he and his wife were Jewish and they both believed Jesus Christ was the Jewish Messiah—but not the Messiah only. He was God come to Earth!

If I had thought they were troubled before, I now knew they were troubled. A man cannot be God. Every Jew knows that. Every Jew knows that you cannot look on God and live.

The young man gave me a little flyer that read: "If being born hasn't given you much satisfaction, try being born again." Next to those words was a sketch of a little happy face.

I tried desperately not to show it, but that flyer shot a knife through my heart. I was brand-new in California and newly hired by an advertising company to open up a San Francisco branch office. I had been in business for fifteen years in New York and earned a great salary. I had a great social life. I lacked nothing this world could give. Nothing.

I had but one problem—which even my best friend did not know—a problem I remember having since I was about ten years of age. No matter how much I had—love, money, success—no matter how much I had of whatever the world could give, no one could tell me why mankind was on the Earth. Nothing and no one could ever fill the deep sense of emptiness, meaninglessness, and purposelessness I lived with my entire life.

And now a little flyer was telling me I could be born again? Go back into my mother's womb and come out again?

"Ros," they tried explaining, "God exists, and you can know that."

Come on, I thought, *how can anyone know that?*

"Not only can you know God exists," they said. "You can know Him personally."

"What are you talking about?" I came back at them, angered at their fantasy. "You believe what you believe so strongly that you forgot you believe it. You think you know it! You know God? You talk to Him? He answers you?"

Yes, they insisted. God created us for a relationship with Himself, that we could know Him.

I went home that night and remember thinking, *What if there really is a God? I thought there was, but what if I could know that? Could knowing make a difference in my life? But what if I could know Him personally?* Twilight Zone!

Just in case these troubled Jews were on to something, I followed them around for several months. I spoke with them and attended some of their meetings, all of which were deeply upsetting to me. They told me in every which way that Christ died for my sins, for their sins, and for the sins of the whole world. I spoke English, yet I could not make sense of those words: "Christ ... died ... for ... our ... sins."

I took every word to a dictionary. I found out that "Christ" is not His name, but rather the English translation of the word "Messiah." That blew me away a bit. Next: "died … for … my … sins." I looked up every word trying to understand that sentence, but to no avail.

The night that changed my life forever took place at a Hawaiian restaurant in Santa Monica with twelve of those Jews for Jesus. Twelve of them … and me. Twelve Evangelical Protestant 'Jews for Jesus' and me. I didn't know what an Evangelical Protestant was. I don't think I had ever heard those words before.

They started in on me. "Ros, Christ died for your sins, our sins, and the sins of the entire world."

"Would you please hold it right there?" I finally said. "You have been trying to tell me this for months. I have no way of understanding that language. I know the words, but I do not know what you're saying. For the sake of this discussion, let's say that what you believe happened: Christ died for my sins, your sins, and the sins of the world. My question is … why? Why did He do it? What was in His mind when He did that? What would be in a man's mind to go to a cross and die for the sins of the world?"

With that question, those twelve Jewish believers took me through the sacrificial system of the Old Testament, which I never knew through all my years in synagogue. What they told me in two and a half hours, I will tell you in short order here. I've got it down pat! It changed my life forever.

Responding to my question of "why?" they began: "God, Who exists, is holy. We are sinful."

I knew that, but I knew nothing else they told me that night.

"We come into this world separated from God because of original sin," they continued.

Judaism teaches about original sin, but I had no idea of the consequences it had on our lives. They explained that we come into the world separated from God through the sin of Adam and Eve. And if we leave this world in that state, we will be separated from God for all eternity, because the wages of sin is death.

I later learned they had quoted a verse straight from the New Testament (Romans 6:23). But those Jewish Christians knew better than to tell me they were quoting the New Testament. They knew I would have nothing to do with what I believed was a non-Kosher book. So they did not identify the Bible verses they quoted that night. But "the Word of God is living and active, sharper than any two-edged sword, piercing to the division of soul and spirit, of joints and marrow, and discerning the thoughts and intentions of the heart" (Heb. 4:12). And those verses shot right through me.

The wages of sin is death. I did not respond to their message aloud, but inwardly I thought, *The wages of sin? What is a wage? A wage is a salary.*

A wage is something you earn. You deserve it; you've worked for it; it is coming to you. What they were saying to me, therefore, was that if God gave us what we deserve, what we have earned, we would be dead.

They explained death to me. "Death is separation from life. If you stick a pin in a corpse, there is no response because death is an inability to respond to life. It is the same with spiritual life. Stick a spiritual pin in you, Ros, and there is no response because you are spiritually dead. The things of God are foolishness to the natural man." (1 Corinthians 2:14, another Bible verse they sneaked in).

They showed me from the Old Testament (which to me was the only Testament) how without the shedding of blood there can be no forgiveness or remission of sin. Blood had to be shed. I never knew blood had to be shed. We had a dried lamb shank on our Passover table. We killed no lamb. There was no sacrificial system or temple.

"He is a holy and just God," they continued, "Who must punish sin." But then they added, "He is also a loving God Who created us for a relationship with Himself."

During that life-changing night, those twelve Jewish Christians told me how God in His love—without compromising His holiness—provided the way for us to come back into a relationship with Him.

They took me through the Exodus, the story of the children of Israel: God parting the Red Sea and Moses leading them through the sea to the foot of Mount Sinai. Before that, in the tenth and final plaque, the Israelites had to take a lamb—a male lamb a year old, without spot or blemish. When the Angel of Death passed over Egypt that night, all the firstborn of man and beast would be killed—all except those Israelites who had the blood of the lamb sprinkled on the door posts and lintels of their houses. The lamb had been killed in the place of the firstborn.

Arriving at the foot of Mount Sinai, God had Moses set up an altar to which the Israelites would bring offerings of goats, lambs, whatever the sacrifice for sin required. If it was a lamb, such as the Passover lamb, it would be a male, a year old, without blemish or spot. In other words, a holy, perfect offering for a holy God. The individual would come to the altar and stand before the priest with that spotless lamb. He put his hand on the head of the lamb, an act that would be symbolic of the sin passing from the individual onto that little lamb. That lamb, who was innocent but who symbolically had taken upon itself the sin of the individual, was then slain. Then the blood of that lamb was shed on the altar as an offering to God in payment for that person's sin.

I listened to all they explained and again asked, "Why? Why would God do that? Why would God put an innocent animal to death for my sin? Put *me* to death!" It made no sense. But it began to sink in that sin is no light issue to God, and He would do that.

They explained further that the blood of goats, bulls, and lambs through fifteen hundred years of the Mosaic sacrificial system could never take away sin. Not only could those dead animals not remove or forgive sin, they had no power to change the heart or to perfect the worshiper. The individual would go home and sin over and over again, and then return to offer sacrifices over and over again.

Not the blood of one lamb or of millions of lambs throughout fifteen hundred years could take away sin, they explained. But *every* lamb and all of them together were a sign, a sign to point to the One who would one day come and take upon Himself not the sin of a single individual for a time, but the sin of every man, woman, and child who ever lived, for all time.

They then went to one verse in the New Testament, a verse I had never heard. It was when Jesus came into the Jordan and John the Baptist looked at Him and said, *"Behold, the Lamb of God, who takes away the sin of the world!"* (John 1:29)

With that one verse, my life was shattered on the spot. I started shaking. I couldn't speak. I couldn't stand up. I could not believe what I had heard. It was as if someone had pulled the curtain and exposed the stage for me. I knew it happened. I knew it was true. My hang-up all that time was that a *man could not be God.* I realized that night that I was right: *a man cannot be God.* But if God exists, if God is, God could become a man. God could do anything He wants to do.

I was shattered to the core. Even so, it took a few months more for me to work through fear and pride and whatever baggage I carried, and give my life to that incomparable Lamb. I did that in 1976. I remember the night I gave my life to Christ, asking Him to take my life. For me it was all or nothing at all. It was like jumping off a cliff. Either He was God and it would be okay, or He wasn't, in which case I didn't know what I would do. But I asked Him, if He was real and all this I had come to believe was true, to take my life and make of it what He wished, what He intended in creating me.

I had no sensible experience that night. It was an act of trust and a feeble attempt to give God, through Christ, my all. It is many years later now and I have but an inkling of how much I yet haven't given Him. But back then, in the sincerity of my fearful heart, it was my all.

I went home and told myself not to worry, that I would not rush God. I went to sleep that night feeling the same. But on waking the next morning,

I opened my eyes and, for the first time in my life, said, "Good morning, Lord." I knew He was God, and I knew I would never be alone again. The pain and emptiness of my heart were absolutely gone. On my way to work I looked at the hills, the trees, and the sky. The world was new, and I was a new creation in it. "Of course," I exclaimed aloud, "who *else* made all of this?"

I wanted a ladder tall enough to reach the moon to tell the world of such a Savior. I jumped into the Evangelical church to which those Jewish believers had introduced me. Yet, I waited a few weeks before calling my brother, David, who was still searching. I wanted to be sure it "took."

When I finally told David, he said, "You sound like an Evangelical."

"What's *that?*" I asked.

"Actually, Ros, you sound like a Fundamentalist."

"What's *that?*" I had never heard either of those terms before. I knew only that I was a Christian, a follower of the Christ, the Messiah.

Years later, when I began looking into the Catholic Church—after having tried to "save" Catholics for eighteen years—I was embarrassed that I had not done my homework and looked into the Catholic Church on my way into Christianity. Once I realized, however, that God did not establish thirty-thousand-plus denominations, but *one* Church, I did not feel so badly. I had met Jesus. I was a Christian. But I learned that I indeed *was* an Evangelical ... and pretty much a Fundamentalist, as well.

My first Bible study was taught by an ex-Catholic, who was taught by an ex-priest. That was another *Oy veh!* They taught me that the Catholic Church was a cult, a false religious system that was leading millions astray. I believed them. They supported their beliefs from their end, and for the next fourteen of my eighteen evangelical Christian years, I tried to save Catholics from what I believed was a false religious system.

One year after I gave my life to Christ, David, through the Baptist church his wife had been attending, gave *his* life to Christ. We rejoiced on the phone between New York and California for five hours. During that conversation, David said, "Ros, I believe Christ is God, and that the Bible is God's Word. But something is wrong."

He had read our Lord's high-priestly prayer in John 17, in which Jesus prayed that we would be one, as He and the Father were one. "How," David asked me, "can so many good and godly men, thousands of Protestant pastors—who study the Word of God with humility and sincerity, and with all the tools of biblical interpretation—come out with such different interpretations of Scripture, and in such crucial areas? God is not the Author of confusion. If He left us His Word, His written Word, wouldn't He have left us with a way to know what He meant by what He said?"

"Oh, David," I responded. "You are always searching. Just read the Bible. Just be a Christian. Don't worry. We see through a glass dimly now, but one day we will know as we are known."

That was not enough for my brother. Because he *thinks*.

"What human parent," David asked, "would give birth to a child and then leave that child an orphan to fend for itself … to figure out who should feed it what, and who should teach it what? God is a more perfect Father than any human father could be. Would He adopt us into His family, make us His children, and leave us orphans to fend for ourselves? No," David said. "I want to find out if Jesus meant what He said—that He would establish a Church, against which the gates of Hell would not prevail, and which He would lead into all truth until the end of time. I want to know if *that* Church still exists after two thousand years, and if it can be found."

David met some faithful Christians in the pro-life movement, including Catholics who knew their faith. I count that as *phenomenon number one:* Catholics who know their faith. I had never met a Catholic who knew his faith.

It was not long before David began studying with a Franciscan monk from Brooklyn.

Forget that, I thought. I flew to New York from California to rescue David from the monk. I just *knew* the monk was an agent of Satan to lead my brother astray. For three hours, David, the monk, and I discussed the issues of the Reformation and all that separates Catholics and Protestants.

It was Christmas Eve, 1978. I had been a Christian for two years. David had been a Christian for one year and felt drawn to the Catholic Church. "Ros, I am going to midnight Mass. Do you want to come?"

I had never been in a Catholic Church in my life. But I wanted to see what David's problem was. So we went. As we approached the small church in upstate New York, I was struck with the beauty of the scene: pitch black outside, and magnificent stained glass windows with the light of the church gleaming through them; huge, fluffy snowflakes falling in slow motion like in a film. It was a perfect picture postcard. I felt anger well up inside me, and thought, *It is just like Satan to make error look enticing!*

We sat through the Mass. David did not receive Communion since he was not Catholic (yet), and certainly I would not. As we descended the stairs of the church following the Mass, David asked, "Ros, what do you think?"

I was in shock and unable to speak for the entire half hour ride home.

When at last we arrived home, David pleaded, "Say *anything*. Just speak."

When I could finally speak, I said with a sick heart, "David, *that* is a synagogue, but with Christ!"

Excitedly, David responded, "That's right, Ros. That's what the Catholic Church is!"

"No!" I came back at him. "That's *wrong*." What was David's problem? Was he so affected by our Jewish background, by the liturgy, the aesthetics? Didn't he understand that Christ was the end to which all that pointed? It made me ill inside.

One year later, my brother was Catholic. My Christian friends asked, "Is your brother a Christian, Ros?"

"I thought he was, but he's Catholic now, so I don't know." For years afterward, David and I tried to "save" each another.

During the summer of 1990, I visited David in New York. He gave me a magazine called *This Rock Magazine*, published by Catholic Answers (which later became my full-time employer!). "Ros," David said, "it's a Catholic apologetics magazine. I thought you might be interested."

"Catholic *apologetics*?" I responded incredulously.

The word "apologetics" does not mean we walk around saying, "I'm sorry for being Catholic." St. Peter, our first pope—our first Jewish pope—instructs us to "always be prepared to make a defense to anyone who calls you to account for the hope that is in you, yet do it with gentleness and reverence" (1Pet. 3:15).

Apologetic does not mean to be defensive, but to give a reasoned explanation for what we believe. As Catholics, we need to know why we believe what we believe.

I was astonished when David presented me with what he described a Catholic apologetics magazine. "Catholics *have* a defense of their faith?" I asked. "Catholics know why they believe what they believe?" I had never met a Catholic who knew his faith. My Evangelical pastor was an ex-Catholic, as was half our congregation.

But there was something else. I did not know that Catholics cared that anyone knew their faith and thought to myself, *They are wrong because they are Catholic. But if you even think you have the truth, and that truth is the answer for your soul and for the soul of everyone on the face of the Earth, how do you keep it to yourself?* So I had my first measure of respect for any Catholic who would publish what they believed was the answer for the world's salvation.

I took the magazine home with me to California and subscribed to it so I could see what David had "bought into." I thought I would die when the magazine did not come in a brown-paper wrapper. Now I had Catholic mail coming to my mailbox. *Oy!*

In that magazine I saw a full-page advertisement that read, "Presbyterian Minister Becomes Catholic." I had never heard of such a thing in my entire life. A Presbyterian minister becomes Catholic? The article was about a certain "troublemaker" by the name of Scott Hahn. I thought to myself, *I don't care who this Scott Hahn is. I don't care what his title was. He could not have a personal relationship with the Lord Jesus Christ and then become Catholic!*

His background in Calvinistic theology was somewhat similar to mine, so I listened for four hours to a four-part tape series between Scott and the Presbyterian minister who heads Systematic Theology of a Presbyterian seminary. It concerned the major issues of the Reformation that separates Evangelical Protestantism from Catholicism (*Sola Scriptura, Sola Fide, Sola Gratia*—Scripture alone, faith alone, grace alone).

At the end of those four hours, each man summed up his presentation. During the last fifteen-minute segment, Scott Hahn concluded with these words: "For the one who will look into the claims of the Catholic Church, two thousand years of Church history, the Church fathers, and such, to that one will come a *holy shock and a glorious amazement* to find out that what he had been fighting and trying to save people from, was in fact the Church that Christ established on Earth two thousand years ago."

"Holy shock" are the words that describe what went through me physically at that moment. The impact of that split second in time was such that I knew if I did not look into the *claims* of the Catholic Church, I would be turning from God.

It was the second time in my life when I stood paralyzed. The first time was with those twelve troubled (as I thought then) Jews for Jesus fourteen years earlier—the moment it got through to me that God—the unapproachable God of Abraham, Isaac, and Jacob, Whom no man can look on and live—entered history, entered time, and took on flesh for us. This was the second time. I stood paralyzed once more and thought, *Oh no. Don't tell me there is any truth to this.*

That utterly impactful moment began the most agonizing, four-and-a-half-year journey of my life. I had been a women's jail chaplain for ten years and was transitioning from the jail to an Evangelical church in Orange County, California, to head women's ministries. Hardly a week after that life-changing holy shock, I became part of their staff. I taught those women for two years, all the while reading (secretly) everything I could gather on the Catholic Church, often until two or three in the morning—until I knew I had to leave everything and everyone in order to isolate myself and look into the Catholic Church full-time.

I decided to move back to New York, where no one would know of my search except, in time, my brother, who I knew would be ecstatic that his Fundamentalist sister was looking into the Church at last. Before leaving California, I went to a Christian bookstore and asked for everything they had on the Catholic Church, which amounted to everything they had against the Catholic Church. I bought two hundred dollars' worth of books and tapes, hoping that these Protestant authors, mostly pastors, would rescue me from becoming Catholic. I packed up the materials, moved to New York, and got a waitress job in an Italian restaurant whose owners and staff were … Catholic.

I poured through those books. Within four months, I was utterly and desperately alone because I had read too much. Those Protestant pastors were not fighting the Catholic Church. They were fighting *a straw man.* In a statement from Bishop Fulton Sheen, which I first heard from Scott Hahn, he says, "There are not a hundred people in America who hate the Catholic Church, but there are millions who hate what they mistakenly think the Catholic Church teaches."

That was true both of me and of those who taught me. I put away the Protestant materials and began reading solid Catholic books, which my Catholic brother was happy to give me. I began to discover a Church more whole, more magnificent, and more beautiful than anything I could have imagined was God's design for His Church this side of Heaven. I looked into every single thing that separates Protestants and Catholics. In the end, two things were my greatest difficulties. They made me Catholic, and they keep me Catholic.

People often ask, "Was Mary your problem?" No, she wasn't my problem. I could not believe anything until I could believe everything, but I had already read enough about Mary. For the time being, I put all things having to do with her on a shelf. I saw an advertisement that read, "If you read only one book on Mary, read this book." So I got it. I figured if the Church wasn't true, I didn't have to read it. If the Church was true, I only had to read one book. The title of the book was *True Devotion to Mary*, by St. Louis de Montfort. *Oy vey!* How do you call a creature "my life, my sweetness, and my hope"—language fitting for God alone?

I then read the chapter on St. Louis' love for the Lord Jesus and thought *I should one day have such love for the Lord Jesus as St. Louis de Montfort has.* But how can you have such love for Jesus, and such devotion at the same time for a creature, even the Blessed Mother? Would not devotion to her rob us of devotion to Jesus?

I know differently now. Whenever someone asks me about Mary—especially my Jewish friends—I tell them not to be afraid. She's a *Jewish mother.* She would say, "*Do I have a Son for you!*" You'll never meet a Jewish mother who doesn't want you to know her son!

No, Mary was not my problem, but two matters were: the sacramental nature of the Church and the nature of the Mass. No small matters.

The sacramental nature of the Church: Why would God use things as a means of giving us His grace? Why would He use His very creation? Why baptize through water? What can *water* do? It simply gets you wet. Water has no power to do anything. We learned under Calvinistic thinking that everything is corrupt, utterly corrupt. Why would God use corrupt matter as a means of giving us His grace? Grace is the very life of God in our souls.

But then I began to think: why did Jesus change water into wine at the wedding feast of Cana? He didn't have to do that. He didn't have to use water. If they were out of wine, He could have said "poof" and created wine on the spot. In fact, He didn't even need to say "poof." He spoke, and the world came into being. God creates by His Word. Why did He use water? Why did He pick up mud and spit to heal a blind man? He didn't always heal the blind that way. Why did He do that? And why the Incarnation? Why did God take on our flesh?

I began to understand that everything is fallen but not utterly corrupt. Fallen from grace, yes. But through the cross, God has reconciled all things to Himself and restored us and His creation to the dignity, the beauty, and the purpose for which He made all things.

"Things" are neutral. God said all that He made was good. Things are not bad; it is our use of them that distorts them. God Himself uses His own creation as a means of giving us His grace.

What is a sacrament? If you read the *Baltimore Catechism*, you probably memorized that a sacrament is "an outward sign, instituted by Christ, to give grace." What is water? It is a sign of cleansing. You wash yourself with it. God uses water as the outward sign. As a Protestant I believed it was merely a sign. As a Catholic I came to understand that, through the sign, God does what the sign signifies. As water is a sign of cleansing, it is through the water that God, by His Spirit, cleanses us.

I came to understand that the sacraments give grace. The Eucharist, however, was another matter. The Eucharist, Catholics believed, doesn't merely give grace; it doesn't merely give the life of Christ. Catholics believe that the Eucharist *is* Christ.

After a few years of agonizing over this, I finally gave in and went to a priest. It was difficult for me to trust a priest. I was taught that the Church was Satan's system. Was I going to trust a priest and say to him, "Excuse me, is the Church true?" No.

However, I was finally led to a fine priest in upstate New York, Monsignor James O'Connor. Simply addressing this priest without calling him "Father" (another difficulty for my Protestant understanding) I posed the question: "We Evangelicals have Christ, you know. He is the indwelling Christ. Jesus said, 'I will never leave you or forsake you.' Do you Catholics *get* Christ on Sunday in the Eucharist, and then do you *lose* Him during the week and come back the next Sunday and get Him again? How do you get Him if you have Him? Does God come in parts?"

Father O'Connor answered simply and kindly, "No, we Catholics have Christ. He is the indwelling Christ. We have the indwelling *Trinity*, and yes, He will never leave or forsake us. But as in a marriage relationship, a husband and wife *have* each other. They love each other all the time. Sometimes, however, they go about their mundane chores in life and are not so aware of that love. But in the intimacy of the marital union, it is the beloved giving to his beloved, the bridegroom giving himself to his bride in a total act of intimacy, of self-giving love that is unique to that time."

Then he said, "That is the Eucharist. We have Christ. We have a relationship with Him all of the time. But sometimes we go about our mundane chores in life and are not always so aware of that relationship. But in the Eucharist, it is the Bridegroom, Christ, giving himself to His Bride, the Church, in a total act of intimacy; of self-giving love, that is unique to that time."

I silently sat before that priest, trying to take in what I had just heard. I don't think I had heard anything more beautiful in my life. "Okay then," I said. "One more thing …"

This "one more thing" was the second matter that kept me from the Church. It concerned the nature of the Mass, the nature of the sacrifice of Christ. My beloved and well-meaning Protestant pastor, for whom I will be eternally grateful, would stand in the pulpit, hold up his Bible, and exclaim, "Don't those Catholics know that the book of Hebrews says that Christ was sacrificed *once for all?* They re-sacrifice Christ at every Mass!"

I had already come to understand, however, that the Catholic Church believes and has always taught that Christ was sacrificed *once*—for all men and for all time. The Church has never taught anything other than that, and they never will. Furthermore, I learned they *wrote* the book of Hebrews! The Scriptures came from the Church, not the Church from the Scriptures.

I had already come to understand from Catholic teachings that the Mass is not the *re-sacrifice* of Christ but the *re-presentation* of the once-for-all sacrifice of Christ on Calvary. Christ was sacrificed two thousand years ago in time. But God exists outside of time, and His sacrifice is an eternal sacrifice. He is the Lamb slain before the foundation of the world. It is that one sacrifice of Christ that, at the words of consecration through the priest at every Holy Mass, is brought through time, down on every altar of every Catholic Church and will continue until the end of time. Christ is not re-sacrificed but re-presented —the one eternal sacrifice made present on every altar of every Catholic Church, and will be to the end of time.

I had already come to understand *that*. However, I would sit in the back pew and listen as the priest invited the parishioners to join their sacrifices to the sacrifice of Christ—through Him, with Him, and in Him to the Father. In my heart I screamed, *Wait a minute! What are you saying? We join our sacrifices to the sacrifice of Christ? Don't you Catholics believe that the sacrifice of Christ was sufficient for the sins of everyone who ever lived—past, present and future—for the sins of the entire world, forever? Don't you believe that?*

If I join my sufferings and sacrifices to the sacrifice of Christ, I reasoned, I was adding to the sacrifice of Christ. And if I added to the sacrifice of Christ, wasn't I saying, "Lord Jesus, thanks a lot for dying for me, but You didn't finish the job? I need to add to it"? If the Catholic Church believed that the sacrifice of Christ was not sufficient for the sins of all mankind, for all time, then, good-bye, Catholic Church!

For a solid year I asked every Catholic I met, "Do you add to the sacrifice of Christ?" Every Catholic answered, "No, we don't." They wanted me to understand that the Catholic Church teaches that the sacrifice of Christ was sufficient for the sins of all mankind for all time. But it was not the language of the Mass I heard.

Finally, I asked Father O'Connor, "Do you add to the sacrifice of Christ?!"

He looked at me and said, "Yes, we do." And then he said, "Yes, His sacrifice was sufficient. No, He doesn't need ours, but yes, we add to it."

My first inward response was, *Thank you very much. The truth is out. I've been rescued from ever becoming Catholic. I really appreciate that.*

My subsequent response, however, came after sitting in front of that holy priest for I don't know how long—ten seconds, five minutes? I don't remember. But what he said became the most beautiful thing I had ever heard outside of learning of the death and resurrection of Christ for me.

Years before, I had taken a course on the life of Christ. We were up to the point where Mary washed Jesus' feet with her hair. The professor said that, "Our ability to love is in part measured by our ability to receive. When we give, we are in control. But to *receive* can be humbling, awkward, and a bit uncomfortable at times. But Jesus received as freely as He gave when Mary washed His feet."

I remember thinking, *I don't love like that.* I did not love like that then and I don't love like that now. I thought, *I put Jesus on the cross. He died for my sins. Would He now receive me into the very sacrifice that I caused?*

I thought of a mother in the kitchen baking a chocolate cake. She has all the ingredients; she is sufficient for the task; she needs nothing; and she needs no one. But into the kitchen comes her three-year-old daughter: "Mommy, can I help you?" What does love do? Love receives. "Yes, sweetheart." So the little one comes and throws in an egg, some flour, etc. Did the mother *need* her help? No. Was the mother sufficient for the task? Yes. Was it a true addition? It was.

In my Protestant years a couple of the songs I came to love were, "Jesus, Lead Me Near the Cross," and a line that Billy Graham made famous in "Just As I Am": "Oh Lamb of God I come to Thee." I put Him to death, my sins did. But now that He brought me to love Him, if I could go back two thousand years and be at the foot of Calvary, as our Blessed Mother was—where, in effect, I yelled, "Crucify Him!" with that crowd—if I could be at Calvary now that I love Him and crawl up on the cross with Him and give myself to Him who was giving Himself for me … would I not want to do that? I thought I would.

And then I realized: that is the Mass. It blew me away. All of us in effect yelled, "Crucify Him!" He died for our sins; He died for the sins of the world. Who killed Jesus? The Jews? Yes. The Romans? Yes. Both were players, so to speak, at the time. God alone knows the accountability of each soul. But it was sin that killed the Savior. He died for the sins of the world.

And so we who in effect cried, "Crucify Him!"—but now by His grace have come to love Him—we don't go back two thousand years to Calvary. The sacrifice of Christ on Calvary is brought to *us* through time and down on the altar at the words of consecration. And we who in effect yelled, "Crucify Him!"—but now by His grace have come to love Him—can crawl up on the altar of Calvary made present and give ourselves *through Him, with Him, and in Him to the Father.*

"What manner of love is that?" I asked myself. It is beyond all that is human. We couldn't have invented it. It absolutely consumed me, and it still does.

I began praying to Mary, trying out this "communion of saints" thing. I told Father O'Connor that I was doing that, and he told a priest-friend of his, who also came from a Jewish background. That priest responded, "If she's praying to Mary, she is finished." And I was. I was in the Church six weeks later.

To the woman at the well Jesus said, "If you knew the gift of God, and who is saying to you, 'Give me a drink,' you would have asked him, and he would have given you living water" (John 4:10). And so I say to the one who doubts, "If you knew the gift of God and who it is who says to you, 'Take and eat, this is My Body,' you would have asked Him, and He would have given you Living Bread."

Every Holy Mass is the presentation—the re-presentation—of the Passover, the Passover fulfilled in the Passover Lamb, Who is Christ. It is a magnificent truth that we who receive that Lamb—Body, Blood, Soul, and Divinity—can go from every Mass singing, "Next year in Jerusalem," where we who eat the Body and drink the Blood of the Lamb will live in the presence of that Lamb for all eternity.

If you are Catholic, you have an inestimable treasure, an inheritance beyond all that this world can give or hold. He longs to give Himself to you at every Mass, and waits for you in every Tabernacle of every Catholic Church where, as the Prisoner of Love, He longs for our adoration, our love, our friendship, our life.

If you are not Catholic, perhaps not even a Christian, don't be afraid. Seek the God of Abraham, Isaac, and Jacob. Ask Him to help you to know Him. He will not fail to lead you all the way. Through the prophet Jeremiah, God said, "You will seek me and find me; when you seek me with all your heart" (Jeremiah 29:13).

I use to sing this little chorus to the women at the jail—it is one of my favorites too:

"He loves you just the way you are today,
But much too much to let you stay that way.
And when He's changed your life from what it was before,
He still won't love you one bit more."

Because He is a God of love, and all you need to do to get loved is to get in God's way.

God bless you. I'll see you in Heaven, you hear?

Bio–

A series of *holy shocks* led Rosalind Moss from her Conservative Jewish roots to her discovery that Jesus Christ was the long-awaited Messiah. After eighteen years of ministry in Evangelical Protestantism, she entered the Catholic Church at Easter 1995. She has a Master's degree in Ministry and worked as a Staff Apologist for Catholic Answers. She has traveled the world speaking and teaching. She is a prolific author, editor, and has been the co-host of EWTN's *Household of Faith*, *Now That We're Catholic!* and *Reasons for Our Hope*.

Having been strangely affected as a young Jewish girl in New York by the shortening of nuns' habits, Rosalind's long-desired dream of returning the hemline to the floor and the habit to the world was realized when, in 2008, the *Daughters of Mary, Mother of Israel's Hope*, now based in Tulsa, Oklahoma, under His Excellency Bishop Edward James Slattery, took root. Rosalind's name as a religious is now Mother Miriam of the Lamb of God.

Elyse O'Kane

G od is full of surprises. He delights in taking ordinary things and transforming them into the extraordinary. We often think of ourselves as just wives, mothers, grandmothers, teachers, doctors, or office workers. We think we live ordinary lives. But God has a special plan for each of us, a plan that was in His mind before we were born; a plan that has to do with building up the kingdom of God.

That is anything but ordinary!

In 1995, Blessed John Paul II wrote the following words in his letter to women:

"... Emphasis should be placed on the genius of women, not only by considering great and famous women of the past or present, but also those ordinary women who reveal the gift of their womanhood by placing themselves at the service of others in their everyday lives. For in giving themselves to others each day, women fulfill their deepest vocation."

There was a time when I was unaware of God's presence working in my life. I had no idea He had a plan for me. Even though I was baptized a Catholic, went to Catholic schools, memorized every prayer the good sisters taught me, I did not have a personal relationship with the Lord. I didn't even know what that meant.

However, little by little I began to come to an understanding of how much God loves me. Jesus revealed Himself to me through an ordinary person, and I will never be the same again. Meditating on my own personal Magnificat draws me to that famous canticle found in the first chapter of the Gospel of Luke and the woman who spoke it: "My soul proclaims the greatness of the Lord, my spirit rejoices in God my Savior."

What example did Mary give us as she spoke her Magnificat? First, she uttered one word that changed the history of mankind. She said "yes" to God. She gave the ultimate surrender of her life, not knowing exactly what it would entail. Then, not thinking of her own needs and concerns, she went to serve her cousin, Elizabeth. Mary was, in her own words, a lowly handmaid. Finally, she maintained an attitude of praise and thanks to God in the midst of difficult circumstances.

God chose Mary and she said "yes" to bring the Savior into the world. God has also chosen us. He calls each one of us to be Christ-bearers, to carry Jesus in our hearts wherever we go and bring Him to a broken world. As strange as it sounds, God needs us, lowly handmaids, to be willing servants ready to say "yes" when He calls our name. We must be willing to surrender our will to His will and to have hearts full of gratitude no matter what we are going through in our lives.

My story is about the word *yes*. It's not only about my yes. My story is also about how the *yes* of others deeply impacted my life.

We all would like our lives to be simple, uncomplicated, comfortable, free from worry and pain, and full of fun. Now, think of Mary. Think of the saints. Think of your own life. We all have crosses to carry—some have very heavy crosses. But God's promise is: "All things work together for the good for those who love Him" (Rom.8:28). He uses our sufferings to draw us into a deeper relationship with Him. No matter what the cost, no matter how hard it is, our motto must be an echo of Mary's words: "Yes, let it be done to me as You say."

I am a wife, married to my husband John for over forty years, a mother of three grown sons, Matthew, Tony, and Stephen, a mother-in-law to three amazing women, a grandmother, and a teacher. I am grateful to God for the ways He has drawn me into a deeper relationship with Him through this vocation. However, in 1991 something extraordinary happened. Seemingly out of nowhere, I began to compose music.

It seems impossible that someone with no formal music training could do this. But God had been preparing me all along, and I just didn't know it. He was wise not to tell me what He was up to. Had He told me years ago that I would someday write and arrange music, record a CD, and visit different cities to talk about the great things He has done in my life, I would have said, "With all due respect, Lord, I think You may have the wrong person. I'm not equipped to do such things. It's not possible."

But nothing is impossible for God. He allowed me to go through a number of experiences in my life: times when I wandered away from the Church, times when I didn't know where God could be found, times of great sorrow, times when I encountered His love and healing power in my Christian brothers and sisters, and times when His awesome presence in the Blessed Sacrament took my breath away.

Only through these experiences could I write songs like "I Am Waiting for You," "A New Creation," and "I Love You, Lord Jesus." However, taking the songs God gave me privately in prayer, recording them, and making them public was one of the biggest surrenders I had to make. That was when I had to face my fears.

I had a lot of fears: fear of rejection, fear of failure, fear of being humiliated, and the fear of not being good enough. I had to look all my insecurities in the face—the ones I had carried around for years—and completely trust God.

My background is a humble one. My mother and father were immigrants from Italy. We didn't have many material possessions, but I never felt we were lacking in anything. My parents were thrilled to be living in America, the land of opportunity. I think my dad's idea of being rich meant that his four daughters were healthy and well-educated, and that his wine cellar was stocked. They were wonderful people, caring and loving, generous, and prayerful.

I was born to my parents late in their lives. While growing up, it was a little embarrassing at times. Many people thought they were my grandparents. They loved me very much; perhaps I was loved and protected to a fault. I was their "baby."

My three sisters were much older than I, and it was as if I had four mothers. One mother is enough; four is *way* too many. They made most of the decisions for me. My life was basically held under a microscope. I suppose they were strict because of the fear that something bad might happen to me.

As a result, my activities as a child and teenager were limited. My mother would have been content if I never left the house. Asking permission to do something caused me a tremendous amount of anxiety. For example, when I was in high school (I went to a small, all girls' convent school—you don't get any more protective than that), my senior class planned a beautiful prom. A good friend of mine planned breakfast at her house afterwards.

However, my curfew was midnight, and my father was unmoving. A discussion about attending wasn't even allowed. The entire class had been invited, and I was the only one who couldn't go. Everyone felt sorry for me. The other students signed a petition asking my father's permission for me to attend. They rolled it into a scroll and tied it with ribbons with the school colors. He still wasn't impressed, not until he looked at the last signature. He finally gave his permission. Thank you, Sister Mary Frederick!

I had always wanted to study theater, but it was decided that I would be a teacher. My sisters were teachers. It was the respectable thing for a daughter of immigrants to do. Even though I vehemently protested the decisions my family made for me, in the end I always accepted them. My father had a way of raising one eyebrow when I went too far with my arguing. That was my signal to stop. In retrospect, I have to say that my father knew best. But I became a person who lacked confidence in herself, and I feared making decisions. They had always been made for me.

At twenty years old, I met and fell in love with a wonderful man. John was smart, handsome, quiet, gentle, confident, and he knew what he wanted to do in life. He was very Irish, and we were different in many ways. But somehow our differences complemented each other. We were married two weeks after I graduated from college. When John asked my dad for my hand in marriage, my father poured a toast and said, "Congratulations! Now she's your worry."

I went from my parents' protective home into marriage, with no wild and crazy travel adventures to brag about, no living on my own, no time to find myself. Poor John! He had a wife who had lots of fears and who was very insecure about herself. But he loved me anyway, and the fact that I loved to cook Italian food canceled a lot of negatives.

I loved married life. John was a wonderful, supportive husband who was extremely patient with me. Everything was wonderful. We had a good marriage, a beautiful son, and we were expecting our second child. It was then that things started to fall apart.

We moved from Cincinnati, my home town, to Atlanta because of a job change for John. Even though we were leaving family and friends, John and I were excited about buying our first home and experiencing the adventure of a new city. But soon after we arrived in Atlanta, I began to have serious problems with my pregnancy. I was rushed to the hospital, where I was ordered to have complete bed rest or I would lose our baby.

The doctors hoped I could carry the baby to six months, but they were doubtful. We were in shock, and I was devastated. The pregnancy was only four-and-a-half months along, and we were facing some hard times ahead. We were away from our families for the first time, we knew no one, and John had a brand-new job. In addition, we had a two-year-old to care for, and I was on complete bed rest. Our safe, secure little world was beginning to unravel. We were frightened about what might come.

However, what happened next was the awakening of our spiritual eyes.

Growing up, John and I had been immersed in our Catholicism, but we had fallen asleep at the faith wheel. We only went to Mass when it was convenient, and our prayer life was next to nothing. We were in our own world, and there was not a lot of room for God. We had not consciously rejected Him. Going to church was just not a priority. When our first son was about two years old, we felt a pull to get back into our faith. We started going back to church, but the move to Atlanta interrupted that.

Now, we were in a new city, under terrible stress, and we needed something, someone to help us. Our parents were too elderly to come, and our siblings had jobs and children of their own. Everything seemed to be crashing down around us.

After calling all the social services in the phone book, looking for home childcare, in desperation I phoned our new parish. We had not even had the chance to attend, but I hoped someone could help us. I cried over the phone, telling the secretary everything that had happened, that I was terrified of losing our baby, and that I needed help caring for our two-year-old.

Within days of that conversation, many women came to our door, cleaned our home, cooked our meals, and took care of Matthew. This went on daily for two months. It was the most unbelievable thing I had ever seen! The women didn't know me, yet they cared for me as if I were a member of their own families.

As I lay in bed during that time, afraid and wondering if I would lose my baby, I began to read spiritual books the women had brought over. I started reading the Bible. I just opened it up to different places and found it utterly amazing. I have never forgotten some of those Scripture passages.

I read, "Do not be surprised, beloved, that a trial by fire is occurring in your midst. It is a test for you, but it should not catch you off guard. Rejoice instead in the measure you share in Christ's sufferings" (1 Pet. 4:12–13). Then I read, "Dismiss all anxiety from your minds. Present your needs to God in every form of prayer and in petitions full of gratitude" (Phil. 4:6).

I had no idea that the Scriptures, written so long ago, could be relevant in my present situation. How, after years of Catholic education, could I not realize the wealth within these pages? I began reading more and more. It became a tremendous source of comfort to me. I wrote the words down and read them over and over whenever I became discouraged.

Several weeks later, I received a phone call from Connie, a woman from our church. "I heard about your situation," she said. "Do you mind if I come over?"

Connie was one of those "ordinary women" Blessed John Paul referred to in his letter. She was a housewife with five children of her own. She didn't come to clean or cook or babysit. She came to pray over me for healing. God had been preparing me for that moment.

Connie read to me from the Gospel of St. Mark about the woman with the hemorrhage. This Scripture passage holds such meaning and power for me.

"There was a woman afflicted with hemorrhages for twelve years. She had suffered at the hands of many doctors and had spent all she had. Yet she was not helped but only grew worse. She had heard about Jesus and came up behind him in the crowd and touched His cloak. She said, 'If I but touch His clothes, I shall be cured.' Immediately her flow of blood dried up. She felt in her body that she was healed of her affliction. Jesus, aware at once that power had gone out from him, turned around in the crowd and asked, 'Who has touched my clothes?' But his disciples said to him, 'You see how the crowd is pressing upon you, and yet you ask, 'Who touched me?' And he looked around to see who had done it. The woman, realizing what had happened to her, approached in fear and trembling. She fell down before Jesus and told him the whole truth. He said to her, 'Daughter, your faith has saved you. Go in peace and be cured of your affliction.'" (Mark 4:25–34)

The power of those words from holy Scripture—combined with Connie's faith (not mine!) and her obedience to come and pray over me—healed my condition. My doctor, a wonderful Catholic physician, confirmed my miracle and told me I could get out of bed and resume normal activities. I delivered a healthy baby boy, Anthony Joseph, eight weeks later. This experience changed my life.

Many times I stopped and asked myself, "What would have happened if Connie or any of those beautiful women hadn't obeyed the prompting of the Holy Spirit to come and minister to me? What if they had worried about what I might think of their boldness in bringing me Scripture and spiritual reading? What if there had been no prayer for healing?"

They never asked me if I went to church every Sunday, or when I had last gone to Confession. It didn't matter to them. They simply lived their faith, and God did a mighty work. Their hands became His hands, their encouraging words His words. Their kindness became His way of allowing me to encounter Him in a personal and profound way. God used those women as instruments of His incredible and unconditional love. Their yes opened my eyes to see God's love and mercy all around me. He came to me in such a powerful way that I would never be the same again.

Most people don't need to experience such a dramatic event in order to encounter Christ in a personal way. But He knew my weaknesses and saw how I had been moving away from Him little by little over the years. Sometimes God allows us to experience difficult times. It's during those rough and dark times when we begin to search our hearts. We see what's lacking and what's really important. And we begin to long for peace and joy and inner healing. We long for the presence of God in our lives. That's what happened to me.

I was so overwhelmed with gratitude to the Lord for my healing that I wanted to give Him something back. Psalm 116 says, "How can I make a return to the Lord for all the good He has done for me?"

The first thing I did was to go to the Sacrament of Reconciliation. It had been a long time. I was terrified of the priest's reaction, but I knew I had to go back to this sacrament. To my surprise, the priest didn't bat an eyelash. Thank God for priests who don't act surprised or shocked about how long it's been since our last confession or what we confess.

This was just the beginning of rediscovering the treasures of my faith that I had forgotten. Our Church has so many treasures. We have been given our Mother, Mary, the angels, the saints, the sacraments, and most importantly, we have the gift of His Real Presence in the Eucharist. We cannot appreciate these gifts fully unless we are away from them for a while. I had gone to Catholic schools all my life, from kindergarten through my second year of college. But now I was able to understand and appreciate my faith for the first time.

Doors began to open, and opportunities to grow in my faith were set before me. My parish was a thriving one. It always bustled with activities, and there were many ministries and classes. I attended a Life in the Spirit seminar. Connie had spoken to me about the power of the Holy Spirit, and I became very interested in the charismatic gifts. I was eager to understand how miraculous healing occurs, since that is how God had gotten my attention.

I felt such a hunger within me to receive all that God wanted to give me. We seem so concerned about our bodies—eating the right foods and exercising to stay healthy. But our spirits must be nourished and cared for too. We can't let our spirits go unfed, and mine was starving. I didn't realize it until I started to taste and see how good it all was.

I became immersed in the life of my parish. I couldn't get enough of it. The Church became my second home, and the kids were always in tow. I loved this new life. It energized me. And my husband was walking this road right along with me. I praise and thank God that we were traveling together spiritually. Our home was being built on stone and no longer on sand. That was important because more storms were coming.

Our third child was on his way when I learned I had another high-risk pregnancy. I had a very unusual blood type—something that had not been discovered earlier—with both a positive and a negative factor. This condition is considered one in a million.

I was watched carefully throughout the pregnancy, but everything proceeded normally. Our third son, Stephen Francis, was born and seemed fine. Within a week, however, things drastically changed and his condition became critical. Because he had positive blood and mine had a negative factor, and because our blood intermingled during delivery, the antibodies my blood was making were destroying his red blood cells. The condition is called hemolytic disease. His blood counts were so low the doctors were in disbelief as to how quickly they had dropped. He was rushed to the children's hospital for an immediate transfusion.

While we waited for what seemed like an eternity for the blood, the priest from our parish arrived to baptize our nearly lifeless baby. Then a steady stream of friends began to surround us and pray over little Stephen for healing. These friends had become our family, our faith family. Once again, our heavenly Father was showing His love for us through the body of Christ on Earth. He wanted us to know beyond the shadow of a doubt that He is real, that when you ask, you receive, when you seek, you find, and when you knock, the doors are always opened to you.

After twelve long hours of waiting, the blood came and the transfusion began. Stephen's little body regained color and life, and we were able to go home the next day.

Through both of these healing experiences, my faith continued to grow. Prayers for healing became an ordinary event in our home. Whenever the kids got sick, we immediately prayed over them. When my husband got sick, the children and I prayed over him.

Our homes are little, domestic churches. The Scriptures tell us that when someone is sick, the elders of the church should pray over the one who is ill, and they will be healed. The Lord was ever faithful and showed me over and over again that His healing power was available whenever we asked.

Even though we faced many difficult times—the death of my father and mother, the death of my mother-in-law and father-in-law, the death of one of my students, job insecurities, depression, and financial difficulties—I learned that His love, mercy, and grace are sufficient for enduring any trial. Our trust in God and the prayers of our faith-family carried us through it all.

Because of my hunger for God's Word, I joined a weekly Bible study. Our teacher showed us how to put God's Word into daily practice. It was wonderful and I learned so much. After a few years, many of the women became interested in praying the rosary. That particular method of prayer was definitely out of my distant past. It had been years since I had prayed a rosary, probably not since my high school days with the nuns.

I was perfectly content with my relationship with Jesus, and now I thought Mary was going to complicate everything. Even though I grew up with the Blessed Mother all around me in my home and in Catholic school, I had never developed a devotion to her. She was too good, too holy, and too perfect. I felt incredibly inferior to her. I was *not* good, *not* holy, and definitely *not* perfect. I could not relate to her at all. As a result, I was unsure about the direction this group was going. But these women were important to me, so I decided to go along with it.

Initially, it was painful. The slow recitation of the *Hail Mary* made me want to climb the walls. But my real problem was that I felt so unworthy to approach her. And while the other women's rosary chains were all miraculously turning gold, I still belonged to the silver club. While they devoutly prayed, my mind usually drifted to other things, like what I needed to pick up at the grocery store, what we would have for dinner, or how much longer this rosary was going to take.

One time, though, my thoughts took me to a totally unexpected place. As the women prayed their *Hail Marys*, in my mind's eye I saw myself as a little girl sitting off to the side as other little girls played nearby. They were dressed beautifully and looked so happy. I, on the other hand, wore an old, tattered dress and felt very alone. I had a sense of our Lady being near, but I felt ashamed of how I looked. I didn't want to raise my eyes to see her. But I couldn't help but look up. To my surprise, she was looking right at me with this incredibly beautiful, loving smile. She wasn't looking at the other girls. She had her eye on me. I felt she wanted me near her, so I went and sat next to her. She spoke no words, but I felt an immense love from her and realized it was a mother's love.

It was a pivotal moment for me spiritually. It wasn't some extraordinary vision, but I believe it was simply my Mother, Mary, getting in touch with her long-lost daughter. In those precious moments, my mistaken idea of Mary as being the untouchable, unapproachable, sinless woman changed into Mary, my loving Mother, my friend.

Whereas before I felt I had nothing in common with her, now I realized I had something wonderful that I did share with her. We were both moms. I loved my children even when they were rebellious and disobedient. I always wanted to protect them, encourage them, guide them, and point them in the right direction. Many times they turned a deaf ear to my voice and wanted to go their own way. They made mistakes, sometimes serious ones. But I never stopped loving them. I never gave up on them.

I suddenly realized that's how Mary always felt about me. Even though I couldn't relate to her for all those years, she had always been there and had always loved me.

I believe what happened next was a natural progression I made the decision to make a total consecration to Jesus through Mary. This is the St. Louis de Montfort consecration, also known as an entrustment. Blessed John Paul II encouraged this devotion. I didn't completely understand what it meant to surrender my life to Jesus and Mary, and to give God permission to do with my life whatever He desired. But I realized all He had done for me. Presenting to Him the gift of myself was a very small return.

More than anything I wanted to be used as an instrument in His hands. I wanted and needed the Lord to be in total control of my life and I said, "yes." It was a timid yes, a fearful yes, but I don't think God really cares *how* we say it.

In July 1990, I made the consecration in front of a large image of Our Lady of Guadalupe at the Monastery of the Holy Spirit in Conyers, Georgia. In July of 1991, one year almost to the day, something extraordinary happened. As I was driving home from Mass I began to sing, "My soul proclaims the greatness of the Lord and my spirit exults in God, my Savior, for he has looked with kindness on His lowly handmaid. All ages will call me blessed." I was singing Mary's Magnificat.

When I stopped the car, I wondered *what in the world had just happened. What was that song? Did I know it from somewhere?* I sat there for the longest time, and it dawned on me that this was a brand-new melody. It sounded middle-eastern and joyful. I liked it!

For seven months that tune floated around in my head. I never told anyone about it. I didn't understand why this song wouldn't leave me alone. This all happened about the time my prayer group was working on bringing the Magnificat ministry to Atlanta. However, I never considered that the song, "Magnificat," and the ministry, Magnificat, were in any way connected—not until I was asked to be the chairperson for the music for our new chapter.

I told our coordinator I had a song that might work for the ministry, and I sang it to her. She liked it. Then I went to my friend, who was a gifted musician, and sang the melody to him. I told him what it sounded like in my head. I could hear the mandolin and the klesmer clarinet with a wonderful Hebrew sound.

That's how my song, "Magnificat," was born.

The rest is history. It continues to be an amazing gift from the Holy Spirit. So many people have embraced the song, and it has now become the theme song of the worldwide ministry. It is also the opening song for the radio program, *Magnificat Proclaims*, another outreach of this ministry, and broadcast all over the world. Whenever I hear this song played or sung by another group, I get excited and remember that July day in my car. I praise God for it.

After that, melodies and lyrics began to fill my head. I wasn't sure what was going on, but it was something I enjoyed. Many songs came to me during Eucharistic Adoration. I wrote them in my journal or on any piece of paper I could find. My husband kept telling me I needed to record them. It was a wonderful idea but impossible, and I told him so. Besides, I didn't know how to do that. I had many scraps of paper with lyrics on them, and the melodies were all in my head.

Nevertheless, he kept up the pressure. I said that even if I wrote out the songs, we didn't have money to record in a studio. Not only would it cost thousands of dollars, but we'd also need someone who knew how to work with sound engineers, studio musicians, etc. In my mind it was impossible.

I have a very stubborn husband (remember, he's Irish), but he is also a loving, prayerful man who truly felt this was God's will. I was reluctant. I told John that these songs were only for *me*, that they had been given to me in prayer. It was, in essence, my prayer life.

John told me that when God gives someone a gift, it's not only personal but for the entire community. That was hard to hear because I was afraid my music might not be accepted. I wanted to do whatever God wanted me to, but how could this happen?

I began to pray and ask God, "If this is really Your will, bring someone into my life who can help me."

God answered my prayer rather quickly. Mary Welch Rogers was our first Magnificat speaker in Atlanta. Ironically, she was the first person to sing my "Magnificat" song. She was also a songwriter and a recording artist, and we eventually became friends. In the past I had shared with her about my music. I thought about asking her to help me, but I didn't want to put her on the spot.

"No," I told the Lord. "If she's the one, she'll have to ask me."

One evening when we went to a Christian concert together, Mary said, "I really like your music. Would you like me to produce a CD for you?"

I just stared at her. I didn't know what it meant, but I knew it was something good. After she scraped me off the floor, we began to make plans to get together each week and work on arrangements. It was so much fun! We loved the same musical things, we had similar ideas, and the creative juices flowed. Later on, she told me she had never produced music for anyone else before.

The big recording day finally arrived. It was December 12th, the feast of Our Lady of Guadalupe. *A good sign*, I thought. It couldn't be a coincidence. But I was terrified about going through with this project. What was I thinking? I walked into the studio and saw professional musicians, professional background vocalists, professional sound engineers, and my producer all ready to record my music. I thought, *I must be out of my mind!*

Right then, all my fears and all the lies I had believed about myself for years were coming back at once. Negative thoughts filled my head: *Who do you think you are? You? Record a CD? You think God is calling you? You're a nobody. What do you know about music? You don't know how to do this. You're way out of your league!*

There was a kernel of truth in those lies. In the eyes of the world, I was out of my league. But God doesn't look at the world like we do. If I was obedient to my calling then I was right where I should be, and I was learning that God really does care about everything.

As I struggled to understand how it all would come together, I prayed that God would place His healing touch within the lyrics and music of each song. He had given me healing during my difficult pregnancies, and I had seen His marvelous healing power many times since. I witnessed many answered prayers.

Perhaps God would use me as an instrument of healing through my music. He can, and will, and desires to touch and heal His people. I didn't know if anyone would ever even listen to this CD, but I prayed that whoever did would feel His peace, His love, and His healing power through it.

By the grace of God I entered that studio. Some days were harder than others. Insecurities overwhelmed me. I often called my dear friend and said, "I can't do this. It's too hard. I don't know what I'm doing, I'm not a professional singer." Each time she read to me from Scripture or gave me an encouraging word.

One day when I was feeling overwhelmed, she said, "This is the meditation for the day." She then read, "The Lord of Hosts says, 'Get on with the job and finish it!'"

My mouth fell open. I said disbelieving, "It does not!"

"You have been listening long enough," she continued to read. "Take courage and work, for I am with you, says the Lord of hosts." The Scripture for the day was, "I can do all things through Christ who strengthens me" (Phil. 4:13). With that command and with the encouraging Scripture, I completed the project.

I am still amazed and in awe of what happened. The album, *With All My Heart*, is now in over twenty countries. Additionally, four of my

259 of M is 336

songs have been chosen for publication by World Library. Recently, my song, "Come, Holy Spirit," was put into booklet form and sent out to choir directors all over the country.

Thinking this was all that God had in mind for me, I was surprised when more songs began coming to me. I don't know if I will record another album, but I am working toward that goal. Additionally, the Lord has been leading me in the area of an intercessory prayer and healing ministry. Over thirty years ago I received miraculous healing through the touch of an ordinary woman. She was simply the instrument God selected. Providentially, I recently prayed over a young mom who had the same problem in her pregnancy as I had experienced. The doctors held little hope for her baby, just as they had held little hope for mine. Praise God that this young mother received the same healing I did. She carried her baby boy to term.

God does such wonderful works, but believe it or not, He needs our help. He asks us to be His hands, His feet, and His voice. We must be willing to allow His Spirit to use us. We have to say, "yes." It's hard sometimes. It can be terribly frightening; we think we don't have what it takes, that we aren't prepared.

I still battle these thoughts at times. But there's a great saying, "God doesn't call the equipped. He equips the called." As Christians we are called in different ways to do specific works for Him. This call requires a response. In order to say "yes" to unconditionally surrender our lives to the Lord, we have to trust Him. In order to trust Him, we have to know who He is. In order to know who He is, we have to spend time with Him.

This is where the challenge lies. We have become so busy with the things of this world that the temptation to push prayer time aside is always there. But we need periods of solitude—times alone with our Lord—so that we can hear His voice speaking to us. Those moments with Him restore our energy. Our vision of what God is inspiring us to do is renewed and affirmed. What we give to others will drain us unless we ask Him to replenish us.

It is in those still places where God speaks, where He guides, where He gives peace to our souls, strengthens our spirit, and readies us for what He is calling us to do. God has a purpose for each of us, but how will we know what it is unless we are listening to Him?

Take a look at how the tiny word yes has impacted your life. Mary's yes, the yes of others in your life, and your own yes have brought you to this point in your spiritual journey. It can be painful to look back on your life, but it is important to see God's hand in all your experiences—joyful and sorrowful. He has used all of these things for your good and for the good of others. We have a heavenly family that is cheering us on, ready to help us along our journey, ready to enable us to live fruitful lives just as they did.

God has given each person a unique gift, and the call to work alongside Him continues to go out. The call to minister may be within your own family. It may be taking care of your children or grandchildren and teaching them about God's love. It may be to sit with a sick family member or neighbor and to bring them a smile and a word of encouragement. It may be to minister to the people at your job, to be a light that shines in the darkness. It may be a call to missions or to the consecrated life. For Connie, it was to minister to a stranger in need. Like Mary, Connie carried the Holy Spirit within her and went to proclaim the greatness of the Lord.

This is what we are all called to do.

I believe the Magnificat that Mary proclaimed is a prayer each one of us needs to call our own. We need to take hold of the joy Mary had, even in the most difficult times, and declare the great things God has done for us.

St. Teresa of Avila said, "Christ has no body on earth but yours; no hands, no feet on earth but yours. Yours are the eyes with which He looks compassionately on this world. Yours are the feet with which He walks to do good. Yours are the hands with which He blesses all the world. Christ has no body now on earth, but yours."

Who will you touch today? Who will benefit from your relationship with Christ? Matthew 9:37 says, "The harvest is plenty but the laborers are few." Is the God of the harvest speaking to your heart? What is He asking? What will your response be?

The word *yes* is powerful. With that *yes*, God can and will do mighty and extraordinary things with our ordinary lives.

Bio–

The fruit of ten years of music ministry and an active prayer life formed the basis for Elyse O'Kane's first CD, *With All My Heart*. Raised in a traditional Italian family listening to opera, Elyse studied musical theater for two years before majoring in speech pathology and beginning a career as a special education and resource teacher. While raising a family in Atlanta, Georgia, she served the music ministry of her parish, sang at Eucharistic congresses in the Archdiocese of Atlanta, and for ten years led the music ministry of the Atlanta Magnificat chapter. Her first beautiful composition, "Magnificat," came spontaneously to her in 1991, and the song is used at many Magnificat chapters and in churches across the United States. Since the release of her CD, Elyse has continued to write music, is involved in the ministry of intercessory prayer and healing, and enjoys speaking to groups about her faith journey and music.

Marilyn Quirk

Mary said, "My soul proclaims the greatness of the Lord, My spirit rejoices in God my Savior … The Mighty One has done great things for me, and holy is His name." (Luke 1:46, 49) When we give God permission—when we say "yes" to Him just as Mary said "yes"—He takes our lives and does more than we could ever ask or imagine.

I was born in New Orleans to wonderful parents. My father was pure Italian; my mother was pure English. It was quite different, the merging of two nationalities. My paternal grandparents came from Sicily and barely spoke English, but my grandmother was a very spiritual woman. She got up early every morning to begin her day with prayer and then walked two miles to go to Mass. She had seven children: one boy and six girls. My father was the only son, and he held a special place in the family—especially with my grandmother.

My grandmother on my mother's side was an Episcopalian—one of the most Christian women I have ever met in my life. Her faith and her life were an inspiration, and it was contagious.

My father and mother loved each other very much, but they had a turbulent marriage. My brother was three years younger than I, and it was traumatic for us living in that situation. Because of the prayers and the inspiration of my grandmothers, I knew Jesus. I can't remember not knowing Him. He was personal, and He was my confidant.

I prayed and saw miracles happen within the relationships of my family. But it was always an on-and-off, unstable situation. It was because of my faith that I was able to hold together and function in a normal capacity. In those days no one discussed turbulence in a marriage. I couldn't talk to anyone about it, but I could talk to Jesus.

I was baptized a Catholic and made my First Communion in the Catholic faith. My father did not go to church after they were married, and my mother was Episcopalian, so she wanted to take me to her church. My father agreed. After I made my First Communion, they pulled me out of Catholic school and I went to a public school—even though New Orleans is a strongly Catholic city with a quality Catholic education system.

I was in high school when I began to think that somehow God was calling me. I felt I had some kind of a vocation, some kind of a pull or call to give my life to God in some capacity. I went to my Episcopal minister and asked, "What can I do? How can I respond to this call?"

He suggested the possibility of my becoming a medical missionary in the Episcopal Church, so that is the course I decided to pursue. I went to Louisiana State University (LSU) in Baton Rouge and studied medicine.

I lived in a dorm at LSU and made many friends of both genders. Marriage was not part of my plan, since I was focused on becoming a medical missionary. Down the hall there was a group of girls—all Catholic—and they asked me if I'd do them a favor and go on a blind date with this really great guy. I had canceled plans for the night and didn't want to go out at all, but they prevailed upon me and I finally agreed to go … just this one time.

My blind date turned out to be someone I will never forget because he's now my husband. He was the first Catholic I ever dated, which was unusual considering the fact that I lived in New Orleans, even though I grew up among non-Catholics and went to a public school. The only Catholics I had met previously were nominal, who explained they attended church only out of duty.

However, this Catholic fellow was different and strong in his faith, and we became friends. Through him I met the Catholic chaplain at LSU, Father Stanley J. Ott. After Pete and I went out a number of times, I felt an attraction to him and I began to think, *I've got to find out what God really wants in my life. I don't want to fall in love with someone until I know it's God's will for me to consider marriage.*

Looking back, this was such a grace. I asked Father Ott if I could meet with him, and he agreed. I explained I had a big problem. I was attracted to a young man (he probably knew who I was discussing).

"Well?" he said.

"You see, I have a vocation. I'm studying medicine to become a medical missionary."

He said, "Marriage is a vocation."

This was before Vatican II, and I had never heard that marriage was a vocation.

"Yes, Marilyn," Father Ott said. "There is a need for the witness of a Christian family, a Christian marriage in the world today. There's a great need for that to be a witness." He continued, "If God calls you to this, be open to it." He offered to bring me through a series of exercises, where I could discern God's will for me to be open to marriage or not.

As I look back, I realize the extraordinary gift to have a priest who was able to lead me in what I didn't understand at the time to be the spiritual exercises of St. Ignatius. When I ended the period of days (or weeks) going through these spiritual exercises with this holy and humble man with a Doctorate in Theology, my discernment was to be open to marriage.

But then I had a bigger problem. Pete and I had never talked about marriage. I was planning ahead because I didn't want to let my heart fall in love until I knew it was God's will. I met with Father Ott again and said, "If I marry a Catholic, I'm not Catholic and I don't understand about the faith."

"That's simple," Fr. Ott said. "I'll be able to teach you the faith."

I thought that would be a good idea. If Pete and I married, I wanted to raise our children to be good Catholics. I didn't want them to be nominal Catholics. So Father Ott proceeded to teach me the faith for about eight or nine months. Needless to say, through his teaching and through the grace of God and the gift of faith, the scales fell from my eyes and I fell in love with the Church—even those things I didn't fully understand.

One of those was Our Lady. I didn't understand the role Mary played. Neither did I understand the role of the pope. But it was through Divine Grace, being obedient to faith, that I came to see the gift that the pope was for the Church: to lead the Church in the matter of faith and morals and to bring unity. I fell in love with the Church even more.

By this time Pete and I were engaged. I became a Catholic shortly before we were married, and we had a wonderful, sacramental marriage that was graced in every way. The Sacrament of Marriage is very real.

Pete was an engineer with an oil company, and for six years we were away from New Orleans. Six years and four wonderful children later we moved back to the city. When we returned to New Orleans, there was a little more money. We also had family to help with the children, and that kernel of faith—that fervent faith I had within me—began to be absorbed by the cares and riches and pleasures of life.

If we don't nurture our faith, if we don't pray, if we don't place the Lord first in our lives, then gradually our hearts become filled with weeds. The gift of faith can be choked amid the cares and riches and pleasures of life. I became more concerned about where I was going to go and what I was going to do and what I was going to wear. I still went to Mass on Sunday, but my heart was far from the Lord. He wasn't the center of my life.

It can be explained this way: Picture three circles—one with the cross outside that circle (Jesus is not a part of your life); one with a cross just inside that circle (Jesus is a part of your life but not the center of it); and finally a circle with the cross right at the center (Jesus is the center of your life.) Well, Jesus was not the center of *my* life. He was not the treasure of my heart. He was not the pearl of great price to me. I had a love for Him, but it wasn't a fervent love.

As my children grew and were busy with school and various functions, I found myself living the good life and going the way of the secular world. I lived a life of leisure in those days. By the end of 1969, an acquaintance began inviting me to a prayer meeting at Loyola University. While I thought it was nice of her, I had the excuse of being too busy. Truthfully, I wasn't the least bit interested.

However, she persisted. Week after week she called me and asked me to accompany her to the prayer meeting at Loyola University. Week after week I gave an excuse, until after a month or two I finally thought, *She's going to wear me out unless I go* (like the unjust judge in Luke 18). So, I finally agreed to attend this prayer meeting.

About sixty or seventy people had gathered in the upper room of the student center of Loyola University in New Orleans—all sitting around in a circle. They sang songs; someone read a Scripture passage; others stood up and gave a little praise report or shared what God had done in their lives; and then we had a beautiful Mass.

While I was sitting at that prayer meeting I began to weep. It was as if the realization of how far I had gone away from God crashed in upon me. These people really believed Jesus was present there. They truly loved Him. He was the center of their lives, and I had drifted far away from that experience. My copious tears of repentance flowed the whole evening. I just sat there, saying, "Lord, forgive me. Lord, forgive me."

It was a great grace. I remember thinking about that passage in Revelation 3, where Jesus was speaking about those who are lukewarm— neither hot nor cold. That's what I was at that time. Lukewarm. I wasn't cold, but I sure wasn't hot. I felt God wasn't pleased with that; He desired me to love Him first. God is rich in mercy because of His great love. He brought me to life in Christ even when I was dead in sin (Ephesians 2:4–5).

I began going up to Loyola with these women and finally asked for the grace they were all talking about ... this Baptism in the Holy Spirit. Father Harold F. Cohen, S.J. was one of those who prayed with me. This was before there was any Life in the Spirit seminar. The Life in the Spirit seminar is a wonderful thing. If it is available in your area, I encourage you to take advantage of the opportunity to attend one. Your life will never be the same.

The group prayed with me. I expected to have an extraordinary experience. Nothing happened—except my whole life changed. I began going in a different direction. The Scriptures meant much more to me.

Daily Mass became important to me—I wanted to go to Mass. I had the desire to do spiritual things. I wasn't making myself do it. There is a vast difference. I no longer did things because it was simply the right thing to do but because I *desired* to do it.

I learned that when we say "yes" to God, He changes our hearts, puts those desires there, and inclines our hearts to do the things He wants us to do as we continue to say "yes" to Him.

So here we were—a group of women going in a big van to attend the prayer meeting together. Afterward, we'd sit in the vehicle praying for others, reviewing a Scripture passage, and talking and sharing for an hour or so. We finally realized it was not safe for us to sit in a car late at night. I offered my house for us to meet one day during the week. They all eagerly agreed, and about twelve of us met at my house on a Wednesday morning. It was simply glorious! They wanted to meet again the following week. So we met then—and the week following, as well.

By now the group had grown to around twenty women. *What if a style show or a luncheon or something important comes up and it's on a Wednesday and I'm not able to go? I mean, this sounds like a commitment,* I thought. A little sense in my heart (that I didn't recognize it to be necessarily of the Lord) was telling me, "Say 'yes,' and I'll do the rest."

Since I wasn't leading the group—which I didn't feel capable of doing anyway—I agreed. "Okay, I'll say 'yes' and open the door. I'll let the ladies come in and ask them to lock up when they leave."

I actually did that a couple of times, but what began to happen was with my "yes," God began to change my heart. I wanted to be there with these women more than I wanted to be any other place on that particular day.

There was so much happening in our lives as women. We enjoyed not only the fellowship but also praying together. We were growing in our appreciation of being women, and it was extraordinary. The group grew to sixty or seventy women all jammed together. Sometimes we'd have Mass; sometimes we'd just have a prayer meeting, but it was an incredible time of God's grace.

Other women attended our prayer meeting and wanted to begin something similar in their own area. Remarkable as it might sound, there were eventually thirty to forty women's prayer groups that sprang up around the greater New Orleans area. We realized this was something God was doing.

The woman who had brought me to my first prayer meeting was leading the group at my house. It happened that she could no longer come regularly because her husband was going to run for political office. She needed someone else to lead. A few of the women encouraged me to do it, but I demurred, saying, "There's no way I could lead a prayer meeting." But they persisted and insisted that I try.

The thought came to me that the Lord was saying, "Are you saying that My power is not great enough that it can use you? Are you saying that?"

I had to admit, "Yes, I guess so, Lord."

Chastened by these thoughts, I agreed to lead the group. I knew I didn't have the gift to do it, but the Lord did and He could do it in me. This experience brought me into a deeper connection with Him, and to be dependent on Him.

There's a line in Scripture in John 15:5 where Jesus says, "Apart from me you can do nothing." I discovered that in Christ we can do anything He asks us to do. In Magnificat we like to say, "He doesn't choose the qualified, but He qualifies the ones He chooses." That's exactly what God does. He chooses us to do things that are beyond our capability. If we say, "yes" to Him, His Holy Spirit empowers us to accomplish the task.

As I began to lead the prayer meeting at my house, I thought it would be nice to gather all the leaders from the other prayer meetings together, as well. We all came together under Father Cohen, who was the liaison to the Catholic Charismatic Renewal at the time. We talked about how women of the time (mid-1970s) were being evangelized more by the world than by the Word of God.

We realized that the gift God had given to us needed to be given as a gift (Matthew 10:8). Over and over again we heard that it wasn't for us to keep to ourselves but to share. When Mary was overshadowed by the Holy Spirit, it wasn't for her to keep but to give, and she ran immediately in haste to bring the good news of salvation to her cousin, Elizabeth. With this in mind we began sponsoring Days of Renewal for women, Life in the Spirit seminars for women, teachings for women. We had a whole network of women from all the prayer groups with numerous, inspiring events going on. It was awesome!

During the middle of all this—with our four older children ranging in age from sixteen to twelve, Pete and I building a new home, and so much happening with the women's prayer groups—I discovered I was pregnant. *Why would God call me from the important work I'm doing to draw me aside to have another child?* I thought.

God's answer was eye-opening. "Marilyn, let's sit down," the Lord said. "Your thoughts are not My thoughts, and My thoughts are not your thoughts. Having a child and bearing a child is a very important work in My day. Say 'yes' to this call that I have on your life at this time, and you will be blessed. And the child will be blessed, as well."

It was incredible for God to speak to me in this way and for me to embrace it. I would have embraced it, but not with the joy He was helping me to achieve, or to understand that this was important. The prayer meeting that met at my house moved into the parish hall and has remained there, which is what the Lord desired. I had this precious fifth child. Four years later we had our sixth child.

Around this time (mid-1970s), a group called Women's Aglow came to the New Orleans area. It's a wonderful, interdenominational outreach to women. A Presbyterian friend of mine, Bobbie Byerly, began coming to our Wednesday morning prayer meetings because she desired fellowship. Bobbie was instrumental in bringing Aglow to the New Orleans area. She later went on to become the National President of Women's Aglow.

Aglow took off like wildfire in New Orleans. Over half of the women who attended Women's Aglow events were Catholics. Because of the large number of Catholic women, they wanted a Catholic priest to be a spiritual advisor to Aglow, but Archbishop Philip M. Hannan didn't think it was a wise idea.

The Aglow leadership wasn't happy with that answer, and Bobbie asked me if I could help them in any way. About this same time, Father Ott was now Bishop Ott, and he was brought into New Orleans as auxiliary bishop. Father Ott was like a father in Christ to me. He had brought me into the faith; he'd been a close friend to Pete and me before we were married; and he continued to be a close friend. He attended our wedding ceremony; he was just part of our lives.

"I know the auxiliary bishop, Father Ott, very well," I told Bobbie. "I'll make an appointment to see him and try to explain what the problem is and how it would be a good thing." I thought that since the majority of the women attending these events were Catholic, it would be good for a Catholic priest to be present to answer any questions that might arise. They had also asked me to speak at an Aglow event, which I was not going to do unless I got the bishop's approval.

I was five months pregnant with our sixth child at this time.

The bishop said, "Yes, Marilyn, I see what you're saying. I'll talk to Archbishop Hannan. I think he'll agree with me that it would be good to have a representative there. But," he continued, "the archbishop and I discussed that it would be great for something like Aglow to begin for Catholic women."

At his words, thoughts just tumbled around in my head! *Oh my goodness, I don't hear that to be from God.* For one thing, it wouldn't be a good thing if I went back to Aglow and said, "I think they're going to approve a priest to become spiritual advisor, but they'd like to begin something for Catholic women." That would sound like competition. I felt like Elizabeth in the Scriptures; I wanted to go into seclusion. "Stop the world! I want to get off."

I thought about the team I worked with. "Oh, my dear! We are all so busy handling the prayer groups and handling other events. No way am I going to be 'visionary Marilyn' coming up with some big new plan of what we should do." So I concluded, "I'll tell no one about this. I'll leave the bishop's office happy, but I'll tell no one."

Two days later I went to my OB GYN, Dr. Jim Seiss, a real man of God, who happened to be a state advisor to Women's Aglow. While I lay on the table waiting to be examined, the doctor was washing his hands. "Marilyn, I was praying for you the other day," he said.

"Oh, you were? Thank you, Jim."

"Yes," he continued. "I thought that something like Aglow should begin for Catholic women."

I almost fell off the table! *Oh no! How did you know?* Then I told Jim that the bishop had just told me this.

"Praise the Lord," Jim said. "You know, there are a lot of Catholic women who wouldn't go to anything that wasn't Catholic. There are also a lot of Catholic women who would go to something interdenominational, but they're not strong enough in their faith and might be evangelized or brought to faith in that arena and maybe become weak in their Catholic faith. Why should they be deprived?"

I closed my eyes and thought, *Oh, Jesus, I say "yes," but not now.* I felt overwhelmed—it was just too much.

That was near the end of 1978. It was not until the beginning of 1981, when our youngest was two, that I could hold my head above water and feel like life could go on. There was talk in the Church about evangelization and how to reach out, and the thoughts the bishop had expressed two and a half years earlier came to mind. The team of five from local prayer leaders were already active in many areas, but I mentioned the bishop's idea to the team and—to my surprise—they thought it was great.

I called Bobbie Byerly, who by then had ascended to national leadership in Aglow, to run the idea by her.

Bobbie said, "Marilyn, I believe it's of God." She offered to call the leaders of Aglow and ask them to place at our disposal any information that would help us in any way to get started. They didn't see it as competition but rather like a big sister helping a little sister. That's how we looked at it too. From International President Jane Hanson on down, there's always been that kind of a blessing upon Magnificat, for which I thank God to this day.

Next, I called my dear friend Patti Mansfield and bounced the idea off her. Patti immediately suggested, "Why not call it 'Magnificat'?" Her husband, Al, advised us to look at the visitation in Luke, Chapter 1, and to meditate on that scene.

It was amazing how everything came together. When I advised Bishop Ott of what we were thinking, he was delighted. "Awesome!" he said. His advice was, "Begin small. Plan the event around the Feast of Our Lady, take one step at a time, and God will do the rest."

With the bishop's blessing we had fliers printed. A lady, an artist involved in the prayer group, took the name and the concept to prayer and came up with the design for our logo. Everything just fell into place! One team member said, "You know, it's like we're daughters baking a cake with our mother. Mother Mary, who is so present with us, is orchestrating the whole thing. She brought all the ingredients, all of the gifts together, and we just stirred the bowl a little bit and helped her put it in the oven. When the finished cake came out, we thought we had baked it, but we didn't. It was Mary. It was her ministry."

We chose the date October 7, 1981, to begin. It was a convenient date for us. We often look back on this Feast of the Holy Rosary and marvel that this was all orchestrated by God and is part of His divine plan. The Feast of the Holy Rosary is relevant to our present time. It was set by Pope Pius V in 1571, after the defeat of the Moslems at the famous sea battle at Lepanto.

As the Moslems were on route to conquer Christian Europe and impose the faith of Islam upon all there, a small force of Christian men, mainly out of Spain, rallied together to defend Christian Europe. Pius V had the whole continent of Europe praying the rosary for Our Lady's intercession. The Christian forces carried a banner of Our Lady of Guadalupe aboard the lead ship to ask Mary to come to the aid of the Christians. Against all odds there was a decisive victory for the Christians that inspired the pope to inaugurate the Feast of Our Lady of Victory, later renamed the Feast of the Holy Rosary.

We are convinced that there is a connection between this feast and those of us in Magnificat. We began in a Knights of Columbus hall in St. Dominic's Parish in New Orleans. The facility was built to accommodate one hundred fifty people comfortably, and we were told that possibly two hundred could fit. We had two hundred tickets printed. Before the fliers hit the mail, two hundred tickets were sold.

Now we had a huge problem. People were going to get fliers and call up for reservations, but there were no more tickets. I called the chancery office to alert the bishop that he might be hearing complaints about this.

But the bishop said, "Oh, Marilyn, that's marvelous! Next time they'll know to get their tickets early."

"Next time?" I questioned.

"Oh yes," he replied. "This is going to continue and grow all over."

The day of the meal was, in fact, a glorious day. The bishop proved to be prophetic. From that day there were those who wanted to bring this back to their local area. We said to each other, "We don't even know if we're going to have another one." But over a period of time we were convinced that was what the Lord wanted, and we sponsored more prayer meals.

As the ministry grew, we were told to incorporate, to get copyrights, and to write statutes. Again and again God brought those gifts together in just an awesome, amazing way. In 1998, at the Vigil of Pentecost, Pope John Paul II said that when the Holy Spirit intervenes, He leaves people astonished. He brings about events of amazing newness. He radically changes persons and history. He changes us and does incredible things. We've seen this happen at the beginning of each chapter and never cease to be amazed at God's timing and the beautiful way God works in our midst.

In Song of Songs 4:12–16 we read, "You are an enclosed garden my sister, my bride … Arise, north wind! Come, south wind! Blow upon my garden that its perfumes may spread abroad." God has truly blown upon Our Lady's garden. Magnificat, a ministry to Catholic women, is now a private association of the Christian faithful, canonically placed within the heart of the Church under the jurisdiction of each local bishop.

At the time of this writing (2014), there are eighty plus chapters located in twelve countries on three continents, plus twelve more areas with chapters in formation. Membership is of a spiritual nature. We only ask that members agree with the objectives of Magnificat, try to incorporate these objectives into their daily lives, and that they pray for all of the members.

The spiritual benefits are enormous. When a woman signs her name to a Magnificat membership card, she is connected to a vast network of women all over the world who are praying for her and for her intentions … as she is praying for them. This prayer connection is powerful!

By God's grace and blessing through Magnificat, I have come to realize how God has honored my quest to serve Him. He has given me the privilege of visiting almost all of the Magnificat chapters, so in a certain sense, I have become a "missionary." The "medical" part pertains to the spiritual medicine that comes to us through our prayer connection with our loving God, as well as from the honorary degree that mothers naturally acquire through experience.

Magnificat was called forth, I believe, for such a time as this, a time in which women need to be reaffirmed in their true identity as women. We see the power of a woman's influence throughout the Old Testament and the New Testament—for good or for evil. I believe that God is addressing himself to women especially today.

In his beautiful apostolic letter, "On the Dignity and Vocation of Women," written on the occasion of the Marian Year 1988, St. Pope John Paul II said that many times in order to intervene in the history of his people, God addressed himself to women. "In the Spirit of Christ," St. Pope John Paul II concluded, "women can discover the entire meaning of their femininity and thus be disposed to making a 'sincere gift of self' to others, thereby finding themselves." It is only through Christ that we realize that we are of value and that we have unique, unmatchable gifts as women.

At the solemn closing ceremony of the Second Vatican Council (December 8, 1965), we read a beautiful message for women that states, "But the hour is coming, in fact has come, when the vocation of woman is being achieved in its fullness, the hour in which woman acquires in the world an influence, an effect and power never hitherto achieved and that is why … women impregnated with the spirit of the gospel can do much to aid mankind in not failing."

This is in direct contradiction to the false teaching being given to women today that they need to find liberation in seeking themselves. The truth is that only in Christ can we know our true identity. Only in Christ can we know true liberation, free to be the person that God has created us to be.

We look to Mother Mary as our model of the truly liberated woman, truly free in Christ, truly free to be all that God has called her to be. Eve said "no" to God, but Mary said "yes" and thereby untied the knot that Eve had tied. As we say our "yes" in obedience to God, following His plan for our lives, we too can be instruments of grace in the world. To do that we need to nurture His gifts by being open to the power of the Holy Spirit. We need to hunger and thirst for more of God.

I truly believe that God's desire is for us to have an intimate prayer life with Him. He wants us to walk with Him and talk with Him and to seek His kingdom every day through prayer and His Word. Then we become new creations in Him. And He will give us joy beyond anything this world can ever give.

"Now to him who is able to accomplish far more than all we ask or imagine, by the power at work within us, to him be glory in the church and in Christ Jesus to all generations, forever and ever. Amen" (Ephesians 3:20).

Bio–
Marilyn Quirk is the founding Coordinator of Magnificat, in which capacity she served for thirty-one years. She is now Coordinator Emeritus of its Central Service Team. While studying to become an Episcopal medical missionary in 1958, Marilyn converted to Catholicism and has been involved in the Catholic Charismatic Renewal since 1970. She has served as a member of the Steering Committee for the Southern Regional Conference and has served on the National Service Committee of the Charismatic Renewal. She and her husband, Peter, have six children and thirteen grandchildren, and are members of the Knights of the Holy Sepulchre and Legatus. On January 29, 2000, Marilyn received the Pontifical award Pro Ecclesia et Pontifice from St. John Paul II for her FIAT to nurture and grow the Magnificat ministry.

Dr. Carol Razza

I want to begin by praising the Lord. "Thank You, Lord. Thank You, Lord. You are a marvelous God! God is good, and He is good all the time." A song has been coming to my mind and has been on my heart for a while now. It is the worship song, "I'm Amazed by You." I am constantly amazed by what God does. One morning, the thought occurred to me as I was praying and I said, "What a marvelous God you are, Lord!" I was in California, and my husband was praying in Florida, and yet our prayers were united.

I see this in Magnificat as well—it is an international ministry, and we are united as women and men across the miles. There are many men who are supportive of Magnificat, and it can only be attributed to God.

I have a sense that God wants us to recognize that unity. I want to challenge you and me to look outside of our own fears, our own concerns, and our own lies, specifically beyond the lies formed in our own lives. I truly believe God is moving in our world today. God is calling His people to come together and do the things He ordained them to do. He has called us from the womb to do His will. He is an amazing God because He gives us exactly what we need to accomplish His calling.

Let's pray. "Lord, we are amazed by You. We are amazed that You love us. You have loved us throughout our lifetime and You continue to show love for us each and every day, Lord. We don't have to be perfect to receive that love. In fact, we are so short from perfect and yet You continue to love us. You continue to draw us out of our wounded-ness. You continue to draw us out of those places that we thought were so secure and safe but really weren't. They were places of bondage. You continue to draw us out into freedom. A freedom that You, and You alone, can only give. We thank You for that, Lord. I make this prayer in the name of the Father and of the Son and of the Holy Spirit. Amen."

Jeremiah 1:5 tells us, "Before I formed you in the womb, I knew you." Before you came to birth, He consecrated you. He is talking about *us*. I have discovered in my life that God knows us, loves us, and has gifts and plans for each and every one of us.

Jeremiah 29:11 says, "For I know the plans I have for you. Plans for your welfare and not for woe. Plans to give you a future full of hope." Full of hope! That means God has a plan for our welfare and for the welfare and advancement of the kingdom. The devil will do whatever he can to try to stop the fulfillment of God's plan. He doesn't care about us, but he does care that God has a plan. If God's plan is truly activated, and if each and every one of us takes our rightful place in the body of Christ, Satan is in trouble!

I call the devil a boogie-man. The only thing he can do is scare us. "Boo!" he says, and we say, "Uhhh!" When I read Revelations 12:17, I recognize this, as Mary is running and God is protecting her. The devil is after her baby. He wants that baby. He wants Him destroyed. Mary is safe (the church) and the devil wages war against all the people who love God.

It is so empowering to read these words in verse 17: "And he took up his place on the sand of the sea." The devil has been placed on sand. We stand on the Rock. So, is the devil a boogie-man? Yes! But we have to stand our ground. The only way we do that is to allow God to move in our life, to embrace the fullness of who we are in Him, and to allow Him to activate the gifts He gave us in the womb of our mother.

Everyone has a story. My story includes one sibling, my sister, Jackie. She is twelve years older than I am. During those twelve years, Mom and Dad couldn't get pregnant. I can't ask this question now because Mother and Dad are celebrating life with the Lord. Besides, she would probably be too ashamed to say "yes," but the story goes that Mom had the one and only glass of red wine she would ever have. And so, here I am!

I was raised in an environment where Mom and Dad did not go to church, but the love of God was strong in my home. Mom and Dad loved each other desperately for fifty-eight years. Dad died first. Then Mom caught up with him, and they celebrated sixty years together in heaven.

There was love in my home. It was easy for me when I recognized who God was to translate the love of what I experienced at home into the love God has for me. While there was love in the home, it wasn't church. As a little girl I was drawn to the TV to watch *Save the Children*, where Christian groups went into Africa. Before the show started they had gospel singers, and I would love it. I was four years old, dancing with the gospel singers. Now, we have twin baby girls and we call them Song and Dance. One likes to sing and one likes to dance. And oh can they get into it! They call me Nonnie. Their Nonnie is rubbing off on them.

I heard stories from my cousins about my sister while she was growing up. My sister is fair-skinned with strawberry-blonde hair. I am dark-skinned with dark hair. My cousins said, "When Jackie was born, she was beautiful.

When you were born, you scared the life out of us." Can you imagine "scaring the life" out of someone? So, the lies started to form at a very young age. Sometimes we don't realize the impact of words. I didn't hear this from my parents, but I heard it from the world. I was absorbing, "you are ugly." That is the message I started to embrace.

In addition, my mom was an immigrant from Sicily. She was five or six years old when she came from Marsala, Italy. My father was second-generation. They might have completed the third grade in school, or maybe fourth. I started school at the age of four. It was very difficult for me because I was always too young for my grade. I attended public school, so I was picked up by bus and taken to our religious education classes.

In second grade, I met Sister Mary Margaret (God bless her!). She was a St. Joseph sister, who in those days had their faces half hidden. There she was, all covered in black with big rosary beads around her waist. I wasn't quite sure how she was going to beat us up with them. She was about twenty-five years old, but I thought she was ancient. We had to study the *Baltimore Catechism* because I was preparing for First Holy Communion. My parents helped me study some, but it wasn't that important that I study, although it was very important that I go.

By the time I stood before Sr. Mary Margaret to recite from the *Baltimore Catechism*, I shook. What if I got it wrong? I was paralyzed, trying to remember the answers. I couldn't repeat anything. She looked at me and said, "You, Carol LaPonzina, are too stupid. You will not make your First Holy Communion."

I sobbed. I was seven years old and I really didn't understand what First Holy Communion was, but I sure wanted to be a bride. I wanted to wear that dress, and we were all ready to have a party. I was excited to do that. As I sobbed, God in His graciousness allowed Fr. Dennis O'Brien, the pastor—a big Irishman—to walk in.

"Sister, what is happening?" he asked.

"She is too stupid," Sr. Mary Margaret said. "She cannot make her First Communion next week."

The priest looked and said, "Oh, sweetheart, come with me. Excuse us, Sister." We walked outside; we sat; we shared; and we talked. When we finished, he said, "Honey, you know everything you need to know about Jesus. You will make Communion next week."

"Tell her!" I said." You are the pastor. Come on, Father, let's go tell her!"

And he did. Very graciously he said, "There must be a mistake."

But for me, there was another lie. Now, to add to "you are ugly," I was also stupid.

I want you to allow God to bring to mind the lies that you are still holding on to, those lies still rooted in your life. I know without a shadow of a doubt that the devil keeps those lies captive. The longer he can keep them there, the longer we believe the lie, and the less chance we have of activating our gifts. I was gifted in the womb of my mother just as everyone else. Those gifts were there, but they were buried inside a very shy, a "painfully shy," little girl. For those who know me, there is nothing shy about me now!

When the Holy Spirit takes hold of you, He doesn't let go. Think about those words. Think about those lies that have formed from past hurts. Most people don't know that it is critical for parents and grandparents to interpret their children's world for them. My parents would say things to me like "you are so beautiful. You are so smart." They didn't know this other stuff was going on inside of me, but I also knew they didn't have any education. My teachers were the smart ones. They were the ones who could evaluate me. My parents also thought I was tall. When I stand behind a podium to speak, the audience can barely see me. But to them I was tall. Mom was four-foot-eleven, and Dad was five-foot-three, so it is all relative.

One of the graces God gave me was a blessing my mother prayed over me. She didn't know she was doing that. She was just telling me the truth. I had asked her, "You know, Mom, you named me Carol. Why?" We are an Italian family, and usually you are named after someone in the family. I wasn't named after anyone.

She said, "Oh, I just love Christmas carols. They bring me such joy." So you see? The gift that I received at my Baptism in the Holy Spirit was supernatural joy.

If you look it up in the Catholic Catechism, you will see it is an imprint on us that brings supernatural joy. It is a joy so deep inside of us, recognizing that no matter what we go through in life, God is present. That is exactly what it was for me. Any trial I had to face, I knew God was there. He was in the midst, and that was certainly a blessing my mom prayed over me without even knowing it. What is dangerous is the reverse, when parents, grandparents, or other significant people in authority place word curses on people such as "you'll never make anything of yourself" or "who do you think you are?" This is dangerous and damaging.

A number of years ago when I had my practice in psychotherapy, a man came in to talk to me. During prayer, he remembered he was lazy in school and he wanted to play and be out with his friends. So he didn't do what he needed to do in school, like study. One day, his parents said, "You will become nothing but a garbage man." And in fact, that is what he did. They put up the benchmark that he achieved. In New York, garbage men clean up, but they also make great money. So he did pretty well financially. But the reality is their words were so negative and hurtful. We must be aware that we set the benchmark for our children. Teachers can wound and they can encourage. It is important, and we need to learn how to draw out the gifts in one another.

With the lies of being ugly and stupid, my personality was being formed. Those early years are crucial for children. We were all children at one point, each and every one of us. It doesn't matter how pure and Christian the home is. The reality is the world out there is cruel!

I remember one man I prayed with who was in his forties. He wasn't married. "Who would marry me?" he told me.

I didn't understand that. "What do you mean 'Who would marry you'?"

He looked at me and asked again, "Who would marry me?"

When we prayed together, the Lord gave me a vision of a little boy on a playground, sobbing. As soon as I shared this with him, he began to sob. He said, "I remember that day. I was new to that school and in the first grade. My parents had recently moved and I didn't know any of the kids. A little girl came up to me and she said, 'You are so ugly. You have the biggest nose.'" From that point forward he thought of himself as ugly.

It is then that a lie is formed, and it becomes a magnet. No matter what people say to you after that, such as, "I don't like that color on you. You look better in bright colors rather than dark colors," you don't hear that. What you hear is "you are ugly." The negative words stick to you like a magnet. Then something else comes along, and it is attached too. It makes the lie real. If you are talking to someone and you notice their eyes are someplace else, you think, *Oh, they don't want to hear what I have to say because I am stupid.*

I have an absolute privilege to work with the formation of seminarians to the priesthood. One of the seminarians told me that he couldn't get past one of the lies that he had absorbed in his life. We prayed together, and I took it into prayer, and God revealed something to me about him. I called him back into my office and shared it with him. On the spot God broke the chain that was keeping this young man in such bondage. I am so grateful because now when he goes through ordination he is ready.

Our priests are under such extreme attack. Without them we have no Eucharist, and without the Eucharist we have no Church. They are in the front line, and I want these men to be prepared before they go out into the world.

People's words may not wound you as much as an adult as they did when you were a child, but they sure will pull up everything you had locked away. That is what the lie does. Those early years are critical. As men and women of faith, we have a responsibility for these children that come into our lives, to encourage them and not look only at their behavior. I realize sometimes children have horrible actions, but we need to put on the eyes of Christ to look beyond their behavior and look into the hearts of the children we are working with. We need to encourage them.

As time was moving forward in my life, I became more interactive in school and social activities, but in a quiet way. My parents told me I could do anything. I remember Dad saying, "Anything you want to be, you can." I believed that, even though I still believed the lies which were ingrained and very real to me. It was something I contemplated every day. Many times we don't have the words to the lie but we have the behavior. The lie is a wound on our soul.

I finally learned the *Baltimore Catechism*. It teaches about the faculties of the soul, which are memory, intellect, and the will. The memory is the picture book of our life. If we take our photograph album, those pictures with nothing attached to them, no emotion, that is the memory. Our understanding or intellect is, "How do I interpret those pictures?" That is where the wound lies.

I remember one man saying that every time he looked at a particular picture he remembered just seconds before that his mother beat him up. "Can you imagine? My mother beat me up." He was so sad, even though he said this as he was smiling.

The third faculty is the will. How do we live it out? In my early years, I was living out an understanding of myself as ugly and stupid. Who would want to look at me? Who would want to hear what I had to say? I lived it out by being shy.

I am always amazed by God because He took that shy, wounded little girl, who believed she could accomplish nothing, and brought her into an environment where she became a psychotherapist. I have been in practice for almost thirty years, and I only closed it to go into full-time work at the seminary and because I was traveling so much more. People normally look at psychologists and psychotherapists as people of wisdom, so look at how God plays games with the enemy. He says, "You are going to try and stuff it in, and I am going to bring it out."

Some people have their conversion right on the spot. Something happens to them and life is different. My conversion was such a gentle wind. I am sure our Mother was accompanying me. I didn't know her then but she knew me. She was walking and accompanying me saying, "Come on, come on, little one. I want to introduce you to a man who is going to tell you who you are. He is going to teach you who you are."

God has a way of doing the amazing.

At sixteen I met a wonderful young man. Paul was my childhood sweetheart, and with tears I can say he is my sweetheart today of almost forty-five years. He knew and saw something in me that I couldn't see. He had his own wounds, but he knew and saw something special in me. When he looked at me, he looked at me through God's eyes and he saw beauty. If you ask my husband today, "What did your girlfriend wear when you went to the party?" he will tell you. He will tell you exactly what I wore, the perfume, everything. God started to use him.

I was a teenager and I didn't know God yet. Sometimes Paul and I went to church. Sometimes we took the envelope his mother used to give him to take to church, opened it up, and used the two dollars to get tea and a bagel. Needless to say, my husband was surprised after a year of doing this when his mother got the statement from the church in the mail. He never imagined the church did this. She met him at the door to smack him and said, "Where's the money I gave you?" You can imagine our surprise. We finally confessed.

Because of the loving encouragement of my husband, Paul, and the seeds that were planted by my parents, I finally believed I could do whatever I chose to do. And with that I started college part time. I took only one or two classes at first. As I got into the master's and doctorate programs, I moved a little faster, but it took me twenty-seven years to get my doctorate!

When I started to college, I was still shy and not outspoken. Every time I got a test back, I thought, *Oh, I hope I did as well as the next person.* God used my professors to write little notes like "this is so insightful" or "I never heard this before." I believe God can use anyone He chooses to bring truth, even college professors. He used all of these people, and I was hungry to hear the positive comments. I wasn't healed, though, because I had not been introduced to the Lover of my soul.

God used the chosen field I love, psychotherapy. I have prayed over the years as I worked with people that God would use me to do good. But the reality is that psychotherapy doesn't heal anyone. Jesus is the healer. I can introduce people to Him; help them to be open; help them to look at the lies in their lives; but the reality, the truth is, the only healer is Jesus.

I wasn't healed at the time, but I was walking in a good direction. The Lord kept my then-boyfriend and me chaste. We built a beautiful relationship, were best friends, and continue to be best friends today. I can share anything with him, and he can share anything with me.

We were married on February 9, 1969. It was glorious, except we had a snowstorm—the biggest blizzard in New York at that time. We went on our honeymoon, and when we came back we had the reception. As the years went on, we had two beautiful sons, Paul and Timothy.

When we had Timothy baptized, the priest asked us, "Why did you name him Timothy?"

"I just liked that name," I said.

He said, "Your oldest son's name is Paul, and this one is Timothy. You need a third son named Barnabas."

"I don't know if I like that name," I said.

We didn't have a third son, but today if I did, I would name him Barnabas.

I was married to the love of my life and things seemed perfect. Yet, there was a yearning. It wasn't about the marriage relationship … it was different. In 1969, after we were first married, friends of mine invited us to go to Manhattan to see a new play. It was *Jesus Christ, Superstar*.

"Yes," I said. "I would like to see a play."

I went with a Jewish girl and a Catholic. We sat in the first mezzanine. For those who are unfamiliar with the play, *Jesus Christ, Superstar* is an opera. It includes singing and jumping all over the place … and lots of nonsense that isn't in the Bible.

But for me, something happened during that play.

At the crucifixion, when Jesus was lifted on the cross, I rested in the Spirit. I didn't know what that experience was, but now I can identify it as resting in the Spirit. I knew He did that for me!

When the play was over, we were on 42nd Street and Broadway. I began jumping up and down like a crazy woman. "He did it for me! He did it for me!" I said, "He did it for you, too!"

"What?" they asked.

"He died for us!"

"Oh, that? No, he's an actor," my friends tried to explain. "He's coming back tonight to do it again."

My friends didn't get it. Truthfully, I didn't get it, either. Not really. But I knew something special had happened to me. I ran home, ran into the house, grabbed my husband, and said, "He died for us!"

He said, "Oh, that's nice."

Seriously, I acted like a lunatic. I didn't know what to do with this knowledge; there was no one around to pick that yearning up and nurture it. It wasn't until a few years later when we had our sons that someone invited us to go to a Marriage Encounter. Timothy was only ten months old.

While we were there, my husband and I were getting a little bored with the teaching. Much of what was taught centered on good marital communication, and that was something we already did well as a couple. It wasn't in our nature to hold things back.

Then something changed. The priest started to speak, and when he did our hearts were convicted. We knew for the first time that God had called us into this marriage to exemplify Jesus, to show the love of the Trinity.

We left there as disciples. We left saying, "Oh, this is what marriage is about." We didn't understand the depth of that before. We thought you get married because you are in love. But it is so much more. We thought, *What is this all about?* We didn't know the most important part! We were just so filled with God's love. We went to church and joined an image group—a support group for those who have attended a weekend. We started to grow in our faith and marriage through the Marriage Encounter ministry.

Then we moved to Florida and took another step. We made it to a Cursillo retreat. The Cursillo ministry allowed us to move into a personal relationship with Jesus. My eyes couldn't get any bigger. I remember walking out of Cursillo and seeing things as if for the first time. It was like a fine-tuning of the world, which had just been turned on. Everything looked so bright and so clear.

Two weeks after my Cursillo, I realized I hadn't said one curse word. I come from New York. The adjectives used in New York are used like no other place in the world, and I was just as good as the rest of the population in expressing myself. But for two weeks I hadn't.

That's when I heard the Lord say, "If you are going to preach about Me with that mouth, you are not going to say those other words." Wow! I couldn't believe the Lord was talking to me, but I still didn't understand exactly what He was doing. It was as if He cleaned me up on the spot in that area.

Right after Cursillo, we experienced the Baptism in the Holy Spirit. The Lord was moving! In 1980 we went to our first Charismatic Renewal conference in Miami. It was exciting because I had never seen so many people so full of joy. They were my people. We danced together. We jumped and did all sorts of acrobatics in the Spirit. It was wonderful.

Then a woman preached. I had never heard a priest preach like this, but when Auntie Babsie from Trinidad spoke, it was as if I could have shrunk to the size of a pea and let her swallow me. I couldn't get enough of this woman; I wanted to get closer.

During my childhood I had a hunger for a "mammy." It was wild. I had a mommy, and she was a good mommy, but I always wanted a chubby, dark-skinned woman as a mammy. The Lord was saying, "Here she is. She is your mentor." Auntie Babsie didn't know me, but the Lord took care of that a few years later.

When she stepped off the stage, the Lord did something profound. My husband is very quiet in his faith. He looked at me and said, "Someday, I am going to see you up on stage like that."

"What will I say?" I asked.

"I don't know, but you are going to be there."

The Lord gave him the prophecy for ministry for me. He has come into ministry, as well, because of the places God has taken me. Paul comes when he can, if it is not too expensive for the two of us to travel. I love that the prophecy came through him, just as the Lord planned.

Thirty years later, my husband is still my prayer warrior and my encourager. Every time someone asks me to speak, I go to Paul and say, "Are you still on the same page? Do you want me to do this?"

He says, "Absolutely! This is where God is calling us."

Do you see how God used him? He inspired Paul at that time.

Now that we had the Baptism in the Holy Spirit, I knew life would never be the same ever again. While things were good in our life, Jesus was my Lover, and it just couldn't be the same. I couldn't do things the same way. I couldn't say things the same way. For those who have had this type of conversion—when you come into that love of the One who loves you the most—you experience the same thing.

I break into song as I write this: "I will never be the same again. I will never return. I close the door. I will walk the walk. I will run the race, but I will never be the same again."

I couldn't return. I didn't want to. Life was so much more exciting. Certainly, there were people who looked at me as if I had lost my mind. I *did* lose my mind, but it was okay because I lost it in a good way! I have a good Daddy, Who is the Father in heaven, and a good brother in Jesus. The Holy Spirit continues to reveal the love of the Trinity to me. I publicly professed Jesus as my Lord and my Savior.

I knew God had a plan for my life, but I didn't know what it was exactly. He spoke it through my husband, and I knew everything was okay. My sons were little, but I knew they were going to be okay and I didn't have any fear. I didn't wonder, "What if this happens, and what if that happens?" We must be careful to watch the words that come out of our mouths. We can give the enemy lots of ammunition to play havoc in our lives and within our families.

Over the years I have prayed with people who said, "My greatest fear was that my children would become drug addicts." And, of course, they did. The parents gave the enemy information. But I knew in my case that God had everything in control. He loved my sons much more than I loved them. He loved my husband more than I loved him, and God continued to nurture our family. Our words can damage, so speak the truth, always the truth. We know the truth is out of the Word of God.

God is our fortress; He is our strength; He is our courage; He is the One who protects us; He wants us to be whole. Put on the armor of Christ. Put it on for your kids, but be careful in speaking out those fears. Remember that the fears come from the lies. The more we allow God to get into the crevices of our lies and free us, the more the fears go away.

If you are a person who worries a lot and holds on to things that are upsetting, recognize that this is not from the Lord. It is a type of control. If you worry, then you think it won't happen. The reality is if you worry, if this is what you talk about, if this is where your focus is, you are tying up your guardian angel. I believe we have angels that want to do God's work for us. Instead, we tie them up by the lies we believe and by our fears.

You may have heard this story: a bear was captured when he was a cub, and whoever had captured him put him in a small, six-foot by six-foot cage. For years, the only thing this bear knew was six feet up, six feet over, six feet back, six feet up, and six feet over. He knew that cage.

Finally, the time came when the animal activists said, "We need to open this cage and let this bear out. He is too big for this cage. It is not fair. He needs to be in the wild." They opened the cage thinking it would be a celebration. But it was not. The only thing the bear could do was move six feet over, six feet back, and six feet up. They pulled the cage off of him, and he still could only move six feet up, six feet over, and six feet back.

God took our cages away! He took our cages away over 2,000 years ago. He is saying, "You need to walk beyond six feet." He invites us, "Let Me lure you into My love."

I believe there has been an assault on our ears. We hear words that have no substance. People say, "I will always love you." Then they leave.

"You can always trust me." Then we learn we can't.

"I'll forgive you." And they turn their backs on us.

The reality is that when God says it, He means it. He tells us that in Scripture. But if we hold onto our lies, we will never hear it. I believe that is why so often we go to Mass, receive Holy Communion, but leave the same way we came. We really don't believe the power of that miracle that happens on the altar ... I mean *really* believe it. I don't mean believe it with head knowledge, but with our hearts. When we read the term "understanding" in the Scriptures we think cognitively with our Western minds. I understand, I "get" it. But that is not the way it is meant to be understood.

In the understanding of Scripture, "understanding" the word means using the five senses. It means to truly embrace with every part of our being, giving it all I have with every cell and fiber of my body. I need to realize that when God says it, He means it and He acts on it. He doesn't keep us stuck in that same place. That is not how He functions.

We need to give it all to Him. We need to be crazy in love with the Lover of our souls because then we give Him permission to operate the way He wants to operate in our life. To operate in drawing us out and operate in severing the things that need to be severed.

The Holy Spirit is a surgeon. He goes into those places that are damaged and cuts away all the bad. But He can't if we keep pushing Him away and saying, "Oh, no don't go there, or there. That is too sore," or "I don't want to look at that again." No! I urge you to look at it again, but look at it with God's eyes. He has a new revelation for you. Give it all to Him; surrender it all, give Him permission.

Again I want to sing: "Lord, I give You my heart. I give You my soul. I live for You alone. Every breath that I take. Every moment that I am awake. Lord, have your way with me." I want to pray this for you: "Lord, have Your way with us. Have Your way with us this day."

Life, since Jesus, is life I could never have imagined. Things continue to happen as I continue to surrender my will for my life into His hands. He allowed me first the healing of the lies. All of a sudden it was clear it was a lie! I pray for each of you reading this right now that God will go into those dark areas of your soul and shed light so that you can see clearly and hear from Him. You won't believe it from me, but you will believe it from Him, when He gives you the truth of who you are in Him. We have to ask ourselves, "Are we living the abundant life or does worry, anger, depression, and fear have a hold on our life?"

So many Christians live in depression. They say to me, "I love Jesus, but depression is a family disease. My mother was depressed. My grandmother was depressed."

In answer to that I say, "That is a *lie!* Today is a day of freedom."

I certainly don't want to diminish the hurts that people have in their life. But the only one Who can heal, Who can soothe, and Who becomes the salve is Jesus. Normally, He is the first One we push away. We say things like, "Lord, You disappointed me." He didn't disappoint us. This world may have. Our choices may have, but He didn't disappoint us. He is right there to rescue us.

Sometimes people say, "I prayed for my husband for months and I gave up." For months? He said He was coming back soon, and it has been over 2,000 years. Jesus is not on the same time scale as us. Every day we have to remind ourselves of the promises of our baptism to live as priest, prophet, and king. That is the promise of our baptism—to be sensitive to the movement of the Spirit. With all of the burdens I carried around, He turned my lies into pearls. At my baptism God knew exactly what He was calling me into.

I remember asking someone, "With a name like Carol, I don't have a saint to model. What is my saint?" People would say, "Oh, my saint is so-and-so. This is my feast day." What was mine? I had no idea. I wanted one, and someone spoke wisdom to me when she said, "Yours is St. Charles Borromeo." I didn't like that name, so I never bothered looking up information about St. Charles until I was an adult. On November 4th, his feast day, the priest spoke on St. Charles Borromeo. That is when I learned he is the patron of seminarians in formation and missionaries. Isn't that prophetic?

My middle name is Jean. In French John is Jean. The Cure of Ars, St. John Vianney, is the patron of diocesan priests. Did God know? Of course He knew! And if He knew for me, He knew for each one of us at the time of our baptism.

He took the heart of that little girl who hungered to be with those babies in Africa. Those babies were bigger than I was at the time, and He brought me there. He sees the desires in our hearts when we are young. That is a foretaste of where God is taking us. It is a foretaste, so if you dare tell yourself "I am not gifted. I don't have what God needs to use me," then look back and remember that little child, because it wasn't God that took away that desire.

Maybe it was this world; maybe it was hurts. Whatever it was, it wasn't God. With God there are no time limits. In order for me to get to Africa, it took until I was almost sixty years old. It didn't happen right away. The same with the seminary. God revealed to me years before that I would be part of the formation of seminarians, but it took almost fifteen years. I put it aside. I said, "Lord, I trust You. Whatever it is, it is. I will get there when You ordain it."

And that is what He says to each and every one of you. I am a missionary. I go throughout the world. The list of the places I've been gets longer and longer. Could I have ever designed this? Never.

Sometimes people say, "I want to do what you are doing. How do you get there?"

I said, "I don't have a clue, and I don't know. I go one place and then I find myself someplace else." In January, I visited India—a first for me. I go where God leads me. Half the time my husband and I have to take out a map and find out where I am going. We don't know where it is, but God does.

I've had the privilege to see the most incredible miracles happen in Africa. People were healed; some were throwing away their crutches. They came in on beds and went home walking. I remember a man, Peter, who was so beautiful. He didn't want to come to the conference. He didn't want to bring shame to his wife since he couldn't walk. The doctors said that when they went home, he would have his legs amputated. Two days into the conference, I turned and was shocked to see him standing alongside me.

"Peter!" I said.

He said, "I know. My wife doesn't even know yet. God healed me!"

Our God is a good God!

One of the first things I felt in Africa was a sadness and a burden in my spirit for the division in the tribes. I didn't realize how tribal they are, especially in Kenya. Up until 2007, they were still massacring each other. The last time I was there, there was prayer and a reconciliation of the tribes at this conference. It was incredible to see what God was doing in the heavenlies, and we trust what He will do outside of that environment. People came together and embraced each other and asked for forgiveness. These were people who had lost their homes and their families to another tribe, and now they were forgiving each other. It was absolutely beautiful.

God has a purpose and a plan for each and every one of us, but we have to trust in God, and God alone—no matter where your journey takes you. It doesn't matter where you are right now in your spiritual walk, God still has more. Sister Nancy Keller is famous for saying, "God has more. He always has more."

Sometimes we think we have gotten to a place and we're comfortable, and that's it—we've arrived. He always has more for us, He is the God of the supernatural. He is supernatural. When we embrace Him, when we open ourselves up to the Holy Spirit, we recognize that we are a part of the supernatural.

Another time I was in the Dominican Republic, where the Lord sent me to do a lot of work. I don't speak Spanish, but I always have a translator. In my travels, I find some translators are better than others. At one particular conference, the translator didn't get it right. No matter what I said, it wasn't coming out in the way I thought the Lord wanted, which was confirmed when someone who understood English explained the translator wasn't interpreting the words correctly. "He doesn't have it. He isn't saying what you are saying."

There was nothing I could do. The conference was over and I was asked to minister to 250 young people waiting for me. I explained to the interpreters as clearly as I could to translate every word exactly, "It is a simple message of salvation, but I want the kids to get it. I want them to receive the Lord this day."

The interpreter answered, "Yeah, yeah, I'll say everything."

About two hours later, all the kids came up to receive the Lord. Many of them were healed that day. They were resting in the Spirit.

"Richard," I said. "You didn't say one word. Two and a half hours we were here, and you didn't say one word."

"Oh, I didn't have to," he said.

"What do you mean, you didn't have to?"

He explained, "You spoke perfect Spanish."

I was shocked. "Richard, I don't speak Spanish!"

He nodded. "Yeah, I know. That's why I was looking around to see who was feeding you the words. But there was no one there."

"Okay," I said. "Tomorrow when I come back to these kids, we are going to be praying for a Baptism in the Holy Spirit. I'm bringing my friend, LeeAnn."

The next day, she came. "LeeAnn," I said. "Please, if I have a word of knowledge for one of the kids, we want them to know what God is saying to them."

"Oh, yes," she responded, "I am going to say everything."

Once again we completed the entire prayer service. "LeeAnn," I exclaimed. "You didn't say a word!"

"Oh," she said, "I didn't have to. You spoke like a native. Not like an Anglo, but like a native."

Even today we can have an upper-room experience. I didn't hear myself speak Spanish. That would have shocked me, and I wouldn't have understood myself. But the kids understood. They understood because the Lord willed it and we had the upper-room experience.

God is good. He has allowed so many wonderful privileges as I continue to journey, as I continue to grow, and as I continue to be open to His movement in my life. Once, when working at a conference in Scranton, an anorexic woman came up to me and asked if I would pray with her. "The doctors say I only have a few more months to live because I can't eat," she explained. "My body won't accept food, and they don't know what is wrong."

As we sat down and prayed, God revealed that she was harboring unforgiveness toward her siblings. I didn't know she had siblings, but I asked, "Do you have brothers and sisters?"

She answered, "Yes."

I questioned, "Are you not forgiving them?"

"They treated my mother very poorly."

I told her, "The condition you have is not physical. It comes from this lack of forgiveness. Will you choose to forgive them?"

She agreed, and we prayed. The next morning she ran to me and explained the previous evening was the first night in months she slept well. She ate a full dinner and nothing bad happened. She added, "This morning I had breakfast, and I feel wonderful!"

God healed her. Is that considered a miracle? Of course it is! Do you believe He wants you to be a part of it? Yes, He does. I can relate story after story, but I believe He is calling you to recognize your own giftedness. He has called each and every one of you, because there is a mission field that needs you. It might be your home. It might be your workplace. It might be going to the nations.

I have a ministry in Africa. They named it *Swahiba*, which means "a friend closer than a brother." The seminary where I work is totally supportive. They set up an account for people who want to donate to the African mission by donating to the seminary's fund. It is for those who have a heart for the missions. I pray that you consider the Swahiba, because God is doing a great work there that needs our help.

Being used by God started with my prayer of surrender. It began with my acceptance of Jesus as my Lord and Savior, knowing that He really was the Lover of my soul.

I believe the following prayer by Fr. Jim Ferry, who died in 1989, introduces us to that Lover, and we can hear the call of Jesus in this prayer. I pray you hear Jesus speaking directly to you as you read these words:

"Come to Me, My friend.
I call you to a deeper surrender of yourself.
I call you to come to Me.
I call you to come to My freedom.
Unloose you heart, surrender again to Me today.

Come to Me, my friend.
I will give you all you need.
Believe and trust in Me.
I know you will not understand.
Only know My way is the perfect way.
My plan is a perfect plan for your life.
Turn yourself to Me again today.

I wish to deepen My life in you.
I wish to give you My love.

My friend, I want to transform you.
To make you a new creation, ever new, ever changing.
I want to bring you into a deeper truth, a deeper freedom.
I want you to believe in My power
to transform you, to heal you.
Do not limit what I can do.
There is still so much more I want to do
with you and through you.
I call you to a deeper faith
that I may be still more powerful in you."

Bio–

Dr. Carol Razza is a full-time faculty member and formation advisor at St. Vincent de Paul Seminary. She also serves on the Advisory Team for the International Magnificat, and on the National Catholic Charismatic Council. She is licensed by the state of Florida in Mental Health Counseling and has worked in private practice as a psychotherapist for over twenty-five years. She has written two books, *Sonblock, How Christians Unknowingly Shield Themselves From Grace*, and *Parent Me ... Please*, a book helping parents to parent their adolescents. Carol also presents at seminars, conferences, workshops, and retreats both nationally and internationally. Carol's greatest blessings include her marriage of over forty years to her husband Paul, their wonderful sons and daughters-in-law, and grandchildren.

Jan Tate

O ne human life: a series of choices, of yes and no answers and relationships with others. Those choices, those answers, those people make all the difference. This is the story of my life and of the people and choices that have led me down many pathways. It is unique because I am a unique and unrepeatable person, created in the image and likeness of God.

I open the door of my heart so that you who read this may have a glimpse into the road I have traveled and the manifestation of God's presence that I have discovered waiting around every corner and along each part of the path.

I was born July 16, 1950, on the Feast of Our Lady of Mt. Carmel. I have always treasured the fact that I was born on a Marian feast. I hope to die on a Marian feast, as well. From my earliest days, I was taught to love and revere Mary as the Holy Mother of God. She has been my constant companion and spiritual Mother.

At this point in my life, I have two great passions, two motivating forces in my mind and heart, that guide me in my decisions and choices each day. It is from these two passions that I speak and minister. They form the wellspring of my prayer life and draw me closer to Christ. These two passions shape the way I see everything. They are my Catholic faith and my marriage.

When I look back over my life, I can see that the Lord placed people and events that ignited those passions within me. As I embraced the ways of the Lord, one "yes" led to other "yeses." Steadily, brick by brick, the Lord, through the power of the Holy Spirit, built my life.

A Scripture verse that has long been one of my favorites comes from Hosea 11:3–4: "Yet it was I who taught Ephraim to walk, who took them in my arms; I drew them with human cords, with bands of love …"

These words of the prophet Hosea speak to the way of the Lord with me: God has drawn me to Himself *with human cords, with bands of love.* My personality is such that the Lord knew I would respond best to His invitation through people and relationships. Thomas Aquinas was probably drawn to the Lord through knowledge and truth, while others are drawn to the Lord through beauty, art, music, or logic. The way the Lord draws us is consistent with our unique personalities and temperaments. How blessed we are to be loved, guided, and shaped by a God who loves each of us so personally.

Because of the ministry that I have been involved in, I have become deeply aware of the tremendous impact our families of origin have on us. We don't get to choose our family. God sends us into a particular family situation. The influence on us by the people who raised us is profound and lasting. Our basic identity is shaped, initially, by them. It is from the way they treated us that we understand what it means to be a woman or a man; what in life is of value; and what those "unbreakable unshakeables" are that guide our thoughts and choices.

Dr. Larry Crabb, a prominent Christian psychologist, wrote: "Values that are naturally lived by people we watch become more a part of our soul than those values we are specifically taught." That's why most of us have had the experience as we grew older of saying: "Gosh, I sound just like my mother/father." Almost unwillingly, we repeat the past because the values we observed became the values we absorbed.

I am not saying we have no control over ourselves with regard to the patterns we learn from our families. What I do know, however, is that changing those values and patterns takes deep soul-work, acute personal awareness, and focused intentional work. The relationship patterns we learn growing up become like our second skin. Therefore, in telling my story I must reflect on those early influences that shaped me. They were the first *human cords* the Lord used to draw me to Himself.

My parents were committed Catholics, who considered the practice of their faith and service to the Church as non-negotiable. They had an amazing passion for one another and a deep love for their five children. They valued education and loved reading, music, people, and fun times. They believed that life should be spent in service, not in selfishness, and both demanded excellence from themselves in all they endeavored.

My dad started his own floor-covering business when he graduated from Loyola University in New Orleans, and he worked tirelessly to support my mother, who stayed home to raise the five of us. My mom was a great "CEO" of our household. She taught me the value of self-discipline, creativity, and hospitality.

She and my dad were not perfect, however. Some of their brokenness meant that I absorbed messages that were not healthy or true. Some messages that play over and over in my mind come from my family of origin such as:

"Idleness is the devil's workshop."
"Autograph your work with excellence."
"To whom much is given, much is expected."
"Sleeping late is 'wasting daylight.'"
"Work before play."

As I look at those messages and see them all together, I realize that a great deal of who I am and what I have achieved is due to the fact that my family programmed into me a certain work ethic and belief. Because I was given much by God, I was expected to make a return and do so with excellence.

At first blush this seems like a good message. However, after a while it got twisted up inside of me. I began to think that my worth was based on my performance, and that I had to be perfect in order to be loved. I also got wrapped up in a strong pattern of competition with my older sister for the love I wanted, and bam! I had all the makings of an over-achiever, who had difficulty believing in the free, gratuitous love of God and the precious gift of salvation in Christ.

Much of my adult faith journey has been spent untwisting those lies within me and on learning that love—real love—can be trusted. God desires to lavish His mercy and grace upon me even though I am not perfect.

My mom died from cancer at the young age of fifty-nine. As I look back over the legacies she and Dad gave me, the two I am most grateful for are their consistent modeling of an alive and growing Catholic faith and their passionate commitment to each other in the Sacrament of Matrimony. They planted the seeds in me that made the garden of my soul ripe for harvesting my two great passions.

My parents were one of the pioneer couples who started marriage preparation in the form of Pre Cana in the Archdiocese of New Orleans in the 1950s. Their love for each other and their commitment to raising and educating their children while serving the Church and their extended families was an example I embraced. Indeed, it was the seedbed the Lord used for the development of my own work ethic and my two great passions.

As I grew older, the Lord used other people, other *human cords,* to draw me to Himself. I attended an all-girls' Catholic high school in a suburb of my hometown of New Orleans. Sometime during my freshman year, I responded to an invitation on the bulletin board to attend Sodality meetings at Jesuit High School, an all-boys' high school. I admit I went mostly because I was interested in meeting some guys who might be eligible dating prospects. God took my mixed motives, however, and introduced me to a Jesuit priest who became one of the greatest influences in my life.

Father Ken Buddendorff was a fairly new priest at the time, and we took an immediate liking to each other. I went to everything the Sodality sponsored. Gradually, a group of guys and girls formed a core group. We socialized, prayed, and learned from Father Bud and from each other for the rest of my high school days. My parents loved Father Bud and trusted him completely. He began taking me along with him to speak at retreats and days of reflection. Father Bud introduced me to the world of the Jesuits in Grand Coteau, Louisiana, home of the Jesuit novitiate.

I look back on this and marvel that my parents trusted him so much, and that he trusted me so much that he invited me to share ministry with him. Father Bud called forth my gifts and believed I could do things I never dreamed I could do. He imparted to me a real love for the Scriptures and introduced me to Ignatian spirituality. He was my sole confessor for almost fourteen years, and I grew to treasure the Sacrament of Reconciliation because of Father Bud's love and mercy toward me.

One of my pivotal experiences occurred during my senior year, when I accompanied Father Bud to a youth convention in Mississippi. I got up to speak and experienced what I know now was the Baptism in the Holy Spirit. It was the first time in my life that I felt completely possessed by the Spirit while giving a talk. The Spirit just washed over me. I remember sitting down when I finished my part of the presentation and seeing absolutely stunned looks on people's faces, especially on Father Bud's. I cried for hours afterwards.

I had no idea what had actually happened, but I knew that something had been born within me. It wasn't until ten years later in 1978, when I took my first Life in the Spirit seminar, that I began to understand what had happened to me. I can only praise God for pouring out His Holy Spirit so freely on me at such an early age, when I did nothing to deserve it.

When Father Bud became director of Our Lady of the Oaks retreat house in Grand Coteau many years later, he invited me to share ministry with him by preaching Ignatian retreats and by giving presentations to his interns in spiritual direction. With deep wonder and awe, I thank God for this priest, this *human cord* who helped me become the woman God designed me to be.

In March of my freshman year at Loyola University, New Orleans, where Father Bud was campus minister, I began dating an upperclassman. He was tall, handsome, and intelligent. His name was Lloyd Tate. Lloyd's dad, an alcoholic, had committed suicide when Lloyd was only seven. By the time we met, Lloyd was a responsible, resourceful person with a love for the Lord despite the pain of his past. He had a tremendous gift for music, as well as for academics.

Our dating years were a mixture of fun and faith, study and work, and lots of guitar music, since Lloyd played in a band to help pay for his education. Besides being the first person in his family to attend college, Lloyd earned a master's degree in business and passed the CPA exam the first time he took it. I finished college in three-and-a-half years, and we married in February 1972. At the age of twenty-one I was married to the man of my dreams and pregnant just one month later. Thus began our long journey toward holiness through the Sacrament of Matrimony.

When I reflect on my married life with Lloyd, I am struck by several experiences the Lord used early on to influence us and shape us into a couple He could use for His honor and glory. I see these moments of grace as free gifts from God. We surely did not have the wisdom to know what we were doing in those early years!

On our honeymoon I discovered a letter from my parents in my suitcase. In the letter, Dad wrote something quite profound: "From now on, your married life is all that matters. If something is not good for *both* of you, it is not good for *either* of you."

God used those words over the years to shape the way Lloyd and I made decisions. Dad's advice pointed us in the direction of building unity as a couple instead of choosing to go our separate ways on issues. We did not always follow Dad's advice, and our relationship suffered when we didn't. From our missteps, we learned to value the wisdom of his counsel and to strive for deeper unity in the way we lived out our marriage—in imitation of the Trinitarian union.

From the first night of our marriage, and for the first six or seven years afterwards, we said our wedding vows to each other every night before going to sleep. This practice enabled us to stay committed and helped us focus on our relationship during the early years of struggle and selfishness. We continue to say our vows often, even after forty years, and especially when we are struggling to understand one another. This refocuses our attention on God's plan for a Sacramental marriage.

After only four-and-a-half years of marriage, Lloyd and I were humbled and shocked when Father Bud invited us into the ministry of preparing engaged couples for marriage in the Catholic Church. That "yes" became the dominant influence that shaped our choices going forward. That "yes" exposed us to other married couples and priests, who expanded our horizons and taught us about love, sacrifice, and ministry in beautiful ways. Now that we have served in this ministry for over thirty-eight years, we can see the Lord's hand in fashioning our marriage through the people who drew us to Him and to each other with *bands of love*.

The more we work with engaged couples, and the more we minister to married couples in retreat work, the more I am convinced that the Lord called us into ministry early on so that He could fashion our marriage into a reflection of His love for the Church, as St. Paul so eloquently explains in Chapter 5 of his letter to the Ephesians. This can only happen when we are living an intentional married life, and when we are focusing our energies on God's plan for married love. The relationship Lloyd and I share today reflects a lifetime of grace, work, prayer, and sacrifice. What a tremendous blessing from the Lord!

It is through this ministry within the Catholic Church that the Lord taught me that His call for me is to live the vocation of marriage. In essence, it is the path to live out my Baptismal commitment. It is not just that I am living out my faith and happen to be married. No! Marriage is a "lifestyle" Sacrament. For those of us called to this Sacrament, it is the primary means for us to attain holiness. My marriage, then, deserves as much of my time and energy as my relationship with the Lord, or any ministry I do for the Church.

Lloyd and I were blessed to raise five children. Our two sons and three daughters have also been key influences in shaping my life. They taught me many things and caused me to look deeply into myself. Children have a way of revealing our great strengths and our glaring weaknesses. They expose our innate selfishness.

The gift of my motherhood drew me closer to Mary. Along with Lloyd, I sought to share the Catholic faith with my children in an authentic way. God used these children to teach me to surrender my self-will to Him and to turn to the Holy Spirit for guidance and wisdom. The words of Pope Benedict XVI resonate within me: "Faith grows when it is lived as an experience of love received and when it is communicated as an experience of grace and joy." However imperfectly I did that, it was my deepest desire to do so.

Raising children also brought Lloyd and me face to face with our respective family of origin patterns of alcoholism, depression, and suicidal tendencies. We struggled to help our children through their own trials with the dysfunctions that left their mark on both of us, and that work continues to this day. No family is immune from suffering. Ours was not. With the grace of God, some excellent counseling, and constant prayer, we are making daily progress toward wholeness in every aspect of our lives. As diligently as we practiced our Catholic faith and taught that faith to our children, not all of them presently embrace the faith in its fullness. Our prayers for them and their journey to Christ continue.

All of our children are married, and most have children of their own. The Lord has used my "in-law" children to stretch the boundaries of my love. The precious grandchildren He has given us are truly the reward of old age. I am deeply indebted to all of these *human cords.*

Two major relocations as a result of Lloyd's career introduced us to new and varied *human cords.* The first was to New York, where the Lord drew us into a Life in the Spirit seminar in our Church parish in New Jersey. Being baptized in the Holy Spirit expanded our prayer life, our love for Scripture, and our enthusiasm for service.

The second move was to Charlotte, North Carolina, where we made our Cursillo Weekends. Through that experience we met an even wider circle of "on-fire" Catholics. After a four-year absence, with both of us in our early thirties, we moved back to New Orleans and prepared for greater involvement in the Catholic Church.

It became readily apparent that the Lord uses every experience and every person from many walks of life to show forth His Face. I learned—however slowly—to be open to others and to search for the Face of Christ in everyone I meet and to whom I minister.

I suffered a miscarriage two years after our fourth child was born. Losing a baby was one of the most profoundly sad experiences of my life. My heart goes out to all women (and men) who have shared that pain and sense of loss. God graced us with one more child before I had to have a hysterectomy. It was a bittersweet time for Lloyd and me. The privilege of bearing life is humbling and awe-inspiring. I am filled with the deepest gratitude.

Beginning at age thirty-seven, I started making yearly, directed retreats at the Jesuit Spirituality Center in Grand Coteau. Through my director, Father Tom Madden, S.J., I was introduced more formally to the Spiritual Exercises of St. Ignatius Loyola. Jesuit spirituality seemed to fit me like a glove.

Four years later, Father Madden spoke to me about the possibility of making the full Exercises, without closing myself off in a retreat center for thirty days, which was the way St. Ignatius initially envisioned it. It became a burning desire in my heart to do so. Through a God-inspired phone conversation with a dear friend from grade school, I met an older laywoman who became my spiritual director. Over a period of eight months she led me through the Spiritual Exercises, and then she met with me monthly for the next seven years. She was a director of great personal holiness. Under her loving guidance, I deepened in my love for God, for His holy Word, and for prayer.

At the time I had no idea God was preparing me for something else. For me it was simply a time to learn the difference between following the dictates of my religion and falling in love with the Lord. The more time I spent with Jesus and His Word, the more I loved Him and allowed Him to express His boundless love for me. The experience of being so totally loved by God brought healing to my childhood wounds and filled me with greater joy and zeal in my service to the Church.

What a tremendous surprise awaited me in 1995, when the Lord began inviting me to consider becoming a spiritual director myself. Through another series of amazing "God-incidences" (not coincidences), I was accepted into a two-year internship in 1996. Upon completing my training, I was invited to serve on the staff of the Archdiocesan Spirituality Center. This center serves the priests, religious, and laypeople of the Archdiocese of New Orleans, offering ongoing spiritual direction and spiritually enriching programs.

During my years of serving as a spiritual director, I have listened to the spiritual journeys of many beautiful and generous people. I have been invited to preach retreats and to walk with seminarians and lay people through the Spiritual Exercises. The Lord has taken this very extroverted personality and fashioned a person who thrives on great solitude and stillness. This transformation by the Lord into a person who craves silence and solitude is a testimony to the Holy Spirit's action in my life. It is not a transformation I would have requested on my own or even thought possible.

I continually hear the prompting of the Lord to "Come aside and rest awhile" with Him so that I can be refreshed enough to minister to the people He delights to place in my path. The pull of the world toward activity and accomplishments remains very strong within me and is difficult to resist. I have felt the sting of the unholy spirit's darts in my mind whenever I choose to collect myself in silence before a directee comes to see me. I have also experienced the strength of God's grace and mercy, which enables me to triumph more times than I fall.

In addition to offering ongoing spiritual direction to others, I have also traveled to foreign countries and proclaimed the gospel and given witness to the Catholic faith. My husband and I co-authored a manual for *In-Home Marriage Preparation*, which is used in many dioceses and Catholic parishes. We preach couples' retreats on an ongoing basis and continue to prepare many couples for marriage in the Church.

We do it all because of God's grace and His invitation. All of this is due to the power and presence of the Holy Spirit. All of this is directly attributable to God's divine mercy and gracious goodness. In every place, in every face, we see God's goodness reflected and recognize the intense longing in the human heart for meaning and purpose, for love and acceptance. We humbly respond to each invitation and await the surprises God has in store for those who seek Him.

At each juncture along the journey of my life, God places a person to communicate the next step. Truly He woos me to Himself with *human cords, with bands of love.* Because of my involvement with Magnificat, I have met incredible women across the world and have watched God work miracles of healing and grace.

Pope John Paul II and his writings, especially in the area of sexuality and married love, have been major influences in my life and marriage. Lloyd and I have dedicated many hours to the study of the Theology of the Body. Through God's grace, our own hearts and minds are being transformed as we seek to be conformed to God's likeness in human flesh, the Lord Jesus.

Because of the enduring friendships we have formed, I know the comfort of having soul sharers and ministry partners. In the end, these *human cords* have helped me survive the deaths of my mother, my brother, and our miscarriage. These friends, our "truth speakers," have encouraged us through difficulties with our children, disappointments with ourselves, and moments of discouragement with the Church and the world.

I understand more clearly now the significance of being part of the Body of Christ. We were never meant to exist alone. We need each other to make God "come alive" in our everyday lives. Our God truly is an awesome God! He can take an ordinary human life and mix it with grace and mercy to accomplish extraordinary things. For my part, I must give my "yes" and then surrender control to the Lord. The daily surrender of my will is required … nothing more and nothing less. But it makes all the difference.

The words of St. Paul capture my reality as I ponder the journey of my life thus far:

> "Take yourselves for instance, brothers, [and sisters] at the time when you were called: how many of you were wise in the ordinary sense of the word, how many were influential people, or came from noble families? No, it was to shame the wise that God chose what is foolish by human reckoning and to shame what is strong that he chose what is weak by human reckoning; those whom the world thinks common and contemptible are the ones that God has chosen—those who are nothing at all to show up those who are everything. The human race has nothing to boast about to God, but you, God has made members of Christ Jesus and by God's doing he has become our wisdom, and our virtue, and our

holiness, and our freedom. As Scripture says: 'if anyone wants to boast, let him boast about the Lord.'" (1 Cor. 1:26–31)

I am neither wise, nor influential, nor noble by birth. However, I am wise in the power of the Holy Spirit, influential in ministry through the grace and mercy of Jesus Christ, and noble by my rebirth in the Sacrament of Baptism.

It doesn't get any better than that!

Bio–
Jan Tate is a native of New Orleans, Louisiana, and a lifelong Catholic. She and Lloyd have been married since 1972 and have five children and are the proud grandparents of fifteen! Lloyd and Jan have shared in the preparation of engaged couples for marriage in the Church for over thirty-eight years. Jan graduated with honors from Loyola University New Orleans with a degree in Communications. In conjunction with the Family Life Office for the Diocese of Baton Rouge, Louisiana, Jan and Lloyd published their own *In-Home Marriage Preparation* manual in 2002. Jan is a trained spiritual director on the staff of the Archdiocesan Spirituality Center of New Orleans and finds herself called to honor the Lord by being part of the spiritual journeys of others. God has enabled Jan to serve Him by combining her two great passions in life: her Catholic faith and her Sacramental call to Matrimony.

Maria Vadia

Proverbs 29:18: *"People without a vision lose their way."*

When describing who I was before I found the Lord, it is not a pretty story. Not only did I not have a vision for my life, but I was a lost soul—totally blind and deaf. If I had died during that time, I would have gone to hell. I looked good and I smelled good, but I was absolutely rotten on the inside. I was living for myself. I didn't know Jesus. I had no idea of what Jesus had done for me, and I didn't really care at that point in my life. I went to a Catholic school and reached all my milestones. I received the sacraments and later, when I married, it was in the Church. But I had no idea about a personal relationship with Jesus.

I had seen Jesus on the cross from my earliest memories, but I was totally desensitized to what that signified. I did not understand anything. I likened myself to being a "baptized pagan." My immediate family was no different. They too were "baptized pagans." In my home I never saw my parents pray. I never heard the name of Jesus. I never saw a Bible. However, to anyone looking in, we looked good on the outside.

I come from a very intellectual family. There are brilliant doctors on my mother's side. On my father's side was lots of money; my family consisted of lawyers, businessmen, etc. My upbringing was focused on worldly goods and successes. I was gripped by the spirit of the world—the spirit of materialism—which is a wrong way of thinking. Worldly thinking focuses on self and materialism and goes against the Word of God. I was filled with darkness!

We came to America in the first wave of Cubans, arriving in Miami, Florida. We thought we would be back in our own county of Cuba within three months. We thought we were taking a short vacation, but that three months has turned into more than fifty years now.

I praise God because I found Jesus in Miami. Thank you, Lord. Alleluia!

My parents made the decision to leave Cuba because of the political unrest, and they left absolutely everything behind. When we arrived in

America, they didn't turn to God in any way. They were gripped by self-reliance and self-sufficiency. Their attitude was "we can make it on our own. We can come out of this setback because we are highly intelligent. We can rise up and succeed."

Life continued. I attended the University of Miami and graduated, but I had no thought of God. I was totally in love with the world. I married a Cuban-American who was much like me. He too loved attaining worldly and material success. Everyone thought we made a great couple. We married in the Church. Where else would a Catholic get married except in the Church? It was expected of us. However, we did it for all the wrong reasons. The Lord was not part of my life or my marriage. I truly was in total darkness!

My husband was a wealthy man. His family was a multi- multi- and multi-millionaire. My father-in-law was very smart and when Castro took over the country, he took his money out. He quadrupled his money in America. I was given a blank check, and I could buy anything. I could travel wherever I wanted. We had the best cars; we had the best homes. Our home appeared in architectural magazines. All the trappings of extreme wealth were visible. I had the life people in America dream about having. I literally had money coming out of my ears. Money was the least problem in my life.

In a year we had two babies, and then I got pregnant again. In my worldly way of thinking I said, "I'm not having this baby. It is too much. I can't cope with another baby." I said this in spite of the fact that I had help at home.

Then I made a decision I still regret today. I went to the hospital and had an abortion. In my way of looking at things, "it" was just cells. I had learned at the university that the first three months of life "it" is just a blob of blood cells. I believed there was no life there, but now I know better. It was wrong, very wrong. We now know that a baby is a baby from the very first moment of conception. At that time I was living a lie.

After my abortion, life continued onward. I had two more children. I watched our wealth continued to grow. We purchased more homes, more cars, and everything money could buy.

During this time in my life, my older sister had a personal encounter with Jesus. She was filled with the Holy Spirit, and she couldn't wait to share Jesus with me. She wanted to share the Good News! She knew I was on my way to hell and not to heaven, and she came to share Jesus with me.

I thought my sister had lost her mind! It was Jesus in the morning, Jesus in the noontime, and Jesus in the evening. I thought, *I don't have anything in common with this sister of mine anymore.* What I did not know is that for the next seven years she would go to church and pray with her Bible class specifically for me.

I did not know any "saved" Catholics; I did not know anyone who loved Jesus. The people I associated with loved money. That's what I did, and that's what I lived for. I had money, convenience, and a wonderful, comfortable life.

My sister was the first person I met who had a personal relationship with Jesus Christ. During the years when she prayed for me, I began to experience an emptiness in my heart. I realized that my life had no meaning and no purpose.

I began to question and search for answers. "Why am I alive? Why am I here?" Life seemed so monotonous. I had my children, but I acted more like a chauffeur driving them back and forth from school. There had to be something more.

My feelings of loneliness and emptiness with no life purpose became stronger and stronger. I would weep and say, "This life does not make sense." The turmoil was terrible. What I was experiencing was foreign to me. I could not understand the changes taking place within me. I had everything money had to offer, and yet I was in misery. I was so lost that it did not occur to me that Jesus was missing in my life.

In 1987 my husband gave me tickets for Pope John Paul II's visit to Miami. He said, "Go. We have given enough money to the Church. Take the VIP tickets and go."

I went, but I didn't pray beforehand. Prayer was a foreign idea to me at the time. It was not part of my vocabulary to say, "God, touch my heart and heal me." As incredible as it may sound, I went to see the pope because I thought he was cute. I went for all for the wrong reasons.

Perhaps some of you reading this were also in Miami during Pope's John Paul II's visit. If you experienced his visit, you may remember it rained, it thundered, and there was lots of lightning. We were even asked to leave because of the dangerous weather conditions.

While a storm raged outside, another storm was raging in my heart that day. To me it was beautiful, and God touched me! I was filled with the love of God from head to toe. Suddenly, He came down upon me and filled me with His love. All I could do was thank Jesus and claim, "Alleluia!"

Just being in an atmosphere of people who loved God touched me. I didn't pray (I didn't know how), yet the Spirit of God came over me with showers of love. Suddenly, I loved people. I knew something was odd because this was not typical. I had a long list of people I hated and resented. But now that was gone. I just loved people!

After this time, a friend invited me to a charismatic prayer group at St. Therese of the Little Flower Church. When my friend said the word charismatic," I said, "What? Charis ... charis ... what?" I had never heard the word before.

"These Catholics are different," she explained. "They follow Jesus like during the time of the early church."

I agreed to go to the prayer group that night with my friend, and what a sight I was! I was dressed to the hilt in a mini-skirt, and just about everything was showing. I even had a punk hairdo. I looked like a rooster. But I thought I looked really cool. Yet, these people welcomed me with open arms. They did not say, "You are not dressed properly." No, they just loved me.

I was touched as I watched the men praising God. They stood with their arms raised high, spontaneously praising the Lord. It was a new experience. These men said, "Jesus, I love you!" "Jesus, You are my Lord and Savior. Jesus, I surrender."

I was in awe! These men were saying they needed God. Of course they did—but I did not know that at the time. They were asking as if Jesus was right there in front of them. Of course He was. The Scripture backs up this claim, "For where two or three are gathered together in My Name, there am I in the midst of them" (Matthew 18:20).

I was amazed and floored not only by what these men were praying, but that it came spontaneously. It was coming from deep within. It was not a holy card or rote prayers. Please know that I am not putting down memorized prayers. I actually won the prize every year in school for memorized prayers. But these men were praying from deep-down, from the heart. It was flowing from the inside. This is what Jesus says in John 7:38: "Those who believe in me out of their innermost being will flow rivers of living water."

I saw something flowing from deep within these men and it was beautiful. Then they began to pray in some unknown language. I thought, *This is not Spanish, this is not English, what is it?* And then they began to sing in tongues. I thought, *This must be what heaven sounds like.* I fell in love with what I was seeing and experiencing.

So many things caught my attention. These Catholics were happy! I was used to a depressed church. Whenever I walked into Mass it was like a funeral. Long faces were everywhere. Misery was everywhere. But these Catholics were dancing, and they were rejoicing. They were joyful. They had happy faces. They had something I had never seen before. They had something I did not have.

Another thing surprised me. They had Bibles.

I was invited to a Life in the Spirit weekend seminar, and it was there that I understood with my heart—not with my mind—what it says in John 3:16: "For God so loved the world [me!] that He gave His only Son, so that everyone who believes in Him might not perish but might have eternal life." That verse touched me deeply.

Then I read in Ephesians 1:17 that the Holy Spirit is a Spirit of revelation. Suddenly, I understood what Jesus did for me. It is not that I received the Holy Spirit; the Holy Spirit grabbed me!

I told the Lord that day, "Lord, I have lived thirty-seven years for myself. Now I give You the rest of my life. Take my life and do with me whatever You want. I'm yours. From now on, I will live for You." The Lord took me at my word. I was so filled with joy. It was beautiful.

As I was driving home I thought, *My husband is going to love what happened to me tonight.* I was naïve and like a baby in diapers. I was so happy. I was filled with joy. I entered the house, excited to tell the one person I loved most in the world about what had happened to me.

I was shocked by his reaction. "I don't want to hear about it," he said. "I don't give a hoot about what happened."

I didn't understand this and I began to wonder what was wrong with him. I thought, *No one is going to take this away from me. I have found God. I have met Jesus, the One who loved me and died for me. I am not going back. I am not turning back. I am going to move forward.* All I could say was, "Thank you, Jesus!"

My kids were blessed by my transformation. One of them told me, "Mom, you have become a nicer person." Another one told me, "You haven't screamed in three days." Praise the Lord. This happened within three days after being baptized in the Spirit.

For those who do not understand what Baptism in the Holy Spirit means—it is to be totally immersed in the Holy Spirit, filled and transformed. The Holy Spirit changes and transforms us. He cleans us up. He gives us meaning and purpose. That is what happened to me. He started to do a work in my life.

One of the things that immediately happened was that I was filled with joy. I had never experienced that kind of joy before … ever. I felt so much joy to know I belonged to the Lord. I was happy, happy, happy! Then another wonderful thing happened. I had a hunger for the Word of God. I read the Bible for hours and hours, and I would weep.

Jeremiah 15:16 says, "Your words were found and I ate them. And they became for me the joy and the rejoicing of my heart." I read the Scriptures and must have spent a year repenting. When I read these words it was the Lord speaking to me. I could understand them and it was so beautiful. I could understand the Word of God through the Holy Spirit speaking directly to me.

Then there were more changes. I started to go to the sacraments. I joined a Bible study and was a member of a prayer group. I spent a lot of time praising God and spending time with Him. It was a total turnabout, radical, and I had a "fire." I had a fire to tell people about Jesus. I didn't even have to take an evangelism course.

The fire I had was to share about the Lord and how one could enter into the kingdom of God. I had to speak out of necessity, because all of my friends were lost. Almost everyone in my family and in my husband's family was spiritually lost. This was totally new to me.

The Lord led me to the Genesis House. It was a house for the homeless with AIDS. We ministered there and saw many miracles. We led many of these people to Jesus. It was a wonderful, wonderful time. I told people about Jesus everywhere I went.

This went on for three and a half years. My only deep sorrow during this time was the fact that my husband didn't want anything to do with my new life. Can anyone relate to that pain? You know the Lord; you love the Lord, but your husband is still in darkness. It is a deep, lonely pain in your heart—it was in mine.

Three and a half years after I met the Lord, two storms came against us. One of the storms was financial—we were losing all our money. This storm was like the *Titanic*. This should never have happened. This was never supposed to happen. Not only were we losing our money, but it all came out on the front page of the *Miami Herald* newspaper! We were going down the drain financially, and the economic downturn problem made it worse.

My husband's behavior became unacceptable. Without going into detail, I soon became a single mother with four children.

I had met Jesus in the best of times; now I was going to meet Him in the worst of times. I had faith in Jesus for salvation; now I was going to have to trust Jesus for everything else. I had to meet Him as the Good Shepherd. I had to meet Him as my Healer. I had to meet Him as my Protector. I had to meet Him as my Provider. I was totally forced to trust in Him. I had to make sure that every day I was filled with the Holy Spirit.

This was radically different than when I first met the Lord. However, I had eaten so much of His Word that now I had to make a decision. "God, either You are a liar or Your Word is true. I am going to make a decision that I am going to trust in Your Word. I am going to start trusting in Your Word for everything."

This was the first step in another new direction, that of a single mom. I had the Holy Spirit. I had Jesus. Every night when I went to bed, I proclaimed Psalm 127:2: "The Lord grants sleep to His beloved." I thought, *Lord, if I look to the left or look to the right, I won't be able to sleep. Lord, I just trust in You.* I slept like a baby! I began to trust more in Him and in the power of the Holy Spirit.

I had received the gift of tongues when I was prayed for during the Life in the Spirit seminar. This is an amazing gift. It is so underrated. In 1 Corinthians 14:4, Paul says, "When we pray in the Spirit, we strengthen ourselves." I spent a lot of time praying in the Spirit so I could remain strong—strong for my children and strong in the Lord.

I knew God had plans for my life. Proverbs 29:18 states, "A people without a vision lose their way." I already had a vision for my life. I knew the Lord had called me to the nations. He had called me to this nation. He had given me visions of maps of America. I was receiving visions of these maps, until one day I realized what the Lord was showing me.

I finally got it! I thought, *Okay, so You want me to proclaim Your Word in America.* After this, I began getting visions of remote areas—very primitive areas—and I saw myself preaching. I had dreams of preaching in those areas. It was so strange then. However, as I write this I'm happy to say that through Jesus all things are possible and all of this has come to pass. What can I say but amen! Alleluia! Praise the Lord—thank you, Lord!

Right after I met the Lord, a wonderful charismatic priest, Fr. Harold Cohen, S.J., from New Orleans, prophesied over me: "God has amazing plans for your life. He is going to take you places that you haven't even imagined." In the worst moments of my life, I remembered Fr. Cohen's prophetic words to me. His words gave me the strength and courage to move forward. I knew I was under attack from the enemy, but I knew that with Jesus I could conquer and move forward. I had the grace of God. Once again I was so thankful that I proclaimed, "Thank you, Lord! Thank you, Jesus."

I often spent time before the Lord in the Blessed Sacrament for three hours at a time. When people left, I would begin claiming the Word of God aloud over myself. "Death and life are in the power of the tongue" (Prov. 18:21). I began proclaiming blessings over my children as well. I was very concerned for my children. I am happy to report that my God has provided for everything. Matthew 6:33 states, "Seek first the kingdom of God and His righteousness, and all these things will be given you besides." My children are all doing well, and God is taking care of them.

Trusting in the Word of God, standing on the Word of God, believing that the Holy Spirit is really inside me became my reality. If it wasn't for the help of God, I would have committed suicide or killed my husband. Neither is a good option, but it was only by the grace from the Lord that kept me standing. It was the Lord who kept me in my right mind. I thank Jesus for His provision, and I learned to trust the Lord for everything.

One testimony about God's providence came during my first Christmas after the separation. My children were used to presents under the Christmas tree, from the floor to the ceiling. I was a compulsive shopper, and with all that money I bought and bought and bought. You can imagine my state of mind that first Christmas without money. I didn't even know how I was going to support all of us. I thought Lord, *I know that You are the reason for the season, but it would be nice to have a few presents under the tree for my children.*

I soon received a phone call from a friend of mine who didn't know what was going on in my life. "The Lord told me to come and see you," she said. "He told me to give you this money. It's for your kids." It was $700.00! So, I had money for Christmas gifts for my children.

The Lord called me to a prison ministry. Every Saturday we went to the women's jail. Many miracles happened there. We went into the prison and preached the Word of God. One day while we were worshiping and praising God, I saw the Lord standing in front of one of the inmates.

Later, I told her, "Sister, I saw the Lord standing in front of you."

She said as she wept, "Yes, I came in here with a tumor on my breast, and now the tumor is gone."

Thank you, Jesus! The miracles and the signs and wonders continued. "Go into the whole world and proclaim the gospel to every creature" (Mark 16:15). To *every* creature!

Even inside the Church there are many who do not know Jesus. He said, "These signs will accompany those who believe: in My name they will drive out demons, they will speak new languages. … if they drink any deadly thing, it will not harm them. They will lay hands on the sick, and they will recover." (Mark 16:17–18).

This is why we are here, why we are on this planet. In Matthew 10:7–8, Jesus told His disciples, "As you go, proclaim the kingdom of God is at hand. Heal the sick." Jesus didn't say, "Pray for them." He said, "Heal them. Cast out demons, cleanse the lepers, and raise the dead." This is our job description. This is for every child of God.

I began to understand by revelation the power of the cross. He shed His blood there. "Without the shedding of blood, there is no forgiveness of sin" (Heb. 9:22) and "He was wounded for our transgressions; He was crushed for our iniquities. The punishment for our sins was upon Him, and by His wounds we are healed" (Isa. 53:5).

Christ not only took our sins, but He took every sickness, every disease, every pain, and every addiction so that we could be healed. He has provided for our well-being—our spirit, soul, and body. He carried our shame (Psalm 69:7). We don't have to carry it. He became a curse for us so that all the curses coming down the family tree could be broken and we could be healed and blessed. "On the cross Jesus became a curse for us" (Gal. 3:13).

I come from a family of diabetics—my mother, my father, my grandmother, and my grandfather. When I was expecting my second baby they told me I was a pre-diabetic and as I grew older I would probably become a diabetic. But you know what? I found Jesus, and I broke that curse, and I am not a diabetic. I say, "Alleluia. Thank you, Lord." There is alcoholism in my family tree. You know what? I found Jesus, and I broke that curse. My children are clean and free. Alleluia!

Jesus won the victory on the cross. Jesus won an inheritance for you and for me. We are different. We are in the world, but we are not of the world. Colossians 1:13 says, "He took us out of darkness into the kingdom of light." We are citizens of the kingdom of God. He has given us the kingdom. "I will not leave you as orphans" (John 14:18). "We are children of the kingdom" (Luke 12:32).

On the cross He took our poverty so that we could enjoy the abundant life. Jesus said in John 10:10, "I come to give you life, and life more abundantly." He took our rejection and our abandonment so that we could be adopted into the family of God. Ephesians 1:5 says he predestined us for adoption. This is our identity. We are sons and daughters of the Most High God.

We all grow through the trials in our life. Even though I knew the Lord, the pain I felt when my marriage broke apart was like a crushing, physical pain. I felt that my heart was bleeding. It was very difficult, but there is One who is bigger than any difficulty, any trial, or any pain in your heart—the Holy Spirit.

Romans 8:11 says we have the spirit of resurrection. The same Spirit that raised Jesus from the dead dwells inside of you. We have the same Spirit. We are temples of the Holy Spirit and we carry His glory.

Psalm 144:1 says that the Lord trains my hands for war and my fingers for battle. He truly did train me when we were selling our home in 1992. It was a huge, expensive house, and there was an economic crisis at the time. The real estate market was not selling, people were not spending money, and everyone predicted, "You will not sell your house. This is the wrong time." It seems that the enemy always sends someone to give you a negative report, especially on a bad day.

I said, "Lord, I have to sell this house, and You are going to have to show me how. Everyone is saying the real estate market is not moving, and Holy Spirit, you are going to have to show me the way." Jeremiah 33:3 says, "Call out to me and I will answer you and I will show you great and mighty things that you do not know."

The Lord gave me the strategy to sell the house: "Go around the house seven times like Joshua marched around Jericho." I prayed a covering over the land, claiming the blood of Jesus—north, south, east, and west. I broke any curses over my house, and my house sold in less than two and a half weeks. "Alleluia!"

I could go on and on with testimonies. This was a time of training. He was training my hands for war and my fingers for battle for what lay ahead. I said "yes" to the Lord in 1987 and I knew in my heart He had called me. I could never go back and be a "pew potato," just sitting there. There was a call on my life, and by the grace of God I kept my eyes on Jesus. The promises He made, the visions He gave me, and the prophetic words have all been fulfilled.

At the time of this writing, I have been to twenty-nine nations. This sounds crazy, even to me. In the past I detested speaking in front of people, but now this is what I do. I never enjoyed writing, but now this is what I do. When the Holy Spirit comes, He invades our lives. He changes everything around so we can become the kind of people God created us to be.

God not only forgives our sins, but He forgets them. It is beautiful to live a new life free of condemnation. "There is therefore no condemnation for those who are in Christ Jesus" (Rom. 8:1).

I have seen many miracles in the nations where the Lord sent me. In Uganda we held a worship conference. It was absolutely glorious, and the presence of God came upon us. We held a healing service as well. In the Spirit I saw heaven open up. Body parts and body organs came down. I saw eyes, I saw knees, I saw livers, I saw a pancreas, and I saw kidneys. All these body parts came raining down. He gave me the interpretation of this vision. God was saying, "I am not only going to heal people, I am going to heal and make new body parts."

An elderly man of seventy-one years old came in with a cane; he was hardly able to walk. He wore thick glasses and could barely see. This man received a new set of eyes and a new set of knees! He started to dance in front of everybody. He doesn't need his glasses anymore.

To see this man without his cane and dancing was amazing. Not only did the Lord heal him physically but he also healed him spiritually. He began to receive visions. Every day he received a vision. "You know what?" he confessed. "I used to laugh at you charismatics and make fun of you. I used to think you were wasting time. But now look at what the Lord has done for me!"

People need to see the power of God, a kingdom of power and a kingdom of glory—not a kingdom of misery and depression. As citizens of His kingdom we need to reflect Him. We represent Him.

Another time through the word of knowledge, the Lord revealed to me special information there was no way I could have known without the Holy Spirit. In faith I said, "The Lord is touching tumors, and growths are disappearing from your body." Three ladies came up and said their tumors disappeared. Nobody touched them. Doesn't that show the goodness and mercy of God?

We were on our way from one province to another when my friend, who was driving, received a desperate phone call from a friend. "My father was in a car accident and just taken to the hospital. A bus hit his car, and he went into a ditch. I am so desperate. Please pray."

As it turned out, we passed only a few yards away from where the accident took place! My friend parked the car on the side of the road. Her friend came over to her, weeping. She thought her father was going to die. We prayed. We made bold declarations that her father would not die but live and proclaim the greatness of the Lord. We sent healing and victory in the name of the Lord. We prayed, "Holy Spirit, come and release the healing of the kingdom of God into his body, into every affected area. We just stand on Your Word, Lord, that 'by your wounds he has been healed'" (1 Pet. 2:24).

It also happened that this same woman had a baby with an enlarged head. We prayed for the baby, who was having surgery on Friday. The accident happened two days before, on a Wednesday. We prayed for this baby and released the healing of the kingdom of God.

Both cases were long-distance prayers, with no laying on of hands. We believed in the healing of the kingdom of God into this baby. "Lord, touch him and go back into the womb, whenever that defect took place," we prayed. "Heal that problem. Release healing into that baby. Surround that baby with angels."

Two days later we received a phone call from the lady. Her father walked out of the hospital with just a pain in the ribs. Additionally, the baby was taken to the hospital for surgery on Friday and the doctor said, "I am not doing surgery. Something has changed since I saw the baby." We began praising the Lord, saying, "Thank you, Lord!"

This is the great God whom we serve. The Holy Spirit is looking for people who will work with Him. Second Corinthians 6:1 says we are co-laborers with God. This is why the passivity needs to be broken. The Holy Spirit is looking for people who will say "yes." Often we say, "If God wants it, He will do it."

No! It is time to get up and take action! Stop waiting on Heaven. Heaven is waiting on *you*. Why do you think we have the Holy Spirit? Why has God anointed us? Why has He equipped us? Why has He given us the various gifts of the Holy Spirit? So we can remain passive? No, you have a calling on your life. There is a purpose for your life. If I did not have a vision for my life, and if He didn't have something specific for me, I probably would have gone back into the world of self-centeredness and idle pleasure. You need a vision for your life.

There is something specific God wants you to do; something specific He wants me to do. God wants you to give birth to His purposes on this planet. He wants to release Heaven on earth. This is how Jesus taught us to pray: "Let Your Kingdom come, let Your Will be done on earth as it is in Heaven" (Matt. 6:10). He didn't say as it is in hell; He said as it is in *Heaven*. You have that gift to release Heaven.

I love going to a certain town in Uganda. Only two percent of the people are Catholics and Christians. Ninety percent are Muslims. The Muslims come to the meetings because they are desperate, and they come usually at night. They are like Nicodemus. They come searching for Jesus at night so that no one will see them.

One time a mother brought her thirteen- or fourteen-year-old daughter. She carried her because for at least two years the girl had not been able to walk. She was paralyzed from the waist down. We ministered to her. We told her to get up, and she began to take steps holding our fingers. "Silver and gold have I none but what I have I give to you. In the name of Jesus of Nazareth, rise up and walk" (Acts 3:6).

Then the young lady started to take steps on her own. She walked wobbly but then she said, "Let's run!" And we went running! It was glorious. It was amazing. I felt Heaven clapping and shouting with joy that the kingdom of God had entered into that place.

The next morning another Muslim family brought their daughter. This girl had never walked. She was crippled. We prayed and she started to take steps with us, but then we had to leave for another province. We left the girl with a charismatic nurse, and within two days she was walking on her own in her own house. Her father was a Muslim imam. Mohammad couldn't heal his daughter, but Jesus, the Great Physician, did. The word spread and more Muslims began coming for healing.

It is amazing what God can do through a person who says "yes." See what God did in my life! He took me out of the pit of the world. I was blinded, materialistic, a lover of money, and I had no knowledge of Jesus. Now I have said "yes." Now He has used me to bring thousands of people into the kingdom of God and to release His Holy Spirit.

All you need to do is say "yes." It is not about our qualifications. It is about our "yes." God is satisfied with our "yes." He can do the rest, and He will.

In Tanzania, a paralyzed, eleven-year-old girl needed healing. We began to pray for a release of the healing power of the kingdom of God. At first nothing seemed to happen, but within twenty-four hours the girl was running up and down the road. Her father was a Muslim and her mother was a Catholic. The father had never allowed his daughter to be baptized, but the girl said, "I want to become a Catholic. I want to give my life to the God that healed me."

It is a new day. It doesn't matter what your past has been. If it has been rotten, wonderful, or just so-so, it doesn't matter. The Lord is here to do something new. Jesus is looking for a friend (John 15:15). He is looking for a people who will take time for Him. He is looking for people who will spend time with Him. He is looking for people to share His secrets with and to share the plans He has. When we say "yes," He will do the rest. He wants a personal relationship with each one of us. You should look at your life and see a history of "yes, yes, yes." If we say "yes," and we are faithful to that "yes," He will do the rest.

In 2009 I went to see the Pygmies, the little people in Africa. The year before, the Lord said, "I want you to go to look for the Pygmies." So the following year I traveled to Africa with a priest, a catechist, and a friend. We parked the car and started walking through the wilderness. When we found a group of Pygmies I was shocked by what I saw. I should have looked them up online to find out more about them, but I didn't have time. I saw human beings so dirty, and dressed in rags, with no shoes. I didn't know the last time they had bathed themselves. They were used to living in the forest and picking the fruit from the trees, but now they were like fish out of water. Their houses were just enclosed spaces covered with grass, and they had no protection against the elements. Our pets in America lived better than they did!

I began to proclaim the gospel to them. I was so excited! I talked to them about Jesus, His love, and what He had done for them. I got no reaction—no response to the Good News. They all looked hopeless. They had such sad faces. I was telling them about Jesus, but my words were having no impact.

I stopped and I thought, *Lord, there is a problem here. The message is not penetrating. What do I do next?* The Lord said, "He who did not spare His own son but freely gave Him up for all of us, how would He not freely give us all things?" (Rom. 8:32). Then I understood! *I am here to give them something.* The gospel, of course, but was there something I could give them that was tangible?

"What do you want?" I asked them, but they could not answer. They were so hopeless. They could not imagine that anyone would help them. They were a people abandoned and rejected by the rest of their nation. They were miserable.

Finally, the oldest Pygmy said, "I want to be like everyone else. I want a new house. Our houses are falling apart. I also want a cow so that I can drink milk every day."

I said, "If you want houses, my God is big enough to give you houses. If houses are what you want, I will give you houses because my God will supply."

They became so happy! They started to dance and then they were open to the gospel. Every one of those Pygmies opened their hearts to Jesus. They were filled with the Holy Spirit and began to dance. It was amazing. It was like a well of joy that broke open where there was no water. It was beautiful.

At the time of this writing, they now have over thirty houses. One of them told me, "It is so beautiful when it rains now. It is like music to our ears." They no longer have to run and find shelter when it rains. We are building them houses of bamboo and eucalyptus wood with metal roofs.

I pray this testimony will encourage you to say "yes." You will see the fruit. You will give birth to something that is dear to the heart of God. We should not be living on this earth in hopelessness. We have a purpose for our lives. The Lord has a plan for you and for me. He has good works planned for us from "before the foundations of the earth" (Ephesians 2:10).

No matter the size of the problem you are going though, God is bigger. We have a God Who will take the rubble of our lives and make something beautiful. Romans 8:28 says, "God changes all things for the good of those who love Him, of those who have been called according to His purpose." He will turn around the worst thing in your life for good. He will change all things for good for those who love Him, in order for us to say, "Thank you, Lord."

I want to share a passage from Isaiah for those reading this who have problems with their husbands, or have a broken marriage, or have felt rejection, abandonment, or loneliness:

"Fear not for you will not be put to shame.
You need not blush, for you shall not be disgraced.
The shame of your youth you shall forget,
The reproach of your widowhood is no longer remembered.
For He who has become your husband is your Maker.
His name is the Lord of Hosts.
Your redeemer is the Holy One of Israel,
called God of all the earth." (Isaiah 54:4–5)

Amen! The Lord wants to become your *all in all.* No matter what you are going through, open your hearts to Him. Let Him come and sit at the center of your heart. Begin thanking him each day like this: "Thank you, Lord. Thank you, Lord!" Know that God has a plan for your life. He wants to move through you and bless you more abundantly than anything you could ask for or imagine.

If you have never openly proclaimed Jesus as your Lord and Savior, I invite you to pray and ask the Holy Spirit to come in power. Romans 10:9–10 says, "If you confess with your mouth that Jesus is Lord and you believe in your heart that God raised Him from the dead, you will be saved."

Salvation is a gift from God. We cannot save ourselves, which is why He had to send Jesus. If you have never surrendered to the Lord in this way, I ask you to pray yourself, or find a friend to pray with you. Today is a day of grace. Right now, this moment, it is an invitation. It is an invitation for you to open your life to Jesus, to open your heart to Jesus. Let Him come in and take control of your life.

Jesus is calling for surrender, not just for you to be a church attendee. There is a difference. He is not looking for church attendees. He is looking for people who will surrender and start living for Him.

Thank you, Lord. Praise be to Jesus!

Bio—

Born in Havana, Cuba, Maria Vadia was ten years old when she and her family fled to Miami, Florida, to escape the communist regime. She attended Catholic schools and was a "Sunday" Catholic with no personal relationship with the Lord Jesus Christ. Later married to a wealthy man, she was gripped with materialism; yet in the midst of everything that the world had to offer, she knew that something was missing. Maria was baptized in the Holy Spirit in 1987 and is active in the Catholic Charismatic Renewal of the Archdiocese of Miami. She has spoken at many charismatic conferences and has traveled extensively around the world bringing a message of faith, salvation, and healing. She is founding Coordinator of the Miami chapter of Magnificat and a member of the Magnificat International Advisory Team. She is the founder of The Glory of God Foundation, which helps the Pygmies with new houses in Uganda, and has authored seven books. Maria is mother to four grown children and grandmother to seven.

Baptized in the Holy Spirit

by Rev. Harold F. Cohen, S.J.

In Loving Memory

[Father Cohen was the first Spiritual Advisor to the Magnificat Central Service Team—his explanation of the Baptism in the Holy Spirit is timeless.]

Prior to His ascension, Jesus told His apostles, "Before many days you shall be baptized with the Holy Spirit." He added, "You shall receive power when the Holy Spirit has come upon you; and you shall be My witnesses" (Acts 1:5,8).

The apostles prayed for the coming of the Spirit with Mary, the mother of Jesus and a group of about one hundred and twenty. On Pentecost, they were "baptized with the Holy Spirit" and were transformed into new creatures, bold witnesses for Christ.

Pentecost comes to each of us in the Sacraments of Initiation: Baptism, Confirmation, and Eucharist. In Baptism, we receive the Holy Spirit and become God's children and members of the Body of Christ. In Confirmation, we receive a new fullness of the Spirit and are empowered to serve the Church and bear witness to Jesus. In the Eucharist, we receive the risen Jesus Who fulfills His role of communicating the Spirit to His friends.

Often, we do not allow the Spirit we have received, to be as active in us as He wants to be. To use an analogy, He is like chocolate syrup poured into a glass of milk: it goes to the bottom of the glass until stirred up. But when it is stirred up, it permeates the milk and transforms it into something new.

We can learn how to "stir up" the Spirit (and how to receive more of Him) from Jesus in the Gospels:

"If anyone thirsts, let him come to Me, and let him drink whoever believes in Me. As the scripture has said, 'Out of His heart shall flow rivers of living water.' Now He said this about the Spirit which those who believed in Him were to receive" (Jn. 7:37–39). "If you then, who are evil, know how to give good gifts to your children, how much more will the heavenly Father give the Holy Spirit to those who ask Him!" (Lk. 11:13).

The Lord teaches us that first we must thirst for God, we must desire more and more of His Spirit. Then, we must believe that Jesus is faithful to His promises and will indeed give us His Holy Spirit. Finally, we must ask God for the Holy Spirit. We must pray with perseverance, asking, seeking, knocking, believing that "everyone who asks receives, and he who seeks finds, and to him who knocks it will be opened" (Lk. 11:10). We can follow the example of the early Church by praying for the Spirit, in union with Mary and the apostles, as they did at the first Pentecost (see Acts 1:12–14).

What can we expect when we are "baptized with the Holy Spirit"? We can expect an immediate or gradual experience of deeper union with God, our loving Father and with Jesus, our Lord and Friend; a fresh appreciation of Scripture; a greater love for others and a desire for Christian fellowship; the fuller presence in our lives of the fruit of the Spirit: love, joy, peace, patience, and more (see Gal 5:22–23); the reception of one or more of the charismatic gifts of the Spirit such as discernment, service, prophecy, praying in tongues, healing (see 1 Cor. 12–14).

This gift of a new fullness of the Holy Spirit is, I believe, the grace of our age. "Ask and it will be given to you!"

Contributor's Contact Info

All contributors retain their individual rights to copyright, use, and licensing of their individual testimonies, and have granted Magnificat Central Service Team, Inc. copyright permission to use their testimonies in this collective work. For reprint or re-use rights to individual testimonies, please contact the appropriate contributor(s). For reprint or re-use rights to the collective work, please contact Magnificat Central Service Team, Inc., 1629 Metairie Road – Suite 3, Metairie, LA 70005-3926.

Annette Miriam Baber
Email: Tbaber@aol.com
Phone: 435-503-5638

Diane Bates
Email: magnificatcst@aol.com
Phone: 504-828-6279

Kathleen Beckman
Email: Kathleenbeckman@aol.com
www.foundationforpriests.org

Johnnette Benkovic
Email: info@womenofgrace.com
www.womenofgrace.com
Phone: 800-558-5452
PO BOX 239
Oldsmar, FL 34677-0239

Babsie Bleasdell (deceased)
Contact Paula Owolabi
Email: paula.owolabi@bell.net
Phone: 416-284-6976

Dorinda Bordlee
BIOETHICS DEFENSE FUND
Email: dbordlee@gmail.com
www.BDFund.org
Phone: 504-231-7234
Like BDF on Facebook

Kitty Cleveland
c/o Christiaria, LLC
PO Box 843
Madisonville, LA 70447
Email: kitty@kittycleveland.com
www.kittycleveland.com

Sharon Lee Giganti
Email: info@sharonleegiganti.com
www.NewAgeDeception.com

Marilyn Heap
Email: mnrheap@cox.net

Elizabeth J. Kim, Ph.D.
Brain Fitness Center
13030 Euclid St., Suite 118
Garden Grove, CA 92843
Phone: 714-537-5400
Email: ekimphdoc@gmail.com
www.brainfitness.org

Kathy MacInnis
Email: magnificatcst@aol.com
Phone: 504-828-6279

Patti Mansfield
Email: mansfield@ccrno.org
www.ccrno.org
www.amordeus.com
Phone: 504-828-1368

Sr. Briege McKenna, O.S.C.
St. Clare Sisters Retreat Ministry
PO Box 1559
Palm Harbor, FL 34682, USA
www.sisterbriege.com

**Mother Miriam of the Lamb
of God, O.S.B. (Rosalind Moss)**
Daughters of Mary, Mother of Israel's Hope
www.motherofisraelshope.org
466 S. 79th East Avenue
Tulsa, OK 74112

Elyse O'Kane
Email: Elyse@elyseokane.com
www.elyseokane.com

Marilyn Quirk
Email: magnificatmq@gmail.com

Carol Razza
Email: drcarolraz@yahoo.com

Jan Tate
Email: jantate72@bellsouth.net

Maria Vadia
Email: thegloryofgod@hotmail.com
www.thegloryofgodministries.com

PROCLAIMS

A collection of powerful, inspiring testimonies

For ordering information, visit our website at
www.magnificat-ministry.org.

Notes

Notes

Notes

Notes

Notes

Notes

Notes

Notes

Notes

Notes

Notes